CAMBRIDGE LIBR

Books of enduri

CW01574655

Can

The city of Cambridge received its royal charter in 1201, having ...
to Britons, Romans and Anglo-Saxons for many centuries. Cambridge University was founded soon afterwards and celebrated its octocentenary in 2009. This series explores the history and influence of Cambridge as a centre of science, learning, and discovery, its contributions to national and global politics and culture, and its inevitable controversies and scandals.

A History of St Catharine's College, Cambridge

A History of St Catharine's College, Cambridge, by W.H.S. Jones, was originally published in 1936. The book documents the history of the college, which was founded in 1473 by Robert Woodlark, then the Provost of King's College. It is thought the name was chosen in honour of Catharine of France, the mother of King Henry VI, although it is also possible that it was named as part of the Renaissance cult of St Catharine, a patron saint of learning. The book charts the history of the college from the foundation to the 1930s, and is divided into chapters on topics including domestic history, key figures, and a section on documents, including statutes, income, authorities and correspondence. The book is generally acknowledged to be the authoritative text on St Catharine's College and will appeal to anyone interested in the University of Cambridge.

Cambridge University Press has long been a pioneer in the reissuing of out-of-print titles from its own backlist, producing digital reprints of books that are still sought after by scholars and students but could not be reprinted economically using traditional technology. The Cambridge Library Collection extends this activity to a wider range of books which are still of importance to researchers and professionals, either for the source material they contain, or as landmarks in the history of their academic discipline.

Drawing from the world-renowned collections in the Cambridge University Library, and guided by the advice of experts in each subject area, Cambridge University Press is using state-of-the-art scanning machines in its own Printing House to capture the content of each book selected for inclusion. The files are processed to give a consistently clear, crisp image, and the books finished to the high quality standard for which the Press is recognised around the world. The latest print-on-demand technology ensures that the books will remain available indefinitely, and that orders for single or multiple copies can quickly be supplied.

The Cambridge Library Collection will bring back to life books of enduring scholarly value (including out-of-copyright works originally issued by other publishers) across a wide range of disciplines in the humanities and social sciences and in science and technology.

A History of St Catharine's College, Cambridge

Once Catharine Hall, Cambridge

William Henry Samuel Jones

Cambridge
University Press

CAMBRIDGE UNIVERSITY PRESS

Cambridge, New York, Melbourne, Madrid, Cape Town, Singapore,
São Paolo, Delhi, Dubai, Tokyo

Published in the United States of America by Cambridge University Press, New York

www.cambridge.org
Information on this title: www.cambridge.org/9781108008969

This edition first published 1936
This digitally printed version 2010

ISBN 978-1-108-00896-9 Paperback

A HISTORY
OF
ST CATHARINE'S COLLEGE
CAMBRIDGE

St Catharine's College
Main Court

A HISTORY OF ST CATHARINE'S COLLEGE

ONCE CATHARINE HALL CAMBRIDGE

By

W. H. S. JONES, Litt.D.

President, late Bursar

CAMBRIDGE
AT THE UNIVERSITY PRESS
1936

PRINTED IN GREAT BRITAIN

CONTENTS

ERRATA

p. 102 l. 22. *before* "Addenbrooke" *add* "after his death this interest survived in the College, and".

p. 135 note 3. There should be inverted commas to mark off the first pamphlet, which was written by the Master of Christ's College.

p. 337 l. 1. Major Luard meant to write 5.30.

p. 375 l. 20. The date (of which there is no written record) may be 1920, not 1919.

p. 386 l. 17. *for* "Pleasant" *read* "Pheasant".

ILLUSTRATIONS

Illustrations

PREFACE

THE real history of a college is a thread spun out of the lives of those who have lived together within its walls. It is, however, only during the last century that the community life of St Catharine's has been recorded with any degree of fulness; down to the nineteenth century at least much more is known of "Catharine men" after they left the College than when they were in it, and of those who died while they were members of the Society most are shadowy figures. Every now and then the common will of the College manifests itself in some corporate act, or its efforts at self-expression appear in disputes, whether amicable differences of opinion or passionate quarrels. But events like these are occasional. This history, therefore, is episodic, a sequence of incidents usually to all appearance disconnected and separate. Doubtless the links are always there, but only sometimes are they seen by us; more often they have been lost for ever in the mists of oblivion.

A college history, therefore, must be annalistic in character, and nothing is gained by disguising this truth instead of frankly admitting it. Only occasionally is it wise to attempt to connect one episode with another, and then only tentatively and with every possible precaution. The spirit of a period, its mentality, is the true bond between one event and another, and it cannot be caught, except partially and with much uncertainty.

If this continuous thread of human lives could be reconstructed, the history of a college would be as interesting as a novel. The annalist is often tempted to exercise his constructive imagination when he finds that all that remains of a period is a dull list of dates and events. He is, however, in duty bound to keep himself in check and to chronicle only the bare facts. But no such restraint is placed upon the reader; he can, if he be a devoted "Catharine man", have no more delightful task than that of attempting to clothe in flesh and blood the skeleton that is all the historian can give him for most of the life of the College. If a reader asks: "Why this dull account of Overall's election instead of entertaining matter like 'Robinson's vote'?" the answer is ready. The entertaining matter exists in the latter case, but in the former it is wanting; the historian must not invent, but the reader may, if he likes, and he will derive great pleasure from his efforts.

The dullest parts of the history have been grouped together in Part II under the title of "Materials". The name was chosen after very careful consideration. It indicates that, at least from most of the sections, material can be extracted to feed the fancy. Especially fruitful are the letters, which have been selected for their intrinsic interest, though some of them do not concern St Catharine's at all. Only want of space has prevented the inclusion of many more.

In spite of its fragmentary nature, a college history has certain lessons to teach. Of these perhaps the most obvious and the most important is that a college serves best each age and generation when it is true to itself, and tries to realise the ideal set before it in its statutes. This ideal may not, in fact often does not, commend itself to posterity, but a worthy posterity will see to it that a new and more enlightened ideal is embodied in fresh legislation. A second lesson, at first sight inconsistent with the one just indicated, is that a college must never think only of the present; unless it realises its duty to posterity it may prove a "dead hand" in very deed, cramping development and compelling the future to be content with less than its best. A selfish college may do more harm than a lazy one. A really great college is always true to itself without forgetting its successors.

It was found to be unwise to observe a rigid uniformity in modernising obsolete methods of spelling. These are sometimes irritating and a hindrance to the reader, especially in long documents and in letters; at other times the old spelling is an aid to a true understanding by giving the appropriate atmosphere. A delicate sense of the fitness of things is necessary if one is to decide rightly when modernisation is, and when it is not, desirable, and I cannot hope to have been consistent in my inconsistency.

Another apology is perhaps due for grouping the incidents of the history under four main heads, after having adopted a quasi-annalistic method, and for treating certain subjects in separate sections or appendices. I can only say that to break the rule of annalistic treatment does at times appear to make for greater clearness and a closer sequence, although it involves a certain amount of repetition. Neither has it been possible to keep strictly to these four divisions; in particular, many financial matters are included in Chapter II because they concern closely domestic history.

I hope too that I shall be forgiven for attempting to mark the peculiar position of "scholars" at St Catharine's for two hundred years by using a small "s" instead of a capital in the part of the history where our earliest Scholarships are described. "Scholarship" I have always printed with a capital, except in quotations.

My thanks are due to the Master and Fellows of the College, who have undertaken the expense of printing the work. The Master, Mr D. A. Winstanley and Dr G. G. Coulton have helped by advice and criticism, while Mr E. A. B. Barnard, whose name ought to be on the title-page, has catalogued our muniments and ransacked the London collections of manuscripts for new evidence. He has moreover been generous to a fault with invaluable help and suggestions, and has compiled the index of names. To the staff of our College Office, in particular to our chief clerk Mr J. F. Ablett, more than a mere expression of thanks is due. They have all worked hard at the tiresome labour of typing; they have searched through ponderous tomes to find a quotation; and Mr Ablett actually read three out of the four volumes of *Alumni Cantabrigienses* to collect the references to St Catharine's men. Without the devoted help of this loyal staff the present history could never have been attempted.

No words of mine can express what I owe to the labours of Bishop Philpott and Bishop Browne. The former left the materials for a history of St Catharine's; the latter wrote one. My debt to both I gratefully acknowledge; the present book is but the effort of a pupil to carry on the work of his masters, and to add a record of the period they did not live to see. My thanks are due to Messrs Hutchinson and Co., the publishers of Browne's *St Catharine's College*, for kind permission to make use of it, and to quote from it several long passages.

The best thanks of the College are due to several photographers, especially to Mr W. Tams, for their careful work, and to the officials of the University Press for their untiring patience.

W. H. S. J.

April 1936

EPOCHS IN THE HISTORY OF ST CATHARINE'S COLLEGE

WITH A LIST OF MASTERS

The old ideal; St Catharine's for its Fellows

1473 Robert Woodlark
1475 Richard Roche
1480 John Tapton
1487 John Wardall
1506 Richard Balderstone
1507 Thomas Greene
1529 Reginald Bainbrigge

The period of change; St Catharine's begins to be a teaching institution for the young

1547 Edwin Sandys
1554 Edmund Cosyn
1559 John Mey

Quarrels

1577 Edmund Hound
1598 John Overall
1607 John Hills

Tutorial System at its best

1626 Richard Sibbes
1635 Ralph Brownrigge
1645 William Spurstow
1650 John Lightfoot
1675 John Eachard
1697 Sir William Dawes[1]

Decline

1714 Thomas Sherlock
1719 Thomas Crosse
1736 Edward Hubbard[2]
1741 Kenrick Prescot
1779 Lowther Yates

Progress

1799 Joseph Procter
1845 Henry Philpott

Decline

1861 Charles Kirkby Robinson

Modern Regeneration

1909 Claude Hermann Walter Johns
1920 Thomas Wortley Drury
1927 Frederick Margetson Rushmore
1933 Henry John Chaytor

THE LIST OF MASTERS IN THE REGISTER OF DANIEL MILLES

Richardus Roche natus Tauntoniae...huius Collegii prefecturam primus obtinuit.

Ioannes Tapton...non alio ornatus titulo quam Magistri in Artibus.

Ioannes Wardall...Bacchalaureus sacrae Theologiae.

Richardus Batterston...sacrae Theologiae Bacchalaureus.

[1] Before Dawes there was elected Dr Peter Fisher, who resigned before admission.

[2] Before Hubbard there was elected John Sayer, B.D., of Queens' College, who resigned before admission.

Masters in Register of Daniel Milles

Thomas Green sacrae Theologiae Professor.

Reginald Bainbrigg sacrae Theologiae Bacchalaureus.

Edwinus Sands...aliquot annos huic Collegio praefuit, sed regnante Maria Pontificiorum furori cedens diu apud exteros latuit donec mitiora Elizabethae tempora eum in nativum solum revocarunt, et non multo post ad Archiepiscopatum Eboracensem evexerunt.

Edmundus Cosins in Iure Civili Doctor.

Iohannes Mey sacrae Theologiae Professor...postquam optimum prudentiae et integritatis specimen apud nos praebuisset ad Episcopatum Carliolensem evectus est.

Edmundus Hownd sacrae Theologiae Professor in alieno solo natus, nempe Gallorum Caleti seu Gessoriaci.

Ioannes Overallus vir profundae eruditionis hanc Prefecturam, simulque Cathedram Theologicam pro Rege in hac Academia tenuit. Cuius rara et recondita Doctrina tantum apud omnes percrebuerit ut post alios Dignitatis Ecclesiasticae titulos primo in sedem Lichfieldensem nec multo post in Norwicensem suffectus est.

Ioannes Hill sacrae Theologiae Professor in Comitatu Cantabrigiensi natus Prefectus Duodecimus.

Richardus Sibbs sacrae Theologiae Professor, omnium quos praesens aetas viderit pientissimus, Concïonator mellitissimus, qui haud paucorum corda suavitate dicendi emolliit, et vivendi sanctitate ad bonam frugem plane rapuit. Hic erat qui Collegium istud partim temporum injuria, partim Praefectorum socordia et avaritia bonis suis spoliatum, et omni honore exutum ad pristinam famam et Dignitatem restituit, quaque erat apud omnes pios autoritate maxima, largam Benefactorum messem, in hoc vacuum Gymnasium faeliciter deduxerit. Adeo ut non nudo Praefecti nomine dignus videatur, sed alter ffundator censeri debet.

Radulphus Brownrigg, Ipswichi Suffolciensium Decus ingens et gloria, maximo totius Academiae comodo in Magistrum decimum quartum electus est. Vir supra communem mortalium sortem eruditus, ingenio plane mirabili, Judicio exquisitissimo, quibus morum suavitas, et candor accesserit singularis. In concionibus facundissimus, pariter ac copiosissimus, in Disputationibus acutissimus, in re Collegiali prudentissimus ac diligentissimus. Ad maxima quaeque negotia aptus natus, et nihil minus spirans quam Episcopum in quorum sacrum ordinem Anno 1641 assumptus, Episcopus Exoniensis consecratus est. [*Mistakes uncorrected.*]

PART I

THE HISTORY

Chapter I

SITE AND BUILDINGS

ST CATHARINE'S COLLEGE was founded in 1473 by Robert Woodlark, Provost of King's, whose life and work are given in Chapter II.

The site chosen by Woodlark for the new foundation was quite close to King's College. If one were to take Queens' Lane, the north wall of the Hall, and lines drawn at right angles to these from the centre of the lawn, the rectangle thus formed would probably include all the original buildings. Browne says that during the drought of 1877 "we saw very clearly on the grass of the College Court the lie of the Chapel walls and the corner buttresses; they extended about half way across the grass-plot from west to east, and about half way also from north to south".[1]

Some preparatory steps were taken at least as early as 1459, for on 10 September in that year Woodlark bought two tenements in Milne Street, situated in the parishes of St Edward and St Botolph, between the tenement of John Rasour to the south and a tenement belonging to Michael House on the north. They abutted on a tenement of Corpus Christi (le George) to the east, and on Milne Street to the west. The northern boundary was 90 feet, the southern 107 feet 2 inches. The tenements were subject to a quit rent of 3 shillings a year payable to the Master and Scholars of Michael House.

Milne Street ("the street of the mills") was the old name of Queens' Lane, once one of the main thoroughfares of the town. The boundary between the two parishes passes through the entrance to the present D staircase. So there can be no doubt about the position of the original buildings, which, according to an entry in the College Register,[2] occupied the site of these two tenements, and of another, acquired 9 September 1460.

This third tenement was leased from the Master and Scholars of Michael House for 99 years, at a yearly rent of 8 shillings. The property was purchased in 1471. It is described in the conveyance as a tenement with a

[1] Browne, p. 14.

[2] *Register*, I, 119.

garden, in the street called "Millestrete", between a tenement of Robert Woodlark on the south and a tenement or hostelry called the Black Bull on the north. The Register says that on this site was built the Library.

On Michaelmas Day 1472 Woodlark acquired a lease of a tenement and garden to the south of the other properties, and separated from them by the brewery of John Rasour. The lease was for 99 years, renewable in perpetuity. It was granted by a chantry of St Mary and St Nicholas in the Church of St Clement.

The property, called "Wodhows" in the Register, was thirty-six and a half yards long by ten broad.[1] It had two chambers on the ground floor, and a garden. The lease describes it as in Milnestrete in the parish of St Botolph over against the White Friars (*erga fratres albos*), between Queens' College garden on the south, and the property of John Rasour on the north.

This intervening property was not acquired till 1516, when it was bought for £50 from Alice Ray, widow of John Ray, a burgess of Cambridge.[2] The conveyance describes it as the "Inne called the Swanne" along with "a voyde Grownde lying and beyng byhynd the said Tenemente called the Swane". The inn, together with the house on the south side of it, the acquisition of which is of unknown date, was sold in 1556 to John Mere for £50. Many years later these properties were repurchased for a much larger sum.

On the site of the first three properties Woodlark built his little college. It was quadrangular, with the Chapel at the south-east corner and the Library apparently at the north-east. The entrance was from Milne Street at the point where now is the entrance to D staircase. It was probably of two storeys, and built of wood and stone. This may be inferred from Woodlark's reference to stone-cutters, and to the timber he had collected long before building was begun.[3]

[1] The length was the measurement from east to west, the breadth that from north to south.

[2] *Register*, I, 91.

[3] *Memoriale Nigrum*, fol. 50, "Memorandumque... de meremio empto in certis domibus framiatis emptis de Sturgyn et alterato a Coton usque ad Hornyngsey et recariato Cantebrigiam ad fabricam aulae praedictae diu ante fabricam predictam remanente." There is doubt as to the correct extensions of contracted words in several places, but the meaning is in no place uncertain.

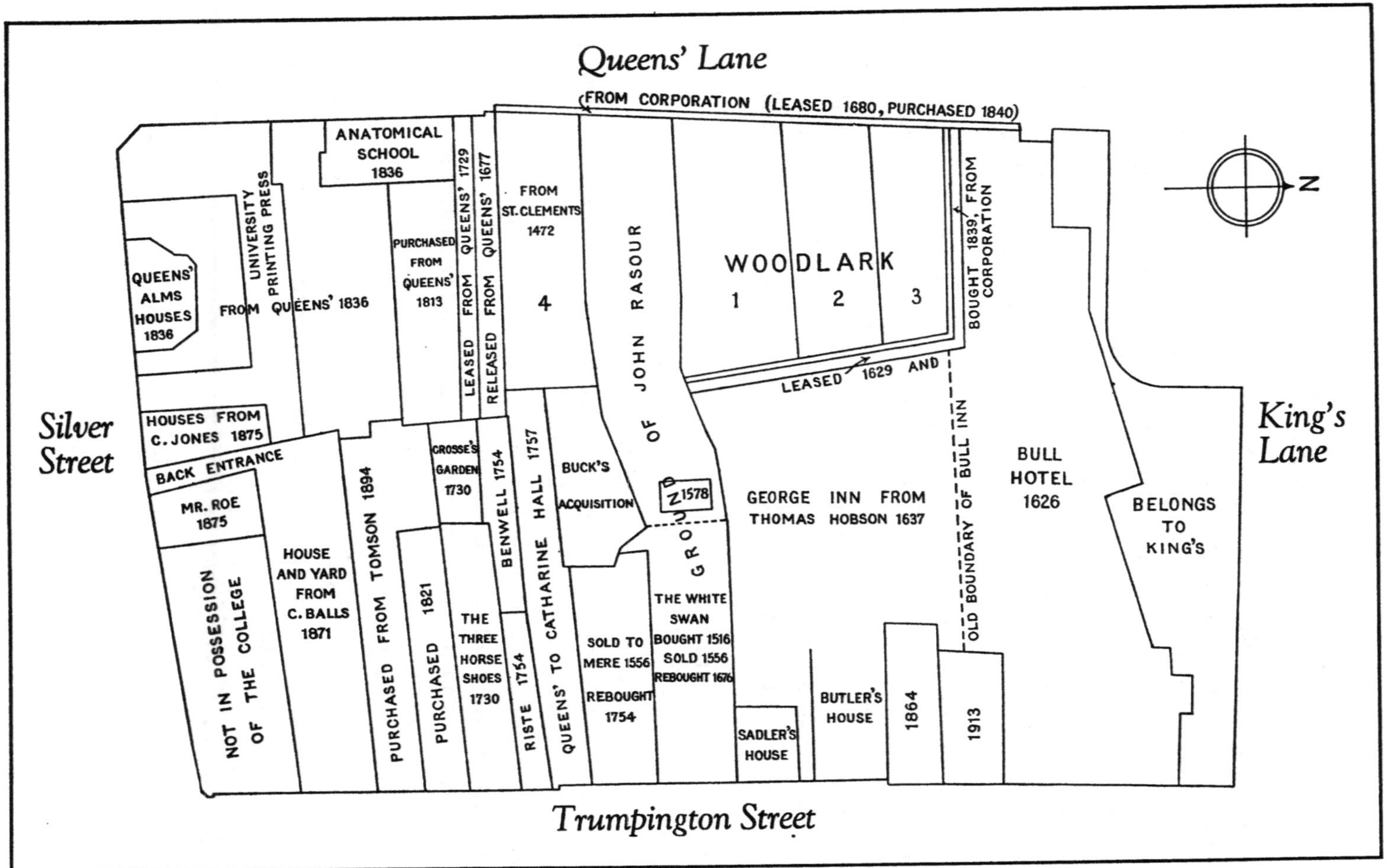

The Site and its Acquisition

The early statutes refer to the Tower, where the Treasury was. It would certainly be near the Lodging of the Master, who was its Keeper (*custos*). If the not unnatural assumption be made that the Hall, Kitchen and Buttery have remained roughly on their present site since the foundation, there remain as possible sites for the Tower the corner by the Library and the corner by the Chapel. It does not appear possible to decide definitely between the two sites, but as our old records closely associate the Master's rooms with the Library there should perhaps be given a slight preference to that corner of the Court.

The question now presents itself: which were the rooms reserved for the use of the Master? Willis and Clark mark as the Lodge that part of the College now occupied by the Screens, but G. F. Browne, in a charming *Historical Sketch* prefixed to the first edition of the *Year-Book and Register*,[1] shows good reason for believing that a great part of the Lodging was on the east side of the quadrangle. The extant evidence is to be found in the statutes and in two inventories.

The Founder's statutes reserve for the use of the Master:

(1) The "chief" chamber (*camera principalis*);
(2) The "better one over the Hall" (*melior super aulam*);
(3) Another room between the last and the Library (*alia camera intercepta inter praedictam cameram et librariam*).

Freedom of choice, however, is left to the Master, in case he should find it convenient to make other arrangements.

In the Edwardian statutes the rooms assigned to the Master are:

(1) The "chief" bedroom over the Hall;
(2) A bedroom between this and the Library.

In the inventory made by the Fellows in 1623 to protect themselves against possible dishonesty on the part of the Master, the following are specified as the rooms of his lodging:

(1) The Master's great chamber;
(2) The Master's bed-chamber;

[1] Compiled by the Rev. W. T. Southward and Messrs R. R. Conway and F. M. Rushmore, Cambridge, 1902.

(3) The chamber next the Library;
(4) The gallery;
(5) The "old rome at the stayers foote leadinge to the Library".

There is another inventory in the first Audit Book, dated 19 October 1636. This mentions under the heading of the Lodge:

(1) The outward chamber;
(2) The great chamber;
(3) The chamber next the Library;
(4) The entry next the bed-chamber;
(5) The bed-chamber;
(6) The gallery.

It is interesting to note that the first item in the list of College property in the great chamber is "I Wainscott Portall at ye Entrance into ye Chamb Libra".

"The other facts we know", says Browne, "about this (north) side are, that the Hall had a chamber over it, that the Library was upstairs, and that there was a chamber between it and the chamber over the Hall."

"Now the whole length of the east side of the original College, intercepted between the north side and the south side, was 54 or 55 feet. The suggestion that the Master's gallery or principal chamber ran along the length of this side, no doubt on the first floor, with a window at the south end looking into the Chapel,[1] seems very natural. The entrance to his lodgings was presumably at the north-east corner of the quadrangle, and his guest chamber on the ground-floor below the gallery, perhaps leaving a covered entry to the Chapel between its southern end and the Chapel; the rest of his rooms were on the north side, one over the Hall, another, still on the first floor, between that and the Library, and another on the ground-floor at the foot of the steps up to the Library. These steps may have been his private way to the Library, a convenience which other Masters had. For the two first-mentioned guest rooms he turned to the right when he entered from the Court; for the others he turned to the left."

[1] We know that there was a "windowe looking into ye chappell", and Browne remarks that "we can scarcely think that the Chapel would be commanded from any room except one in the occupation of the Master".

If this reconstruction be accepted, Kitchen, Buttery, Hall, Library and Master's Lodging occupied two sides of the quadrangle, leaving for students' chambers the other two sides, which would give about eight sets.

The inventory of 1513 in the Register clearly states that the College was built on the southern two of the three tenements purchased by Woodlark, and the Library on the one to the north. These statements make it at least likely that the Library stood out from the rest of the buildings, and as it was certainly upstairs, the ground-floor may have been occupied by the cloisters which are so hard to fit in the original plan.[1]

The Chapel and Library were not completed at the opening of the College, probably for want of funds, as the benefactions of William Cotte and Clement Denston were intended to be devoted to the completion of these two buildings. The William Taylard bequest (26 Oct. 1505) of £100 was for the "building, repair and maintenance" of the College.[2] Dr Thomas Greene, Master of the College, gave (29 April 1517) £10 "towards a new structure of four chambers to be built on the south side of the College".[3] Alice Lupsett, widow of Thomas Lupsett, goldsmith, of London, gave (5 August 1523) £10 for the same purposes as William Taylard.[4]

These benefactions appear to show, not only that the original buildings were incomplete and without due provision for their maintenance and repair, but also that the need of new chambers was pressing. It is hard indeed to understand why this should be so. If the rule of "two in a set", laid down by Woodlark for Fellows, were applied to Fellow Commoners and students of lower rank, the original buildings would have accommodated at least sixteen, besides the Master. In 1558, when the College had not only established itself but increased in size, it mustered but eighteen, including the Master.

Perhaps it was becoming convenient, even at this early date, to allow a separate chamber to each Fellow. Even though the Edwardian statutes contemplated two Fellows to each chamber, it might be considered wise to retain this regulation when it was possible, and perhaps desirable, to adopt a more

[1] Fuller, p. 168, calls the College "complete in chapel, cloisters, library, hall etc." The order of the buildings is perhaps significant. [2] *Register*, I, 18.

[3] *Register*, I, 64. The number 4 confirms the estimate of 8 in the original building.

[4] *Register*, I, 32.

generous policy in assigning rooms. Certainly Marmaduke Monson in 1577 had a set of rooms to himself.[1]

Be this as it may, a range of chambers called Greene's Building was built on the Milne Street front to the south of the original quadrangle, on the site acquired in 1516.

John Cragge, the business Fellow of the College during the second half of the sixteenth century, built a "gallery"[2] opposite Greene's Building and extending southwards from the Chapel. This was pulled down in 1611 to make room for a new block of chambers called the Claypoole Building. This addition to the structure of the College is noteworthy in at least two respects. In the first place there is the original contract with John Atkinson, which enables us to reconstruct the building with tolerable certainty; in the second place it shows that the College was beginning to find in students' chambers a profitable investment.

The building is to be two storeys high, each storey being nine feet from floor to ceiling, and the breadth eighteen feet from the inside of the brick wall to the outside of the groundsill in the lower rooms, and the second storey as broad as the said brick wall will allow it to be. The rooms are to be six in number, with partitions for study and bed-chamber, and there is to be a case of stairs without the building, of such convenient size as to carry to each room a fair pair of stairs. Each room is to have a fair bay window on the College side; at the end there is to be a bay window, and convenient lights on the other side by clerestories. The builder is to take down and use "the gallerie wch Mr Cragg buylt and now standeth in the said Coll: to his owne proper use comodity and behoofe, with all thappurtenances". The whole work is to be completed within twenty days after the next Michaelmas, and the builder is to be paid £60 at once, and 100 marks on 22 October.

The amount of cash paid for this building was £126. 13*s*. 4*d*., and of this Sir John Claypoole found £120. By an indenture dated 31 December 1613

[1] *Register* C, and p. 227.

[2] It is not known to what uses this gallery was put. The need was present, however, as is shown by the mention of a gallery in the inventories of 1623 and 1636. It is possible that it was used as a common room on the occasion of a feast. *Aula sive parlura* is a frequent expression in our old documents; perhaps the gallery served as a *parlura*.

he gave to the Master and Fellows the aforesaid sum "for and toward the edifying and erecting of certain lodgings and chambers in the said College or Hall commonly called the New Buildings". The Master and Fellows on their part are to maintain two scholars out of the rent, allowing each one half of £5. 6*s*. 8*d*.

The number of students had greatly increased during the past fifty years, and was about to increase still further, so that more accommodation was becoming a pressing necessity. About the same date there was built another block of chambers with the £100 left by Mrs Rosamond Payne for "the purchase of land or rent in fee simple for the maintenance of one or two scholars in Catharine Hall". The recipients are to maintain two scholars, paying to each five marks a year. The money was made over to the College by James Frampton, executor to Mrs Rosamond Payne, by an indenture dated 4 July 1610, but it is not known when the Payne Building was put up nor where it stood. "Ross: Paynes Court" is mentioned in the Bursar's accounts for 1624–5, but the rooms were probably built at least twelve years earlier. As to the position, Willis and Clark suggest that the block ran westward from the southern end of the Claypoole Building. If this view be adopted, there was a small quadrangle to the south of the original buildings, the sides of which were formed by Greene's Building, the south side of the original quadrangle, the Claypoole Building and the Payne Building. The four sides enclosed the College Garden, in which was the Dove-house.

The period following the completion of the Claypoole Building owes much to the enterprise of Thomas Buck, Fellow, Bursar, Esquire Bedell, and University Printer. The site east of the Claypoole Building was not in the possession of the College, with the exception of a piece west of the Chapel and of a small piece purchased in 1578 for £5.[1] During the period 1622–4 Buck, by much skilful manœuvring, managed to bring within the control of the College practically the whole of what is now the south-east quarter of the grass-plot. The details are obscure to a degree, but the main facts are clear enough. On 24 October 1622 Buck obtained a lease of the property to the

[1] See *Register*, I, 79, where power of attorney is given to John Cragge to take possession of part of the "Hay House" in Cambridge. This was part of the White Swan tenement.

south of the Swan, and on 15 June 1624 leased to the College the western half of it. At the expiration of this lease the College in 1648 obtained another from Cornelius Archer, who had acquired the property in 1623. It was finally bought by the College on 3 May 1662 for £30.

On 14 October 1622 Cornelius Archer conveyed to Thomas Buck for £6. 13*s.* 4*d.* a little piece of ground towards the north 2 feet in breadth, towards the south 3 feet 9 inches in breadth, and in length from north to south 20 feet 3 inches; also one other piece of ground, on the north side in length 11 feet 7½ inches, on the south side in length 12 feet, and in breadth throughout 10 feet. On 5 August 1623 Thomas Hobson conveys to the College a small parcel of ground on which a wall and stack of chimneys were built.

Somewhere on the area now controlled by the College, probably next to the Claypoole Building, a new range of buildings was in progress in October 1622, for the conveyances referred to in the last paragraph speak of the "new building now erecting towards the west" and of the brick wall and chimney stacks "lately erected and builded". The whole made up the New Court, which included what are called Archer's Court and Buck's Court. The Fellows of this period referred to this court as "the back Court by Archer", "the Court behind the chappell", and perhaps "the Pump Court". The rent paid to Buck was £3.[1]

The accounts also mention the "Old Buildings", the "Court next ye Streete", the "Little Court", the Garden and the Cloisters. An attempt must be made to identify these, although certainty in some cases is not possible.

The strip of land leased from the town of Cambridge in 1629 is said to lead to the old building. The College accounts have the following entries:

1637–8	For mending the Storehouse wall next ye bowling greene etc	00. 02. 07
1683–4	ye old building at ye end of ye chappell.	
1688–9	the old building at the end of the chappell.	

[1] Accounts for:

1623–4	To Mr Bucke for the yeares rent for ye ground of ye New Court	3. 0. 0
1628–9	For the rent of the court behind the chappell	3. 0. 0
1630–1	For rent of the backe court by Archer	3. 0. 0
1631–2	For rent of the back court by Archer's house	3. 0. 0

As the bowling green ran from near what is now the centre of the grass-plot towards the present Ante-chapel, Willis and Clark infer that by the old buildings are meant the stable, storehouse, etc. which stood near the Chapel. It seems more likely that "old building" means just what it says, and that any old part of the College could be so called. At any rate the 1688 accounts refer to an old building next the street, and those for 1623–4 under the heading "In ye old buildings" include "ye tiles over the Master's lodging and bedchamber", and also "Mr Lothians chamber".

By the Little Court is meant, according to Willis and Clark, the original court constructed by Woodlark. In it (accounts for 1623–4) was the staircase of Mr Perne, Bursar in 1624–5.

The Court next the Street was probably the one enclosed by the buildings of Greene, Payne and Claypoole, in which were the Garden and the Dovehouse.

> 1623–4 In the garden. For mending the Dovehouse doore.

There remain the Cloisters, which are mentioned by Fuller. From the accounts for various years from 1636–7 we gather that they had a door, a seat or bench, windows and chambers. The most interesting entry is in the accounts for 1648–9:

> Allowed Mr Lynford for ye Income of the middle study in
> the furthest chamb^r^ of ye Cloister-building 4. 2. 6

"As however we have already accounted for all the space within the College, it could only have stood on part of Hobson's ground; a theory which is strengthened by the fact that no entries concerning it are met with before 1636–37."[1] Hobson's house and ground were acquired in 1637, and this theory of Willis and Clark assumes that within a few months there was put up in Hobson's yard an elaborate structure of cloisters and chambers, including the chamber of a Fellow, without the slightest trace of a record in any of the College documents. No theory as to the position of the Cloisters is free from difficulty, but if it be assumed that they were under the Library, there are perhaps fewer difficulties than on any other hypothesis. It would be

[1] Willis and Clark, II, 94.

tempting to identify the Cloisters with Buck's Building of 1622, were it not for two entries in the accounts for 1685–6:

repairing the chambers in the Cloysters[1]	0.	10.	6
repairing the Northside of Bucks building	0.	10.	2

The College records abound in references to the work of Buck at this period. He was Bursar in 1622–3 and again in 1628–9. Perhaps the first book of Bursar's accounts, which commences with the year 1622–3, at a time when the College had doubts of the integrity of the Master, was due to Buck's business ability and attention to detail.

On 4 January 1622/3 the College agreed to pay back to Thomas Buck all moneys expended by him on the new building.[2] On 9 April 1623 there was paid to him £31. 8*s*. 8*d*., in part payment of £140 due to him upon a bond given him by the College. There is no such bond in the Register, but the part payment is an entry in the accounts of the year. On 27 January 1623/4 a bond was given to Thos. Buck, Steward of the College, for £143. 6*s*. 0½*d*. disbursed by him out of his own purse for the building and repairing of the College. On 10 December 1624 a bond for £30 was given to Thomas Buck—the money to be repaid before 1 January 1627. In the accounts to Michaelmas 1628 is an entry of £21. 6*s*. 8*d*. "paid to Mr Bucke in full discharge of a debt due to him from ye Colledge". The sum of £21. 3*s*. 1½*d*. was paid to Mr Buck in 1630 in part payment of a larger sum due to him *pro aedificiis nuper extructis*. A further bond for £277 was given by the College on 7 January 1630/1, the money to be repaid on the first day of the following May, while an entry occurs in the accounts of the year 1635–6 of £7 "P^d^ to Mr Thomas Buck in full discharge of ye Coll: debt". Among the receipts for the year 1636–7 occurs the entry: "Left of the money which Mr Buck gave to the Colledge—04 08 00". In 1625–6 "P^d^ for a salt-seller

[1] Perhaps these "Cloysters" are the new ones referred to by Bonnell. See p. 30.

[2] "Whereas we, the Master and Fellows of St Katherine's Hall in Cambridge, have appointed and assigned Mr Bucke, Fellow of the said College, to oversee the building and repairing thereof, we now also do, with our full consent, conclude and agree that what monies soever he already hath and shall disburse for the finishing of the said building already begun shall be paid again unto the said Thomas Bucke or his assigns by the said College." [4 January 1622/3: draft in Buck's handwriting except the date.]

which Mr Bucke bought for y^e^ Colledge—4—0—6". At the end of the accounts for 1672–3 is a note: "The fourty pounds wch Mr Thomas Buck gave to our Library were thus laid out viz." There follows a list of the books bought.

The College in Lyne (1574)

Buck was evidently an interesting character, ready to give but readier still to lend, ever willing to carry out on his own responsibility, and in his own name, what he thought would ultimately be to the advantage of the College, waiting patiently until his colleagues were willing or able to take over from him what he had done on their behalf.

The old plans of Cambridge, made by Lyne (1574), Braun (1575), Hamond

(1592) and Fuller (1634?),[1] are so confusing and at the same time so interesting that they deserve a section to themselves. Of St Catharine's in Hamond the latest work on these plans says:[2] "The tiny entrance court has no building on its western side, but is parted from Queens' Lane by a wall,

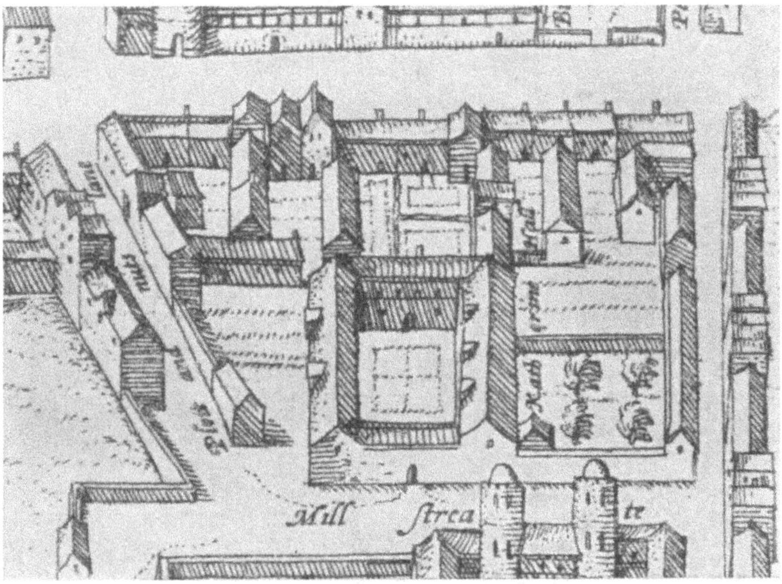

The College in Braun (1575)

in which there is a low door. On its other sides it is enclosed by buildings: those on the north and south sides are prolonged eastward beyond the court, and in the northern prolongation is contained the Chapel, which is marked by a large window in the eastern gable. The position of the Hall, in the northern half of the building which fronts the entrance from Queens' Lane, is clearly indicated by a single large window and by the door of the screens passage, seen in the plan on its eastern side. South of the entrance court, and larger than it, is shown the interior court, contained by ranges on three sides, and on the south side separated by a wall from a garden."

[1] *Old Plans of Cambridge*, 1574–1798, by Clark and Gray, Part I (text), Part II (plans): Cambridge 1921.

[2] Clark and Gray, I, 62, 63.

The position of the Hall is largely a matter of conjecture. There would be a great convenience in building the new Hall, which was opened in 1675, on a different site from that of the old; building on the same site would force the College to have its meals in another place during a long interval. On the

The College in Hamond (1592)

other hand the Kitchens,[1] which were put up about 1634, served the old Hall for forty years. Is it likely that meals were carried across the court? Is it not more probable that the Kitchens were built near the old Hall? The question must remain unsettled.

But the position of the old Chapel is scarcely a matter of uncertainty. Either Hamond has put it on the north end instead of on the south, or else

[1] These are still used, and are on the extreme north-west of the main court.

Clark and Gray are wrong in saying that the Hamond building is the Chapel.

John Atkinson in 1611 contracted to build a two-storey range of six chambers as long as is "between the Chapel and the utmost part of the ground

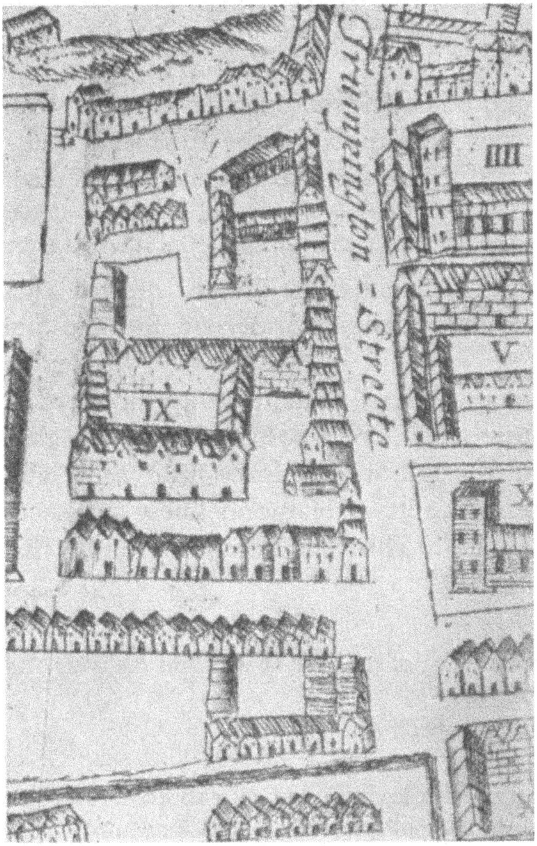

The College in Fuller (1634?)

towards Queens' College orchard; to be set up in the place where the gallery now standeth".[1] This must mean that the Chapel was at the south-east, not the north-east, corner of the original court.

[1] See Willis and Clark, II, 111.

Again, Hamond's "Chapel" lies, in part at least, upon the site of the present Hall.[1] Therefore by 1675 the old Chapel, if Clark and Gray are right, must have been demolished. But we know that it was not, and that money was spent upon repairing it[2] until the new Chapel was built.[3]

Carter, whose *History* was published in 1753, speaks of:[4] "The Flower-Garden, where stood the old Chapel". This garden was in the centre of the present court.[5]

It is necessary to quote this evidence in order to show where the old Chapel stood; that it was *not* on the same site as the present Chapel, or even partly on it, is proved by the petition of the Master and Fellows to the Bishop of Ely, praying him to consecrate their new Chapel. In it they say that the Chapel could not be built in a regular manner, "without altering the situation of the Chappel", and further that they have "erected a Chappel, in a new place, much more convenient and decent for the public worship of God".[6]

As to the wall facing Queens' Lane, it is not indicated in Lyne, Braun or Fuller. There is, moreover, strong positive evidence against it. In a rental of chambers which, though at least forty-four years later than Hamond, deals with the original court as Hamond knew it, the rent is given of a chamber "over the gate". This rental is so interesting that a copy is given below.

[1] It seems to occupy the east of the present Hall and the west of the present Chapel.

[2] Willis and Clark, II, 97.

[3] It was opened in September 1704.

[4] Carter, p. 204.

[5] "A handsome Portico, that leads into a Court about 60 Yards long and 40 broad, in the Middle of which is a pretty Flower-Garden paled round." *London Magazine*, 1748, p. 162. *Account of the Colleges and Halls of the University of Cambridge*. It is likely enough that, when the old Chapel was pulled down, the Society adopted the plan of planting this garden, "paled round" to mark that the spot was once holy ground.

[6] See Willis and Clark, II, 107 and Cooper, *Annals*, IV, 67. It is just possible that the building that Clark and Gray would identify with the Chapel is the old Library, which was, according to all the documentary evidence, on or near the place where Hamond's "Chapel" stands.

[Endorsement to a rental of date 1636]

The Quarterly Rent of the Studies in the College.	*s.*	*d.*
For the Chamber in the New building	5	0
Except the 2 Upper which pay 2*s.* and pay [?] for every study ...	4	0
The Chamber over the kitchen, 4 studies	5	0
The Chamber above that	4	0
The Chamber against the Lodge stairs	4	0
The Chamber against the Pump	3	4
The Chamber above the Lodge	1	0
The Chamber over the Gate	5	0
The Porter's Chamber	0	0
The old Building next to the street	3	4
Except the lower Chamber over the left hand as you are in	5	0
Ex. the mid Chamber [2*s.*]	6	8
Ex. [Sir John] Claypole's Building	5	0
Except the over chamber on the right hand as you are in	3	4
Of building next to Hobson's	5	0
Except the [? middle] chamber which pays quarterly for every study 2*s.* 6*d.*	10	0

The three plans mentioned in the last paragraph agree in showing dormers on the north and south sides; Hamond's has no dormers. Lyne, if not the others, appears to indicate two storeys on these sides with dormered attics over them. Fuller, while showing the 1634 building, has no trace of any other addition to the original court; Greene Building, Claypoole Building and Payne Building are all absent.

In order that the reader may judge for himself, reproductions have been made of the four earliest plans of St Catharine's. The writer's own view is that little trust can be placed in the accuracy of the details in any of them. In general outline they all give fairly accurate information, and thus tantalize the curious by raising false hopes of solving interesting problems.

With Buck's Building of 1622 what we may call the first stage of the growth of the College came to an end. All the buildings, old and new, mentioned in the preceding paragraphs were pulled down during the period of reconstruction, but one range of chambers, built round about 1630, the last of the old and the first of the new, was spared, probably because it fitted in with, if it did not actually suggest, the style of the new quadrangle begun in 1673–4. It still remains in practically the same state as it was originally.

This building was made possible by the bequest of the Bull Inn, left to the College in the will of John Gostlin, M.D., Master of Gonville and Caius College. The will is dated 9 October 1626,[1] and Gostlin died soon after. The property reached from Milne Street to Trumpington Street, and the profits from it were for seven years to be paid to William Gostlin, the executor, who, however, on 10 April 1630, gave up this claim in return for an annual payment of £40 for 3½ years.[2]

On 16 August 1629 the Town of Cambridge leased to the College a strip of land, lying behind (i.e. to the south of) the Bull, "whereon part of the new buildings...are sett..., conteyning in breadth at the end next the Bull gate fower foote and a halfe, and in length from the said Bull gate to the ould buildings of the said Hall one hundered Sixtie eight foote". The lease was for 500 years, and the rent 12 pence a year. The land was conveyed to the College, more than 200 years afterwards, on 7 February 1839. On the western part of this strip and of the Bull yard, together with part of the original site, the new building was erected.

This block of chambers, called to-day E staircase, forming the west side of the court known now as the Bull Court or Walnut-tree Court, but once as Dr Gostlin's Court, is eighty-seven feet in length, with the Kitchen at the southern end. The windows facing Queens' Lane have been altered to match the windows of the Eachard Building to the south, and the small

[1] The following items from the Audit book of 1626–7 are of interest:

For a supper to enterteyne Mr Gostlin	1. 01. 0
For another supper to enterteyne Mr Gostlin and others	1. 04. 3
for wine and tobacco then	0. 06. 0

[2] The College had use of part of the Bull yard in 1629, for among the payments of 1628–9 we note:

For the rent of p^t of the Bull grownd from Lady day till Midsummer 4. 0. 0

room[1] shown in Loggan as projecting over the Bull yard has been taken down, but in most other respects the block remains as it was when first erected. It is mentioned in the 1629 lease from the Town and in a lease of the Bull Inn granted in 1631, where a "faire building of stone and brick enclosed with a brick wall on the north and east side" is said to be "now erected". Willis and Clark, relying on three entries in the Bursar's accounts, believe that the statement in the Bull lease was a fabrication. The items are these:

1630–1	For carriage of 170 loade of earth out of ye new court	2.	2.	6
1631–2	To Mr Williamson for pavinge the back entrie of the bull, and building the wall towards the garden	7.	13.	4
	For sweepinge Dr Gostlin's court	0.	0.	6

These entries seem insufficient to prove a gratuitous lie in the lease of 1631, especially when the work was probably done months before payment was brought to account. In all probability the building was fairly advanced in 1631, but progress was slow, as some difficulty was experienced in finding the money required. The completion of the work is marked by certain items in the accounts for 1636–7:

For red oker for the new building	0.	1.	0
For three load of sand and six hundred of bricks att 1*s.* 10*d.* per hundred for the new building	0.	13.	6

The main "new building" expenses are brought to account in the year 1634–5. The whole charge amounts to £260. 5*s.* 10*d.*, and the receipts include £200 from Mr Stafford and £50 from Mr Spurstow, the Bursar of the preceding financial year. The accounts for 1636–7 record that £8. 5*s.* 6*d.* was spent "for repairing Mr Spurstow's building", but we do not know who Mr Stafford was. In 1627 Mrs Stafford, wife of Mr Alexander Stafford, left property to help four poor scholars, and there is no account of payment made from this source before 1689, so perhaps the profits of this bequest were diverted for a time. It is possible that the sum of £277, lent to the College

[1] See 1640–1 accounts: "To Masons and Labourers for worke on the wall built to support the studdy over the Bull-gate 2. 5. 4." The wall from which the "studdy" projected is still weak where the room once stood.

by Thomas Buck on 7 January 1630/1, had some connection with the building scheme.[1]

The oldest buildings in the College were by this time somewhat decayed. It would seem from the accounts that defects were tinkered with, and that the College lived more or less from hand to mouth in respect of repairs. On two occasions, however, more systematic attempts were made for a thorough overhaul. In 1638–9 the sum of £93. 2*s.* 2*d.* is brought to account for "Enlarging of the Chappell and Lodge", most of the money being spent on labour. In 1657–8 a sum of £60. 3*s.* 8*d.* was expended "in the Extraordinary repaires of the Colledg. viz. for slating and sparring ye Chappell, ripping both buildings in ye old Court, part of ye Lodging, cloysters, and building in Archers Court; ripping all the new building, and taking down ye Chimnys, new runing and repairing the leads in the new building, etc." To pay for these repairs the sum of £61 was taken "from the Treasury"—a transaction that throws some light on College finance in pre-banking days.[2]

[1] The Bursar's accounts for 1634–5 give the following details with regard to the "New Building".

For bricks	34.	0.	10
for lime	16.	7.	6
for hair, sand, lath, ? nails, painting, slate and tiles	27.	0.	4
for lead	26.	13.	5
for timber	37.	18.	5
the smith	16.	17.	6
the mason	27.	10.	0
the glazier	2.	18.	7
for workmanship	70.	19.	3
	260.	5.	10

In one of the attics of this building is an oak beam with the following initials roughly carved:

R.L. 1634
I.P. 1639

Robert Long entered Pensioner in 1633, and John Pew entered Pensioner in 1638. The first entry shows that the room was fit for habitation in 1634.

[2] See p. 263, note 2.

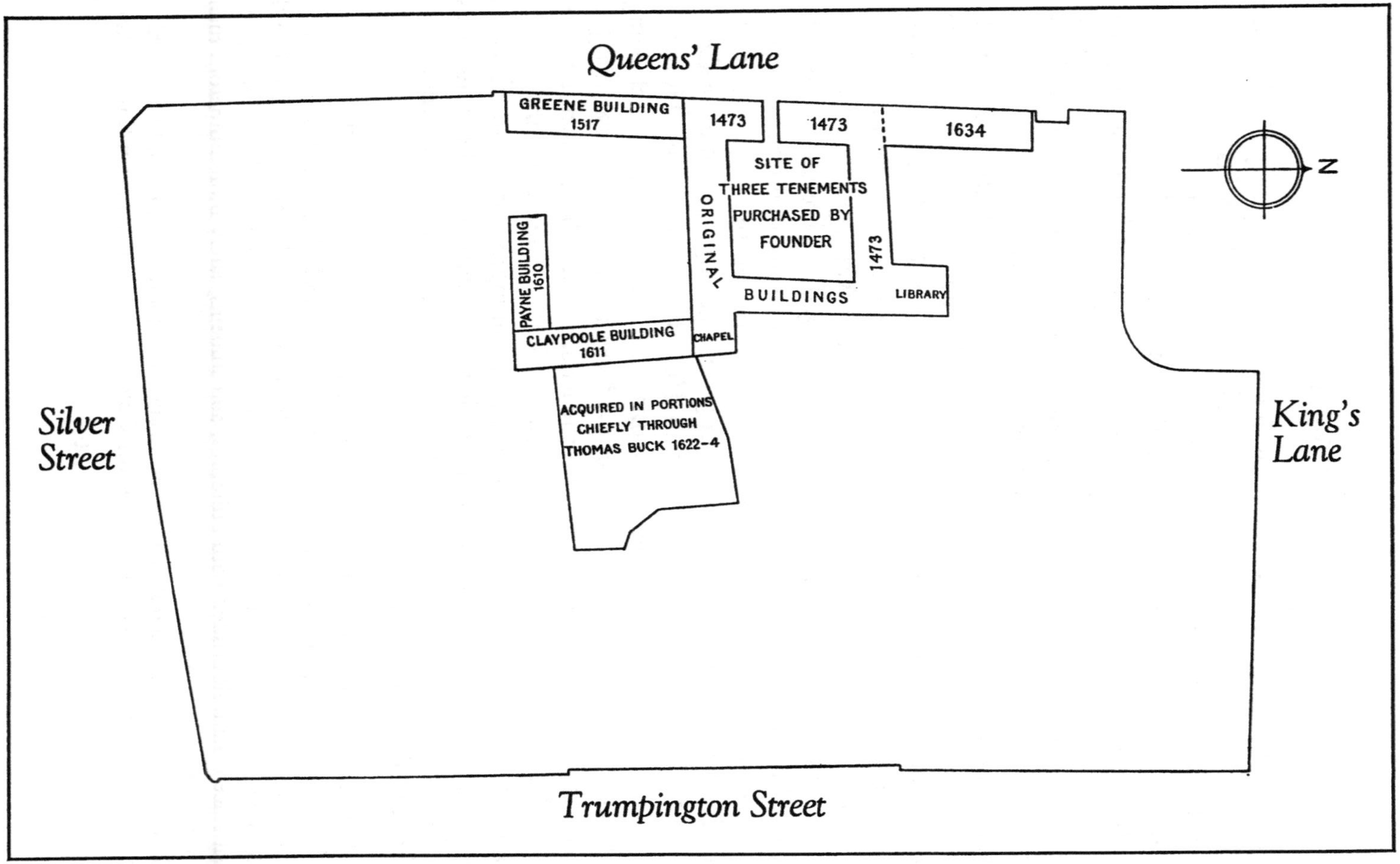

The College in 1634. The strips leased in 1629 are not shown. The date of the Payne Building is doubtful.

Fuller,[1] writing about this time, calls St Catharine's a "pretty Hall" (*Aula bella*), and says that its poverty is its only blemish, and hints that the bequest of Gostlin has helped it to grow both in numbers and in size. But it is obvious from the Bursar's accounts that the old buildings at least were almost past repair, and no surprise need be felt that a scheme for rebuilding was soon to be launched. The surprising fact is that the necessity of rebuilding was not seen earlier, at the time when the buildings of 1610–22 were being erected, only to be pulled down some seventy years later.

One important addition to the acquisition of the present site remains to be noticed before the great rebuilding that was begun in 1674. This was the famous George Inn, lying between the Bull on the north and the White Swan on the south, the boundary between it and the White Swan separating also the two parishes of St Botolph and St Benedict. It was acquired about 1637, but the conveyance no longer exists. It had belonged to Thomas Hobson, the carrier, who died on 1 January 1630/1, leaving it to his grandson, who sold it to the College. The only means we have of dating the transfer is to be found in the accounts for the years 1636–7 and 1637–8, which refer to Hobson's yard, the barns and stables in Hobson's ground, and Hobson's house. The house is called by various names in the accounts, the chief being "Hobson's" and "Sadler's". The rent paid was at first £3, afterwards £4, which was divided as dividend among the Master and Fellows, although the taxes and repairs were charged to College Stock. The house and stables occupied a frontage of 60 feet exactly in Trumpington Street northwards from the junction of St Benet's and St Botolph's parishes. The house was pulled down in 1760; the stables, in the opinion of Bishop Browne, were on the site of the modern Chapel.[2]

[1] "Lowness of endowment and littleness of receipt is all that can be cavilled at in this foundation, otherwise proportionably most complete in chapel, cloisters, library, hall etc. Indeed this house was long town-bound (which hindered the growth thereof) till Dr Gostlin that good physician cured it of that disease, by giving the Bull inn thereunto, so that since it hath flourished with buildings, and students, lately more numerous than in other colleges." P. 168.

[2] Philpott was much interested in the acquisition of Hobson's house and yard, which gave, as his notes say, a back entrance to the College from Trumpington Street. There

On 22 March 1648 Cornelius Archer leased to the College for 21 years a piece of ground with a house thereon built, lying on the south side of the College and extending to Sir John Claypoole's Buildings towards the west, in length from east to west 75 feet 8 inches and from north to south in the middle 26 feet in breadth. The Master and Fellows agree to pay 20 shillings rent yearly and at the end of the term to build a sufficient wall of good material to fence and sever the said ground from the College ground and yard. This was the property part of which Thomas Buck, as we have seen, leased to the College in 1624. When it was finally bought by the College on 3 May 1662, the purchase money was £30, which seems a very low figure.

The credit of first conceiving the idea of rebuilding the "ruinous structure" (as it is styled in Eachard's epitaph) of the old College belongs[1] to Matthew Scrivener, Vicar of Haslingfield, *alumnus* of St Catharine's and benefactor of the new Chapel. He appears to have influenced John Lightfoot, the Master, for the work of rebuilding was begun on 23 February 1673/4, as we learn from the rough accounts kept by Eachard, who succeeded Lightfoot as Master in 1675.

But it was after the death of Lightfoot that the work began to move apace. His successor was an indefatigable collector of subscriptions, and succeeded

are various items in the Bursar's accounts for 1636–7 showing that the College at that time (as it was later) was busy repairing and improving the property. Similar entries occur in the accounts for the years ending 1640, 1645, 1648, 1652, 1654, 1655. In all except the first it is called "Sadler's". In July 1766 the Court of Chancery ordered that the sum of £72, with interest at 4 %, should be secured on the Barton farm (bought with Mrs Ramsden's money) as a compensation to the Master and Fellows for their loss. Philpott adds: "I have not found any title deeds of Hobson's house and yard, nor any conveyance of them to the College.... There are no accounts at all of the receipts and expenditure of the money in the Treasury, which was more immediately under the control of the Master: many benefactions were given to the College, such as Dr Sibbs', Lady Cocket's, Mr Shirland's, Dr Gouge's, Mr Colson's, Mr Jordan's, Mr Alured (*sic*), Mr Mustard's, and the lady Rebecca Romney's, but no account has been preserved of the receipts or of the expenditure."

[1] See the inscription under Loggan's engraving of the College (1688). Scrivener entered the College as a Sizar in 1637, and died in 1688. Evelyn, too, writing in 1654, calls the College a "meane structure". See Cooper, *Annals*, III, 460.

in inspiring others with his energy and zeal. At his death the rebuilding was unfinished, but it was well advanced, and the accounts he kept tell us plainly how the money was raised and expended.

Although financial information about this, the greatest building scheme in the College history, is fairly full, it must be remembered that, according to modern ideas, accounts of this period are unsatisfactory and imperfect. Single entry is the method employed, and there were no checks applied to prevent waste and peculation. The only safeguard was the probity of the executive officials, though it must be confessed that, as far as we can see, confidence was rarely misplaced. Nevertheless it is with something of a shock that we discover that at his death in 1697 Eachard had spent upon his building scheme £950. 17*s.* 5*d.* of University money, over which he had control when Vice-Chancellor. No secret was made of the transaction, no objections were raised, and no scandal occurred either during his lifetime or after his death.

The legitimate means of raising money adopted by Eachard were subscriptions, loans, annuities and sale of plate. These will be discussed in a later section of the present work.

The scheme for rebuilding made it necessary to extend the site of the College to the south. Accordingly the College applied to Queens' for a lease of part of the garden which was situated south of the southern boundary of Woodlark's fourth tenement. After some delay an answer was given 17 February 1676 that Queens' had no objection to leasing a strip 10 feet in breadth and about 36 yards in length, "provided that the said Master and Fellows of St. Cath. Hall do at their own charge procure the hands of 6 Serjeants at Law, or the King's Counsel, to satisfy Queens' College that it may be lawfully done, and shall further procure his Majesty's Royal leave for the greater satisfaction and security to the Society of Queens' College aforesaid".

Seven lawyers[1] were consulted and the leave of Charles II obtained;[2]

[1] They were Francis Pemberton, Thomas Waller, Thomas Hanmer, John King, Thomas Exton, William Jones, Lestrange Calthorpe.

[2] See Willis and Clark, II, 80, where the letter is printed. A copy of it endorsed "To our Trusty and Well beloved the Master and Fellows of Q[ueens] C[ollege] in our University of Cambridge" is among the St Catharine's muniments.

Plate I

Queens' College from the Master's present Garden
(about 1830)

and very soon afterwards some sort of a lease must have been granted, for the strip concerned was built over when the Master's Lodge was built, but it is strange that the first extant lease is dated 25 February 1706/7.

Although the seven lawyers agreed that Queens' might safely grant the lease, five of them signed a separate opinion, which ended with a warning: "It will concern the Master and Fellows of St Catherine's Hall to be well assured before they build, that the College will not afterwards avoid the lease, as they may do, until eleven years are passed, and a new lease made at the rent that shall then have been paid for the greatest part of one and twenty years."

The anxiety of Queens' about parting with its original possessions in the immediate vicinity of the College buildings brings to mind a similar anxiety felt by St Catharine's, when that Society sought through an Act of Parliament (1756) permission to adjust its site to make room for the buildings of the Ramsden Trust.

The annual rent paid to Queens' under the lease of 1707 was 20 shillings. In 1729 another lease was granted of the piece of ground along with another piece, 123½ feet long and from 7 feet 2 inches to 8 feet 9 inches broad, for 21 years at an annual rent of two pounds. Another lease of both pieces at the same rent was granted in 1751. This lease was allowed to expire, but about 1789 Queens' thought it was time for St Catharine's to take out a new one, at an advanced rent. St Catharine's demurred to the increase on the ground that the original contract implicitly fixed the rent in perpetuity. One cannot avoid the suspicion that much of the wrangling that ensued was due to the love of quarrelling so common in the University at this period. The sum involved is so trivial, and the equity of the case so clear. Finally a lease was agreed to for 21 years from Michaelmas 1789 at a rent advanced by one shilling a year.

In 1799, Queens' being now able to sell under the Land Tax Act, the two Colleges began to discuss the question of purchase. The price asked by Queens' was £530 which, for 252 square yards, was at the rate of over £10,000 per acre. St Catharine's submitted a case to Sir John Mitford, the Attorney-General, and asked for his advice, whether to settle at once or to wait for the lease in force to expire. The Attorney-General advised that it would be probably wise in every way to pay the £530, but if the Master and Fellows decided to wait it would be prudent also to avoid all observation on the conduct of Queens' College in the meantime. "For however unconscionable the demand may be...yet it is easy to imagine that it will cost Catharine Hall more than £530 to procure for themselves elsewhere the same accommodation which they now enjoy by means of the ground in question, supposing that accommodation could be procured by building on another spot for the same purposes."[1]

St Catharine's waited until 1810, when the lease expired, spent over two years in talk, and finally (1813) bought the two pieces, along with another to the south of them, for £1372. A sum of £152. 6*s.* 0*d.* was paid as rent for the two pieces during the two years and a half that had elapsed since the expiration of the lease.

The lay-out adopted by the architect of this building scheme has given to the present court all its distinctive features. First came the modern Hall, Buttery, old Combination Room (now a gallery to the Hall) and Library[2] (1675–7), then the old Lodge (ready 1676–8) and finally D and C staircases (the shell finished by 1679, but probably not ready for occupation before 1687). The Chapel was added in 1704, while the foundation of B and A staircases was not laid until 1757, when Mrs Ramsden had given her generous bequest to the College.

The buildings occupy three sides of a quadrangle, about 200 feet from east to west and 110 feet from north to south.[3] The west side abuts on Queens' Lane, the gateway in which was the main entrance until the Ramsden chambers were erected in the middle of the eighteenth century.

One of the chambers next to the archway was the Porter's Lodge, the Porter being, as we have seen, an undergraduate down to at least 1743. Thus Dr Crosse gave to the College his income of the chamber "up two pair of stairs on the south side adjoining the gate-house", and an order of 19 October 1710 decides that the chamber of the Frankland Fellow shall be "the ground

[1] The case and opinion are among the College muniments. [2] Over the Hall.

[3] The south-west corner has an acute angle, so that the northern range is 15 feet shorter than the southern. This irregularity adds a peculiar charm to the quadrangle by softening the hardness of its severe lines.

chamber on the right hand betwixt the Butteries and the gate-house". It was probably the chamber on the right hand as one enters C staircase, which has a curious passage leading towards the wall of the archway. A door in this wall would enable the occupant of this chamber to carry out his duties with comfort and efficiency.

The east side is open to Trumpington Street, with a fore-court of a breadth of over 50 feet, the site of the tenements once lining that street. Loggan's print shows that it was at any rate suggested to complete the quadrangle by a range of chambers on this site, and Carter, whose history appeared in 1753, says[1] that "the College is now purchasing several Tenements in Trumpington Street...to make room for a new Building wherein are to be Apartments for the new fellows and scholars, with a Library in front". The project was abandoned, probably for lack of funds, and the space was planted with a grove of elm-trees. These, with the iron palisades and entrance gates behind them, formed a beautiful foreground to the three-sided court, but in 1921 the trees were found to be rotten and dangerous, and had to be cut down. A new range of buildings begun in 1930 at the north-east corner, which will presently be described, helps partly to fill up the gap thus created, and when a corresponding wing has been erected on and near the present Porter's Lodge, there will be no appearance of either bareness or deficiency.

The general style of the whole College is modelled on that of the building erected in 1634. Both design and structure of this range of chambers were certainly very different from those of the old quadrangle. For thirty or forty years the Master and Fellows had before their eyes the old and the new, and were impressed with the superior beauty and excellence of the latter. These they resolved to perpetuate in their reconstruction, thus fixing the character of the Ramsden Building and also of those buildings recently erected. The "notes" of this character are dark-red brick, relieved by a little stone-work, three storeys with attics over them, and tiled roofs with dormers.

The solidity of the walls is worthy of a passing notice. At the base these are, at least in places, six feet thick, as workmen engaged on modern plumbing have found to their cost.

[1] See *History*, p. 199.

Internally, a set consists of two or else three rooms, an arrangement which seems to indicate that each set was designed for either one occupant or two.

Neither the official records nor Eachard's private note-books make it clear what architect was employed, or even whether an architect was employed at all. This is regrettable, but perhaps less so than our ignorance of the genius who designed the 1634 building. Willis and Clark point out that the College accounts of 1673–4 to 1676–7 mention payments to two "surveyors", Mr Elder and Robert Grumbold. The latter had been employed at Clare in 1669, and was, according to a tradition long current in the Society, mainly responsible for the work.

An old member of the College, James Bonnell, revisiting it 17 November 1679, wrote to his friend Strype an amusing letter, preserved in the Cambridge University Library.[1] It tells us that the end of the College next Queens' was finished at the time of Bonnell's visit, but the letter raises a most perplexing though interesting problem. For a little later he goes on to describe "the new buildings, which are walled, but not covered: they are very lovely, but the tower cloister is much too low; which was occasioned by Dr Barrow's intending to have a wall run through the middle of it lengthways, and then the height would have seemed tolerably well; but this being since converted into pillars, which in truth are better than a wall, yet serve to make the walk seem too low".

Where in the "new" (that is the present) buildings is the "tower"? Where is the "cloister" with pillars down the centre of it? The only part of the present building that could be called a tower is the Library staircase north of the screens, and if ever there was a cloister near it only one record, other than Bonnell's letter, has survived. It so happens that in the Bursar's accounts for the same year as Bonnell's visit there is an item of nine shillings for "4 New Wicker chairs in the Cloyster chamber".[2]

At Eachard's death, the funds for the rebuilding of the College were found

[1] See p. 307.

[2] The problem is all the more obscure because the old buildings, like the new, included a "cloister". See p. 13. To which of the two cloisters does this item refer? It seems impossible to say.

to be in a very embarrassed condition. This is not surprising, as Eachard, although a man of great ability and energy, was anxious for fame and glory at any cost, and cared not who paid the bill so long as he won a reputation for himself. At last an appeal was drawn up, and circulated in January 1698–9. It runs as follows:

"Whereas the Reverend and Worthy D[r] John Eachard, Late Master of Katharin Hall in the University of Cambridge, out of his great Zeal to promote Learning and Piety, did Design to Rebuild the said College or Hall, which through length of Time, was very much gone to Decay; and being thereto Encourag'd not only by the concurrent Advice and Approbation, but the Generous and Charitable Contributions of many Worthy Gentlemen and Divines, as well such as had been Students of the same College, and his own Pupils, as others in divers parts of the Kingdom; and having through his own indefatigable Industry, and great Expence, added to the liberality of other Contributors, made considerable progress towards the accomplishment of his intended Building, was still encouraged by the repeated Advice, and renew'd Promises, and large Subscriptions of many Prudent, Pious, and Charitably dispos'd Persons, to go on in a Work so greatly tending to the advancement of Learning and Piety: Accordingly, in the latter end of the Reign of King Charles the Second, he undertook a very Large and Chargeable Building, hoping that the Continuance of his own Care, Pains, and Expence, and the Promises and Subscriptions of others, who had engag'd themselves to be Benefactors, would enable him to finish this Great and Costly Work, as well as what he had formerly begun: But the sudden and unexpected Death of that Prince, and the Measures which his Successour took, in particular relating to the University's, raised such just Fears in the Hearts of Such, who otherwise were forward to promote This, and every good Work, least their well-meant Charity should be abus'd to serve the ends of Popish Superstition and Idolatry, as gave occasion to some to withdraw their Subscriptions, and others grew very cold and indifferent: Whereby it came to pass that a very great Debt was contracted, towards the discharging of which, notwithstanding his utmost Care and Pains, and the entire expence of all the proffits of his own Estate, his Mastership, and all his Preferments, he could make but slow advances. For the mighty charge which lay upon the Nation, towards the carrying on a long and rigorous War; and the great necessity of a very large Charity towards the support and relief of our Persecuted Brethren from abroad, rendered such as were willing, less able to assist and further him in his work. When therefore all other ways fail'd, 'twas at length, (not inconsiderately and rashly) but upon Mature Deliberation, Resolv'd to Engage in the building of a Chappel, this being thought the best Expedient, not only to discharge the old Debt, but likewise successfully to carry on and finish his intended work. Pursuant hereto, such Funds were thought upon, and in some part settled and compleated, as gave great hopes and encouragement. But the great difficulties which soon arose from the non-currency of Money; and the stop which was put to his own diligence and endeavours, by his lingering sickness, and at last his immature, and much lamented Death have unfortunately occasion'd that a very great Debt remains: Towards the clearing of which, the late Reverend Doctor (valuing the Public Good, more than the Private Interest of his Relations and Friends) has by Will, intirely bequeath'd his whole Estate of Inheritance, to the value of a Thousand Pounds and upwards; but this falling very short, we whose Names are here under written, being extremely sorry that a Series of unforeseen unlucky Accidents should have retarded and hindered so good a Work, and not willing that any discouragement should ly in the way of any future Patrons of Learning, and Benefactors to Mankind, do, as well towards the discharging of the said Debt, as carrying on the said Chappel, contribute in manner following."

This appeal, helped by the powerful advocacy of Sir William Dawes, the Master, was successful, and the building of the present Chapel was begun. It was consecrated on 1 September 1704 by Simon Patrick, Bishop of Ely, and the sermon, printed the same year, was preached by John Leng, Fellow of the College, and afterwards Bishop of Norwich. The site of the new Chapel lay east of the Hall, the old position, as the petition of the Society to the Bishop of Ely explains, being out of keeping with the general lay-out of the College. G. F. Browne believed, with much reason, that the position of the Chapel roughly corresponds to the site of Hobson's stables. The accounts of the time throw but little light on the details of the building. The most striking feature of the interior is the fine woodwork, for which John Austin received £350, while Francis Woodward was paid £110. 15*s*. 0*d*. for the carving.

There were two additions to the site in 1730, when the Three Horse Shoes was acquired, along with a small garden, bought by Dr Crosse for the use of the Master, immediately to the west of it. These were the last additions to the site before the benefaction of Mrs Mary Ramsden, who left her estates to the College for erecting chambers, and for providing stipends, for six Fellows and ten Scholars. It was her wish, as her Rules and Orders show, for the new buildings to front Trumpington Street,[1] but this suggestion proved impracticable, as did a similar suggestion in 1913. But the College set about acquiring the properties the possession of which would make her wish possible of fulfilment. In 1754 they bought for £416 from Alice Appleyard the eastern portion of the ground leased to Buck in 1622. Very soon afterwards they bought for £160 from George Riste the house to the north of the Three Horse Shoes and the tenement west of it from Anne Benwell for £140. Three years later, in 1757, they acquired the intervening property from Queens' College on condition of paying a perpetual annuity of £8.

The architect of the new building was James Essex, but he had little to do except continue the style of the existing buildings. His original task, sixteen sets and a library, was reduced through lack of means to twelve sets, B staircase (8), A staircase (4). The Trumpington Street front was left open and planted with elms, which, as we have seen, were cut down in 1921. The foundation stone of the new chambers was laid 1 July 1757, and the estimated cost of the whole was £7300. The present lawn was laid out after the completion of the Ramsden Building, though it is impossible to discover the exact date.

We have seen[2] that a writer in 1748 describes a garden "paled round" in the centre of the court formed by the new buildings. Edmund Carter in 1753, describing this same garden, says:[3] "The *Flower-Garden*, (where stood the old Chapel, and the Bones which were there dug up, were buried in the present Chapel) is a small but pretty spot, and kept very neat, and on a Pedestal in the Center, stood a Statue of Charity, with a Child at her breast, and two more by her Side; but was a few Years ago taken away, tho' I think it was an Ornament to the Garden." Dyer too, writing in 1814,[4] calls this garden "a little spot, but neat and elegant, 50 years ago a statue of Charity stood in the midst".

At the same time as the Ramsden scheme was being carried out the boundary between the Bull and the College was altered to make room for the offices, still in existence, between the Chapel and the Bull yard.

[1] See Carter, p. 199: "The College is now purchasing several Tenements in Trumpington Street...for a new building...with a Library in front."

[2] See p. 18.

[3] *History*, p. 204.

[4] *History*, II, 179.

No material change took place in the appearance of the College for a hundred years. Then in 1868, in order to make the High Table more comfortable, an oriel window was added to the Hall, which gave by its projection into the Court over four feet of length to the dais on which the Society dines. To prevent the discrepancy between the two styles being too glaring, the windows, together with those of the Buttery, Combination Room and Library, were taken out and replaced by others with Gothic tracery. In 1869 the interior of the Hall was wainscoted with oak. The cost of these changes was £1770.

One other slight addition to the College should be noticed here. On 7 February 1839 the reversion of two strips of land was conveyed by the Corporation of Cambridge for £31. 10*s*. 0*d*. The first of these strips had been leased to the College since 17 August 1629, and had made possible the building of the present E staircase. The second strip, leased to the College since 29 September 1680 (renewed 1 June 1724 and 8 May 1809), was void ground in the street on the west side of the College, about three feet in breadth and "ten score and seven" feet in length, on which were set up the "noble palisadoes" (still standing in 1936) presented by Dr Sherlock.

In 1875 the present Master's Lodge was begun. To provide a site, the lodging houses built in 1837 on the south-west corner of the island site were pulled down, and in addition a tenement was bought to provide room for a gateway and stables on the Silver Street front. The architect chosen was Mr W. M. Fawcett. A great deal of care was taken to find a suitable model to serve as a pattern. The Bursar's accounts for 1873–4 contain an item of £3. 2*s*. 9*d*., expenses of the architect and Bursar on a visit to Aston Hall; finally Sawston Hall was chosen. Like the rest of the College the Lodge is of red brick, with a not unpleasing exterior. Internally it has all the defects of Victorian domestic architecture, relieved in part by the handsome panelling. That in the dining-room came from the famous Cromwell House in Castle End, that in the study from the Buttery.

The total cost was about £9000. When we add to this the cost of acquiring the site and the loss of income from the lodging houses pulled down, over £20,000 was expended to erect what has proved a white elephant from the first. It is easy to be wise after the event, but those who were responsible for the new Lodge cannot have seen anything of the future needs of the College. Their vision was confined to the needs of the moment; a recon-

Queens' Lane about 1840

struction of the interior of the old Lodge would have satisfied modern requirements and left a magnificent site free for possible future developments.

 3-2

For many years the old Lodge was used as Fellows' chambers, but in 1921 it was converted into undergraduates' sets, the kitchens and cellars being turned into baths and a boiler house.

The parts of the island site acquired since the Ramsden enlargement were bought at the following times.

1821. The "house next the Butler's" (68 Trumpington Street) was bought for £900. It was rebuilt in 1852 for £1098. 10*s*. 5*d*. Incorporated with the College 1933.

1836. On 2 April there was purchased from Queens' College for £7700[1] a messuage in Silver Street, with outbuildings lately used as the University Printing Offices and also a brick building called the Anatomical School with the yard and appurtenances, also the almshouses adjoining the said messuage all being part of the estate known in Queens' College records as Andrew Dockett's estate. The College added a part of the ground to the Master's garden, leased two small pieces to Balls and Tomson (see below) respectively, and built nine houses fronting Silver Street and Queens' Lane on another part of the site. The cost of the building was £4378. 17*s*. 3*d*., the architect being Mr William Walter. These houses were pulled down in 1875 to make room for the new Master's Lodge.

1864. No. 66 Trumpington Street, pulled down 1930 for Hobson's Building.

1871. No. 70 Trumpington Street, the back part of which, with the rooms over the shop, were incorporated into the College 1933; once "Balls' House".

1875. Tenement in Silver Street pulled down to make room for part of Master's Lodge outbuildings.

1894. No. 69 Trumpington Street; once "Tomson's House".

1913. No. 65 Trumpington Street, pulled down 1930 for Hobson's Building.

The property acquired in 1871 made possible the swimming-bath, one of the first in Cambridge. It is noticed in the accounts for 1871–2, and in those for 1872–3 the wages of the bath-keeper (W. Sell) occur for the first time.

The property known as the Sherlock Building, apparently because it was bought out of Library funds, lying north of the swimming bath and east of the Fellows' garden, was for many years used as a Junior Library and Combination Room. After the war of 1914–18 it was turned into sets for undergraduates, and in 1935 was pulled down to make room for a handsome range of chambers running from the Ramsden Building towards Silver Street.

[1] Towards this sum the Master (Procter) and the senior Fellow (Burrell) each gave £1000.

[Made by JAMES ESSEX]

A Plan of the College of Catherine Hall in Cambridge, with the additions thereto according to Mrs Ramsdens Will, as they were finish'd in ye Year 1765

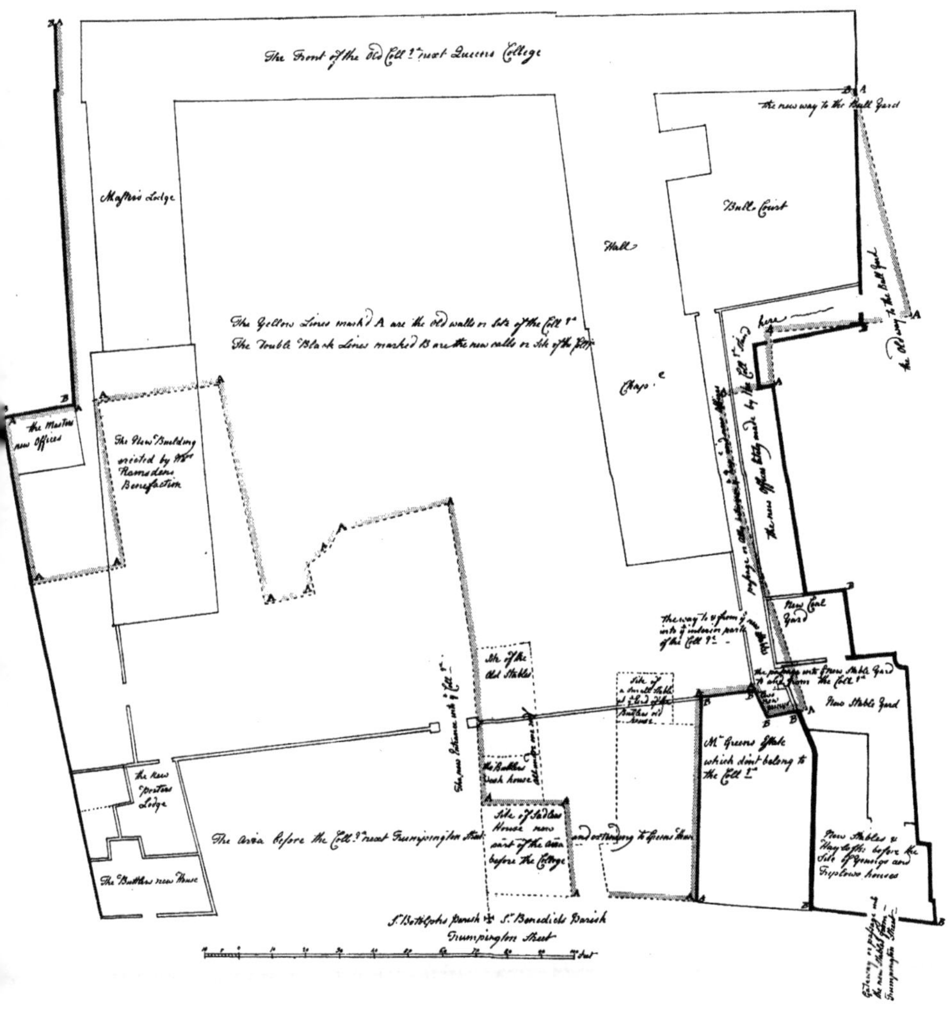

65 and 66 Trumpington Street, site of Hobson Building

Hobson Building

Early in the Mastership of Dr Johns an anonymous donor offered him a large sum of money to build a range of buildings on the site of the grove. The plan was abandoned in 1913, not because of the outcry raised by a small section of the public against cutting down the (already rotting) elms, but because the Fellows, learning by chance who the anonymous donor really was, thought it wiser to refuse the offer. The appeal prepared on this occasion is here reprinted, as the illustration at least may be of some interest.

ST CATHARINE'S COLLEGE, CAMBRIDGE

PROPOSED NEW BUILDINGS

THE Bishop of Bristol in his *History of St Catharine's College* has recorded the growth of the College, and its gradual acquirement of adjoining sites and the development of its buildings. On more than one occasion a large increase in the number of students led the then existing body to enlarge its accommodation at great sacrifice to the Master and Fellows of the time; for the College has always been ill endowed, and still remains, save one, the poorest in Cambridge.

The need of enlargement was never greater than now. In every department the

College is extremely flourishing. The number of undergraduates has steadily risen of late years, and has more than doubled in the last ten years. While only thirty-two students can reside within its walls, the College has three times as many in lodgings. There seems to be every prospect that these numbers will be maintained, if not increased. There are now forty-four men in the First Year.

It must be clear that the corporate life of the College, one of the most important factors in University Education, cannot continue to flourish while such a large proportion of its members reside outside its walls, and that this state of things is likely to affect every side of the College interests.

The College now proposes to complete its ancient plans by erecting a fine building on the site of the Grove, at a cost of some £20,000. An anonymous benefactor has offered to bear one half of this cost, provided that the scheme is carried out without delay, and the College now appeals earnestly to its own members to assist it in raising the remainder.

The rapid decay of the old elm trees, which have so long formed a picturesque feature on Trumpington Street, and the practical inconveniences of a space open to the street at night, have made it most desirable that the Grove should be taken into the College. The opportunity afforded by the above munificent offer must weigh against a sentiment which would preserve old associations and amenities no longer living or vital.

The proposed building, figured above, will give a handsome front to Trumpington Street, in complete harmony with the old buildings. It will comprise a gateway and porter's lodge, a splendid library and two large much needed lecture rooms, four sets of Fellows' rooms and twenty-four sets of students' rooms. The basement will afford bathrooms with hot and cold water for the students.

The transfer of the two existing libraries will set free at least ten more sets of students' rooms, thus more than doubling the accommodation for undergraduates.

Contributions may be paid to the St Catharine's Building Fund Account at The London County and Westminster Bank, Cambridge, or direct to the Master.

C. H. W. JOHNS, MASTER OF ST CATHARINE'S COLLEGE.
E. T. S. CARR, PRESIDENT AND BURSAR.
A. W. SPRATT, SENIOR TUTOR AND DEAN.
W. T. SOUTHWARD, JUNIOR TUTOR AND CHAPLAIN.
F. M. RUSHMORE, ASSISTANT TUTOR.
W. H. S. JONES, FELLOW AND LECTURER.
R. H. BIFFEN, FELLOW AND DRAPERS PROFESSOR OF AGRICULTURAL BOTANY.

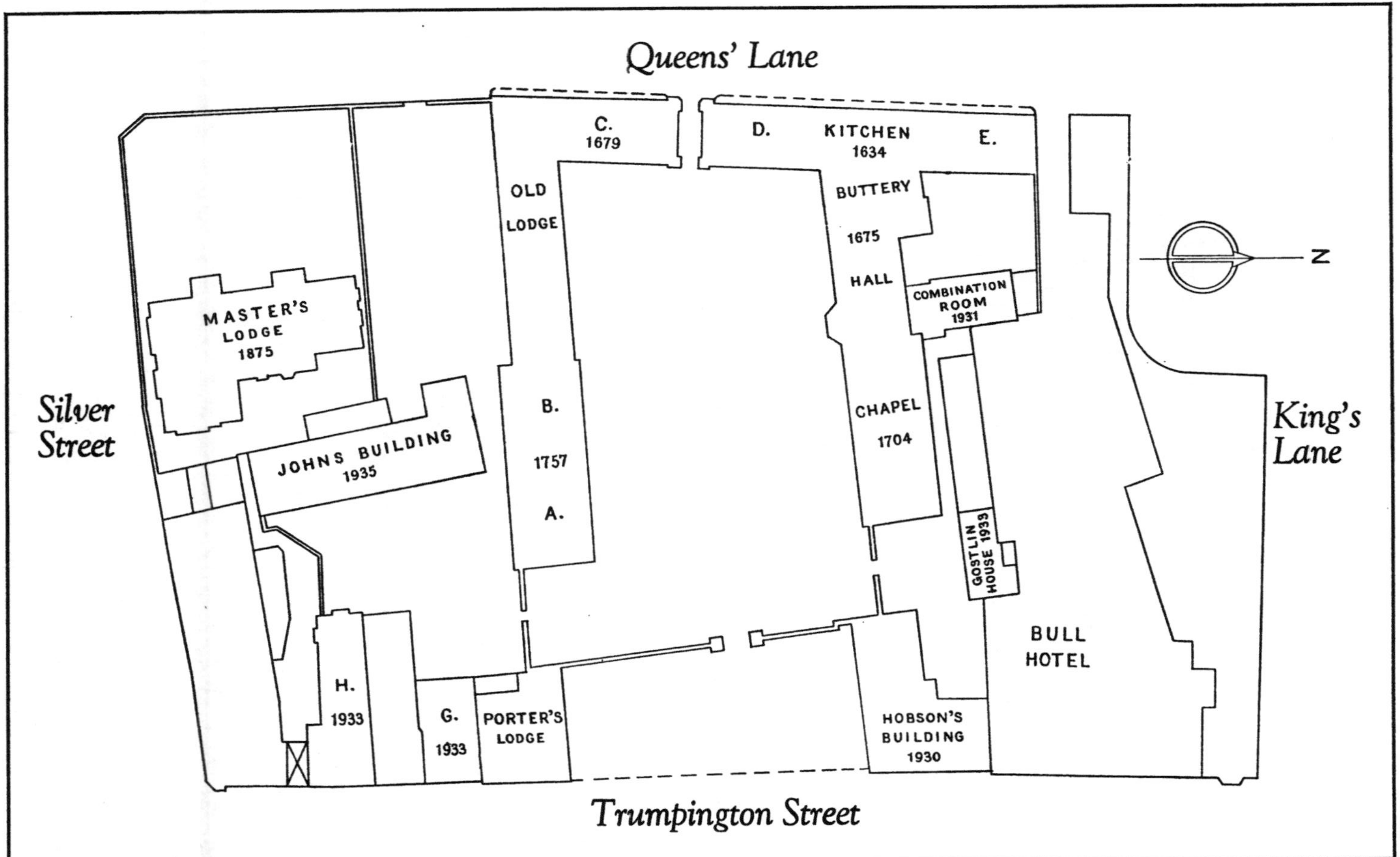

The College in 1936. The Library is over the Hall. *G* and *H* are old houses brought within the enclosure of the College in 1933. The date of the Old Lodge is probably 1678, of D staircase 1679. The Porter's Lodge (once Porter's and Butler's houses) was built between 1760 and 1770.

Mr Mullett's reconstruction of Claypoole Building

Sherlock Building on site of Johns Building

Site and Buildings

As early as 1919 the attention of the Society was directed towards the ultimate development of the College buildings, but it was not until 1929 that the problem was seriously attacked. After consultation with Mr G. L. Kennedy, an architect who had done good work at King's, the Society of St Catharine's came to the following conclusions:

(1) That the front facing Trumpington Street ought to be kept open;

(2) That the Silver Street frontage was problematical, as Silver Street would at some time in the future be widened on the north side;

(3) That the need for new buildings was urgent, as, while the existing buildings could house about 80, the number of residents was nearly 300;

(4) That each subsequent development must harmonize with the existing, and also with the final, lay-out of the island site.

In accordance with these conclusions the following steps were taken:

(1) Hobson's Building, on the site of 65 and 66 Trumpington Street, was erected in 1930.

(2) The Combination Room, situated over the Buttery and Screens, was thrown open to the Hall, forming a gallery that adds greatly to the dignity of the old dining chamber. Incidentally the number of Halls was reduced from three to two, to the great convenience of both the undergraduates and the catering department of the College.

(3) The old Choir Room was pulled down and on its site was erected a new Choir Room, with a new Combination Room over it, in 1932. The interior decoration of the latter was copied from the style adopted at Hitchin Priory, painted plaster with mouldings.

(4) In 1933 Gostlin House was built on a small parcel of ground inset into the premises of the Bull Inn. At the same time Nos. 68 and 70 Trumpington Street were taken into the enclosure of the College.

(5) In the summer of 1935 the old house, once Tomson's, known to many generations of undergraduates as Sherlock Building, was pulled down, and on its site was built a handsome range of chambers

at right angles to B staircase. Unfortunately the swimming pool, so popular in the summer months, had to be given up to afford increased accommodation. The architect was Mr H. L. Mullett.

There still remains to be built the south block to correspond to Hobson's Building on the north, and then Mr Kennedy's main object—to make a setting for the jewel of the old buildings—will be complete in all essentials. But two important problems remain to be solved—a new Hall and a new Master's Lodge. These, however, are questions for the next generation of Fellows.

CONTRACT WITH JOHN ATKINSON, 1611

Articles of agreement made between the Right Worshipful Dr Hills, Master of St Catharine's Hall within the University of Cambridge and the Fellows of the said College of the one part, and John Atkinson of the same town of the other part, the 18th day of April, 1611.

Imprimis the said John Atkinson...does...agree to and with the said Master and Fellows of St Catharine's Hall to build them a good and substantial range of buildings so long as is between the Chapel of the said College; and the utmost part of their ground towards Queens' College orchard; to be set up in the place where the gallery now stands.

The said John Atkinson covenants that the aforesaid building shall be a girt house of two stories high, each of them to be nine feet from the floor to the ceiling, the studs to be 12 inches distant, the breadth 18 feet from the inside of the brick wall to the outside of the groundsill in the lower rooms, and the second story so broad as the said brick wall will suffer it.

The said John Atkinson covenants to make a Staircase outside the buildings of such convenient size as to carry a fair pair of stairs up to each of the six rooms, and that in each of the said six rooms there shall be a fair bay-window on the College side, and in the end a bay-window; and convenient lights on the other side by clerestories; and that the windows shall be well and sufficiently glazed, 14 iron casements placed in the most convenient places; and all the said windows to be coloured with white lead and oil.

The said John Atkinson covenants to make in each of the said six rooms partitions for a study and a bedchamber, with sufficient doors, locks, hinges and staples.

Gostlin House

Bull (Walnut-tree) Court and Senior Combination Room

The said John Atkinson covenants that the several floors in the said rooms shall be boarded with good and seasoned board, either of oak or deal-board; and all the said six rooms shall be plastered with lime and hair inside and out, the whole frame to be cast rough or smooth as decided by the said Master and Fellows.

The said John Atkinson covenants to make in the said building two stacks of chimneys with three fireplaces in each stack, well built for continuance and for casting smoke without annoyance.

The said John Atkinson covenants to remove John Royse's house, and in its stead to make a wall whereupon the building shall run and so provide by means of a cripple roof that the water shall not annoy either building.

The said John Atkinson covenants to make a fair door for entrance by the end of Mr Copinger's chambers, with lock and key and the other appurtenances; and the whole passage to be plastered with lime and hair.

The said John Atkinson covenants that all timber to be used in the said building shall be sound, firm, strong, and of a good seasoning; and all the stone, tiles, glass, iron, mortar, brick and whatsoever else is necessary shall be of the best for durability, and to make it a strong, seemly and habitable building. And that all the said building and every particular item shall be honestly performed and ended within twenty days after the feast of St Michael the Archangel next ensuing.

For and in consideration of these covenants and performance thereof, the Master and Fellows of the said College for them and their successors covenant, grant, and agree to and with the said John Atkinson to pay to him at or before the sealing of these agreements the sum of Sixty Pounds of lawful English money, and on the 21st day of October next ensuing one hundred marks of like current money.

And we further covenant that the said John Atkinson, in consideration of the performance of the said premises, shall be empowered to take possession of, remove, and use the gallery which Mr Cragge built and which stands in the said College; for his own use and benefit, with all the appurtenances, i.e. timber, tiles, glass, iron, wainscott and clay, with all the paling, posts and rails surrounding the Fellows' garden in the said College; to have and enjoy them, himself, his heirs and executors for ever.

In witness whereof the parties above said to these present articles have set their hands and seal the day and year first above written.

JOHN ATKINSON.

Sealed in the presence of:

HENRY KING
EDWARD HILLS.

Chapter II

DOMESTIC HISTORY

ON 15 February 1858 a paper was read before the Cambridge Antiquarian Society by Charles Hardwick, in which is collected all that is known of "Robert Woodlark,[1] Founder and first Master of St. Catharine's Hall". Woodlark was born in the village of Wakerley, near Stamford in Northamptonshire,[2] but nothing is known of his education before he entered on his academical career at Cambridge. There he was one of the first "Scholars" or "Fellows" of the College founded by King Henry VI in honour of St Nicholas. Two years later, in a charter issued 10 July 1443, the King modified his original plan, and authorised the erection of a new foundation, to be called the King's College of St Mary and St Nicholas, the head of which was to be styled Provost instead of Rector. The members of the first foundation were also to be members of the second, and so Woodlark became a Fellow, and then Provost, of King's, his appointment to the latter office dating from 17 May 1452. As a University officer Woodlark was a success, being chosen Chancellor in 1459 and 1462.

In 1452 Woodlark was appointed by the King's letters patent Master of the Works at King's College. His sister Isabella married as her second husband John Caunterbury, who was Clerk of the Works at the same College. His interests therefore might well have centred round the great foundation over which he presided until October 1479. A man in the position of Woodlark was unlikely, one would think, to divert even a part of his energy to founding a new collegiate body. But this is what he did, and what is more, the new foundation was, so to speak, at the very doors of the old. Fuller notices the strangeness of his action. "Herein he stands alone, without any to accompany him, being the first and the last, who was Master of one College, and at the same time founder of another."[3]

[1] In all our early records the name is spelt "Wodelarke".

[2] Earlier historians have (erroneously) Northumberland.

[3] *Worthies*, II, 551.

The *Memoriale Nigrum* tells us little about the reasons that influenced Woodlark, but we may, from the Founder's statutes, conjecture at least two of them. He appears to have held strong views about the education of the clergy, particularly about the secular clergy, wishing such to concentrate upon what we call cultural studies, and to refrain from the professional study of law, whether canon or other.[1] Such a restriction he could not impose upon King's, but the Fellows of St Catharine's were bound, in reading for their degrees, to confine themselves to philosophy and theology. Woodlark was also anxious—perhaps morbidly so—for a special memorial, over and above the distinction of being Provost of King's. In particular he desired prayers to be said for his soul after his death, and elaborate instructions about them are given in his statutes.

Whatever the actual reasons were that influenced Woodlark, they amounted to more than a mere passing whim. Long before the opening of the College he had been engaged in acquiring a site,[2] and in gathering together material.[3] By St Catharine's day (25 November) 1473 the College was ready for habitation, although neither the Library nor the Chapel was yet finished, and on the next day Peter Welde, M.A., and John Wardall, B.A., "entered commons" as Fellows, along with James Wylleborde, M.A., Edmund Bacton, M.A., and certain others as Fellow Commoners.[4] The Founder had intended to provide for a much larger Society, but the ruin of the cause of Henry VI destroyed all such hopes, and "three or more" Fellows only are contemplated in the statutes. There is no mention in the *Memoriale Nigrum* of junior students. But there is, at the end of that document, a memorandum about the Hall of Saint Katerine the Virgin in the University of Cambridge and the diocese of Ely, founded "for a Master and ten Fellows, students of philosophy and sacred theology". This is a note, not of a fact, but of a hope and aspira-

1 "The question whether a university may advantageously concern itself with education of a purely technical character, was one which presented itself to the minds of the thirteenth and fourteenth centuries as well as those of the nineteenth." Mullinger, I, 255.

2 See p. 3.

3 "de meremio empto...et alterato a Coton usque ad Hornyngsey et recariato Cantebrigiam ad fabricam aulae praedictae diu ante fabricam praedictam remanente." *Memoriale Nigrum*, f. 50.

4 *Memoriale Nigrum*, f. 50.

tion. It indicates what Woodlark wished to establish, and what he would have established, had the fates been less unkind.

Browne[1] goes to some pains to show that there were several immediate causes of the selection of the name "Saynt Kateryn's[2] Hall of Cambridge", and gives the following summary:

(1) The reputed learning of the Saint;

(2) The high esteem in which she was held at this period;

(3) The devotion shown to the Saint by Woodlark's patron Henry VI, whose mother's name was Catharine.

If another guess may be hazarded, perhaps the name was merely an accident. If the College buildings became ready to receive their first occupants just before St Catharine's day, the name might very well suggest itself.

St Catharine's was opened at a truly momentous time. The new learning had begun to spread after the fall of Constantinople in 1453, and the Reformation was soon to follow. Browne points out that a year after the opening there was published by Caxton at Bruges *The Recuyell*, the first book printed in the English tongue, while the Licence for divine worship in the Chapel was granted in the year in which there came from Caxton's press at Westminster the first book printed in England, *The Dictes and Sayings of the Philosophers*. Woodlark's young foundation, however, was a confirmation of the old learning rather than a welcome to the new, nor did the Reformers find much support among the early Fellows of St Catharine's.

For some years after the opening Woodlark took an active part in the affairs of the College, even after the appointment of Richard Roche to the Mastership in 1475. He himself is rarely styled "Master" in the old records; the usual title is "Founder" or "First Founder", and Roche is put down as the first Master in the register made by Daniel Milles in the middle of the seventeenth century. Until a charter was obtained there could be (in the strict

[1] See *St Catharine's College*, pp. 6–9.

[2] The spelling in old documents shows every variety the name can assume, Katerine, Katharine, Catherine, Catharine, being the most common forms. "College" and "Hall" both occur. The usual style was "Catharine Hall" for a long period before 1860, when "St Catharine's College" became the official title.

sense) neither Master nor Fellows, and the College was legally Woodlark's private property. Woodlark's task, therefore, was concerned partly with carrying forward the work of building, and partly with securing legal status and recognition.

The arms of the College provide an interesting subject of discussion. Browne gives reasons for believing that the original form consisted of Woodlark's own arms (gules a lion of England or, and azure a fleur-de-lys of France or, parted by a bend dancetty) impaling the Catharine wheel.

On this point permission has been obtained to quote at length from two letters sent by York Herald to the Bursar in July and August 1934.

"I have made a search in our records and find three references to the Arms of St Catharine's College, Cambridge. In each case the Arms are shown 'in trick'. They are 'Gules a Catherine wheel Or'.[1]

The references are:

1. R. 18. (A late 16th Century MSS.)
2. E.D.N. Royal Badges, etc., page 1. The first page is inscribed 'This Booke of Entrances was made by Raffe Brooke, alias Rouge Croix 1590', but the Arms and titles given are mostly 17th Century, including that of 'Aula St. Katherine 1475'.
3. K. 7. page 4—The Visitation of Cambridge 1684, by Sir Henry St George.
   'Catherine Hall Cambridge 7 July 1684.'
   'The Arms of Catherine Hall in University of Cambridge as they have been ancientlie borne and used by the Master and Fellows of the said house, which Hall was Incorporated' (Here follows the name of the Master—John Eachard, Dr in Divinity, and the Fellows.)

In Philpot's Cambridge (1619), page 3, the Arms are also shown in trick as 'Gules a Catherine wheel Or'.

I find no evidence of the Arms being impaled by the Founder as stated in Bishop Browne's 'History of St Catharine's College'.

I have examined our Chapter Book and Treasurer's Book for 1683–84, but do not find any reference to the payment of fees for *registering* the Arms. The payment

[1] Edmund Carter, *The History of the University of Cambridge*, p. 208, says the arms are "Sable a Katherine-Wheel Or". A writer in *Notes and Queries* (29 October 1910) says: "Surely Sable is a misprint for Gules".

was probably made to Sir Henry St George, Clarenceux, at his Visitation, 7 July 1684. As the Arms were entered at that Visitation they are unquestionably authentic, but I cannot find a record of the actual grant of the Arms."

"As regards the number of spokes on the Catharine Wheel of St Catharine's College Arms. There is no blazon (written Description of the Arms) recorded here, and in the absence of a blazon it would appear that the number of spokes is a matter that may be left to the individual Heraldic painter.

There are four representations of the Arms 'in trick', the references to which I gave you in my last letter. The number of spokes (and knives on the rim) as given in the four references are:

1. R. 18. (A late 16th Century MSS)	12 spokes and 20 knives on rim.
2. E.D.N. (Royal Badges, etc.)	6 ,, ,, 12 ,, ,,
3. K. 7. (Visitation of Cambridge 1684)	8 ,, ,, 8 ,, ,, on the rim as *continuations of the spokes.*
4. Philpot's Cambridge (1619)	6 spokes with 6 knives as *continuations* on the rim.

Of these references No. 3 (Visitation of Cambridge 1684) is the most reliable, and I would advise that the number of spokes and knives shown therein be adopted."

The Visitation is referred to in the Bursar's accounts for 1683–4, where occurs the item:

> To S^{r} Fr. St George for registring
> ye Coll armes and seal 1. 10. 0

"Fr." is, of course, a slip on the part of the Bursar for that year.

York Herald's verdict agrees very well with the figure in Ivory's *Foundation* (1672) and with the stone carvings over the Queens' Lane archway and on the left side over the entrance from the court to the screens. The former has eight spokes, the latter six. Both are of about the same date as the Visitation. The wheel over the Trumpington Street gateway (eight spokes) is about a century later.

The Royal Charter of Incorporation was granted by Edward IV on 16 August 1475, and on 22 November of the same year Woodlark conveyed to the Master and Fellows all that he had provided for the young College.

KATHARINE *Hall.* 1475.

ROBERT *Woodlark*, born at *Wakerly* in *Northumberland*, D. D. the last Fellow that King *Henry 6* placed in Kings Colledge, third Provost of the same, Chancellour of this University, founded this Colledge or Hall in a place called *Milnstreet*, over against *Queens* Coll. Orchard, formerly known by the name of the *Carmelite Fryars*, of four Tenements which were purchased for that purpose: he dedicating the same to the Honour of S. *Katharine* the *Virgin* and *Martyr*, obtained of King *Edward* 4 a Licence of mortmain for the endowment thereof; which was confirmed to him and his Successours for ever. Wherein he established a Master, and 6 Fellows. Since it hath been enlarged by the liberality of *Isabel Canterbury* widow, *Will. Taylor*, *Katha. Myles*, *Rob. Simpton*, *Hugh Pemmerton*, the Lady *Eliz. Bernardiston*, *John Leach*, *Rich. Nealson*, *Rob. Shorton*, D. D. Master of S. *Johns* Coll. in this University, Dean of *Stoak*, &c. after Master of *Pembroke* Hall; *Hugh Garret*, *John Chester*, *Tho. Green*, D. D. Master of this House, Dr *Thimbleby*, Dr *Middleton*, *Rosamond Payn* widow, *John Cholmley*, *John Duke*, Sr *John Claypool* Knight, *John Gostlin* Dr of Physick, late Fellow and Master of *Gonvil* and *Caius* Colledge, Vice-chancellour 1618, who died Vice-chancellour *October* 21, 1626, a large and bountifull Benefactour: *Thomas Buck* late Fellow of this House, Seniour Esquire Bedle, Master *Christopher Shirland*, Mistris *Stafford*, Master *Thomas Hobbs*, Master *Peter Phesant*, *Anne* Lady *Cocket* widow, Mistris *Jurdayn* widow, *Anne* Lady *Bernardiston*, *William Gouge* Doctour of Divinity, Master *Coulson*, Master *Skerne* Esquire, Master *Alured*, Master *Cradock* Citizen and Merchant of *London*, the worthy Company of the Mercers in the City of *London*, *Robert Skerne* Esquire, a great Benefactour, *John Lightfoot* now Master of the same, and many other Benefactours. So as there is now in the same, a Master, 6 Fellows, 18 Scholars, 9 Exhibitioners, besides Officers and Servants of the Foundation, with other Students, being in all 150.

John Lightfoot, Doctour of Divinity. &c. being now Master thereof.

John Ivory's *Foundation* (1672)

But before this he had received two handsome benefactions from outside.[1] The first was 100 marks given by Lady Joan Barnardiston towards the building, and the second, given 28 June 1475, was help towards completing the Chapel and Library, £40, being received from the executors of William Cotte and Clement Denston. These benefactions show that the buildings were not completed on the day when the College was opened.

The charter to which reference has been made recites that Robert Woodlark has founded a "mansio" for a Master and three or more Fellows "studying philosophy and sacred theology". It grants the usual powers of a corporation in respect of ownership, with licence of mortmain up to the annual sum of 40 marks. It orders the Society to pray for the King's health in life and for his soul after death. The witness is Edward, Prince of Wales and Keeper of England, at that time a child about four years of age.

The fine to be paid for grant of this charter was £18. 4*s*. 4*d*. The College apparently had some difficulty in finding this money, amounting as it does to more than the combined annual stipends of a Master and three Fellows, for on 8 July 1476 a writ of *fieri facias* was issued to the Sheriff of Cambridge for the recovery of £1. 16*s*. 8*d*., the remainder due to the Crown out of the fine for confirmation of the Charter of foundation, and the licence of mortmain for 40 marks. The money had to be paid to the Exchequer for the use of Queen Elizabeth on the day after the next Michaelmas Day.

There were two licences granted for worship in the College Chapel, one in 1475 and one in 1478. Henry Philpott believed that the first applied to a temporary chapel used until the permanent chapel was built and furnished. This is a reasonable enough suggestion, but if it be correct the Fellows performed their offices for two years (1473–5) in neighbouring churches, and then for three years (1475–8) in a temporary chapel. One wonders why a temporary chapel, *i.e.* one of the chambers, was not used from the first, as the members of St Catharine's before 1478 could scarcely have exceeded eight or ten. Be this as it may, on 15 January 1475/6 William (Grey) Bishop of Ely granted to Robert Woodlark, "founder of the Hall or College of Saint Katerine recently built in Cambridge", and to the Fellows and others

[1] For an account of these benefactions see p. 205.

willing and qualified, licence for the celebration of divine offices in the chapel built (*constructa*) within the College, *auctoritate nostra pontificali.*[1] It is strange, to say the least, that Roche, the Master, is not mentioned; it is perhaps stranger still that the second licence is granted to Woodlark along with the Master and Fellows. In this document William Pykenham, Doctor of Laws, Vicar-General and Keeper of the spiritualities of the diocese of Ely, the see being vacant, gives to Founder, Master, Fellows and others licence for the celebration of divine offices in the Chapel lately built within the College, "so long as it is decent and tidy and arranged for divine worship", without prejudice, however, to the parish church of the College. The licence is dated from the conventual church of Barnwell.

On 25 May 1476 a charter of appropriation of the church of Coton was granted[2] to the Master and Fellows by King Edward the Fourth, on the condition that they should provide a suitable chaplain for the ministration of the sacraments and sacramentals, and distribute yearly among the poor of the parish a certain portion, to be determined by the Bishop.

The charter recites that the Master and Fellows were already possessed of one acre of land in the field of Coton together with the advowson and patronage of the parish church belonging to the said acre, and empowers them to appropriate the said parish church to their own uses for ever.

Woodlark, as a good business man, was not neglectful of detail. We can see this plainly in the careful arrangements he made for providing the rents of the leasehold tenements fronting Milne Street. These amounted to 19*s*., and from October 1466 he gradually acquired pieces of land, the annual value of which would in his opinion suffice to pay this sum in perpetuity. Then there was the question of parishes. The boundary between St Botolph's and St Edward's practically bisected Woodlark's new quadrangle,[3] and Woodlark had to settle the division of Church dues between the two. An agreement was made whereby the personal tithes went to the Rector of St Edward's, while the praedial tithes were to be divided in the proportion of the grounds in the respective parishes.

[1] See *Register*, I, 77.

[2] *Register*, I, 20.

[3] There is to-day a parish boundary-mark just over the entrance to D staircase.

But a saintly character—the earliest register of the College describes Woodlark as *benignus, mansuetus, humilis*—even when combined with business ability, is not proof against calumny and detraction. As might confidently have been expected, the Founder was accused, in gossip probably, as we hear of no legal proceedings, of misappropriating money belonging to King's College. Woodlark replies with a direct denial. "Not a farthing of King's money was used for St. Catharine's", he says, and adds that Thomas Betts, the auditor, declared that King's owed their Provost £328. 10*s*. 4*d*.[1]

The Royal Charter gave powers to Woodlark and his executors to make statutes for the government of the College. These were drawn up when Richard Roche[2] was Master, for in them he is referred to as such. The last deed in which Roche is mentioned as Master is dated 25 October 1480. So Woodlark imposed his statutes before 1481 and after 1475.

The earliest extant copy of these statutes is in the College Muniment Room. It is clearly a copy, as certain initial capitals are omitted, being left out to be added, probably illuminated, later. It was doubtless written when Wardall was Master, for in the list of Masters at the end the names of Wardall and his predecessors are written in the same hand as the body of the statutes, but later names are in a different hand. Moreover, the list of exequies to be celebrated every year in the Chapel contains only those of Woodlark, Cotte, Denston and Bassett. Those of Hugh Pemberton, for which the College sealed a composition in 1504, are not included. We may thus infer that this copy was made between 20 November 1487 (Bassett's composition) and 14 October 1504 (Pemberton's composition).

[1] *Memoriale Nigrum*, f. 50. "In quibus cum ceteris ad praedictam aulam memorandis nihil ad onus aut de debito collegii Regalis ad valorem unius [the reading may be *minimi*, the writing being here uncertain] quadrantis, ut si opus sit praesto erit solutio, declaratio et responsio."

[2] Appointed by Woodlark himself, as was also in all probability Tapton, the next Master. The statutes require the Master to be a graduate in Divinity, whereas Tapton was only Master of Arts. But Woodlark's statutes reserve to him power to alter or dispense with any of them during his life time. Woodlark died before 1486 or 1487.

The history of St Catharine's for two hundred years is a series of side-lights. There is a glimpse here and a flash there, but only now and then does the light burn with a steady, continual brightness. One of these rare occasions is afforded by the Founder's statutes. It should be observed that these were drawn up, not before the College was founded, however much Woodlark may have pondered over them, but in the Mastership of Richard Roche (1475–80). So they embody the knowledge gained by actual experience of working the College according to the Founder's ideas.

"There is little", says Mullinger, "in the statutes given by Woodlark to the College which he founded, deserving of remark, beyond the fact that both the canon and the civil law were rigorously excluded from the course of study."[1] This is a hasty remark, and the last clause is misleading, for all studies were forbidden by the Founder except those of philosophy and sacred theology. The truth is that scarcely a clause in the Founder's statutes does not throw light on the history of either the University or the College.

A fundamental point about them is that they draft rules only for Fellows and for the Master. The sole exception is that the charges to Fellow Commoners, who apparently are to be restricted like the Fellows to the study of philosophy and theology, are directed to be added to the common stock. No rules are laid down for the studies and discipline of junior students, who are never even mentioned, and implied only once in a rule that during meals a passage from the Bible or the Fathers must be read "per unum puerum sive clericum ad id deputatum, qui biblista sive biblicus vocitetur". We can understand neither the statutes nor the Founder's intentions unless we remember that the Fellows and their education were all-important. The modern conception of a college as a large collection of juniors, whose education is the main work in life of a small body of seniors, is entirely foreign to the spirit in which St Catharine's was founded. It is probable, almost certain, that whatever juniors resided in the very early days of the College were there on sufferance, earning their privileges by serving the Master and Fellows in some subordinate or menial capacity. In modern days there is a great gulf fixed between the attainments required of a Fellow and the

[1] Mullinger, I, 318.

minimum necessary for a degree. The teachers are expected to be on a far higher plane than the "average man". Four or five centuries ago the gap was not nearly so large. Knowledge then was circumscribed, and its acquisition a mechanical process. Students spent all their years of education in mastering a very limited field. But generally it was mastered, and the result was an average level of attainment very unlike the differentiation now possible between the best and the worst of the candidates for degrees. So a large number of students was considered worthy of Fellowships. What is now a rare distinction was then a normal stage in the career of many graduates. In short, the main object of University training was to produce a body of Fellows, and to keep them, for some years at least, engaged in fuller and deeper study. It is significant that during the hundred and thirty-four years following the foundation of St Catharine's ninety Fellows were elected, giving an average of two every three years. As the Society never included more than a Master and six Fellows (with, perhaps, nine to thirty undergraduates), it is clear that a Fellowship was usually, not a career, but a stepping-stone to other things. In short, a Fellowship was an important stage in the education of the best brains of the University. Woodlark evidently considered of great value the years spent in this position, and devoted great care and attention to their supervision. It is therefore not surprising that his statutes were made for Master and Fellows, and that they ignore all classes of juniors.

These statutes require the Master to be of a suitable character, and at least thirty years of age. He must be a Doctor, or at any rate a Bachelor, of theology, and must proceed to no degree in any other faculty. His stipend is to be five pounds *per annum*, paid quarterly.

The qualifications of Fellows are these. They must be born in England, in priest's or lesser orders, Masters of Arts or at least "baccallarii meliores". At no time is the Society to contain more than two Fellows from one county. All Fellows are to proceed to the usual degrees in their faculties, and to debate once a week for at least two hours in philosophy or theology, from which exercise the Master alone is excused. No other branch of study is permitted.[1]

[1] Apparently for a degree. It could scarcely be supposed that a Fellow was precluded from studying other subjects as hobbies.

On election each Fellow swears, among other things, never to reveal to outsiders any secrets of the College to its loss or detriment.

Meals are to be taken in common, and during them in true monastic fashion the Bible or the Fathers must be read without interruption from laughter or conversation. To the Master is given the task of assigning lodging to the Fellows, two sharing a chamber. The stipend is to be four pounds a year, payable quarterly, and Fellows are forbidden to accept ecclesiastical benefices, with or without cure of souls, for more than one year, but they may hold a free chapel in cases where personal residence is not required.

The rules relating to absence are very strict. Permission is required from the Master or, in his absence, the President, whenever a Fellow wishes to go away more than four miles from Cambridge, and no Fellow is to spend the night out of College in Cambridge or within four miles of it without urgent reason. Absence for more than sixty days in one year, whether continuous or not, involves *ipso facto* loss of Fellowship. Entering a religious order, or the acquisition of private means of the annual value of ten marks, involves loss of Fellowship after six months.

Woodlark defines the duties of the Master and of the President, but makes no mention of any other College office. This omission is quite consistent with his ideal of a small, non-teaching society. Bursarial duties were at first carried out by the Master, who was also known as the Keeper. As the College grew, and its teaching duties developed, new offices arose. A *senescallus* (Steward or Bursar) is recognised in a College Order of 1543 and in the Edwardian statutes of 1549. The latter make no mention of a Praelector, but he appears in the (apparently Elizabethan) account of College terms and exercises.[1]

[1] See p. 58. The name "Bursar" gradually replaced "Steward", until in 1792 the Stewardship was made a separate office. The Dean first appears as receiving a salary in the accounts of 1800–1, but his election to the office goes back to the earliest extant College "conclusions". The Praelector is so styled in all Latin documents, but in English he is "Lecturer" until 1851, when he receives his Latin name. The Chaplain was first appointed as the result of Mr Moses Holwey's foundation in 1695 of a "conduct" Fellowship. Before this date the services in Chapel were carried out in turn by the Fellows in Holy Orders.

So the original St Catharine's was meant for a few advanced students, all clerics, being what might fittingly be called temporary monks, whose chief work after study was prayer. About one-eighth of Woodlark's statutes consists of detailed instructions about the prayers to be offered for his soul,[1] and every pre-Reformation benefactor required from the College a Mass, a sermon, or prayers. These religious exercises had the advantage of increasing the incomes of the Master and Fellows; one of them, the chantry of William Myles, founded in 1509, provided an *exhibitio* equal to the annual stipend of a Fellow.

The Library, in days when science laboratories were unknown and text-books very rare, played a most important part in College life, instead of being, as it is now, a museum.[2] Besides the books in the Library, others were kept in the Chapel. Some were "chained", in modern parlance "not to be taken away", others were for the use of the Master and Fellows in their chambers. The Founder's rules were strict, but not more so than we might expect in the case of property at that time so difficult to replace, for his "books" were manuscripts, not printed volumes.

The Tutor is recognised by no College statute or official account-book before 1882, but his office must have existed *de facto* from the time when junior students became numerous. Nearly every Fellow does tutorial duties at certain periods of the seventeenth century.

[1] The instructions include: (A) In the Founder's life: (1) at the celebration of Mass a special Collect; (2) after Mass prayer for the body and soul of the Founder. (B) After his death: (1) After *prandium* and *cena* in Hall the psalm *de profundis* and prayers for the soul of R. W. and for all faithful souls. (2) Every week on Saturday Mass of the B.V. Mary and on Sunday of the B.V. Katerine, the Master and Fellows to be present. (3) After death as soon as possible a requiem Mass with a special Collect. (4) A weekly requiem Mass on the same day as the death with special mention among benefactors of Henry VI, Richard Wodelarke and Joanna his wife parents of R. W., Elizabeth de Burgh and Thomas la War, William Cotte and Clement Denston. (5) An obit day for the Founder, the M. and Fellows to be present at the Mass. (6) A requiem Mass four times a year at the end of each term, the Master to receive 12*d*. and each Fellow 8*d*. for celebrating High Mass *personaliter*.

[2] There is a very good account of the early Library by Dr G. E. Corrie in the Cambridge Antiquarian Society's Publications, vol. 1 (1840). Reprinted pp. 376–385.

(1) All books, whether kept in the Chapel or elsewhere, were to be openly displayed once each term, and to be subject to a similar review each year before the Master and Fellows in residence.

(2) No book was to be sold, given away, exchanged, pawned, or alienated in any way.

(3) No book was to leave the College to be copied in quires (*quaternatim*); books leaving the College to be bound or mended were to be returned with all speed.

(4) At night copyists were to leave their work, but Fellows might continue to study if they took great care.

(5) Strangers were allowed admission only if one of the Society were responsible, and after dark only if the Master or a Fellow were actually with them.

(6) The Library was to have a strong lock, commonly called a *clyket lok*, and to be locked after dark. The Master and each of the Fellows had a key.

(7) Fellow Commoners, with the consent of the Master or in his absence of the President, might have the same privileges as Fellows.

Besides private study there were "exercises", from which only the Master was excused. These consisted of weekly debates, lasting for at least two hours unless the Master or President considered it right for them to last for a shorter or longer period. They took place apparently in the Chapel,[1] and were on subjects either philosophical or theological, others being expressly forbidden.

Of the studies of junior students nothing is recorded before the Reformation, and there is every reason to suppose that there were but few undergraduates, as we should call them. But the Reformation seems to have begun the change which turned the College from a society of student priests to a teaching institution for the instruction of young men, and the College records contain two copies, the earlier in a seventeenth-century hand, of College terms and exercises. The date of the original document is practically settled by the use of the phrase "sacra Synaxis" for Holy Communion; before the Reformation "missa" would have been employed. "Synaxis" is used to denote the Eucharist in the Royal Injunctions of 1549 for Cambridge Univer-

[1] See the composition of Robert Sympson (14 December 1530) "quotiens ex obligatione statutorum disputare eos contigerit in capella dicti collegii, sive problemata observare". The last phrase might be turned (faithfully and idiomatically) "to keep problems".

sity[1]; it was probably a Cambridge expression for the new English Communion Service legally introduced in 1549. Later the term disappears.

In this document the following rules are laid down:

(1) The first term is to begin on the fifth Monday after 13 January (fourth if that be a Monday), the second term on Whitsun Day, and the third term on the fifth Monday after 10 October (fourth if that be a Monday).

(2) On these days, as on Christmas Day and Easter Day, the Holy Communion is to be celebrated, at which celebration all scholars, of whatever rank, are to be present.

(3) On each Monday after the beginning of term at four o'clock the senior Sophisters are to dispute in the Hall, the Praelector presiding.

(4) On each Wednesday the junior Sophisters are to dispute in like manner.

(5) On each Thursday those of the second year are to dispute in like manner.

(6) On each Saturday all junior members immediately after supper (*coena*) are to deliver speeches in the order of their seniority, *per binos et binos* before the Praelector. After the speeches all "except the Sophisters and those delivering speeches on that occasion are to hand up *themata* (summaries of the arguments) written out in their own handwriting".

(7) Failure to observe these rules will bring liability to incur the penalties fixed by custom or by statute.

The "terms" evidently refer to a domestic, not a University, division of the academic year, as a term could be rarely if ever kept before Commencement by one who began residence on Whitsun Day. The reference therefore is to a division of the year into three parts for private convenience, the reason for such division being now unknown.[2]

It is interesting, and significant of the period, that residence was required during each of the great festivals of the Church.

The Praelector[3] had charge of the intellectual education given by the College. The "exercises" consisted of debates and speeches, but even if,

[1] See Lamb, p. 146.

[2] The financial year of the College was from the foundation divided into four quarters. The accounts of pupils, when the Tutors' books begin, are made up quarterly.

[3] Here mentioned for the first time in the College records.

according to modern ideas, too much stress was laid upon oral training, yet some attention at least was paid to written work, whether the *themata* were essays in the strict sense of that word or merely summaries made during or after the delivery of the speeches.

The full text of the document is as follows:

Primus Terminus Initium sumat Die Lunae quinto post 13.um Ianuarii, quod si 13.us inciderit in Diem Lunae, is pro 1.mo Die Lunae numerabitur.

Secundus, ipso Die Pentecostes.

Tertius, Die Lunae quinto post 10um Octobris, Computo faciendo similiter ac in primo Termino.

Iisque Diebus, atque etiam Festis Nativitatis & Paschatis, sacra Synaxis celebretur; ad quam omnes Scholares, cuiuscunque Ordinis fuerint, praesto sint, nisi rationabilis Causa impediat quo minus aliquis adesse possit.

Quovis Die Lunae post initum Terminum, Hora quarta pomeridiana More consueto disputabunt in Aula Sophistae seniores, iuxta Ordinem Senioritatis suae, moderante Praelectore.

Quolibet Die Martis similiter disputabunt Sophistae iuniores.

Et quolibet Die Jovis qui sunt secundi Anni similiter disputabunt, nisi quod non teneantur Respondentes, unam ex duabus Quaestionibus propositis ante disputandum Thesi defendere.

Quolibet Die Sabbati[1] omnes, tam Sophistae, quam reliqui Scholares, immediate post Coenam per binos & binos in Aula iuxta Senioritatem suam declamabunt coram Praelectore. Eique post finitas Declamationes Themata propria Manu scripta tradant omnes praeter Sophistas & illa Vice declamantes.

Quod si quis in praedictis deliquerit, sciat se Poenas subiturum iuxta Mores consuetos & Statuta.

The University statutes of Edward VI,[2] which are of about the same date as the document just discussed, enable us to form a fairly complete idea of the course of studies pursued by St Catharine's undergraduates as they began to

[1] In one copy "Sabbati" is struck out and "saturni" substituted.

[2] See Lamb, p. 125. "Recens venientem a ludo literario primum excipiant mathematica. Illa toto eo anno discet arithmeticen nimirum geometriam et astronomiae cosmographiaeque quantum poterit. Sequens annus dialecticam docebit. Tertius et quartus adjunget philosophiam. Et artium istarum pro ratione temporis domi forisque quisque sit auditor. In hoc quadriennio bis quisque disputato in publicis scholis bisque respondeto in suo grege. Quae si perfecerit et post consuetum examen dignus videatur baccalaureus esto."

grow in numbers. One of these statutes lays it down that in his first year a student is to learn mathematics, that is to say arithmetic, geometry, and as much astronomy and cosmography as possible. During the second year he is to learn logic, during the third and fourth, philosophy. During this period of four years every student is to "dispute" twice and to "answer" twice in the public schools. Then, after the usual test, he may become Bachelor.[1]

We find that in 1500 Peterhouse and St John's House petitioned the King (Henry VII) to be recognised as colleges in order to escape the subsidy from which colleges only were exempted.[2] Probably St Catharine's about this time secured formal recognition from the University, for in 1501 Richard Balderstone served as Proctor, as did William Capon in 1509, while in 1514 St Catharine's was given four turns to appoint a Proctor every forty-four years. Its Master served as Vice-Chancellor first in 1523.

At the Law Hundred or Leet of the town, held on Hock Tuesday 1502, the Master of Katherine Hall, along with those of Corpus Christi College and St John's House, were presented for having the pavement before their tenements broken and ruinous.

One of the fragments of which the early College history is composed takes the form of what we may term a pawn ticket. In itself interesting it shows that in spite of its poverty the College was not too poor to lend a helping hand to a neighbour in difficulties. The document may be thus modernised:

This indenture made the 3 day of April and the 20th year of the reign of King Henry the VIIth [1505] betwixt dame Christian Pope the Prioress of the house and church of the nuns in Swaffham Bulbeck on the one party and Master Richard Balderston, President of St. Katerine Hall in Cambridge on the other party witnesseth that the said Prioress hath laid a chalice in pledge of five pounds to the said Master Balderston of the which five pounds she knowledgeth and granteth her content and paid in lawful money of England of the day aforesaid. And it is agreed betwixt the parties aforesaid that the prioress or her assigns shall pay the five pounds of lawful money of England at the feast of the Annunciation of our Lady

[1] See note 2 on previous page.

[2] Cooper, *Annals*, I, 254.

next following the date of this writing to the said Master Balderston and then she to have her chalice again. In witness whereof the above said have put to their seals.

One hopes that the Prioress redeemed her precious chalice, or if the five pounds—the yearly salary of the Master—were not forthcoming on the appointed day that the College did not make her forfeit the pledge. Swaffham Bulbeck Priory was always poor and needy.

The College archives include a document throwing a side-light on contemporary history in the letters patent granting a plenary pardon to the Master and Fellows for all offences committed before 23 April in the first year of Henry VIII, who came to the throne 22 April 1509. The document is in good preservation; it is very wordy, and enumerates all conceivable crimes and offences.

"Men in high station, or in any public trust, were very solicitous formerly to obtain this mark of their sovereign's approbation, as a security against the malice of those enemies which the management of great and extensive affairs, with whatever integrity and caution they may be conducted, is sure to create; and on the part of the Crown, if no positive delinquency or mal-administration appeared, such favours were readily dispensed."[1]

On 26 March 1511 a deed was executed in which Peter Cheke, Bedell of the University, and John Thirlby, town clerk of Cambridge, declare that certain statements made by Nicholas Glosse, goldsmith, of Sudbury, were not true. Glosse had said that in the preceding June he had been imprisoned in Cambridge by the Vice-Chancellor of the time, William Bokenham, at the suit of the Master and Fellows of the College of St Catharine, and that under constraint and menace he had sealed and delivered a bond to the Master and Fellows for £40. The two witnesses affirm that, believing Glosse to have made these statements in order to evade his obligation, they feel bound to declare their knowledge that he was not imprisoned or menaced by the late Vice-Chancellor or by the Master and Fellows; but that of his own free will he came to the shop of the said John Thirlby and sealed and delivered the

[1] Churton, *Lives of the Founders of Brazenose College*, p. 211.

bond in the presence of Thomas Sharpe, Fellow of the College, John Thirlby and others.

Someone has remarked that in this context Glosse and Sharpe are not inappropriate names. It is perhaps more pertinent to notice the uncertainty which at this period attended business transactions, and the possibility of fraud and misrepresentation. We do not know the details of this particular dispute, but £40 was a large sum, probably more than the revenue of the College for a whole year.

The College on 15 September 1537 sealed a most remarkable document.[1] It was certainly opposed to the letter, and perhaps to the spirit, of the Founder's statutes, and so the King's licence was to be obtained for the carrying out of its provisions. In this document leave is given to Edward Moore, Fellow of the College and priest of the chantry of William Myles, to be student beyond the sea, where it shall seem to him most profitable for his learning, licence of the King's grace first obtained, for three years or four at most; and the Master and Fellows undertake to pay during his absence to his assigns the yearly profits of his Fellowship and chantry, and to procure one of the rest of the Fellows to have the name of the chantry priest and to say the usual Masses yearly in his stead.

The deed recites that the said Edward Moore had a desire and mind to go over the sea that he might study there and increase his learning, but was not able to continue any space with sufficient "exhibition" unless he retained the emoluments and profits which he was then taking from the College.

It is not known whether this College Order was carried into effect, but if it was, and if Moore stayed away his full four years, his leave of absence would expire a short time before the College combined the offices of *collector redituum* (Bursar) and of priest of the chantry of William Myles (6 July 1543).

Whether the permission to travel was used or not, the incident is an interesting anticipation of the modern institution of travelling Fellowships or studentships. As Bishop Browne says, "this was very handsome treatment". Moore was to receive, for four years, a stipend of eight pounds, far more than

[1] *Register*, I, 102.

that of the Master, with no duties whatsoever except to study. Moore must have been an exceptional man to deserve such a magnificent "exhibition". Perhaps the College commissioned him to observe and study the doctrines of the Reformers, to which it was by no means favourable. It should be noticed that the Fellow chosen for this privilege was receiving double the stipend of an ordinary Fellow; in other words, the College could not have made a more expensive choice. We have here confirmatory evidence of the view that the College was, in its early days, intended for the education of "advanced" students, rather than with the comparatively elementary studies of those whom we should call undergraduates. A hundred years later, in the earliest inventory of College plate, mention is made of "Mr Moore's beaker". Bishop Browne remarks: "It is pleasant to hope that this beaker commemorated Edward Moore's gratitude to the College: it would be still more pleasant to have the beaker now."

As has already been pointed out, St Catharine's in pre-Reformation days was concerned mainly with its Fellows. The first endowment to resemble a modern Scholarship was that of the Bible Clerkship, an office that might more fittingly be styled a Sizarship, as duties, some of them menial, were attached to it. The donor, a liberal benefactor of the College, was Richard Nelson, to whom the Master and Fellows grant (4 September 1506), in return for a gift of forty marks and "all his dues from his chamber in the College of St John the Evangelist", the right to nominate to the office of Bibliotista "unus honestus scolaris". Nelson during his lifetime is to fill each vacancy as it occurs; after his death the Master and Fellows agree to appoint to the office an "honestus et discretus scolaris", born in Londisdale, or in Lancashire, Yorkshire or Westmorland, provided that such a person can be found in the University, who must be able to read and to sing pleasantly and well.

The duties of the Bible Clerk are to read the Holy Bible at the usual, fitting times, "as the custom is in the other Colleges in the University of Cambridge", and also to wait on the Master and Fellows at dinner in Hall. Every day he is to say the psalm *de profundis* and other religious offices, and every week the seven penitential psalms. In return he is to receive food and drink, "with semi-commons of the aforesaid College", up to the value of eight pence weekly. There is to be assigned to him a suitable chamber in the College, and the Latin original possibly suggests that this chamber is not to be shared with anybody else.[1]

Exequies are to be kept and Masses said for Richard Nelson, who leaves six shillings and eight pence to be shared by the Master and Fellows when present. An amusing clause is added, insisting that "attendance" must not be taken to mean appearance at Chapel followed by a quick departure.[2] The Bible Clerk is to have four pence every year for attending. Jesus College is appointed to be the "watch-dog" to see that these conditions are faithfully carried out.

The composition of Dame Elizabeth Barnardiston, made the eighth day of March 1514, is in many ways the most interesting, if not the most important, of the early documents relating to gifts and benefactions. In the first place it is written in beautiful, even though legal, English, strongly reminiscent in its phraseology and rhythm of the English Prayer Book; then it is the second benefaction from a lady of the house of the Barnardistons; finally it founds a new office, the details of which are very significant.

The deed recites that Dame Elizabeth had given 100 marks to be employed to the weal of the house towards the purchase and amortisement of a manor called Mawdeberis, with the appurtenances in Coton and the towns adjoining, lately bought of Sir Robert Southwell.

The Master and Fellows agree to retain of the said lands, of the clear yearly value of five marks,[3] for and as lands purely given to them by the said Dame Elizabeth in pure and perpetual alms.

[1] "Praedictus Scolaris, viz.: Bible Clerk, habeat infra nostrum dictum collegium unam cameram sibi decentem et convenientem." Does *sibi* go with *unam* or with *decentem et convenientem*? Probably the latter construction is correct. We should certainly expect a more explicit phrase, particularly in a legal document, if a Sizar were to have a room to himself in a College whose Founder, thirty years earlier, had ordered that two Fellows were to share one chamber.

[2] Attendance is defined as being present (*a*) at the *exequiae*, from the beginning of the second Psalm to the Benediction; and (*b*) at the Mass, from the beginning to the third Agnus.

[3] Some of the Coton land was usually let under the name of "five-mark land", as the leases describe it.

An obit day is to be celebrated with service for the soul of Sir Thomas Barnardiston and others, for which service on such obit day the sum of six shillings and eight pence is to be distributed among the Master and Fellows. "And also the said Master and Fellows and their successors shall yearly for ever in the day and feast of the translation of Saint Thomas at their own proper costs and charges, except necessary expences for horse and man from Cambridge to Ketton and from Ketton again to Cambridge, find and send an honest, discreet and secular person, learned and graduate, to make and declare a sermon in English at the chapel of Saint Thomas within the parish of Kettyngton aforesaid." At this the Barnardiston family is to be remembered, and after the death of Elizabeth an obit is to be kept, "at the which the Master and Fellows and also suggeraunts (i.e. sojourners) being within the limits of the town of Cambridge shall be attendant and personally present upon pain of every of them four pence if there be no cause reasonable". From the five marks are to be provided "wine, bread and wax at all times sufficient and ready for masses and orisons there to be celebrate and done, as well to and for the Fellows and suggeraunts of the same place, as to and for all strangers thither resorting to pray or to sing mass or masses within the said chapel. For all which...the said Master and Fellows by these presents bind them and their successors unto the said Dame Elizabeth, to her heirs and executors, in a hundred pounds sterling."

In addition the Master and Fellows agree to support a Butler. It will be convenient at this point to discuss what we know about early College servants and how long the original customs were, in whole or in part, kept up, even though the annalistic thread of our history be broken thereby.

The College Register contains a copy of the original sealed deed whereby the Master and Fellows appoint, for life, Richard Lychfeld and Alice his wife to be College "Laundress". It is dated 29 April 1517, and is a significant document. It is the first instance on record of external service being employed in Woodlark's austere, almost monastic establishment. In the early days of the foundation (and it was a practice that died out slowly and gradually) a great deal of the work now done by hired servants was performed by junior students, "Sizars", as they were usually called. The Registry list[1] of members of St Catharine's assigns the offices of the Bible Clerk, the Butler and the Cook

[1] See p. 75.

to individual *discipuli*. The deed instituting the Bible Clerk[1] (1506) requires him to wait at the high table, while the Butler is given four pence in the composition of Robert Shurton (1536)[2] for attending Mass. The Barnardiston composition discussed above contains a clause whereby the Master and Fellows covenant

"to receive and to dwell with in the said Hall or College such a child or scholar, conveniently learned in grammar, as the said Dame Elizabeth...shall present;... which child and scholar and his successors shall be accounted, reckoned and named the butler, or else my Lady Barnardiston's child, in the said college, and shall always be attendant to minister and serve all things necessary concerning the buttery to Fellows, suggeraunts and strangers being within the said college. To the which child and his successors the Master and his successors shall at his first coming assign and appoint an honest chamber within the said Hall or College, and also pay and yield weekly for ever to him and his successors meat and drink to the clear value of six pence a week, and also in money once in the year for ever six shillings and eight pence for his linen. For the which the said child and his successors, so enjoying and having the said room and office, shall daily for ever say the psalm of Miserere with De profundis and the collect of Fidelium for the souls above rehearsed."

After the death of Lady Barnardiston the Master and Fellows are to appoint by preference a "child" who is akin[3] to her; failing such a choice, a native of Yorkshire or Lincolnshire is to be preferred. If no such happen to offer himself, they may assign it at their pleasure.

As early, however, as 1629–30 the Butler appears as a servant, who could make a profit or loss on his trading. The Bursar's accounts for that year allow "ye Butler for losses in beare in ye tyme of infection 5. 16. 3½". It is difficult to suppose that a College would give such an independent position to one of its junior students. The "butler's boy" receives a Christmas box of one shilling in 1644, and in the year 1656 both Butler and Cook[4] are deemed to

[1] See p. 63.

[2] See p. 218.

[3] This surely proves that no stigma at all was attached to the office; in fact the fee paid to the Bible Clerk and Butler for being present at Mass shows that both these offices were somewhat of a distinction.

[4] It may be noticed here that the Sizar-cook occupied at St Catharine's a position below the Bible Clerk and Butler. There was no endowment of his office; his presence was not required, as was that of the other two, at religious services; in the Registry list

have given acquittance to the Steward, as the Bursar was then called, for all sums due to them. There is in the Audit Book a receipt, given by the Cook on 17 September 1658, for the sum of £61. 6*s.* 3*d.*, of which £13. 13*s.* 4*d.* is for wages, and £47. 12*s.* 11*d.* for Commons, which at that time certainly included dinners in Hall. So by the middle of the seventeenth century the practice had grown up of appointing a Cook with a fixed wage, who also made a profit on the meals he supplied.[1] This practice did not cease until 1918.

The Registry list does not contain any reference to the *ostiarius* or Porter, but in the Bursar's accounts he sometimes appears as a member of the College, along with the *bibliotista*, and sometimes as one of the servants. This is all the more remarkable as an allowance "for porter's place" is a very common entry in the earlier accounts of the Tutor. The sum allowed was ten shillings per quarter, and it is significant that there is a bursarial charge every year of two pounds for the *ostiarius*. So the Tutor in 1676 calls one "Wood" (Richard Woods, admitted Sizar 30 April 1673) the "Colledge Porter", and allows him "for the porters place till Michaelmas 1. 0. 0." In the same year Husband is given "for porters place ½ y^r 1. 0. 0.", while in his Lady Day to Midsummer account we find among his charges "Porters place receiv'd 1. 0. 0." It would appear that he did not perform his duties; perhaps he was absent during the Lent quarter, as his Steward's bill for that quarter is only three shillings. The large number of similar entries about this time seems to imply duties actually performed, but the hypothesis might be defended that the duties, once real, were now a dead letter, and that "porter's place" had become a kind of Exhibition. Some support is lent to this view by the un-

coquus appears last on the list of *disciputi*, separated in fact from the others. When the offices were taken over by salaried servants, the Butler preserved his precedence. There is an interesting letter sent by J. Sidgwick to Eachard 8 April 1678. In it the writer says "I must request you to put mine own son John's name into your Buttery in the capacity of Sizar". We do not know the relative positions of Butler and Sizar. The Butler was probably the superior in authority.

[1] In the Audit Book the *coquus* appears as a servant till the year 1632–3, after which the entry ceases. Possibly a new method of payment was adopted after that year. Yet the Steward's book for 1629 has items opposite the names of fifteen persons *in statu pupillari*. The last is *Coquus*, and the sum opposite his name is 3*s.* 3½*d.*

5-2

certainty of the Bursars, who are not consistent in the place they assign to the *ostiarius*, and by the emergency measures taken in times of pestilence. During seasons of plague extra help was needed to "keep the gate", and nowhere is it recorded that students were called upon for this work. Thus in the accounts for 1641–2 there was paid the sum of two pounds "Money and Commons to the Porter, the women, Wright and George in the plague time", and the same sum was paid that year to "Goodman Cloude for gate keeping in the plague time besides ye quarters wages". Two items of the year 1665–6 are also informative: "To John Miller for keeping ye gates a fortnight in ye beginning of ye visitation that yeare 0. 14. 0; To him and a man to help him to measure ye coales, 0. 1. 6." Allowances for Porter's place appear in the Tutor's accounts as late as 1743. In 1785–6 there were an "Under Porter" and a "Porter's Boy".

The impression produced by a perusal of all the entries is that there was a servant-porter in the seventeenth century, who needed, however, occasional help. In normal times poor students helped to pay their way by undertaking to relieve the Porter, but under the stress of a "visitation", when students perhaps scattered, or else were carefully isolated from contact with outsiders, recourse was had to faithful retainers and humble friends among the local tradespeople.

Be this as it may, it is certain that no great stigma was attached to so-called menial work during at least the first two centuries of the life of the College. "Sizar's place" brought to the student in poor circumstances two pounds a year, and Ward, admitted Sizar in 1675, was Sizar to three senior members, receiving quarterly allowances for his services of £1. 10*s*. 0*d*. in addition to his Scholarship of the annual value of five pounds. Sizars may well be compared, as far as their duties are concerned, with the "fags" at our Public Schools; they performed personal services[1] for senior members. In addition

[1] Not, however, the routine services performed by *e.g.* laundress and bedmaker. "Bedmaker" is a regular item in early bills, while in the first volume of the College Register is a copy of the appointment of Richard Lychfeld and Alice his wife to the office of College Laundress. The laundress is often a man in the College records, and so apparently were bedmakers, if the "Ladds", often referred to in the Tutor's books as receiving large sums, may be identified with them. It is to be noticed, however, that

they waited in Hall, although probably a Hall waiter was employed before 1799–1800, when he first appears in our accounts. James Bonnell, writing to Strype about his visit to St Catharine's in November 1679, complains of "a formality of being served by gownd waiting men, little dirty pawd sizers".

The number of those who were admitted to the College during the first hundred and fifty years of its existence is a very difficult question. The College records are of the scantiest. There are in existence lists of Masters, Fellows and Bible Clerks,[1] but the earliest record of entries is in the Bursar's accounts for

bedmakers were often women. See Tutor's book Midsummer to Michaelmas 1684: a/c Mr Herring:

Bedmaker	6.	0
Laid out by her for him	7.	2

An extract from Cooper's *Annals* (III, 181) for 1625 may perhaps be quoted:

"On the 19th of December, the Vicechancellor and eleven Heads of Colleges made a decree, reciting that contrary to the ancient statutes of the University and Colleges, within a few years, boys and men ignorant of letters, and altogether unapt to make any progress in the studies of the University; and women besides, had crept within the College walls, to do those works which used to be done by indigent students to help to bear their charges; from whence great damage had accrued to poor scholars, and scandal to the University at home and obloquy abroad. To prevent which evils, it was therefore decreed:

That for the future, no boys, or men, so ignorant of letters, by any means, or pretext, should be permitted to reside or wander about any College, or in any manner, or by any pretext, intrude to do those sort of works; unless they were either Ministers of the College, or peculiar servants, who only do their own master's work.

That for the future, no woman of whatever age or condition, dare either by herself, or being sent for, be permitted by others, in any College, to make any one's bed in private chambers; or to go to the Hall, or kitchen, or buttery, to carry any one's commons, bread or beer to any scholar's chamber, within the limits of the College; unless she were sent for to nurse some infirm sick person."

[1] The lists of Masters and Fellows are in the *Register*, vol. I, and in the compilations of Milles and Prescot; that of early Bible Clerks in the *Register*, vol. I, p. 70.

1622–3.[1] An analysis of *Alumni Cantabrigienses* proves interesting but unsatisfactory. A careful search through its four volumes shows no entries of juniors, but only those of *e.g.* Fellows, before 1544. This fact fits in well with the supposition that St Catharine's was originally intended for the later education of senior students, but it may be due to the lack of evidence, as Matriculation began only in 1544. From 1544 to 1580 the number of entries usually varies from 0 to 5, but in 1550 there were 11; in 1564, 8; in 1568, 12; in 1569, 7; in 1571, 10; in 1572, 6; in 1573, 7; in 1579, 9; and in 1580, 6. Then follow six years during which the entries are large, but consist mostly of migrants from other colleges.[2] They are:

Year	Entries	Year	Entries
1581	9	1584	11
1582	12	1585	6
1583	15	1586	8

The next decade shows eight entries in 1593, six in 1594, seven in 1597 and one, two or four in the other years. The seventeenth century opened with two to four entries a year, but there were nine in 1604 and ten in 1605. The numbers begin to be consistently large in 1613, in which there were six entries, followed by six, ten, five, eight, six in successive years.

[1] The word "year" in this account of admissions means the old academical year, which began in July. The Admission books enter names under such years, often without giving the months, so that it is not possible to discover how many came into residence in any particular October.

[2] The custom of migration introduces an element of uncertainty, though not a large one, into all our calculations. If a man is recorded as having matriculated from college A in one year, and having graduated from St Catharine's three or four years later, we cannot say for certain when the migration took place. I have assumed that a migrant remained one year at his first college. Such guess-work makes unreliable the number of entries given for any particular year, but does not seriously affect the accuracy of total entries for any period of four years or over.

Here follow the entries as they appear in the College records:

Year	Entries	Year	Entries	Year	Entries
1622	14	1662	11	1702	8
3	No record	3	29	3	6
4		4	30	4	12
5		5	19	5	7
6		6	23	6	7
7	24	7	19	7	11
8	23	8	32	8	7
9	9	9	25	9	7
1630	28	1670	23	1710	11
1	23	1	20	1	10
2	20	2	23	2	7
3	17	3	8	3	6
4	20	4	25	4	6
5	17	5	18	5	9
6	14	6	15	6	13
7	27	7	24	7	12
8	32	8	21	8	7
9	25	9	21	9	12
1640	28	1680	15	1720	6
1	34	1	14	1	15
2	20	2	10	2	8
3	34	3	12	3	6
4	23	4	9	4	7
5	28	5	5	5	8
6	14	6	14	6	11
7	11	7	7	7	5
8	20	8	10	8	12
9	12	9	9	9	4
1650	8	1690	6	1730	10
1	10	1	9	1	5
2	14	2	8	2	13
3	11	3	12	3	5
4	17	4	21	4	4
5	10	5	18	5	8
6	12	6	19	6	7
7		7	11	7	7
8	13	8	5	8	8
9	8	9	5	9	4
1660	15	1700	4	1740	6
1	15	1	5	1	4

Domestic History

Year	Entries	Year	Entries	Year	Entries
1742	5	1784	6	1826	19
3	2	5	7	7	26
4	9	6	1	8	33
5	5	7	5	9	25
6	5	8	8	1830	23
7	2	9	8	1	20
8	6	1790	0	2	26
9	8	1	6	3	17
1750	7	2	3	4	25
1	8	3	9	5	25
2	6	4	8	6	29
3	6	5	5	7	19
4	4	6	1	8	31
5	6	7	3	9	27
6	4	8	3	1840	24
7	6	9	3	1	14
8	3	1800	0	2	24
9	4	1	0	3	26
1760	6	2	0	4	18
1	4	3	3	5	25
2	4	4	7	6	23
3	7	5	2	7	21
4	1	6	2	8	22
5	4	7	0	9	11
6	3	8	15	1850	18
7	5	9	4	1	16
8	3	1810	5	2	14
9	3	1	10	3	13
1770	3	2	12	4	10
1	5	3	7	5	6
2	12	4	10	6	10
3	4	5	15	7	9
4	5	6	12	8	5
5	5	7	15	9	10
6	4	8	21	1860	13
7	9	9	23	1	12
8	2	1820	15	2 }	29
9	8	1	10	3 }	
1780	3	2	26	4	11
1	4	3	29	5	12
2	7	4	34	6	21
3	4	5	23	7	11

Year	Entries	Year	Entries	Year	Entries
1868	13	1872	16	1875	11
9	11	3	14	6	26
1870	18	4	19	7[1]	11
1	16				

These figures may be supplemented from the following sources:

Year		Total
circa 1558	Registry 81 11 Master, 2 M.A.'s, 3 B.A.'s, 4 pensionarii, 8 discipuli	18
1564	Cooper *Annals* II 207, from one of the books presented to Queen Elizabeth on the occasion of her visit Master, 13 Fellows (including Fellow Commoners), 7 scholars	21
1573	John Caius *Hist. Cant. Acad.* p. 72 Master, 6 Fellows, 1 Bible Clerk, 3 inferior ministers, 21 pensioners	32
1621	Cooper *Memorials* p. 351 Master, 6 Fellows, 8 scholars with students etc.	56
	Thomas Fuller Master, 6 Fellows, with all students	above 100
1641	Cooper *Annals* III p. 315 Members assessed to a poll tax (7 colleges larger, 8 smaller)	102
1651	*Foundation of the University of Cambridge* (G. Langbaine?) Master, 6 Fellows, 10 scholars, 9 exhibitioners etc.	150

This number cannot be made to agree with the College records.

Year		Total
1672	John Ivory *The Foundation of the University of Cambridge* Master, 6 Fellows, 18 scholars, 9 exhibitioners etc.	150
1753	Edmund Carter *The History of the University of Cambridge* Master, 6 Fellows, 1 Fellow-chaplain, 1 bye-Fellow, 35 scholars and exhibitioners	about 40

[1] At this date a change took place in the method of recording admissions. Just before the Great War these rose to about 40 annually.

Besides these figures we have the following valuations, etc., not giving numbers, but showing a comparison of St Catharine's and other colleges:

Year

1534 Valuation for first-fruits and tenths. See Cooper *Annals* I 370.

Katherine Hall	39. 2. $7\frac{1}{4}$
Trinity Hall	72. 0. 10

Magdalene is not mentioned.

1542 Assessment to provide 10 soldiers to go with the Duke of Norfolk to Scotland. See Cooper I 404 and Lamb *Documents* p. 42.

Katerine Hall	x^s

The next lowest amount is £1. 4. 0.

1545–6 Survey of Colleges for Henry VIII. See Lamb *Documents* p. 69.

AULAE SANCTAE KATERINAE

Magister pro stipend. 5*l*. Sotii sex singuli 4*l*.	29	0	0
Bibliotista unus 1*l*. 14*s*. 4*d*. Coquus 2*l*. 12*s*. 8*d*. lotrix 8*s*. exhibitio unius ex sotiis 4*l*. promus 1*l*. 12*s*. 8*d*.	10	7	8
Eleemosinae 13*s*. 4*d*. exequiae et refectiones 5*l*. 16*s*. 8*d*. sermones 1*l*. 3*s*. 4*d*.	7	13	4
Expens. sacelli 13*s*. 4*d*. Feod. collectoris 2*l*. expens. extraordinariae 2*l*. reparationes 8*l*.	12	13	4

Summa	59	14	6
Summ. clara reven.	55	18	6
Sic expens. excedunt revent.	3	16	0

The *summa* apparently should be 59. 14. 4.

This was the smallest income of any college except Magdalene.

1549 Collection at the visitation of Edward VI. See Lamb *Documents* p. 121.

Aul. Katerin.	6. 8
Magd.	6. 0

1554 Contributions for a purchase of a new Silver Cross. See Lamb *Documents* p. 101. (St. Catharine's 16*s*. 8*d*.; Magdalene 10 shillings.)

1575 On the 30 September of this year a composition was made between the Town and the University, arranging among other things that for better provision against fire Catharine Hall should provide 2 buckets, 1 scoop, 1 long ladder, 1 short ladder. So Magdalene College, the other Colleges having to provide 4, 5 or 8 buckets. Cooper *Annals* II 337.

See also Lamb, p. 299, where Katherine Hall gives two shillings to "the beadles", when Trinity gives £1. 6*s.* 8*d.* and Pembroke six shillings.

It will be useful to give an exact transcription of the Registry list of *circa* 1558, as the copy in Browne's *St Catharine's College* is inaccurate in many details, particularly in placing the word *Coquus* to the left of the student's name, thus suggesting that Nicholas Johnson was not a *discipulus*. He almost certainly was, even though his name is not included in the bracket. The Cook was apparently a brother of the Bible Clerk, who is bracketed with Henry Smith, the Butler. The Pensioners seem to include Fellow Commoners.

Collegium sive Aula Sanctae Katherinae

Mr. Collegii	Edmundus Cosyne
Mri. Art.	Georgius Chatburn Franciscus Doryngton
Baccal.	Joannes Maddoke Radulphus Cowton Joannes Cragge
Pens.	Marmaducus Munson Carolus Parker Joannes Drase Thomas Parker
Discip.	Rolandus Jhonson Bibliot. Henricus Smythe Promus Joannes Coole Guilelmus Dorington Joannes Dorington Guilelmus Chatburne Guilelmus Yaetes
	Nicolaus Jhonson Coquus.

Registry 81 11.

All this evidence tends to show the comparative smallness and poverty of the College in the sixteenth century, its gradual but steady growth towards the end of that century, and its three "peaks" as far as numbers are concerned, namely 1627–45, 1663–79 and 1815–50.

Until recent times applicants for admission to the University came mainly from two classes—rich gentry and earnest, poor students. The latter were willing to work as Sizars, if they were not clever enough to win a Scholarship; the former gravitated towards a fashionable college. In either case much depended upon the energy of the Master and Tutors, far more than at the present time. Slackness and internal quarrels meant small numbers; during the eighteenth century many Scholarships and Exhibitions at St Catharine's were vacant, and the quarrel between Procter and Atkinson resulted in there being no entries in 1800, 1801 and 1802. On the other hand, a vigorous governing body kept the College large in the troublous times of Charles the First; the year of Naseby saw an entry that had been exceeded on only three previous occasions. It must be remembered that numbers did not bring in the substantial profits that they do at the present day, when colleges are run on strictly business lines. In fact one cannot avoid the suspicion that at times during the eighteenth century no effort was made at St Catharine's to fill vacant Scholarships and Fellowships, just because the stipends thus set free were more profitable to the Society than the advantages of a full College.

Many will find little to approve of in a college of seniors, carried on for the sake of these seniors only, and not for the sake of boys still in their teens. This is not the place to defend Woodlark's ideal; but as we review the pre-Reformation period, during which this ideal was on its trial, we are forced to the conclusion that it was a success, in that the system did give the desired results. If it did not produce world-famous men, it at least produced valuable members of the Church. In the short space of twenty-one years three Fellows of St Catharine's became Masters of other Colleges,[1] one of whom was Vice-Chancellor four times. The young College was popular enough to attract benefactions sufficient to establish the same number of foundation Fellowships as there is at the present day. Nor can the Society that gave Edward Moore his travelling Fellowship have been wanting in breadth of view or liberality of opinions. The College may well be proud of its early

[1] Edmund Natares, Master of Clare 1514, Vice-Chancellor in 1517, 1520, 1525, 1526; William Capon, Master of Jesus 1516; Robert Swinburne, Master of Pembroke 1534.

years, during which it proved itself a worthy trustee, not of money only, but of things far more valuable than money.

Although the early "compositions" and similar documents in the possession of the College often anticipate the interruption of Cambridge life by plague or pestilence, yet the details actually given later by the books of account are unfortunately few in number, and extend over a period of only thirty-six years. Nevertheless, the entries in the Audit Book, few as they are, give most interesting information to anybody who will take the trouble to read between the lines.

The entries in the Audit Book are these:

1629–30	Given to severall poore people and towards the releife of ye visited in tyme of ye plague	4	6	9
	for allowance to ye Butler for losses in beare in ye tyme of infection	5	16	3½
1641–2	To the towne poore in the plague time after the Colledge rate	1	0	0
	Money and Comons to the Porter, the women, Wright & George in the plague time	2	0	5
	To Goodman Cloude for gate keeping in the plague time besides ye quarters wages	2	0	0
1642–3	Payd for ye visited of ye plague	0	6	0
1645–6	To Holden for the visited one moneths rate for the poore	0	1	0
1646–7	To Holden for the visited three moneths	0	3	0
1664–5	Expended by ye Servants in ye time of ye visitation[1]	32	2	11
1665–6	To John Miller for keeping ye gates a fortnight in ye begin̄ing of ye visitacōn that yeare	0	14	0

Holden was evidently the officer in charge of organised relief, and to him the College pays the "Colledge rate", without prejudice to the further claims of any victims of the pestilence; the College apparently supplemented the

[1] This large sum suggests that the Master and Fellows left the College for a period during the visitation this year, handing over the care of the College to the servants. This they were permitted to do by the Edwardian statutes.

compulsory contribution by a further allowance. The allowance for beer to the Butler seems rather large, about £40 of our money. Probably, besides the beer that went bad, the College made some compensation for the beer that would have been drunk had the life of its members not been interrupted by the sickness. We must remember too that in the days before tea and coffee became common, the consumption of beer was, to our notions, abnormally large.[1] Two other points deserve notice. First there is the responsibility thrust upon "ye Servants" in a plague year, £32 being a huge sum in those days for a small institution, and then there is the importance of "gate keeping". Colleges at such times were isolated from the rest of the town; nobody could go out, and nobody could go in, except under the strictest supervision.

That the Society of St Catharine's changed from a student body to a teaching body is a fact of history; when and why the change took place are questions difficult if not impossible to answer. The most likely time for the turning point is the Reformation period, when anything that savoured of monasticism was unpopular and new ideas were struggling for recognition. Financial depression possibly suggested to the Fellows that in teaching lay a chance of increasing their revenues, and it is at least a strange coincidence that the year 1550, when poverty in the University was at its worst, saw as far as we can judge a much larger entry at St Catharine's than was usual in the sixteenth century. Unfortunately there is but slight evidence to confirm this view. The Edwardian statutes lay down no regulations for a tutorial system, but the reader at meals, who in the Founder's statutes is "puer sive clericus", appears in the new rules as "puer[2] sive discipulus". More importance should perhaps be attached to the statement of College terms and exercises, which as we have seen was drawn up about the year 1550. In it men of all years have work allotted to them which is to be supervised by the Praelector, an officer here mentioned for the first time in the records. Indeed one might reasonably conjecture that this document had its origin in the necessity of providing some organisation of teaching and study as juniors entered in greater numbers.

[1] See the interesting table printed on p. 400.

[2] "Puer" seems to mean "Sizar". Compare the "child" Butler of Elizabeth Barnardiston's composition, p. 66.

But though by the seventeenth century a tutorial system was fully established, the first Scholarship was not founded till 1587.

Both the Founder's statutes and the Edwardian lay down the rule that two Fellows are to share one "chamber", which seems to mean what is now called a set. In course of time a Fellow had a chamber to himself, but undergraduates shared rooms. It cannot be determined how many lived together during the first two hundred years of the College, but at the end of the seventeenth century it was two. The arrangement of the sets in the new buildings fits in well with this plan, and the literary evidence appears conclusive. Thus Leonard Osborne, writing to Eachard on 7 June 1680, says that he has sent up his "kinsman with his trunke and books, and such necessaries requirable.... The lad is very modest and of a good nature. I wish him a good Chamber fellow".[1] Again, Samuel Crisp, writing to Strype in June 1694, speaks of "one Hill of ye same year with us that was Fuller's Chamber-fellow".[2] The practice of assigning one set to each undergraduate seems to have arisen when numbers fell in the eighteenth century.

The Reformation period was a time of continual interference from the Crown. Each sovereign in turn felt bound to exercise control over the training ground of the clergy and of the other professions. First there is the Commission of Henry VIII, the report of which appeared in 1546. The result of this, as far as St Catharine's is concerned, was a new body of statutes,[3] the date of which was apparently 3 July 1549. Shortly before this (18 May 1549) occurred the visitation of St Catharine's. "With halfe an houres warnynge wente unto saynte Kateryns Hall and made an ende ther before supper and put them to no more cost but ther bever[4] and supped every at home."[5] So runs the quaint account of the proceedings. On 19 January

[1] Eachard, *Letters* 51. [2] Baumgartner I. *S.C.I.* 1, 132 (Add. MSS. 1).

[3] For a comparison of these statutes with the old, see pp. 339 foll. The changes are not great, being chiefly directed towards the elimination of Romanism. A Bursar is now recognised, and an audit ordered. The financial position of the College, as set forth in the Commissioners' report, is given on p. 221.

[4] Beer at 4 o'clock. [5] Lamb, *Documents*, p. 111.

1556/7 occurred the visitation of the delegates of Cardinal Pole. "My Lord of Chester and D. Cole went to Cathryn Hall first into the chapel and herde masse saide...they made an ende at Katryn Hall by X."[1] On 13 January 1554 a letter from the Chancellor (Bishop Gardiner) appointed Mr Cosyn Master in place of Dr Sandys, who had voided that office by marriage.[2]

The Commission of Queen Elizabeth (1559), of which we have no detailed account, probably removed Dr Cosyn from the Mastership and restored the statutes of 1549,[3] which remained in force until 1860. Later, on 28 March 1577, a letter of Queen Elizabeth appointed Edmund Hound as Master.[4]

These events concern the University at large rather than St Catharine's in particular, but some of the regulations imposed on all Colleges at this time are of sufficient interest to deserve a brief notice.

The statutes both of Edward VI and of Elizabeth forbid Fellows to marry.[5] When all Fellows were in orders of the Roman Church legislation on this point was unnecessary, but now Fellows were not forced to take orders (though it was usual for them to do so) and celibacy was no longer required from the clergy.

The Ordinations of Reginald Pole allow "honest women" to take *prandium* or *coena* in Colleges at the taking of degrees and at Sturbridge Fair, but they must not spend the night there. In addition to this privilege mothers and female relatives to the third degree may have *prandium* or *coena* twice a year.[6] That women actually did "dine in Hall" is shown by the report of King Edward's Visitors: "went to Gonwell Hall....Mrs Cheke and her syster supped ther also".[7] Reginald Pole's order was probably to restrict the custom.

[1] Lamb, p. 206.

[2] Lamb, p. 169. It is not known how or when the Master was allowed to marry.

[3] Queen Mary's letter of 20 August 1553 to the Chancellor of the University and the Heads of Colleges, complaining of innovations and demanding a return to the old order, suggests that the statutes of 1549 were for a time in abeyance. See Lamb, p. 165.

[4] *Register*, I, 73.

[5] See Lamb, *Documents*, pp. 138 ("socios collegiorum maritos esse non permittimus"), 293, 352.

[6] Lamb, p. 261. It is possible, though perhaps unlikely, that meals in private chambers are meant.

[7] Lamb, p. 110.

The rather barbarous custom of "salting" freshmen is forbidden by the Injunctions of Elizabeth.[1]

The same sovereign ordained that at the election of Fellows and scholars the sons of poor men, if of intellectual ability, should be preferred to the sons of rich or influential men.[2] No *scholaris* is to be admitted if he has not completed his fourteenth year, and no *pensionarius* unless he has been sufficiently prepared to study logic.[3]

Gates and doors of Colleges must be locked at the 8th hour in winter and the 9th in summer, when the keys are to be handed to the Master or President.[4]

There was a dispute about the office of Junior Proctor in the year 1542. According to the composition of 11 Aug. 1514 the right of nomination of the Proctors for this year was vested in Pembroke and St Catharine's Colleges. These Colleges nominated Mr Briggs and Mr Haggerstone respectively.

Mr Haggerstone, who was a Fellow of St Catharine's College, afterwards resigned his claim to the office and did not present himself for election. It was stated that Mr Edwin Sandys, who wished to obtain the office for himself, prevailed upon Mr Haggerstone to resign by a gift of four marks in money.

When the votes for the office of Junior Proctor were taken in the Assembly House, Mr Edwin Sandys and Mr Matthew Stokys were candidates and Mr Edwin Sandys had the majority of votes. The friends of Mr Stokys disputed the validity of Mr Sandys' election and appealed to the Vice-Chancellor, Dr Richard Standish. The Vice-Chancellor determined that, as Mr Sandys had canvassed for the office contrary to the tenor of the composition, he was incapable of being elected, and that the votes given for him were, therefore, null and void; that Mr Matthew Stokys was duly elected, but that his admission should be deferred till the truth of certain charges, alleged against him by Mr Cheke and Mr Sandys, should have been investigated.

It was subsequently agreed by Mr Sandys and Mr Stokys, with the consent of the Vice-Chancellor, to refer the whole matter in dispute to the Chancellor of the University (Dr Stephen Gardiner, Bishop of Winchester) and the Bishop

[1] Lamb, p. 307.
[2] Lamb, p. 351.
[3] Lamb, pp. 307 and 351.
[4] Lamb, p. 352.

of Westminster (Dr Thomas Thirlby) and that each of them should abide by their decision under the penalty of £20, the decision to be made before the feast of St Martin next coming.

There was a riot in the Assembly House, connected with this matter, 12 Nov. 1542, when Richard Cumberforth, M.A., Fellow of St John's College, laid violent hands on Dr Glyn, the Deputy Vice-Chancellor, as he was sitting in his chair and dissolving the Congregation. The Vice-Chancellor, after vainly citing him to appear, pronounced him contumacious, and suspended him from his degree of Master of Arts till he should be restored by the Chancellor. At the same time he also suspended from voting in the Senate till the following Christmas John Blyth, M.D., and Richard Swayne, M.A., for aiding and abetting Cumberforth in his assault.[1]

The Mastership of Edmund Hound, who was not elected by the Fellows but appointed by Queen Elizabeth 28 March 1577, was a remarkable one in many ways. Hound himself was by nature either over-conscientious or quarrelsome, perhaps neurotic also, as according to tradition he hanged himself in the cellar of his Dorset parsonage. The business Fellow of the College at this time, John Cragge, seems to have been an active man with a craze for novelty. We know a good deal about Cragge, but much that he did on behalf of the College has not been recorded, and it is by a chance reference in the Atkinson contract of 1611 that we learn he was responsible for building a "gallery" from the centre of the present lawn to the entrance of B staircase.

The last twenty-five years of the sixteenth century saw events which were unusual if not unparalleled. These are recorded in their appropriate place, but only a combination of them, however brief, can show how momentous was the time, a kind of prelude to the greatest period (1625–1650) in the past history of St Catharine's.

(1) The extraordinary lease (1577) of certain rooms to Marmaduke Monson, an ex-Fellow.[2]

[1] The documents relating to these matters are in the Registry.

[2] See p. 227.

(2) Letters of attorney to squat on property to which the College had no shadow of a claim (1580 and 1581).[1]

(3) Other unusual letters of attorney to Cragge (1582, 1587, 1591).[2]

(4) Proceedings against Richard Aunger in the Star Chamber (1579).[3]

(5) The deprivation of John Furmary (1580).[4]

(6) The application of the Master to the Vice-Chancellor against four Fellows of the College for abuses in the election of scholars and praying that they may be subjected to the penalties of the Statute 31 Elizabeth cap. 6 (1592).[5]

(7) The appeal to the Vice-Chancellor of Cansfield against his deprivation of Fellowship (1592).[6]

(8) The unusual number of migrants to St Catharine's.[7]

In the College Treasury are the deeds relating to a dispute with Richard Aunger, a Bencher of Gray's Inn, and a tenant of the College. He claimed the right to cut timber and to present to Coton Rectory. For some time there had been bad relations between him and his landlord; on 28 December 1576 he had got a warrant against John Cragge, who apparently was the Steward, and others for threatening to injure him. At last the College petitioned the Queen to have him brought into the Star Chamber on the charge of removing a boundary stone and falsifying a terrier-book lent to him by the College. On 18 June 1578 the Queen issued a commission to the Vice-Chancellor to examine witnesses. On 16 October 1579 a decree of the Star Chamber referred the matter to the Chancellor of the Exchequer, the Solicitor-General and the Dean of Westminster. This seems an admirable trio, but the costs of the action must have been out of all proportion to its importance. The award was given on 11 November 1579. The Commissioners decided that Aunger was not guilty of forgery, but having put the College to considerable expense he must pay the College £30 before Christmas Day and not fell any more timber during the remainder of his lease.

Browne remarks that this was a conclusion satisfactory to the College, but

[1] See p. 222.
[2] See p. 222.
[3] See below.
[4] See p. 85.
[5] See p. 86.
[6] See p. 87.
[7] See p. 70.

does not notice the really remarkable point about this dispute. Why did the College appeal to the extraordinary court of the Star Chamber to settle a dispute which to-day would be brought into an ordinary court? One can only guess that Aunger, a clever lawyer up to all the possible tricks, by his adroitness forced the College to have recourse to desperate measures.

In the year 1578 the College sold to Richard Faune some timber in Bassam's Close Chesterton for £21. 8*s*. 0*d*.[1] The Close had been let to Richard Cobb on a forty years' lease since Christmas 1562, but he had disposed of this lease to Dr Thomas Lorkyn, who sued the College before the Vice-Chancellor for the value of the timber as belonging to him by virtue of the lease. The Vice-Chancellor, Dr Byng, Master of Clare, gave judgment against the College, ordering the Master and Fellows to bear the costs of the suit and to pay Dr Lorkyn £21. 8*s*. 0*d*. The College appealed to the Senate, and on 20 January 1582 pleaded before the Delegates (1) that the lease granted to Cobb had not yet taken effect, by reason of a previous lease, still running, which had been granted by the Prior and Convent of Barnwell for fifty-one years from Lady Day 1535 to Thomas Raynes; (2) that Richard Faune, to whom the timber had been sold, had the right of that lease by virtue of his marriage with Thomas Raynes' daughter; and (3) that the timber being more than twenty-one years old was by law and custom of the country the property not of the lessee but of the owners of the soil. The Delegates reversed the Vice-Chancellor's decision, whereupon Dr Lorkyn appealed to the Senate and succeeded in getting fresh Delegates appointed. The Master and Fellows refused to acknowledge the legality of an appeal from Delegates to Delegates, and on 12 June 1583 assigned their reasons for refusing to plead before the second Delegacy. The Delegates however proceeded with the case, and gave sentence against the Master and Fellows on 13 March 1583/4, declaring them contumacious.

The incident discloses the fact that tortuous dealings in business were openly admitted (and defended) by the College at this date, and Browne's criticism of the College is by no means unmerited.[2] Of greater moment,

[1] See *Register*, I, 79, and University Registry.

[2] See Browne, p. 80.

perhaps, to the historian is this proof of the futility of University Courts. They appear to have lacked the power to enforce their decisions. It is impossible, too, to avoid the conclusion that at this period, as at many others, a quarrel was enjoyed as a means of recreation and amusement.

John Furmary, B.D., Fellow of the College, having obtained leave of absence from the Master, left Cambridge on the day after the first Tuesday in July 1580 and went to Lincoln, where he stayed till Michaelmas Day. On 2 December 1580 the Master, Mr Edmund Hound, put him out of Commons, and on 7 December 1580 declared his Fellowship vacant on the ground that he had been absent from College without sufficient cause for a longer time than the statutes of the College allowed. Mr Furmary immediately appealed from the sentence of the Master to the Vice-Chancellor, Dr Andrew Perne, Master of Peterhouse.

Notwithstanding Mr Furmary's appeal and an injunction issued by the Vice-Chancellor to stay all further proceedings till the appeal was heard, the Master proceeded to the election of a Fellow in the place of Mr Furmary, and a majority of the Fellows voting for John Foxe, the Master declared him duly elected and admitted him as Fellow. The Master acknowledged the jurisdiction of the Vice-Chancellor, and pleaded before him in reply to Mr Furmary's statement on 20 January 1581/2 and again on 2 March 1581/2. In a paper presented 1 February 1581/2 he desires certain questions to be put to John Holden and Edward Maplett, Fellows of the College, who had been called as witnesses by Mr Furmary in his favour; the questions imply that the two witnesses were strongly prejudiced against the Master and in favour of Mr Furmary. Mr Furmary, in a paper presented 27 March 1582, requests similar questions to be put to John Foxe, called as a witness by the Master, in which he is charged with partiality to the Master and to Mr Cragge, another Fellow of the College, who was a declared and open enemy to Mr Furmary.

Judgment was at length given 9 June 1582 by the Vice-Chancellor, Dr William Fulke, Master of Pembroke College. He determined that Mr Furmary had good and sufficient cause of absence from the College between July 5 and Michaelmas Day 1580; that such cause ought to have been allowed by the Master; and that he ought not to have been deprived of his Fellowship.

He declared the sentence of the Master to be null and void, and restored Mr Furmary to his Fellowship; and condemned the Master in the costs of the suit—the expenses were taxed at 240 shillings. On 20 October 1582 the Vice-Chancellor issued a mandate to John Baxter, M.A., and one of the Esquire Bedells, directing him to cite Mr Hound to appear before him on 26 October 1582 in the Consistory at the usual hour to show cause, if any, against the judgment and to see the taxation of the costs.

On 15 December 1582 the Master, Mr Hound, exhibited before the Vice-Chancellor written proofs:

1. That a commission had been issued 19 August 1580 to induct John Furmary into the church of Saltfleetby St Peter in the diocese of Lincoln of the presentation of Robert Mounsie and Elizabeth his wife, and that the tenths of the said church were of the value of 10*s*.
2. That on 26 March 1579 the Dean and Precentor of Lincoln had inducted John Furmary by proxy into the prebend of Wilton Payneshall in the Cathedral church of Lincoln; and that the tenths of the said prebend were 11*s*. 2½*d*.

These papers were intended to show that Mr Furmary's Fellowship was forfeited on grounds other than absence from College.

On 19 July 1592 the Master, Dr Hound, applied to the Vice-Chancellor, Dr Soame, Master of Peterhouse, for proceedings to be taken against four of the Fellows of the College (John Cragge, William Forster, William Moone, John Forby) under the Statute 31 Eliz. cap. 6 "against abuses in election of Scholars", and prayed that they should suffer the penalty prescribed by the Act.

No further proceedings seem to have been taken in the matter. Philpott suggests that the dispute was patched up by the election shortly afterwards of William Foster[1] into the place of Robert Cansfield, whose Fellowship Hound declared vacant in spite of a protest and a notice of appeal. "In the list of Fellows", he says, "I observe that Christopher Cragg was the person elected between John Forby and William Foster, so that the dispute must have

[1] Afterwards Bishop of Man.

related to the election of Christopher Cragg; the name seems to suggest nepotism, at least on the part of John Cragg, perhaps to the exclusion of a man of undoubted merit like William Foster."

The appeal of Cansfield was made 28 July 1592, and Robert Turner, LL.B., appeared before the deputy Vice-Chancellor, Dr Tindall, President of Queens' College, on 31 July as proxy for Mr Cansfield and obtained an injunction on the Master and Fellows to stay proceedings.

A citation having been served by Thomas Smith, one of the Bedells, on William Foster and on two of the Fellows, Moone and Forby, the Master and the other Fellows not having been found, personally to appear before the same deputy Vice-Chancellor Dr Tindall on 3 August 1592, John Cragge, one of the Fellows, and William Foster[1] alone appeared, and that only in their private capacity and not in the name of the College. It was ordered that the Master and Fellows should again be cited to appear on the next day, 4 August 1592.

John Forby, Fellow of the College, alone appeared then, and he only in his private capacity. The deputy Vice-Chancellor pronounced the Master and Fellows contumacious, but extended the time of their appearing to 1 September 1592.

The appeal came on to be heard again 5 July 1593, before the Vice-Chancellor, Dr Thomas Legge, Master of Gonville and Caius College, when the appellant Robert Cansfield appeared in person, together with the Master (Dr Hound) and four Fellows (Cragge, Forster, Moone, Forby).

The Master alleged his belief that at the time of his sentence against Cansfield he was in possession of a prebend in the Cathedral church of York, which could not be held with a Fellowship in the College. Cansfield thereupon proved that he had resigned the prebend 12 May 1592, before the Master's sentence. Quite naturally, the Vice-Chancellor declared the sentence null and void, restoring Cansfield to his Fellowship.

In March 1598 Dr John Overall was elected Master after a series of meetings, the votes of the six Fellows being equally balanced. The three junior Fellows

[1] Possibly the record is wrong here, as the person referred to may be William Forster, who had been Fellow for some time.

then held a meeting and recorded their votes for Dr Simon Robson, of St John's College, but no election was declared. On the same day (10 March) the three juniors applied at 8 a.m. to the Vice-Chancellor, Dr Jegon of Corpus Christi College, stating that as there was no majority of votes Dr Overall's election was invalid, and begging the Vice-Chancellor to issue an injunction. This the Vice-Chancellor did, and summoned the Fellows to appear before him. The three seniors demurred, but appeared under protest, pleading that the election of Dr Overall was good and valid; if not so, the appointment devolved upon the Crown. Three other meetings took place, each lasting four hours. At last at noon on Saturday 13 March the Vice-Chancellor delivered judgment that Dr Robson was duly elected, and announced his intention of declaring his judgment in writing at eight o'clock on the following Monday morning. The three seniors pleaded for delay, urging among other things that "we are required by his Grace (Archbishop Whitgift) not to do anything which may be prejudicial to the election of Dr Overall". Dr Robson was accordingly admitted on the Saturday after the delivery of the Vice-Chancellor's judgment. But he was Master only for a week. A letter was obtained by the seniors from Queen Elizabeth, appointing Dr Overall, who was admitted on Easter Day 16 April.

The seventeenth century opened quietly at St Catharine's after the stormy times under Hound. The Master was now the able and saintly Overall, and the future was full of hope and promise. Most unfortunately Overall resigned in 1607, and his successor Hills was a failure, although more successful as an ecclesiastic than as a don. A Cambridge man, born at Fulbourn, a Fellow of the College for many years before his election to the Mastership, he nevertheless never got on well with the Fellows, differing from them in politics (he voted in 1626 for Buckingham as Chancellor when the Fellows voted for his opponent the Earl of Berkshire) as well as in domestic matters and University affairs.

There is, however, evidence that the differences between Master and Fellows were not entirely intellectual. It is probable that the financial relations between the Master and the Bursar were not at this period clearly defined, so that there were many possibilities of disagreement, particularly at a time when fresh endowments were coming in and new buildings being added to the old court.[1] It so happened that gifts to the College were just beginning to become numerous after the "hard bargains" of pre-Reformation days. The late Master, in spite of his quarrels with the Fellows, had left the Society £100, the receipt of which is dated 1606. Mr John Duke, of Kelsale, Suffolk, by whose generosity the College acquired the advowsons of Gimingham and Trunch in 1592, left the residue of his goods "for the maintenance of most godly students of divinity abiding in the College". Then there were the gifts of Mrs Rosamond Payne and Sir John Claypoole, of £100 and £120 respectively, which the College invested in building new chambers.[2] In addition there was elected to a Fellowship in 1615 a man of strong character, generous disposition and great ability for business, to whose silent genius seem to be due the changes of this period towards cleaner financial administration.[3]

Be all this as it may, the Master felt compelled to execute on 9 April 1623 a deed whereby out of his "love and affection for the College" he did "release the College from all sums duties and demands whatsoever...due to him from the College for any cause whatsoever from the beginning of the world". One likes to believe that this gushing language, as Browne styles it, was due to the Master's lawyer and not to his own hypocrisy, for on 22 January 1623/4 the Society appeared before the Vice-Chancellor and the Master of Trinity in order that this vague cancelling of debts might be subjected to a proper scrutiny. It then appeared that instead of the College being indebted to the Master, the Master was heavily in debt to the College, and the following agreement was accepted by both parties. The Master was to pay:

(1) Within two days the sum of £20, part of £40 due from the late Master;

[1] See Browne, p. 92: "The new buildings, due to the money left for the endowment of Scholarships, involved a considerable amount of intricate management and a good deal of borrowing and repaying. The Master and Fellows advanced money to pay the bills, and obtained repayment when more money came in. The Master naturally held the threads...a most likely source of misunderstanding and trouble, if he was not very accurate, or not very acceptable."

[2] See p. 10.

[3] All the College books of account begin *after* Buck's election to a Fellowship.

(2) £10 or £13 supposed to be due from a late Fellow, Mr Moone, provided that Mr Moone acknowledged the debt or one or two of the late Fellows testified that it had been incurred;

(3) £8 supposed to be due from another late Fellow, Mr Knowles, on the same provisions as in (2);

(4) £10 in full discharge of all other debts due to the College from Dr Hills.

Clause (5) stipulated that an inventory should be taken of all goods and utensils of the College in the use of the Master, this to be placed in the Treasury.

There the inventory lies to this day, and it is here reproduced, as the details are of some interest.

XXXII/3.

A true inventory of all the stuff and goods which are in the Master's Lodging, and that chamber which the Fellows freely have granted to Dr Hills for his own life and no longer, belonging to St Catharine's Hall in Cambridge, made and taken the third day of February, 1623.

Stuff in the Master's Lodging

Imprimis in the outward chamber next the stairhead one table of ash with a frame of six feet belonging to the same.
Item one old joined form.
Item the chamber is all wainscoted about with settles.
Item one side table sometime Mr Bridge's.
Item old hangings of painted cloth.

In the Master's Great Chamber

Imprimis two portals of wainscot, one at the entrance, the other leading to the chamber next the library.
Item one court cupboard of wainscot.
Item one press of wainscot with three cupboards in the top.
Item one old round cupboard with a top of wainscot.
Item two great joined chairs of wainscot.
Item a little side table of wainscot with leaves to draw out, sometime Mr Bridge's.
Item one map with a frame wherein are the arms of our founder, the College's several masters, and the names of our benefactors.

In the Chamber next the Library and the little closet joining to it

Item one joined press with two cupboards.
Item one livery side table.
Item that chamber all lately wrought with wainscot.
Item the closet adjoining to it is wrought and sealed lately in part with old wainscot.

In the Master's bed-chamber which the Fellows have yielded to Dr Hills for his time without rent and no longer

Item all the hangings of Dornix which were those in the Great Chamber left by Dr Overall, and two window curtains of Dornix.
Item a livery table with a falling leaf.
Item four old frame stools of needlework, and two little stools covered with old needlework, sometime Mr Bridge's, and two portals of wainscot.

In the entry next the bed-chamber

Item one joined press of wainscot with two cupboards, sometime Mr Bridge's.

In the Gallery

Item one great barred chest with a new key and locks lately amended to it.

In the old room at the stairfoot leading to the library

Item one old table with leaves.

His testibus

Jo. Hilles
Tho. Bucke
Tho. Goodwin
Andrew Perne
John Lothiane
Robert Meres
John Arrowsmith

[Endorsed:

The Inventory of such goods as are in the Master's Lodging of St Catherine Hall that appurtain to the said College, taken February 3, 1623.]

There is in the University Registry the draft of a receipt given by the Fellows of the College to the Master. The date is 27 January 1623/4. It acknowledges that on this day Dr Hills had paid the several sums of £20 and £10 mentioned and specified in the first and fourth articles of the agreement made and concluded in the presence of Dr Thomas Paske, Vice-Chancellor, and of Dr John Richardson, Master of Trinity College. The sums to be recovered from Moone and Knowles are not mentioned; possibly more time was allowed in which to collect them.[1]

Probably in connection with these disagreeable and rather sordid disputes, on 11 December 1623 Jeremiah Gray, M.A. and Fellow of the College, resigned his Fellowship. For this purpose he went to the chamber of William Hotchkyn, LL.B., in Trinity Hall, between 10 and 11 o'clock in the morning, and in the presence of witnesses read a paper formally giving up his Fellowship into the hands of Dr Hills, the Master of the College. He declared that he made the resignation entirely of his own free will, for right and proper reasons, without any undue pressure from the other Fellows. Gray had been a Fellow for a little under two years, and he appointed as his attorneys to deliver a record of the transaction to the Master, Thomas Buck and John Lothian, Fellows of the College.[2]

Gray was the first of five new Fellows, three of whom were elected on 30 March 1622 and two on 10 April 1623. Evidently, for some reason or other, he lacked courage to face the crisis that was impending.

So ended a little drama often repeated in essentials in college history. Antiquated methods are carelessly carried out by an ageing and forgetful mind. Then there appear on the scene new Fellows, who in the warmth of youthful zeal strike hard, perhaps under the leadership of a middle-aged reformer. The victim of their just but stern action soon gives them a clear path by his convenient death.

For Hills died in 1626. There followed what was perhaps the most brilliant period in the history of the College. His successor was Richard Sibbes, an able, pious man, with a gift of making friends.[3] He was inclined to Puritanism, and in 1615 had been deprived of various offices for that "offence". From this time onwards Puritan tendencies were to the fore at St Catharine's, the

[1] The Bursar's accounts for 1623–4 contain the charge of 13*s.* 6*d.* "to Mr Tabor, for registring our Master's and the Fellows' final accord".

[2] Original paper in the Treasury.

[3] Praised by Daniel Milles, Fuller (*Worthies*) "he left it replenished with scholars, beautified with buildings, better endowed with revenues", and by Izaak Walton.

Fellows including Thomas Goodwin, John Arrowsmith, William Strong, William Spurstow[1] and John Bond. These men were not only Puritans; they were also men of learning and strong character. They attracted both pupils and benefactors. It has already been noticed how the numbers of entrants increased and kept at a high level from the death of Hills,[2] and many benefactions also are recorded in their proper place.[3] As far as can be seen these students were carefully supervised and taught.[4] As soon as the names of Tutors are available we find that pupils are divided among all the Fellows. It was not until the time of Eachard that one Tutor took over nearly all the pupils, leaving the other Fellows with nothing or but little to do.

In the year before the death of Sibbes one of the Fellows, William Strong, was suspended from every degree and banished the University by order of the Vice-Chancellor for contumacy shown in not answering a charge. Strong was a great and good man, who won distinction as a Puritan divine when he left Cambridge.

In the University Registry is a file of papers dealing with the election of a Master to succeed Sibbes, who died on 4 July 1635. The first, dated 7 July 1635, is a royal mandate empowering the Fellows to elect Robert Crichton, the Public Orator, "not imposing any command...but unmoving all impediments by way of Statute". Crichton was not a graduate in Divinity, and so was ineligible.

But the Fellows had already met on 6 July and unanimously[5] elected Dr

[1] One of the authors of the famous "Humble Remonstrance" against the divine right of episcopacy. It appeared in 1641, and was so named because of the initials of its five writers. VVS are the initials of Spurstow. [2] See p. 75. [3] See pp. 238 foll.

[4] The old customs of the College seem to have been kept up, or perhaps revived. See accounts for:

1627–8 for a Latine Bible to be used in ye hall	0	5	0
1651–2 A bible for ye hall	0	4	0

[5] Browne (pp. 101, 102) says that one Fellow was absent. There appears to be no evidence supporting this view. On the contrary, the depositions of the Fellows at the inquiry expressly state that "they all six (being all the whole number of Electors) did

Ralph Brownrigge, a Fellow of Pembroke, who seventeen years before had been suspended by the Vice-Chancellor for holding the view that opposition to the Crown was lawful. At the request of the King this suspension had been removed.

After the election the King suspended Brownrigge from the office of Master, and on 3 August a letter was sent by Lord Holland, the Chancellor of the University, to the Vice-Chancellor and Heads, bidding them hold an inquiry into the circumstances of the election and to send a speedy report. This document asserts that his Majesty had suspended Brownrigge "upon some information of the miscarriage of the said election, which is alleged to be hypothetical and not managed with the respect that was due unto his Majesty's letters of dispensation directed to the Fellows of that Society in favour of Mr Crichton the University Orator and procured by him not without the encouragement of some of themselves".

At this inquiry it came out that only one of the electors, John Lothian the senior Fellow, knew anything about the mandate on the day that Brownrigge was elected. The whole story is a curious one, and the original account of it reads like a chapter from some historical romance.

It appears that Lothian, a Scot who had obtained his Fellowship by royal mandate from James I, had within a few hours of Sibbes' death sent for his fellow-Scot Crichton and asked him to obtain from the King through his friends at Court a mandate appointing him to the Mastership. No other Fellow was present at this interview, though John Buck, a late Fellow, was there as a kind of witness. Crichton replied: "I answered no, I cared not for it; yet thinking with myself that...this might be an occasion for me to live still in the University I desired time of further deliberation." On hearing that the statutes allowed only three days for election, Crichton, who in spite of his coy disclaimer was very anxious to secure the Mastership, acted with really remarkable promptness and resource. "That Sunday

freely and unanimously and according to their Statutes and consciences elect and choose Dr Brownrigge to be Master". Browne seems to imply (p. 103) that being a Scot also debarred Crichton from the Mastership. But the statutes, while requiring Fellows to be Englishmen, lay no such restriction upon candidates for the Mastership. This is a curious fact, and apparently one not noticed before.

night",[1] he says, "I took horse and before the next day at noon I had obtained his Majesty's grant by the intercession of my gracious Lord and Patron the Duke of Lennox and the benignity of my dread Sovereign the King....

"But finding no Secretary of State to attend I was forced...to use mine own hand in the penning of his Majesty's letters, which I framed wholly dispensatory to remove those bars of Statutes." Crichton goes on to give three reasons for the modest terms of the letter he drafted for the King to sign. The date on the letter is 7 July, but the actual date on which it was written and signed was 5 July. He would have been wiser had he adopted a bolder policy and obtained an express command that the Fellows should elect him. For on his return to Cambridge on 6 July he discovered that the Fellows, all of them except Lothian being ignorant of Crichton's visit to the King, had already met and unanimously elected Brownrigge. Neither before nor at the election had Lothian said anything about his little scheme. When the two conspirators met on that Tuesday evening, both must have been rather embarrassed. Lothian explained that he had expected Crichton to return with a letter "mandatory, or at least more powerful and efficacious". He had remained silent at the election because, if Crichton had returned without a letter, no harm was done, if with a mandate, the election was null and void. He urged Crichton to return and try to obtain a peremptory letter, as mere permission to elect would have no influence upon the other Fellows. Crichton, however, resolved to let the matter drop, as he did not wish to be Master against the wishes of the Fellows.

But although the two chief actors in this drama were content that the matter should go no further, the King, or perhaps the Duke of Lennox, naturally wished to know why the royal letter had been disregarded. Hence the full investigation, at which it was shown that the five Fellows and Brownrigge had all along acted in utter ignorance of the attempt to secure a royal mandate. "The Fellows", says Browne,[2] "were, of course, held free from all responsibility of obedience to a letter they had never seen, and

[1] July 4, the date of Sibbes' death, fell on Commencement Sunday. Crichton saw Lothian about 5 or 6 o'clock.

[2] *St Catharine's College*, p. 104.

Dr Brownrigge was duly admitted to the Mastership. Quaintly enough, it fell to the ingenious and secretive Mr Lothian to admit him."

Brownrigge, although a supporter of King Charles, is praised in glowing terms by the Parliamentarian, Daniel Milles, and his character in David Lloyd's *Memoires*, published in 1668, is worth giving in full.

When King *James* (that most learned Prince) was pleased to honour the University of *Cambridge* by his Presence, and to make Exercises of Scholars, the best part of his Entertainment; this person (then a young man) was one of those who were chosen by the University, to adorn the reception of the King. The part he performed was *Jocoserione* (or *Praevaricator*) a mixture of Philosophy, with Wit and Oratory. This he discharged to the *admiration*, more than the *mirth* of the King, and other learned Auditors, who rejoyed to see such a luxuriance of *wit* was consistent with innocency; that jesting was confined to conveniency and mirth, married with that *Modesty* which became the *Muses*.

Among his learned and accurate performances in publick, I cannot but observe, that when he took the Degree of Bachelor of Divinity, the Text upon which he chose to Preach his *Latine Sermon* was Prophetick, and preparatory to his after-sufferings, *Phil.* I. 29. *Vobis autem datum, etc. To you it is given on the behalf of Christ, not only to believe in him, but to suffer for his sake.* Which eloquent and pious Sermon, he afterwards was to fulfil indeed. *Quod docuit verbo confirmavit exemplo.* He made his Doctrine good by his practice, taking up the Cross of Christ, and following him.

He was preferred to be Prebend of the Collegiat Church of *Eli*, by the favor and love of the then Bishop of that Seat, Dr. *Felton*, a very good and holy man: he had also a good Living at *Barlow*, not far from *Cambridge*, a Country Village; After that, this great Lamp was set and shined in a Sphere more proper and proportionate, being chosen *Master of Katherine-hall*. Here it was wonderful to see, how the *Buildings*, the *Revenues*, the *Students*, and the *Studiousness* of that place increased by the Care, Counsel, Prudence, Diligence, and Fame of Dr. *Brownrig*; who had such an eye to all, that he oversaw none; frequenting the Studies, and examining even younger Scholars, that they might be incouraged in Learning and Piety. He kept up very much, as good Learning and good Manners, so the honor of *Orthodox* Divinity and orderly *Conformity*: He kept to the Doctrine, Worship, Devotion, and Government in the Church of *England*: *which*, he would say, *he liked better and better, as he grew older.*[1]

[1] *Op. cit.* pp. 405, 406.

Browne remarks that although admirable as a man Brownrigge did not supervise well the business transactions of the College. In fact a most important acquisition, Hobson's house, situated to the south of the Bull, came into the possession of the College in 1637 without any conveyance or title-deeds being placed in the Treasury, "and no trace of the receipt or expenditure of nine benefactions of money which are known from other sources to have come to the College" can now be found. Nevertheless, his Mastership was marked by prosperity and happiness within the College and by its enhanced reputation without. It comes however as a shock to find that when Master he continued to accept high preferment in the Church, becoming in succession Prebendary of Lichfield, Archdeacon of Coventry, Prebendary of Durham and (in 1641) Bishop of Exeter. He was Vice-Chancellor in 1643, the year of the Earl of Manchester's visitation, being a most suitable person for the office at that time, for his sympathies were alike with the Church of England, the Presbyterians and the Calvinists. Shortly afterwards he lost his preferments, and at last, in 1645, for preaching before the University a sermon in which he supported the Royalists, he was deprived of his Mastership.

Brownrigge was typical of the spirit that pervaded St Catharine's at this epoch. Breadth of view was the dominant characteristic. The Puritan tendency was marked enough to induce Cromwell to send his second son Oliver to the College as a Pensioner, and one of the Fellow Commoners who entered at the same time was Oliver St John, afterwards Lord Chief Justice of Common Pleas and one of Cromwell's Commissioners for the University in 1654. Yet Brownrigge, and after him Spurstow with all the Fellows, were deprived of their offices because of their Royalist views. Their religious opinions commended themselves to the party in power, but politically the Society was suspect.

Some two years before the ejection of Brownrigge, William[1] Dowsing, by whose authority does not appear, "visited" among other places the

[1] Cooper, *Annals*, III, 364, note (4) says: "In the Querela Cantabrigiensis he is called John Dowsing. It is there said that by virtue of a pretended Commission he went about the country like a Bedlam, and that he beat down all the painted glass not only in the chapels but contrary to order in the public schools, College Halls, Libraries and Chambers."

churches and college chapels of Cambridge. He professed to be carrying out an ordinance of both Houses of Parliament directing that in churches and chapels many things should be removed that savoured of Popery; it included instructions that all crucifixes, crosses, images, and pictures of any one or more persons of the Trinity, or of the Virgin Mary, and all other images and pictures of saints or superstitious inscriptions in churches and chapels should be taken away or defaced. Dowsing kept a kind of diary, and here is the entry that concerns St Catharine's:

At Katharine Hall, 1643 Decemb. 28.

We pulled down St. George and the Dragon, and the Popish Katharine and Saint to which the Colledge was dedicated. Dr Brunbrick the Bp. manifested more reverence due to the place called Church then any other place, the Communion Plate not to be used for no other use in any Church, and he said It was an Error to break down John Baptist there and these words "Orate pro Animâ qui fecit hanc Fenestram". "Pray for the Soule of him that made this Windowe."

On the ejection of Brownrigge, William Spurstow, Fellow of the College since 1630, one of the first members of the Assembly of Divines, a devoted son and benefactor of St Catharine's, was made Master by the Assembly. No events of importance are recorded as taking place during his Mastership, although the College continued to be prosperous. He was one of the Commissioners appointed to treat with the King in the Isle of Wight in 1648, but was opposed to his being tried. In brief, while an enemy of Charles he was no enemy of kingship. A crisis soon followed. Neither Master nor Fellows would take the engagement to support the House of Commons "without King and House of Lords", and they were all ejected. Up to Michaelmas 1650 six Fellows received stipends; from Michaelmas to Christmas 1650 neither Master nor Fellows received stipends. John Lightfoot, a graduate of Christ's and at this time Rector of Much Munden, Herts, was appointed Master by order of Parliament on the Thursday before 17 November 1650, and six new Fellows[1] began to receive stipends from Christmas 1650. The Bursar's accounts for the year ending Michaelmas 1648 were not signed,

[1] See p. 200.

those for the year ending Michaelmas 1649 were signed by two Fellows only, while those for the next year were never audited.

It has been noticed by Browne that Spurstow's connection with the College did not entirely cease with his ejection. The College accounts for 1664 contain the entry:

For the entertainment of Dr Spurstow	2	12	0

"Creditable to all concerned," says Browne.

It is surprising that the College prospered during the years that followed. Lightfoot was a profound Hebraist, and a lovable character, but his heart was in his country parish and not in University and College business. He was Vice-Chancellor in 1654–5, but preferred to act by deputy, and appeared to grudge all the time he did not spend among his parishioners. Philpott said of him: "He must have been a very bad Master of the College: shutting himself up at his country living, and buried in literary labours of small value."

Nevertheless the College was successful and happy while he was Master. Perhaps the reason was that though "inefficient" he inspired others by his loving nature. Affection sometimes succeeds where ability fails. Some of the items in the accounts of the first two years of his Mastership are perhaps significant.

1650–1	Given by consent to a poore scholler, prisoner in towne	0	6	0
	Wine on Shrove Tuesday for strangers ith hall	0	1	6
1651–2	For Xtmas boxes to ye women	0	2	6

Numbers remained much as they had been since 1646, and from 1663 onwards were at a high level until Eachard became Master, when, after a few years of prosperity, they fell about 50 per cent.

In spite of the retiring nature of a scholarly Master, the business affairs of the College were managed with energy and, as far as can be seen, efficiency. In 1654 there were proceedings in Chancery about the non-payment of the Cholmley benefaction. The accounts for several years between 1658 and 1663 contain charges connected with this case. In 1661 came Skerne's benefaction. In 1662 a house and piece of land were purchased adjoining the Claypoole Building.

There is an item of ten shillings in the accounts for 1657–8 "for a reference from the Lord Protector about the augmentation of the Mastership". The words "Lord Protector", especially the word "Lord", have been erased by a later hand! This entry refers to a proposed augmentation of the Mastership, in accordance with a previous Act which assigned the yearly sum of £2000 from tithes for such increase of Masters' salaries at Oxford and Cambridge. St Catharine's Mastership at this time was said to be worth £22. 13*s.* 4*d.*, the smallest of all the Masterships. The proposal, which fell through, was to increase it by £90.

At the Restoration Lightfoot visited Brownrigge, the Master ejected ten years before, confessed that he was an intruder, and offered to restore the Mastership. This was refused, as Brownrigge, living a country life in his old age, did not wish to return to the Lodge. He declared that the office, so far as he was concerned, was void. Thereupon the six Fellows, one only of whom remained of those intruded in 1650, met and unanimously elected Lightfoot as their Master. They then set out to meet him on his return from visiting Brownrigge, and escorted him home with rejoicings. "A most creditable proceeding for all concerned", says Browne. It was a sign too of the spirit that animated the College at its rebirth a few years later.

Before we come to this there is one incident to be recorded which shows that even in such an honourable period practices were tolerated that to-day would be regarded as dubious, not to use a stronger adjective. On 9 December 1664 King Charles II signed a letter empowering Samuel Brunning to hold his Fellowship together with the Rectory of Semer in Suffolk, notwithstanding the College statutes. Brunning held his Fellowship for eleven years after this. We do not know if there were any special circumstances in this particular case, but speaking generally it appears dangerous to grant any Fellow out of such a small Society leave to undertake the duties of a rectory at a distance from Cambridge.

On 23 February 1673/4 began the rebuilding of the College. For many years the early buildings had been falling to pieces; additions and repairs had

Plate IV

The Hall from the Old Combination Room, now Gallery

The Gallery (Old Combination Room) from the Dais

been tried and found wanting. At last to someone occurred the idea of pulling down the old and beginning afresh. A tradition, appearing first in the Latin inscription under Loggan's design, points to Matthew Scrivener as the author of this idea. To Lightfoot and Scrivener must be given the credit of seeing that the Bull Court erected about 1634 afforded an excellent model for a new and beautiful college. Lightfoot lived long enough to see the Hall and Butteries completed at Whitsuntide 1675; £119. 14*s*. 11*d*. was spent at the opening. "The stone laid at the commencement of this work was found during the removal of the steps leading to the Hall a few years ago, with the inscription May VIIth MDCLXXIIII: it is now used as the support of the scraper at the door of the new Lodge."[1]

Lightfoot died in December 1675, and was succeeded by John Eachard. Browne says that little is known about Eachard, but this applies only to his life before he came to Cambridge, for of all our *alumni* none before the nineteenth century has left, in letters and other documents, fuller and better information about himself and the College over which he presided.

His greatest title to fame and respect lies in the energy he displayed in the work of rebuilding. In collecting money he was tireless, sparing neither himself nor his friends. An account of the buildings and the methods employed of paying for them have been described elsewhere.[2] From the abundant evidence that has come down to us it appears that Eachard was more active than business-like. Financially he lived from hand to mouth, and the work of reconstruction was a tedious business, carried out bit by bit as funds came in, but unfinished and in part unpaid for at Eachard's death in 1697. Perhaps, however, this lack of system was inevitable, owing to the poverty of the College, and when the ultimate achievement was so satisfactory it is perhaps unkind to carp at the methods employed. Nevertheless it is somewhat startling to learn that Eachard left debts on account of the new buildings amounting to £3100, of which £600 was owing to relatives and friends, and £950 to the University. He had "borrowed" from the University Chest when Vice-Chancellor, leaving his executors to find the

[1] Browne, p. 140. Replaced (1936) in the south wall of the Hall.

[2] See pp. 28 and 245 foll.

money as best they could. They found £409 by selling his share in a lease at Yarmouth to Dr James, President of Queens' and Regius Professor of Divinity. So the University lost over £500. Eachard openly acknowledges his liability in his memoranda, and the University Syndicate appointed to recover as much of the debt as possible was, if we may judge from its official report, strangely unperturbed by the irregularity of Eachard's transactions. The Master was, in fact, a victim of the not uncommon complaint, an irresistible urge to be generous at other people's expense. We are reminded that he again and again satisfied his charitable nature by giving sums of College money to beggars "in my absence", as the Bursar plaintively reiterates.

Eachard was a popular and successful Tutor, and the first extant tutorial accounts are of the same date as the beginning of his Mastership. He was, however, somewhat greedy. He continued being Tutor after he became Master; when he had occupied the latter office for four years, out of a total of eighteen freshmen whose Tutors are known to us, he had twelve under his charge. As we look at the old registers we are reminded of the tourist mentioned in Strype's correspondence, who heard "Eachard, Eachard, Eachard", whenever he asked who was the vicar or rector of the parish through which he passed.[1]

He had views of his own about education.[2] He was interested in science and medicine; Addenbrooke, the founder of the Cambridge hospital, was the first medical Fellow admitted to the Society of St Catharine's. He was also strongly in favour of attaching some at least of the Scholarships at St Catharine's to particular schools,[3] a policy which later had the hearty support of G. F. Browne, and in a modified form has been revived in modern times.

Some light is thrown on the size of the College during the period of reconstruction under Eachard by the receipts for Hearth Taxes, several of which have been preserved at the end of the first Audit Book. In 1673 the College paid for 48 hearths, in 1679 for 49, in 1680 and 1684 for 51, in 1685

[1] See the letter on p. 307. [2] See the letter on p. 324. [3] See p. 242.

and 1686 for 48, and in 1687, 1688 and 1689 for 58. In the accounts for 1684–5 there is an item of £1. 4*s*. 6*d*., "Hearth money paid more than received this year".

The Tutor's accounts for the period of Eachard's Mastership are much more interesting to the historian than those of the eighteenth and nineteenth centuries. In course of time a form of pupils' accounts was evolved which, though simpler and more business-like, was much less instructive. The earlier bills have, in common with the earlier ledgers of the Bursar, a tendency to give details of little or no value to the debtor (or to an auditor) but of great value to the social inquirer and to the antiquarian.

Some of these details relate to the studies of undergraduates, in particular to those outside the usual course for a degree. A common charge towards the close of the century is £2. 4*s*. 0*d*. for a "course of anatomy", which reminds us that the Tutor's scrap-books tell us that Vigani, the first Professor of Chemistry at Cambridge, resided for a time at St Catharine's, possibly as a guest of Eachard, whose note-books contain many medical prescriptions and more or less accurate information about the powers of drugs and herbs. Presumably Vigani gave advice to juniors, for a bill of the year 1695 has the item, "medicins had of S. Vigani 8/." We may note that the hospitality offered to Vigani contains the germ of the idea that in these modern days resulted in Professorial Fellowships.

Considerable attention was paid to geography, French and handwriting.[1] A charge for "maps" is an often-occurring entry, and in a bill of 1692 the character of these maps is indicated by the entry, "a map of England 0. 1. 6." We are not surprised that French was a common extra, and a typical charge is one debited to Sherlock in 1696, "p^{d} monsieur 0. 10. 0." Attention to handwriting was a praiseworthy custom, even though it reflects little credit on the schools of the day. Modern examiners will wish that at the present time candidates for degrees were subjected to a similar discipline.

1692 writing Mr one fortnight	0	5	0
1696 giv'n ye writing Mr	1	5	0

[1] A "singing master" received 14*s*. in 1676. We do not know for how many lessons.

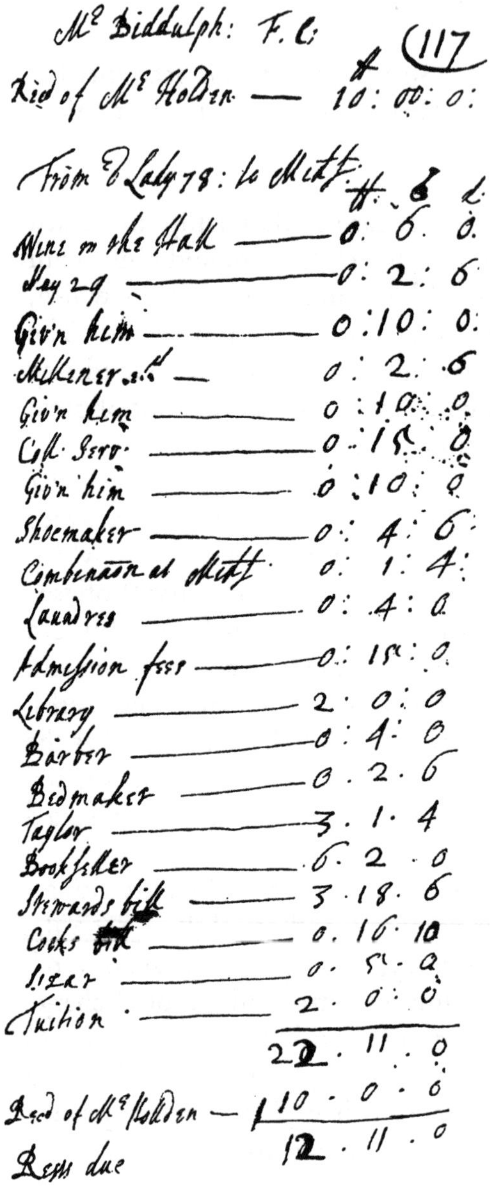

Mr Biddulph: F.C. (117)

Recd of Mr Holden	10	00	0

From Lady 78: to Mich.

	li	s	d
Wine in the Hall	0	6	0
May 29	0	2	6
Giv'n him	0	10	0
Millener etc	0	2	6
Giv'n him	0	10	0
Coll. Serv.	0	15	0
Giv'n him	0	10	0
Shoemaker	0	4	6
Combination at Mich.	0	1	4
Laundress	0	4	0
Admission fees	0	15	0
Library	2	0	0
Barber	0	4	0
Bedmaker	0	2	6
Taylor	3	1	4
Bookseller	6	2	0
Stewards bill	3	18	6
Cooks bill	0	16	10
Sizar	0	5	0
Tuition	2	0	0
	22	11	0
Recd of Mr Holden	10	0	0
Rem due	12	11	0

Fellow Commoner's Account

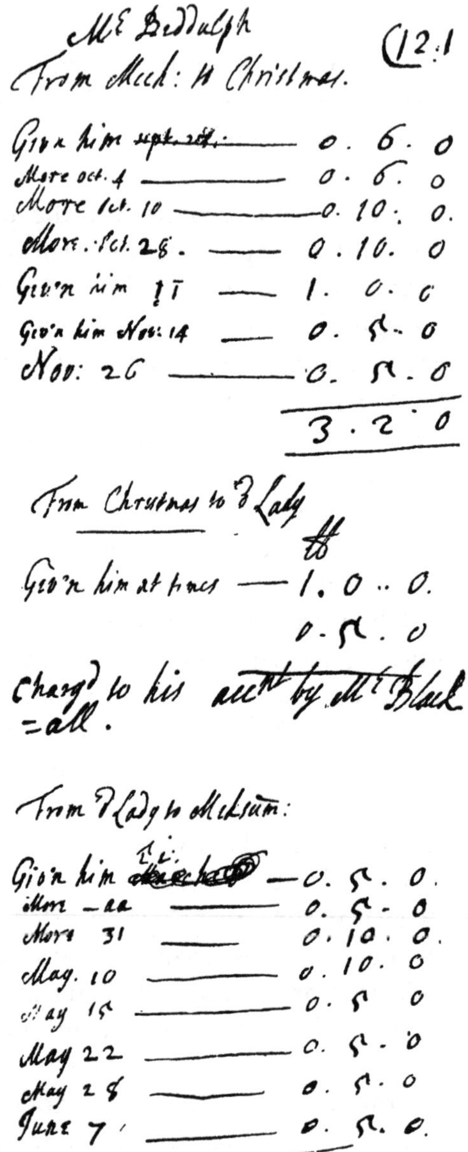

Mr Biddulph (121)

From Mich: to Christmas.

Giv'n him sept.	0	6	0
More oct. 4	0	6	0
More oct. 10	0	10	0
More oct. 28	0	10	0
Giv'n him	1	0	0
Giv'n him Nov. 14	0	5	0
Nov: 26	0	5	0
	3	2	0

From Christmas to Lady

	li		
Giv'n him at times	1	0	0
	0	5	0

Charg'd to his acct by Mr Black =all.

From Lady to Midsum:

Giv'n him	0	5	0
More 22	0	5	0
More 31	0	10	0
May. 10	0	10	0
May 15	0	5	0
May 22	0	5	0
May 28	0	5	0
June 7	0	5	0

Fellow Commoner's Account

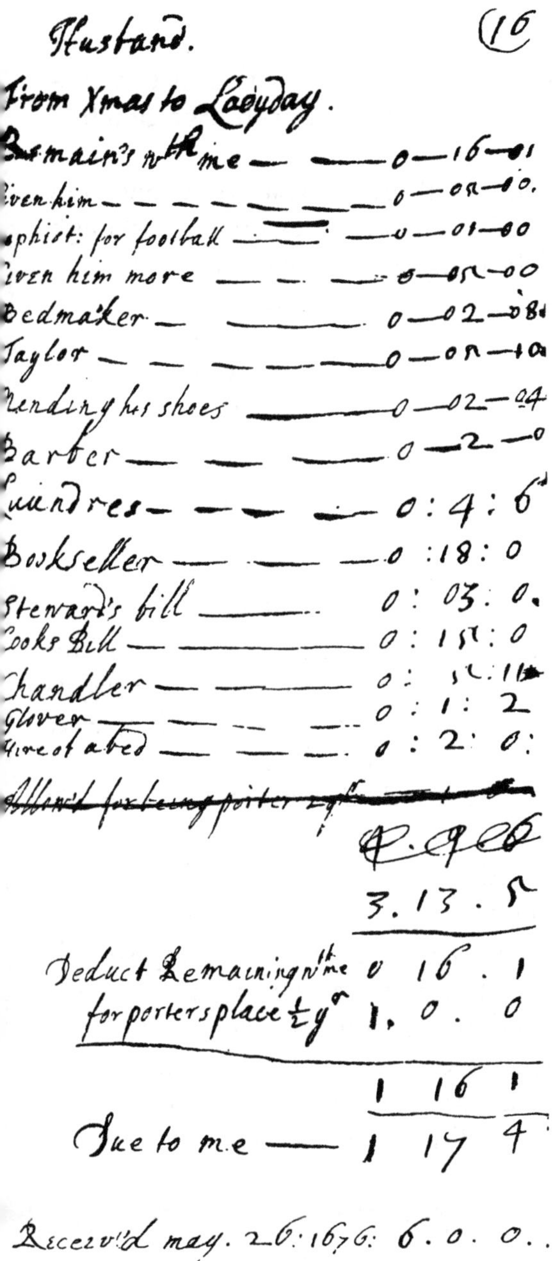
Husband. (16

From Xmas to Ladyday.

Remain's wth me — 0—16—01
Given him — 0—05—10.
Sophist: for football — 0—01—00
Given him more — 0—05—00
Bedmaker — 0—02—08
Taylor — 0—05—10
Mending his shoes — 0—02—04
Barber — 0—2—0
Laundres — 0:4:6d
Bookseller — 0:18:0
Steward's bill — 0:03:0.
Cooks Bill — 0:15:0
Chandler — 0:5:11
Glover — 0:1:2
Hire of a bed — 0:2:0:
~~Allow'd for being porter 2 qr~~
~~4.9.6~~
3.13.5
Deduct Remaining wth me 0 16 . 1
for porters place ½ yr 1. 0. 0
1 16 1
Due to me — 1 17 4

Receiv'd may. 26: 1676: 6. 0. 0..

Pupil's Account

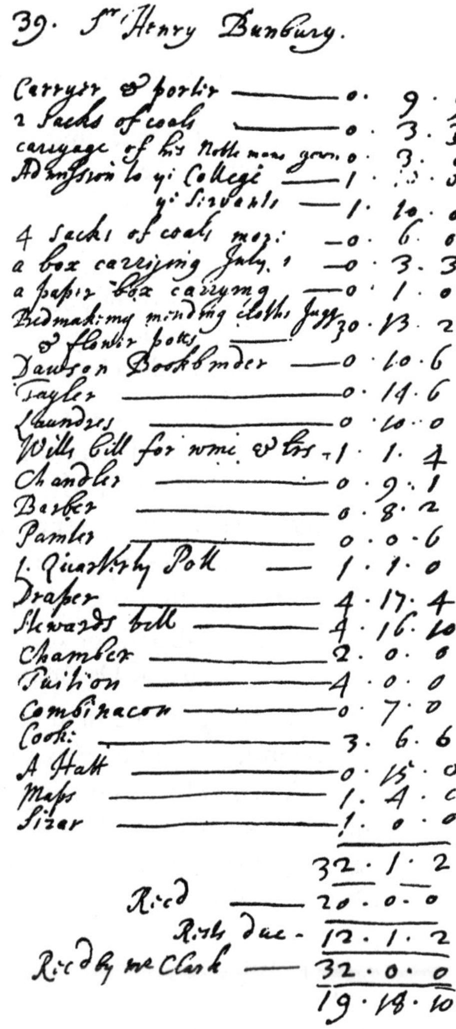
39. Sr Henry Bunbury.

Carryer & porter — 0. 9. 9
2 Sacks of coals — 0. 3. 3
carriage of his Noblemans gown 0. 3. 0
Admission to ye College — 1. 0. 0
ye Servants — 1. 10. 0
4 Sacks of coals more — 0. 6. 0
a box carrying July — 0. 3. 3
a paper box carrying — 0. 1. 0
Bedmaking mending cloths Juggs & flower pots — 0. 13. 2
Dawson Bookbinder — 0. 10. 6
Tayler — 0. 14. 6
Laundres — 0. 10. 0
Wills bill for wine & tea — 1. 1. 4
Chandler — 0. 9. 1
Barber — 0. 8. 2
Painter — 0. 0. 6
1 Quarterly Poll — 1. 1. 0
Draper — 4. 17. 4
Stewards bill — 4. 16. 10
Chamber — 2. 0. 0
Tuition — 4. 0. 0
Combinacon — 0. 7. 0
Cook — 3. 6. 6
A Hatt — 0. 15. 0
Maps — 1. 4. 0
Sizar — 1. 0. 0
32. 1. 2
Recd — 20. 0. 0
Rests due — 12. 1. 2
Recd by mr Clark — 32. 0. 0
19. 18. 10

Nobleman's Account

If we take into account the change in the value of money, we find that charges for such free-lance instruction are to-day much as they were two hundred and fifty years ago.

How did an undergraduate fare when he fell ill? Nowadays serious cases are hurried to a nursing home, but in Eachard's time assistance, although plentiful, was rough and ready. The following entries are significant:

1676	for sitting up with him	0	1	6
		0	3	0
	for watching with him	0	4	6
1678	nurse	1	6	0
	nurse's diet	0	12	0
	apothecary	1	0	3
	doctor's fee	1	0	0
	Dr of physic's fees	3	4	6
1694	to the surgeon	0	10	0
1695	to the chirurgeon	0	10	0

The doctor of physic was probably a consultant, but the "chirurgeon's" fee to-day would bear a different ratio to that of his fellow-practitioner. A night-nurse's duties, for which the usual fee was apparently 1*s.* 6*d.* a sitting, were generally carried out by servants or retainers of the College.[1]

A cap, gown and surplice in 1678 cost £4. 9*s.* 7*d.* But these were often sold to the Tutor when a man went down:

1676	abated for surplice returned	0	8	0
	pay'd Ds Adams for a gowne	0	11	0

A new cap and gown cost at about the same time £2. 14*s.* 7*d.*, and, apparently second-hand, a surplice was sold by the Tutor for 13*s.* and a gown for 14*s.*

The College charges during this period present some surprising differences from those of to-day. The usual matriculation fee was seven pence, while a Sizar paid five pence.[2] Sums of £2. 14*s.* 7*d.* and £4. 7*s.* 4*d.* are paid to the College for the B.A. degree. A fine of half-a-crown was regularly imposed

[1] See p. 164.

[2] Occasionally the charge is 1*s.* 1*d.* or 1*s.* 5*d.*—probably the sum paid by a Fellow Commoner, whose fees were usually about twice those of a Pensioner. A Nobleman paid still more.

for "Christmas absence", a relic of the time when residence was required at each of the three great Christian festivals. Caution money is usually either £3 or £5.

We may conclude with two items which speak for themselves:

1692 given to buy a horse	4	0	0
1696 a sword	1	0	0

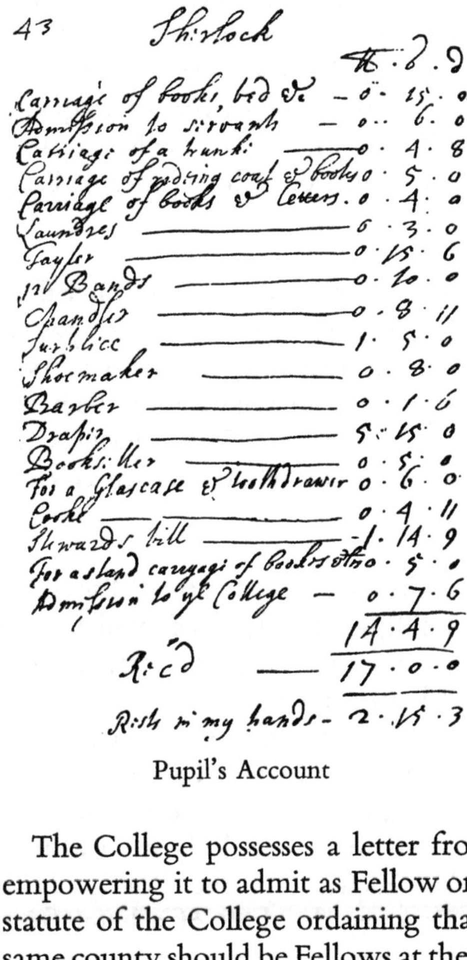
43 Sherlock
li. s. d.
Carriage of books, bed &c — 0 · 15 · 0
Admission to servants — 0 · 6 · 0
Carriage of a trunk — 0 · 4 · 8
Carriage of riding coat & books 0 · 5 · 0
Carriage of books & letters 0 · 4 · 0
Laundres — 0 · 3 · 0
Tayler — 0 · 15 · 6
12 Bands — 0 · 10 · 0
Chandler — 0 · 8 · 11
Surplice — 1 · 5 · 0
Shoemaker — 0 · 8 · 0
Barber — 0 · 1 · 6
Draper — 5 · 15 · 0
Bookseller — 0 · 5 · 0
For a Glascase & toothdrawer 0 · 6 · 0
Cooke — 0 · 4 · 11
Stewards bill — 1 · 14 · 9
For a land carriage of books &c 0 · 5 · 0
Admission to ye College — 0 · 7 · 6
14 · 4 · 9
Rec'd — 17 · 0 · 0
Rests in my hands — 2 · 15 · 3

Pupil's Account

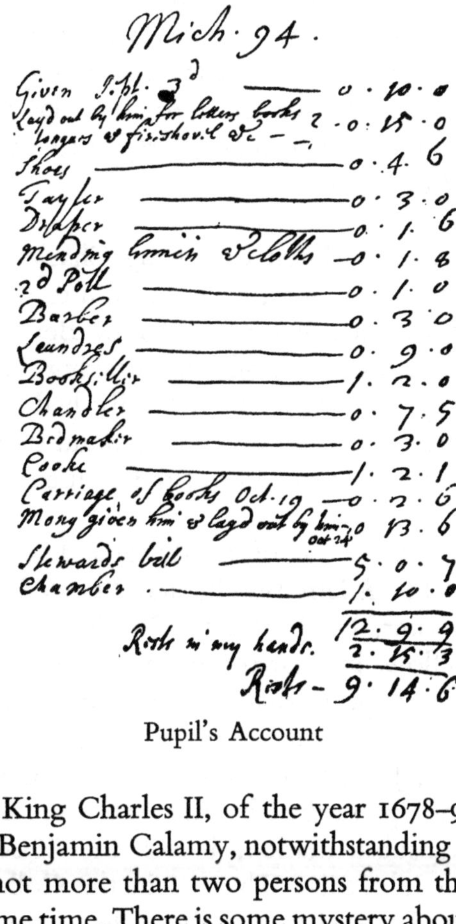
Mich. 94.
Given Sept. 3d — 0 · 10 · 0
Layd out by him for letters, books, tongues & fireshovel &c — 0 · 15 · 0
Shoes — 0 · 4 · 6
Tayler — 0 · 3 · 0
Draper — 0 · 1 · 6
Mending linnen & cloths — 0 · 1 · 8
2d Poll — 0 · 1 · 0
Barber — 0 · 3 · 0
Laundres — 0 · 9 · 0
Bookseller — 1 · 2 · 0
Chandler — 0 · 7 · 5
Bedmaker — 0 · 3 · 0
Cooke — 1 · 2 · 1
Carriage of books Oct. 19 — 0 · 2 · 6
Mony given him & layd out by him Oct 24 — 0 · 13 · 6
Stewards bill — 5 · 0 · 7
Chamber — 1 · 10 · 0
12 · 9 · 9
Rests in my hands. 2 · 15 · 3
Rests — 9 · 14 · 6

Pupil's Account

The College possesses a letter from King Charles II, of the year 1678–9, empowering it to admit as Fellow one Benjamin Calamy, notwithstanding a statute of the College ordaining that not more than two persons from the same county should be Fellows at the same time. There is some mystery about this letter. It was James Calamy who was admitted Fellow in this year, brother of the Benjamin Calamy admitted Fellow in 1668–9. There is no record of the admission of a second Benjamin Calamy. Philpott suggests that the letter of dispensation did not take effect. Perhaps a more likely hypothesis is that owing to a slip of the pen the elder brother's name Benjamin was entered into the King's letter instead of the right one, James. It would be an easy mistake for one to make who knew that a Benjamin Calamy was already a Fellow. Such dispensations were obtained twice more before the century ended. On 7 October 1691 Queen Anne sent a letter permitting the Fellows to elect as Fellow one John Bower, a native of Scotland, in spite of the statute requiring Fellows to be natives of England, and the election on 2 August 1697 of Sir William Dawes to the Mastership, though he was under thirty years of age, was sanctioned by a letter of King William III.

On 15 March 1680 King Charles II sent a warrant to the High Sheriff of Cambridgeshire, ordering him to stay execution of sentence of death passed at the last assizes on James Beversham and Benjamin Beversham, two scholars of the College, for taking the sum of £6 from a butcher on the highway. The Beversham family had been connected with St Catharine's for forty years, and it was an unkind stroke of fate that it fell to Eachard as Vice-Chancellor to commit the accused for trial.

In a meeting of the Master and Fellows on 16 October 1691 the Fellowships of Mr Adam Buddle and Mr William Phillips were declared void by the Master, Dr Eachard. On the same day two other persons were elected Fellows in their room, John Bower and Alexander Bence.

It appears that at the revolution of 1688 there were six Fellows, viz. Nicholas Gouge, Francis Langley, Adam Buddle, William Phillips, Samuel Lea, John Leng. Four of these, Gouge, Langley, Lea and Leng, took the oath prescribed by the Act 1 W. & M. and made the declaration against transubstantiation, before the Master, Dr Eachard, in the College Hall, 30 July 1689. There is in the College Treasury the draft of a letter from Dr Eachard to the Vice-Chancellor 17 October 1691 acquainting him that Mr Buddle and Mr Phillips had not taken the oaths to King William and

Queen Mary and that he had, therefore, pronounced their Fellowships void and admitted two others in their places.

Nearly every item in Eachard's scrap-books is of interest, and well deserves reproduction here, but space forbids us to give in full more than two. These belong to the year before his death, when he was Vice-Chancellor. The first is a copy of the bill presented to Sir William Dawes on taking his degree of D.D. by Royal Mandate. The second is Eachard's rough bill of costs for the Commencement dinner of the same year, 1696. Comment is superfluous, and would detract from the quiet enjoyment to be obtained from contemplating these figures. One may note, however, that Dawes not only supplies a buck, but also pays £6. 10*s*. 0*d*. for his share of the dinner; that the cost of a bottle of wine at this date averaged 1*s*. 8*d*.; that to obtain the cost in modern money it is necessary to multiply by at least three, and that the dinner, if it took place in St John's Hall, was for about 200. Eachard appears to have been on very friendly terms with St John's, and it is interesting to learn that the Bidding Prayer on the fly-leaves of a book in St John's Library, mentioned by Mullinger,[1] is actually in Eachard's handwriting.

Sr Wm Dawes's accompt relating to ye Comencemt. 1696

paid to Dr Beaumont—	1.	6.	0
pd Sr Ch. Caesar's Park keeper—	1.	2.	0
Given Sr William 2 guineas—	2.	4.	0
Laid out by Witt for clerum for Biskett & Wine & letters,	0.	13.	0
To y Colledge for his degree—	5.	0.	0
for registring and to ye register for his letter from ye King—	2.	4.	4
double composition—	16.	12.	8
to ye University besides—	3.	17.	6
Caution for his Act, determination & one opposition—	49.	0.	0
cooks bill for Clerum dinner—	10.	13.	3
Butler's bill for that dinner—	1.	18.	11
Sizings besides—	0.	9.	7
Buck for Commencemt feast—	3.	10.	0

[1] See Mullinger, II, p. 630.

Wine & glasses, & knives & Napkins & wine besides		5. 8. 8
Viz. 4 doz. $\frac{1}{2}$ of Claret at 1L pr doz—	4. 10. 0	
6 bottles of Canary,	0. 12. 0	
2 Bottles of Rhinish & 2 of white	0. 6. 8	
Share of Commencemt Super		6. 10. 0
in all—		110. 10. 9

For this Dr Fisher gave him his Note.

Commencement dinner

To Corn: Austin for altering ye Tables in St John's Hall	1. 5. 0
The upper Cookes bill—sixty one pounds, twelve sh.	61. 12. 0
The under cooks bill for exceedings for ye schollars	3. 3. 0
The Butlers bill for Bread and Beere, &c.	12. 14. 8
Given to Dr Gowers Servts for attending—	0. 10. 0
Mr Potts's bill for a Sturgeon, hammes, &c. 17 odd money,	17. 10. 9
laid out towards ten Bucks more than was given or recd from Commencers: Archbp of Cant gave 2 Bucks Dr Bentley one, Sr Wm Dawes, Dr Jefferies, Dr Smith 3 10 a piece and Dr Bentham 1. 0. 0	21. 5. 6
To Mr Worts for Wine and losse of linnen cutlery &c 49 eighteen and fivepence	49. 18. 5

One of the Strype letters[1] suggests that all was not well with the Fellows of St Catharine's during the period of reconstruction. The writer speaks of the discredit of Catharine Hall, and regrets that it is now debauched, adding that in the days of Lightfoot, although he did not reside, yet the College was not debauched.

This is possibly mere gossip, yet an impartial review of the evidence does not leave the student with a favourable impression of the Eachard period. Energetic but dull, active but selfish, thinking of his own glory and caring little how he satisfied his ambitions so long as they were satisfied, Eachard can scarcely have been a good influence in the Society. But, with all his faults, he rebuilt the College.

At the death of Eachard the Fellows elected as Master Dr Peter Fisher, Rector of Bennington, the home of the Caesar family, four members of

[1] Reproduced on p. 307.

which entered the College as Fellow Commoners between 1667 and 1701. He had been a Fellow from 1672 to 1677, but for some reason resigned the Mastership on 11 August 1697, just one month after the election, and was never admitted. On 18 August Sir William Dawes was admitted Master, King William having given power to elect a candidate under thirty years of age. The new Master had entered the College as Fellow Commoner in 1689. When he became Archbishop of York in 1714 he had rebuilt the Chapel, and also made it certain that a canonry at Norwich Cathedral would shortly be annexed to the Mastership.

Of the events of the early part of the eighteenth century by far the most important was the annexation to the Mastership of a Canonry at Norwich. It is very difficult in these days of "whole-time jobs" to realise how easily two hundred years ago a sinecure office could be regarded as not only permissible but even necessary. The Canonry, however, could scarcely be regarded as a sinecure; its union with the Mastership was rather the amalgamation of two offices, incompatible enough in modern days, but possibly helpful to each other only a few generations ago. Philpott, a clear thinker of sound judgment, believed that "each office was a great support to the fulfilment of the duties of the other".[1]

The income of the Mastership was an urgent matter as early as the middle of the seventeenth century, and this addition to it was due to the influence in high circles of Sir William Dawes. Browne reproduces[2] a most tactful letter written in 1714 by Dawes to Crosse, the President, urging him not to press for the Mastership himself, but to allow it to go to Sherlock. Dawes adds that in this case a Norwich Canonry will be annexed, and delicately hints that it will not be long before Crosse is Canon himself. The Act of Parliament annexing the Canonry was passed 6 June 1714, and there are certain charges referring to the matter, amounting in all to £64. 4*s*. 11*d*., in the accounts for 1715, 1716 and 1718. The Dean of Norwich, Dr Prideaux, fought hard through his friends in Parliament to prevent the Bill from becoming law. Defeated in this attempt, when the next vacancy occurred in 1717, Prideaux maintained that the Cathe-

[1] G. F. Browne, *St Catharine's College*, p. 175.

[2] *St Catharine's College*, p. 173.

dral statutes forbade any person to be Prebendary of Norwich who was Dean or Prebendary of any other Church. Sherlock was Dean of Chichester and Prebendary of St Paul's, and therefore, according to Prideaux, ineligible for a Canonry at Norwich. Sherlock applied for a mandamus, and it was successfully maintained that an Act of Parliament overrode the Cathedral statutes. So Sherlock was admitted Canon (under protest) on 10 July 1719.

The Act remained in force until 1927, when the Canonry was by another Act dissociated from the Mastership. This time the negotiations were perfectly friendly, the Dean and Chapter agreeing to allow the College an annuity of £300 in exchange for the right of election.

On 24 September 1705 the Master and Fellows gave a receipt under the common seal of the College to the executors of Thomas Neale of Bramfield, in the county of Suffolk, for a valuable collection of books, left by him in his will to the College.

The establishment of a chaplaincy in the College by Mr Holwey proved useful, both by setting the Fellows free to carry out secular duties and also by giving an opportunity of testing a man before electing him to a full Fellowship. The first notice of an election to the office is to be found in an Order of 19 October 1710.

Ordered that the Fellow who shall be from time to time in Mr Holwey's Fellowship shall take place among the Fellows of the old Foundation according to his seniority as Fellow, and shall have place in Chapel and Hall accordingly.

Then Nicholas Gouge A.M. was, by the Master and a majority of the Fellows, chosen into Mr Holwey's Fellowship.

Soon after this the estate supporting the Fellowship was found to be "much out of repair", and a College Order of 25 October 1715 requires the prayers in Chapel to be read by the Fellows "as they were before the foundation of the said Fellowship". A fine of five shillings is to be paid by any Fellow who does not "supply the week of his course in his own person". The historian is pleased to get this side-light on the duties of Fellows; he would be yet more pleased to learn the fate of the Fellows who were not in holy orders. Did they read such prayers as their status allowed? Or did they pay their fine? It is not to be believed that they escaped altogether. The lean period did not last long, for there was enough money on 3 February 1717/8 to enable the Society to elect William Pyke into the Conduct Fellowship. At the same time it was ordered that if the Conduct Fellow be absent for more than nine weeks in one year the Master or President shall appoint a Fellow to read prayers for him, who shall receive seven shillings per week out of the stipend of the Conduct Fellow.

So little information has come to us about the discipline kept in the old days by the College authorities that an Order of 17 December 1712 has an unusual interest.

It is hereby ordered by us whose names are underwritten that from the day of the date hereof a sexton or verger be appointed to attend constantly at the Chapel door to prevent any disturbance during the time of divine service, and that the Bursar of the College shall pay the said officer for his attendance the yearly pension of forty shillings.

Tho. Crosse President
Jos. Sparrow
Hen. Stebbing.

If the nature of undergraduates has remained the same during the last two hundred years, it is safe to say that the remedy proposed only aggravated the disease.

The following College Order also is of interest:

11 October 1716

Whereas the Scholars of this College have commonly after the taking the degree of a Bachelor of Arts absented themselves from College and yet have continued to receive the profit of their Scholarships: It is now ordered by the Master and Fellows, that every Scholar of this house shall be resident at least 13 weeks in every year, and if any Scholar shall be absent from College for a longer time in any one year than this order allows, then his Scholarship shall be void and disposed of by the Master and Fellows. And this order to take place from Michaelmas last.

On 5 April 1745 died Mrs Ramsden, whose will is dated 3 November 1743. She left all the residue of her estate to Catharine Hall, much to the annoyance of her Yorkshire tenants, if we may judge from the inscription under her monument in Adlingfleet Church. She wished to found new Fellowships and Scholarships, being influenced probably by the example of her great-uncle Skerne.

Mrs Ramsden was a woman of character and firm convictions. She was, moreover, independent, and fond of superintending details personally. For her Fellows and scholars she laid down certain Rules and Orders, didactic and precise, which are so typical of the donor herself, and of such interest to the historian of education, that they deserve to be quoted in full.

Rules and Orders touching the benefaction of Mrs Mary Ramsden, widow, to Catharine Hall, in Cambridge.

I. After all the other purposes of my will are completely executed and finished, my desire is that with the clear annual rents and profits of my whole estate may be purchased the houses and ground lying between the now erected college and Trumpington Street, in order to erect thereupon a new building for the reception of the fellows and scholars of my foundation; but if such houses and ground cannot be purchased at a reasonable rate, I then desire that the said building may be erected upon any ground already belonging to the college, or that a purchase may be made of any other convenient spot adjoining to the said college, on which such buildings may be erected most ornamentally for the said college.

II. A convenient site being procured and the whole expence in procuring of it defrayed, then with the said net annual produce I would have the said building erected, with sufficient distinct apartments for each fellow and each scholar, if it may be, to front Trumpington Street, if not, to be placed, as above said, in such manner as may be most convenient and ornamental to the said college.

III. When the said building is completed and fit to be inhabited, and the whole expence of it cleared, then the said annual rents and profits shall stand for ever appropriated for the uses and purposes hereafter mentioned; and principally for the founding and maintaining six fellowships and ten scholarships in the said hall or college, to be called by the name of Skerne fellowships and scholarships, to be distinguished in the numerical order of the first, second, third, elected fellowship, first, second, third elected scholarship.

Plate V

Mrs Ramsden

IV. The first general election of the six fellows in the fellowships of this foundation shall be made on the second Tuesday in November after the above mentioned building is finished and fit to be inhabited.

In order to which the master of Catharine Hall, or the president or senior fellow in college in his absence, shall cause notice to be publicly fixed in writing on the gates of the university schools upon the tenth of October, preceding the day of election, that any person duly qualified from any college in the university of Cambridge may appear as candidates at the election.

In the public notice, thus to be given, it shall be signified that all such as intend to appear as candidates shall, ten days at least before the day of election, give in to be left with the master of Catharine Hall, or in his absence the president or senior fellow of the college, their names, their ages, the places of their birth, the schools where they have been educated, the colleges to which they belong, together with proper testimonials from the said colleges of their good lives and characters. And it shall be likewise signified by the said notice, that they are to attend in the combination or common room of Catharine Hall at nine of the clock in the morning of the Tuesday preceding the Tuesday appointed for the election, to undergo an examination touching their abilities and proficiency in learning; at which examination I desire the Vice-Chancellor for the time being, or in his absence his deputy, always to be present and assist.

V. No person shall be capable of being chosen fellow, unless he be Bachelor of Arts complete, Bachelor of Laws, or Bachelor of Physic, or Master of Arts, having taken his degree regularly in the university of Cambridge. But I would have no one capable of being chosen, after he has attained the age of twenty-four years complete, nor any one who has any real estate in possession, or held in trust for him, the annual profits of which exceed the clear value of fifty pounds a year.

VI. In regard that I was born in Yorkshire, where my ancestors have been settled, and that the estates, by which my foundation is to be maintained, lie for much the greatest part in that county, I do direct that, in the first and all future elections the best qualified men, born in the county of York, be preferred, and principally those who, being Yorkshire men born, have been educated at the grammar school at Fockerby in the parish of Adlingfleet in the West Riding of Yorkshire, which school was founded by my uncle Skerne. Provided that such, who claim a preference upon account of this school, bring a certificate, duly attested, that they have been *bona fide* educated there full three years at least in some part of the time of their education; and provided also they be duly qualified for their learning and morals.

VII. If no such scholars appear as candidates from Fockerby school, nor any other born in the county of York, fitly qualified, I would have the next preference given to such as were born in the county of Lincoln. If no candidates appear, fitly qualified, from either of those two counties, I would then have the election open, and any person born in any of the counties of that part of Great Britain, called England, or in any of the counties of Wales, shall be capable of being elected.

VIII. On the day appointed for examination, the candidates shall appear, as above said, at nine of the clock in the morning in the common room of the society of Catharine Hall before the said Vice-Chancellor, or his deputy, the said master of Catharine Hall, president or senior fellow, and the rest of the fellows, that shall be at that time in college, and shall be publicly examined before them in one or more of the ancient Greek and Latin classical authors and in philosophical and academical learning; and each candidate shall write a theme upon some subject, to be given out by the Vice-Chancellor or his deputy; which theme they shall make in the said common room, to be delivered and communicated to all the electors to enable them to judge of the merits of each candidate; and such as, having the qualifications above specified, shall appear to be the best learned, being also approved for sound religion, piety, virtue, peaceable dispositions and good life and conversation, shall be preferred in the election.

IX. The first general election shall be made by the master and fellows of Catharine Hall, that shall then be, or by the major part of them then present, no account to be had of those who absent themselves or do not appear. The master's vote to be reckoned but as the single vote of one of the fellows. If the votes be equally divided, the Vice-Chancellor, or his deputy for the time being, shall have the casting vote; and the master shall immediately declare such person duly elected, who shall have the Vice-Chancellor's or his deputy's voice with any equal number, though the master's vote be not of that number.

By the major part of the fellows is to be understood the major part in respect of any less number. Supposing the electors to be divided into more than two parts, if the division be not equal parts, as, if the electors be six and they all choose a different person, or two choose one, two another, and two a third, the Vice-Chancellor in the first case joining his vote with any one, and in the second case with any two, shall make a good election. But in the same number of six, if three votes be for one, two for a second, and one for a third, the three votes, though but half in respect of the whole, shall be deemed the major part; and the person, on whom such majority falls, shall be by the master declared duly elected; and so in any other like division of the electors.

X. The term and stile of the election shall be in this manner: At the head of a sheet of loose paper shall be written—The election of a fellow into the first of the Skerne fellowships.

The senior fellow of the college then present shall write his vote first in this manner;

I *A. B.* do choose *C. D.* into the first of the Skerne fellowships.

Then the rest of the fellows in order. The master shall underwrite last.

If the master and whole number agree, or the master's vote, added to any other number, make a majority according to the preceding directions, he shall underwrite in this form;

I *E. D.* master of the college, do elect and pronounce duly elected *C. D.* into this first fellowship.

If he differs in giving his vote, and one of the candidates has nevertheless a majority, as observed, without him, he shall then underwrite in this manner;

I *E. D.* do declare *C. D.* duly elected into this first fellowship.

The election thus finished, a transcript of this paper shall be entered into a book, to be kept for that purpose, and the original be put into the treasury or place where the records of the college are kept. In this order they shall proceed to elect into the second, third and fourth fellowships, till the whole number be filled. But if, by reason of the equality of votes in any of the elections, it be necessary to have the Vice-Chancellor's casting vote or his deputy's, who was present at the examination, and whom I desire to attend the elections, he shall, immediately before they proceed to any further election, write his vote for the candidate he judges most deserving. A majority being so made, the master of the college shall without delay admit the person elected, taking the oaths, and doing all other acts by law required, as the fellows of the present society do at their admission.

But for the first election I would have the election of the whole number of six fellows settled before the admission of any of them; and then they shall be admitted into their several fellowships in order as they have been chosen. For it is my intention that in the first election none of the first elected fellows shall have votes in the choice of one another.

XI. In all future elections I will that, within ten days after certain notice shall be had, that any of these fellowships is become vacant, the master of Catharine Hall, or in his absence the president or senior fellow in college, shall cause public notice to be fixed on the school doors twenty-four days before the election, that the election will be held upon the third Tuesday after the day of the date of such notice, that such as intend to be candidates shall, as above directed, give in their names, &c. and certificates, and shall attend to be examined the Tuesday preceding the Tuesday, on which the election is to be made, in like manner, as is above required; and of the day of examination and election I desire especial notice may be given to the Vice-Chancellor or his deputy; for I would not have either him or any other person capable of giving a vote at any election, who was not present at the examination of the candidates. In all future elections of fellows after the first general one, besides the Vice-Chancellor or his deputy, and the master and fellows of Catharine Hall, I will have the fellows of this foundation joined, and have equal votes and attend the examinations preceding the elections. The same form, stile and manner of electing shall be observed in all future elections, as is directed in the first.

XII. For the maintenance of the said fellows I do appoint they shall have clear fifty-two pounds a year, besides their lodgings rent free, and the profits of their fellowships to commence immediately from the time of admission. The fellows of this foundation shall in all things, not herein especially directed otherwise, be subject to all the rules, orders, statutes and discipline of the college, shall be obliged in their turns to perform all college and university exercises, and to stand to all commons in the hall and all other college dues as the present fellows do.

XIII. The fellows shall be obliged to reside in the college at least six months in the year, to be computed from Michaelmas to Michaelmas, by continued residence or at different times. If they have resided six calendar months, they shall be entitled to the full year's profits of their fellowships; if for any less time, they shall be entitled to full profit only for the time of their actual residence; and for every week they are absent they shall forfeit sixteen shillings and eight pence a week, to be employed, as hereafter directed, to the common stock of the college.

XIV. In case any fellow die or quit his fellowship within the year, that is to say, between Michaelmas and Michaelmas, I direct that he shall receive profits only in proportion to the time of his residence in college that year, so that, whoever shall be elected, his successor may enter into immediate profits from the time of his admission for the remaining part of the year; for the rule of allowing the whole year's profits to one, who shall have resided only six months, I would not have take place unless the same person continue fellow for the whole year. The profits during the vacancy I would have be laid aside, as above mentioned, for the common stock of the college, to be applied as hereafter directed.

XV. I would have the fellows of this foundation not be confined, but be at liberty to apply themselves to and follow the studies of any of the learned professions of Divinity, civil and canon Law, or the common Law of England, or Physic, or any other of the liberal arts and sciences, without any obligation upon them to go into orders, unless it be their own free choice.

XVI. If any of the said fellows shall marry, or accept of any living or ecclesiastical preferment of any value whatsoever above twenty miles distance from Cambridge, his fellowship shall be declared vacant; but so that he shall have and be allowed a year of grace from the time of his having quiet possession, as is usual in other colleges in the like cases. But, within twenty miles of Cambridge, I will that any of the said fellows may hold any preferment together with his fellowship, provided it do not exceed twenty pounds a year in the King's books. I will likewise that these fellowships shall be forfeited, if any fellow shall be convicted of any enormous crime, in like manner as the college statutes order.

XVII. For the first election of the ten scholars, I will that the same be made by the master and fellows of Catharine Hall, without troubling the Vice-Chancellor on that occasion. The first election shall be made on the Tuesday fortnight after the first election of fellows; public notice shall be given ten days before the election, that those, who intend to offer themselves candidates at the said election, shall bring their certificates of their ages, &c. upon the Tuesday, and appear to be examined upon the Thursday before the day of election. This first election of scholars shall be made by the master and fellows of Catharine Hall, that shall then be, in the same order and manner as the election of fellows is directed to be made; the majority shall make the election; if they be equally divided, the master's vote, or in his absence the vote of the president or senior fellow shall always decide the matter, in like manner as it is directed the Vice-Chancellor's vote shall do in the election of fellows.

In all elections of scholars after the first, in which the master and fellows of Catharine Hall are only to be the electors, I will that the fellows of this foundation shall be joined with them and have equal votes.

XVIII. The scholars shall be Yorkshire men, and preference given in like manner, as in the case of fellows, to those that come from, and have been educated three years at Fockerby school; if no Yorkshire men, nor Lincolnshire men, duly qualified, do appear as candidates, then the election may be made of such as have been educated in any school or born in any county within the kingdom of England and Wales.

XIX. The stipend of each scholar shall be clear fifteen pounds a year, besides their chambers rent free. The scholars shall be subject in all things to the master and fellows of Catharine Hall, and to the discipline of the college in like manner, as the present scholars are, and shall be in commons, pay all college dues, perform all college exercises and duties in their turns, as those of the like standing in the college are obliged to do. Besides the ordinary exercises of the college, each scholar of this foundation shall every week in term time make a theme upon some subject to be given out by the Master or senior fellow presiding in the hall at dinner on the Monday; and the scholars shall deliver in their themes on the Wednesday following at dinner at the fellows' table. These themes shall be alternately one week in Greek and the other in Latin.

XX. After the scholars of this foundation have taken their degrees of Bachelor of Arts, Bachelor of Law, or Bachelor of Physic, one or other of which I would have always taken when they become of due standing to take the same, I would then no longer have the themes above mentioned imposed upon them, but instead thereof I will that upon the third Friday in every term in the college chapel immediately after evening service every Bachelor fellow or Bachelor scholar shall make an oration a quarter of an hour long in latin upon some subject to be given out by the master or senior fellow in college a fortnight at the least before such oration is to be made. The senior Bachelor shall begin the first term, and the next in order of standing the following term, and so to be continued every term. If there be not a sufficient number of Bachelors of Arts to keep up this exercise every term, I will however that it be kept up as near as may be, and that the Bachelors, who have already performed, may be called upon in order to perform the like exercise, provided the same person be not called upon twice within the same year.

XXI. The scholars of this foundation shall take all such oaths upon their admission, as the scholars of the present college do. No one shall hold any of these scholarships after he is Master of Arts, or after he is of seven years standing, though he does not take that or any other degree.

XXII. The scholars of this foundation shall be obliged to reside every year during every term while they are undergraduates, and the major part of every term after they have taken their Bachelor of Arts degree; otherwise they shall forfeit the profits of their scholarships for the time they are absent at the rate of five shillings a week. But if they keep the whole term while they are undergraduates, and the major part while they are Bachelors of Arts, no deduction shall be made out of their allowance on account of absence during the time of vacations. The forfeitures on account of absences shall go to the common stock of the college.

XXIII. When any of these scholarships shall become vacant, they shall be filled within a month after such vacancy is known, such notices being given and such examinations had as are above directed touching the first general election of scholars of this foundation.

XXIV. I desire that an anniversary day may be held upon the last Thursday in June for the examination of the scholars of this foundation, and I direct five pounds to be spent on that day for an entertainment, to which I desire the Vice-Chancellor or his deputy, the Greek Professor and the university Orator may be invited to be present, together with the master and fellows of Catharine Hall; and that before dinner one of the Skerne fellows shall make a latin speech, the subject to be the usefulness of learning and of public charities given to encourage and promote it. The first fellow to begin, and so in order downwards, the senior fellow who has not made this speech shall make it.

XXV. The scholars, all of them of this foundation, shall make an exercise for that day either in verse or prose on a subject to be given out by the master of Catharine Hall or in his absence the president or senior fellow ten days before, and in the morning of the said day they shall all be examined in some of the Greek and Latin classical authors; which, for the Greek, I am advised should be Homer, Sophocles, Euripides, Demosthenes, Herodotus, Thucydides or Xenophon; for the Latin, Cicero, Lucretius, Virgil, Horace, Livy, Caesar, or Tacitus, some one or more of them in each language. He who appears by his exercise and on his examination to be most deserving shall have five pounds given him in books. The Vice-Chancellor, Greek Professor and the Public Orator, or any two of them, to decide who shall have the preference; if they all three differ, the scholar named by the Vice-Chancellor shall have it.

XXVI. Besides the charge of the maintenance of the fellows and scholars as above mentioned, and the ten pounds for the entertainment and to the scholar in books above mentioned, I desire the Vice-Chancellor or his deputy will please to accept of five pounds a year for his attendance, the master of Catharine Hall five pounds, the bursar of the college five pounds yearly, the Greek Professor and the Public Orator each a broad piece or one pound five shillings in money for their attendance at the examination; and two pounds ten shillings I would have distributed yearly to the poor of the parish in which Catharine Hall stands. These payments I would have annually made upon the anniversary day above fixed by the bursar of the college. The first anniversary day to be kept on the last Thursday in June following the first general election of the fellows and scholars of this foundation.

XXVII. The rents of the estates given for the support of this benefaction I think now stand at a reasonable rate, at which I hope they may be always kept; and as I desire the tenants may always have good and beneficial bargains I would have no attempts, if possible, made to raise them. As they now stand, I hope after all deductions on account of taxes and repairs and charges of management, the payment of the fellows and scholars, and the other small payments charged in the last article, there will still a surplusage remain from the rents and profits of the estates for the benefit of the college, which together with the forfeitures, that shall accrue for the absences and vacancies of the fellowships and scholarships, I would have thrown into the common stock of the college and improved, if it may be, as a fund for the repairs of the college in general, as well the old as the new buildings, or the discharge of any debt that may now lie on the old college on account of the buildings already erected, or the making any additional buildings or buying of books for the library, or other such public use within the said college. But first after all the necessary outgoings for taxes, repairs and management, I would have the fellows and scholars paid before any other disbursements whatever. And if the rents of the estates prove at any time not sufficient to pay the same, I would have the forfeitures for absences and vacancies brought in aid, and pay the whole which is appointed to be distributed, before any thing be laid aside for the common stock of the college.

XXVIII. I would have as above directed my estates always let out as near as may be at the present rents. No lease to be let for longer than the term of eleven years; and no fine or foregift to be taken on account of any lease, the tenant only paying the usual sealing fees to the bursar and the college for the lease.

XXIX. I would have the estates visited once every five years by the bursar and one of the fellows of the foundation to see that the houses, barns and buildings, the woods and fences, and the lands be kept in good order according to the covenants of the leases. The expences of such journeys shall be borne out of the rents and profits of the estates. I would have the accounts of this foundation annually audited, and the audit to be immediately after the common college audit, and the fellows of this foundation to be present at the audit and assist therein.

XXX. I desire and seriously recommend it to the master, deans or other officers of the college, whose duty it is, to see all the exercises above enjoined strictly kept up, and that they by any mulcts or penalties allowed by the statutes or usage of the college effectually enforce the performance of the same.

XXXI. Whereas, since the settling of most of the foregoing rules and orders, I have been informed that some years ago a plan was drawn for the finishing and completing the present college, which plan the college hitherto has been never able to carry into execution, but that however they have from time to time purchased several of the houses and ground, upon which it was my desire the chambers for the fellows and scholars of this foundation should stand, I direct that my trustees shall first of all pay to the college such sum or sums of money, as may be a sufficient recompence for the said houses and grounds; and that the master and fellows do lay out the same in some other purchase or public fund, such as shall answer the rents and profits the college may lose by pulling down the said houses, and be set apart for the same uses and purposes to which the said rents are now applied. For it is my desire that the present college may in no wise suffer by their making way for the reception of the new fellows and scholars of this foundation. And then I would have the new building carried on in the best manner for the completing the said plan. For avoiding also all disputes I would have the fellows and scholars have their choice of chambers by seniority in order, as they have been elected.

XXXII. And whereas I have been informed likewise that there are some of the fellows of this college of bye foundations, who are called fellows, though they have no power or privileges as such; for the avoiding all mistakes in the construction of these orders and rules, wherever the master and fellows of the college are mentioned, I would always have it understood to be meant of the master and fellows of the old foundation only.

XXXIII. Great care having been taken to make these rules and orders explicit and precise, so that it is hoped they cannot easily be mistaken, I therefore appoint no visitor of this foundation. But if any errors or mistakes have been committed, or complaint shall hereafter arise touching the execution of any of these orders or statutes, for the rectifying the same I do direct that application be always made to the Lord High Chancellor or Lord Keeper of the great seal of Great Britain, that the same may be heard by way of petition or such other summary manner as his Lordship in his wisdom shall appoint, and by him to be finally determined.

I do approve, confirm and establish these rules and orders.

MARY RAMSDEN.

Although Mrs Ramsden's intention was excellent and her benefaction generous, a worse deed of gift would be hard to imagine. The minute attention to detail, commendable as it may seem to the general reader, probably resulted in most awkward consequences. One example only shall be given. The common room which is appointed as the examination place for the new Fellows was not very large. It is difficult to see how eight persons could "publicly examine" in it the candidates, who might on any occasion be too numerous for the room to hold them; further difficulty would be caused by the candidates having to make a theme "in the said common room, to be delivered and communicated to all the electors". Such insistence on detail was certain to defeat its own purpose. The benefactress was, for some reason, loath to insist only on essential principles and to leave the immaterial particulars of method to the good sense of the electors.

The preferences too—Fockerby School, Yorkshire, Lincolnshire—would be very difficult to put into practice, and might often result in the election of inferior men, involving a certain loss of prestige to the College. Close Fellowships are in a category very different from that of close Scholarships.

Although Rule XXXII suggests that Mrs Ramsden had discussed the question with the Master and Fellows, she does not appear to have realised that her Fellows would not have the power and privileges of those on the old foundation. If she did realise the point, she made the most culpable of all her many blunders. With the Frankland and Conduct Fellowships there were, when Mrs Ramsden's plans were carried out, eight bye-Fellows with no powers under a Master and six Fellows with full powers. All dined together and lived within the same walls. The foundation Fellows had few duties, the others practically none at all. Unless they married, or were guilty of gross misconduct,[1] all on each foundation held their positions for life. In such a Society quarrels, disputes and bickerings were bound to occur with even greater frequency and intensity than usual. In addition, there was always a surplus,[2] usually a handsome one, to go to the common stock of the College when Skerne Fellows and Scholars had been paid. It was thus to the advantage of the old foundation to restrict the numbers of the new, and so to increase the surplus. The Skerne Fellows, on the other hand, had a fixed income, which, as the value of money decreased, induced them to clamour for something like the dividend that supplemented the income of the older body. The situation soon became intolerable, and we are not surprised that the 1860 statutes almost entirely, and the 1882 statutes completely, amalgamated the two foundations.

[1] A case of this occurred in 1809, and a College Order merely banishes the offender for two years!

[2] See p. 390.

In 1795 occurred a dispute about the election of a Fellow on the Ramsden foundation. The point is rather a mysterious one; apparently the electors to the Skerne Fellowships had chosen a candidate who proved afterwards to be debarred by reason of age, and felt that while a mistake had occurred they had no power to undo it themselves.

A vacancy occurred in March 1794 and the day of election was fixed for 22 April. There were three candidates: Richard Foster, Joseph Hucks and Richard Wadsworth. Of the seven electors six voted for Foster and one (Joshua Wood) for Wadsworth. Foster was declared elected and admitted. Wadsworth appealed to the Lord Chancellor to set aside the election of Foster on the ground of his being "superannuated", and to declare him, Wadsworth, duly elected.

On 14 March 1795 the Master and Fellows presented a petition to the Lord Chancellor, as Visitor of Mrs Ramsden's foundation,[1] praying him to hear an appeal made by Richard Wadsworth against the election of Richard Foster as Skerne Fellow, in the way usually practised by the local Visitors of other Societies without any formality of legal proceedings, and to decide upon and determine it without subjecting the parties concerned to the expense of proceedings according to the forms of a court of judicature.[2]

The result was that an order was served on all the parties concerned to attend the hearing of the appeal in the Court of Chancery on 23 March 1795.

Mr Foster received stipend up to Lady Day 1795, and Joseph Hucks was admitted Fellow on the Ramsden foundation 6 April 1795. One can only guess why Wadsworth was ignored.

The College made a petition to the Visitor that he would relax Mrs Ramsden's Rule V in favour of Thomas Turton. Turton was more than twenty-four years of age, but, the Lord Chancellor relaxing the rule, he was admitted Skerne Fellow on 18 November 1806.

[1] Mrs Ramsden refused to appoint a Visitor, but it was held that the Visitor of the College became *ipso facto* Visitor of the new foundation as soon as it was established—a perfectly reasonable view.

[2] *Register*, VI, 76.

A petition was sent to the Visitor[1] on 6 December 1841 praying that a longer time might be allowed for filling a vacant Skerne Fellowship than was allowed by Mrs Ramsden's Rule XI, and that the age limit might be altered from twenty-four to twenty-eight years of age. On 22 December of the same year Lord Lyndhurst, the Lord Chancellor, extended the time allowed by Rule XI from twenty-four days to four months, but it was not till 16 December 1845 that the same Lord Chancellor granted the alteration of Rule V, and raised the eligible age to twenty-eight. But he ruled at the same time that no person should be capable of being elected a Skerne Fellow unless he were B.A. complete, LL.B., M.B., or M.A. of Cambridge University. The possession of real estate or of estate held in trust beyond the annual value of £50 was to be a disqualification.[2]

Vacancies in the Skerne Fellowships were caused by the death of Charles Hardwick (1859) and by the marriage of William Ogle (1860). The University Commission then sitting granted leave to suspend the elections to these vacancies for one year.

Mrs Ramsden directed that the surplus of the income from her estates, when the Skerne Fellows and scholars had been paid, should be thrown into the Common Stock of the College. The distribution of this surplus was to prove in course of time a matter of dispute between the Skerne Fellows and those of the old foundation, particularly during the lean years at the beginning of the nineteenth century. On the whole one's sympathies are not with the Skerne Fellows, who had many privileges, no duties, a good allowance from their foundress and not ungenerous treatment from the governing body of the College.

The first Order dealing with this surplus is dated 8 August 1777, and directs that the sum of £15 a year be paid out of the said College Stock to the Master and to each of the six Fellows of the old foundation. The same sum is to be paid also to each of the Skerne Fellows, if resident in College for six

[1] Mrs Ramsden (Rule XXXIII), after declaring that she would appoint no Visitor, proceeds to nominate the Lord Chancellor as arbitrator in case of any disputes.

[2] That is, he kept the rest of Rule V.

calendar months, but in failure of such residence six shillings a week only is to be paid for each week of actual residence. £5 a year is to be paid to each Skerne Scholar, if certain conditions of residence be fulfilled; in failure of such residence two shillings a week only for every week of actual residence. The first part of this Order, relating to the Master and Fellows, was rescinded by an Order of 10 March 1790, when it was agreed that instead 11*s.* 6*d.* be allowed to the Master and 10*s.* 6*d.* to each of the Fellows on both foundations, weekly, in lieu of "commons and butters", without any restriction as to residence. A further Order was made on 21 August 1807 rescinding what had been previously ordered respecting the increase of the stipends of the Skerne Fellows and Scholars, and it was agreed that in addition to the provisions made by Mrs Ramsden's Rules and Orders, each Skerne Fellow should receive out of the College Stock at the rate of £68 a year without any restriction as to residence, and each Skerne Scholar £20 a year upon the terms prescribed by the XXIInd of the said Rules and Orders.

This was handsome treatment, increasing Mrs Ramsden's £52 and £15 to £120 and £35, but nevertheless on 25 May 1813 five of the Skerne Fellows, Gresham Verelst, Geldart, Yorke and Maynard, presented a petition to the Lord Chancellor, as Visitor of the College, praying that he would give directions for the increase of the stipends and allowances of the Skerne Fellows and Scholars out of the surplus of Mrs Ramsden's estate, and of the disposal of the residue for the benefit of her foundation. The Lord Chancellor, Lord Eldon, heard counsel both for and against the petition, and (not to our surprise) on 23 April 1814 dismissed it.

But the five were not content with a rebuff at the hands of the Visitor. Perhaps they considered that he was the supreme judge, not of the Ramsden foundation (Mrs Ramsden had appointed no Visitor), but only of the old foundation. At any rate, on 9 June 1817 an information was filed by the Attorney-General on the relation of the five Skerne Fellows, against the Master and Fellows, the heir at law of Mrs Ramsden, Charles Smith, Charles Harrison, also Skerne Fellow of the College, and sundry other persons, touching the management of Mrs Ramsden's property and the disposal of the surplus rents and profits. Judgment was given on 12 February 1820 by the Lord Chancellor, who ruled:

(1) That the directions contained in Mrs Ramsden's will, which require that the rents of her estates should continue the same as at the time of her decease, are void.

(2) That Charles Smith has no right or interest in the real estates, or the rents and profits thereof, by way of resulting trust or otherwise.

(3) That the surplusage of the rents and profits, after the payments and deductions prescribed in the XXVIIth Rule, was intended to be given to the Master and Fellows of the old foundation, and that, as to so much of such surplusage as is not necessary to be applied as a fund for the purposes mentioned in the said XXVIIth Rule, the same belongs to the Master and Fellows of the old foundation.[1]

A final Order was made by the College on 24 February 1854 that so much of the Order of 10 March 1790 as directs the payment of allowances for commons out of the College Stock to the Master and foundation Fellows be rescinded, and that the allowance to every Skerne Fellow, elected after the date of the order, be £48 a year, instead of £68 as fixed by the Order of 21 August 1807.

The impression produced by this series of events is that the relations between the Fellows of the two foundations were none too friendly. The Ramsden bequest was, in comparison with the old foundation, a very large one, and raised points too important and too complicated to be dealt with satisfactorily in the will of a country lady, however talented and intellectual. It was not to be expected that six bye-Fellows could live year after year with six full Fellows, with whom lay all powers of government, without discontent and occasional open quarrels. The difficulties of the situation, great as they were, grew yet more serious when at the close of the eighteenth century there came upon the College the spirit of strife for strife's sake. Doubtless the wars abroad encouraged it; perhaps St Catharine's housed one or two vindictive characters; the period was at the best leisurely and idle so far as University life was concerned. But to these causes must be added the keen enjoyment that the Fellows of those days got out of quarrels and disputes. Little to do, whether work or play, a chance of pecuniary gain, and the pleasant

[1] *Register*, VI, 436.

stimulus of bloodless warfare—these combined are enough to account for the disaffection of Skerne Fellows, as well as for the amusing duel of Procter and Atkinson.

Early in 1790 began the lamentable series of disputes that went on for nearly twenty years.

On 3 February 1790 a writ of mandamus was issued from the Court of King's Bench, directing the Master and Fellows to proceed to the election of a Fellow in the place of Philip Gardner, whose Fellowship had become vacant by marriage.

Mr Gardner received stipend as Fellow to Lady Day 1789, and the next half-year his Fellowship was vacant; Mr Goodwin, elected into his place, received the whole year's stipend to Michaelmas 1790. In the Order Book there is a record (7 July 1789) of the election of Francis Goodwin, M.A. to be a foundation Fellow in the room of Philip Gardner, signed by the Master (Lowther Yates) and two Fellows only, Joshua Waterhouse and W. J. Atkinson. On 1 March 1790 there was held a meeting "in Obedience to his Majesty's Writ of Mandamus lately issued for the Election of a Fellow in the Room of Philip Gardner Clerk late one of the Fellows", and Francis Goodwin was duly elected. The Order is signed by the Master and five Fellows (Joshua Waterhouse, Joshua Wood, W. J. Atkinson, Joseph Procter, Chas. Willm. Burrell).

Mr Gardner had married in October 1788, and according to the custom of the College was entitled to receive his stipend and dividend to Lady Day 1789. It had also been the custom of the College not to elect a new Fellow till after the end of the current half-year for which the dividend was paid to the vacating Fellow.

The Master expressed his intention of proceeding to election before Lady Day 1789, but when some of the Fellows objected he did not proceed. The half-yearly audit was held (as usual) in the following May, and though the audits were the usual times for the election of Fellows, and all the Fellows were present on this occasion, the Master did not mention the election, and took no further step till 6 July, when he gave notice to the Fellows of his intention to proceed to the election of a Fellow on the following day at

9 o'clock in the morning. Procter was in Yorkshire, leave of absence having been obtained from the Master on 28 June. On the next morning Wood and Burrell went to the meeting at 9.15. They found the Master, Waterhouse and Atkinson already present; the Master told them that the statutes had been read, the examination was finished, and that Mr Goodwin was elected. This was a large, one might say an impossibly large, amount of business to get through in a quarter of an hour.

Wood and Burrell protested against the election on the ground that not sufficient notice had been given, and that the Master had purposely brought it on when Procter was away. They refused to sign the minute of the election. Although only one candidate had been examined, the Master knew that there was another.[1]

A College Order was made on 10 March 1790, signed by the Master and all the Fellows except Waterhouse, that not less than fourteen days notice be given by the Master of his intention to fill up a vacant Fellowship, and that such notice be affixed to the Chapel door.[2]

In the Easter Term of 1791 the Master and Fellows showed cause in the Court of King's Bench against a Rule *nisi* for a Mandamus to compel them to declare the Fellowship of Joshua Wood vacant and to proceed to the election of another Fellow.

Wood had been inducted into the Vicarage of Madingley, in which he had the cure of souls, and which was worth more than ten marks a year in the King's Books. He thus had against him no. 9 of the Edwardian statutes.

Erskine, Law and Graham were counsel for the College; Bearcroft, Le Blanc and Yorke argued in support of the Mandamus.

The rule *nisi* was discharged, and Lord Kenyon in giving judgment made history by declaring that disputes of this kind ought to be decided *in foro domestico*. "Therefore," he went on, "with no decided authority or general principle of law against us, but with the convenience of the case and general

[1] Affidavit of Wood, Procter and Burrell.

[2] This Order was rescinded on 22 March 1817, which confirmed the notice of not less than fourteen days, but added that it was to be given at a College meeting. It was also ordered that such notice shall not be affixed to the Chapel door.

principles of law in our favour, we shall do more substantial justice to the parties in this particular case and to the public in general, by refusing to grant this writ of mandamus and by referring this question to the Lord Chancellor than by entertaining jurisdiction over it."

This case is held to have decided that in a private eleemosynary lay foundation, in which category university colleges are included, if no special Visitor be appointed by the founder, the right of visitation in default of his heirs devolves upon the Crown, to be exercised by the Great Seal.

Wood continued to hold his Fellowship until his death in 1816.

About this time an effort was made to get rid of Waterhouse. A petition was presented to the Lord Chancellor, as Visitor, begging him to declare Waterhouse's Fellowship vacant, on the ground of his holding the Rectory of Coton. The College possesses a MS copy of the Lord Chancellor's judgment delivered on 21 December 1795. In it he says that "there were twc grounds on which he saw it fair and just to dismiss the Petition. First, that by the grant from King Edward the fourth of the Rectory of Coton to the Master and Fellows the year after the foundation of the College, they became Rectors of the Rectory; and they, as trustees for their successors, could not present to the Rectory but appoint a Chaplain or Curate; in which situation Mr Waterhouse stood, being misstyled Rector; and therefore being only a Chaplain or Curate, it did not impeach his Fellowship. Second, that it having been the invariable custom for 200 years past, except in one instance, for Fellows to be presented to the living of Coton and to hold the same, under title of a Rectory, in conjunction with their Fellowships, I cannot think of straining the Statute to take advantage of it to the extent of a forfeiture of his (i.e. Mr Waterhouse's) Fellowship, for what had been the constant practice under the conception of being right for so many years, and under which conception so many venerable and respectable characters had acted."

If the College really hoped to rid itself of Waterhouse on these grounds, it must have been either desperate or incredibly stupid.

The election of a Master to succeed Dr Yates resulted in the worst quarrel in the history of the College. Perhaps "feud" rather than "quarrel" is the best word to describe the events that ensued. Yates died on 24 August 1798, and Waterhouse, the senior Fellow, gave notice of an election to be held on Saturday, 1 September. On that day, between 6 and 7 o'clock a.m., there met in the Chapel five Fellows (the sixth Fellowship being vacant), namely, Joshua Waterhouse, Joshua Wood, William Atkinson, Joseph Procter and Charles William Burrell.

Waterhouse voted for himself.
Wood voted for himself.
Atkinson voted for Waterhouse.
Procter voted for Dr John Hey.
Burrell[1] voted for Dr Philip Gardner.

Whereupon Wood, Procter and Burrell requested Waterhouse to appoint a time for a second meeting. This he refused to do, and declared himself duly elected Master.[2] Wood, the next in seniority, in the presence of Waterhouse and Atkinson, then adjourned the meeting to 11 o'clock the same day for a second scrutiny.

At the second meeting only Wood, Procter and Burrell attended; and as no two of them voted for the same person, Wood declared the meeting adjourned to 1 o'clock for a third scrutiny, and sent notice of the adjournment to Waterhouse and Atkinson by the College Porter.

At 1 o'clock only Wood, Procter and Burrell attended the meeting; and as no two of them voted for the same person, Wood again adjourned the

[1] Burrell's vote connects in a way the dispute over this election with the quarrel of 1789. See p. 130.

[2] The Edwardian statutes, under which this election took place, are vaguely worded in the paragraph dealing with the majority required at the election of a Master. It would seem, however, that if five votes were cast, at least three of them must be for the same person to secure a majority: "donec in unum aliquem per majorem partem ipsorum sociorum consensum fuerit et assensum." The Order Book contains under date 1 September 1798 the following entry:

"We whose names are underwritten declare this to be no Election, no one of us having voted for Mr Waterhouse.

Joshua Wood.
J. Procter.
C. W. Burrell."

meeting to the next day (Sunday) at 7 o'clock a.m., and sent notice to Waterhouse and Atkinson by the College Porter.

The next morning (Sunday) Wood left the University and did not return that day. Only Procter and Burrell attended the 7 o'clock meeting, and both voted for Dr Philip Gardner. Procter, the senior of the two voters, then declared Gardner duly elected Master.

The Chapel bell was rung for some time before each meeting.

Gardner and Procter then appealed to the Lord Chancellor (Lord Loughborough), who gave judgment on 20 December 1798. He found that neither Gardner nor Waterhouse was duly elected, and that agreeably to the statutes no further meeting could be held. The appointment thus devolved on him, and he appointed Joseph Procter, B.D.

The next stage in the quarrel is marked by a petition to the Lord Chancellor made by the Master (Procter) and President (Burrell) on 12 June 1801. In it they beg him to interpret certain statutes in consequence of the improper distribution by the Bursar (Wood), and the receipt by Waterhouse, Wood and Atkinson, of the dividends of two vacant Fellowships, contrary to the Master's directions.

The petition also stated that at the audit of 9 December 1800 the Master refused to confirm the election of Wood as Bursar (though supported by Waterhouse and Atkinson) in consequence of his previous misconduct in office, and that notwithstanding the Master's refusal to consent to Wood's election, Wood still continued to act as Bursar, and refused to hand over to the Master the balances in his hands.

The Master also made other charges against Atkinson of having treated with marked disrespect in the College Hall at dinner both himself and Burrell, of having admitted one R. J. Astley, a migrant from Pembroke, without a *bene discessit*, of having neglected his duty as Lecturer, encouraging the said R. J. Astley to continue to attend Hall and Chapel after the removal of his name by the Master from the College Books, and of having encouraged one William Jenkinson to insult the Master and Burrell by promise of advocating his claim to election as a Fellow.

There were further charges of impropriety against Wood of absenting himself without leave from College and College meetings.

One notices with surprise that the Lord Chancellor is asked to pronounce judgment *inter alia* on alleged bad manners.

On 15 September 1802 Lord Eldon, the Lord Chancellor, gave his decision. He ruled that Wood's dealing with the vacant Fellowship dividends was unwarrantable, and directed that such dividends should be restored to the College Stock. He also ordered that the two vacant Fellowships should be filled up, if it could be done consistently with any reasonable arrangement of the College funds.

He also declared Wood's appointment as Bursar void, and that the permission of the Master or President was necessary for absence from College; that the Master had the power of appointing the Tutor, but that the appointment of Dean, Lecturer and Bursar rested with the Fellows, the Master's concurrence being necessary; that the Master was well warranted in refusing to confirm the admission of R. J. Astley; that the consent of the Master, present at an election, is necessary to the election of a Fellow, and that the Master or President alone have the right of putting resolutions to a College meeting. He concluded by desiring information as to the financial affairs of the College, and reserves judgment on other matters pending such information.[1]

A second order of Lord Eldon, given on 24 May 1805, directed that the costs of Dr Procter's and Mr Burrell's petition be paid out of the College Stock, but that no costs were to be allowed to the other parties; that the Master or any of the Fellows were at liberty to lay before the Lord Chancellor plans for the application of the dividends of the vacant Fellowships, the proportions in which the residue of the College revenue is to be divided among the Master and Fellows, and the application of the Patronage Fund.[2]

On the 8 August 1807 Lord Eldon gave his third and final order in the matter of the petition of Dr Procter and Mr Burrell.

(1) The cost of the petition was to be defrayed out of the College Stock.

(2) The dividends of the vacant Fellowships were to be carried to College Stock.

(3) The Master was to receive a dividend in the proportion of £6 to a Fellow's £5.

(4) The Master was to be allowed £45 a year for a servant.[3]

[1] *Register*, VI, 133. [2] *Register*, VI, 377. [3] *Register*, VI, 383.

As a strong Bar was engaged,[1] the costs were heavy. The Bursar's accounts for 1806–7 contain the item of £804. 16*s.* 3*d.* for the "appeal to the Lord Chancellor". Yet at this period the College seems to have been short of money, for in January 1809 we find it borrowing £300 with lawful interest from John Dickon, farmer, of Norton, and £2000 with lawful interest from John Finch, of Cambridge.

Meanwhile several interesting letters were written by Atkinson to Procter, which the latter preserved and placed among the College archives, along with draft copies of his replies. Ultimately the Master declared Atkinson's Fellowship vacant,[2] and Atkinson himself went to Christ's, thus still further prolonging the feud. For Atkinson had been influenced by Dr Browne, then Master of Christ's, in receiving the migrant Astley; so the seat of war changed, while the medium of private letters was abandoned for that of printed pamphlets.[3]

One finds it difficult not to suspect that much of this feud was due to sheer idleness. The Fellows at St Catharine's at this period were not busy with research. They had no undergraduates, or practically none,[4] to teach. Unmarried, they had no home interests. Satan, indeed, found work for idle hands to do. College societies are always liable to quarrel; happy are those which have unimportant trivialities to quarrel about. St Catharine's, unfortunately, has often quarrelled about things that really matter. Nothing could show more clearly the truth of these remarks than the Procter-Atkinson correspondence, to which reference has already been made. Although the

[1] Mansfield, Richards and Bell for the petitioners, the Attorney-General, Romilly and Whishard for the three Fellows (Browne 210). The Visitor was an expensive luxury at this period. The cost of the petition about the Skerne Fellowship (1813–14) was £163. 11*s.* 0*d.*, of that about the living of Ridgewell (1815–16) £133. 14*s.* 4*d.*

[2] The vacancy was filled up by the election of Thomas Turton to a foundation Fellowship (2 December 1808).

[3] "An examination of the Calumnies which have been assigned as reasons for the opposition to Dr Browne's Election into the Office of Vice-Chancellor which took place on the 4th of November 1809. Cambridge 1810. A Plain Statement of Facts: by J. Procter, D.D., Cambridge, 1810." Dr Thomas Browne, Master of Christ's College, became Vice-Chancellor in 1811.

[4] See p. 76.

letters are long and tedious, a few of them are reproduced in an appendix.[1] The length of the feud, the careful if florid style of Atkinson's epistles, and, above all, the utter indifference displayed to the real functions and duties of a collegiate body, are points deserving thoughtful attention.

On a vacancy occurring in the Frankland Fellowship, 8 December 1830 was fixed as the date of the election and notice was sent to Coventry. Five candidates presented themselves, of whom one only, John Inge, B.A., of Trinity College, had been educated at Coventry School. He was then curate of the parish of St John's, Coventry, but had no recommendation from the Mayor and Aldermen. He was examined apart from the other candidates; questions were proposed to him in mathematics, and passages from Greek and Latin authors set for translation into English. He answered but few of the questions and did not attempt the translation at all. Whereupon the Master and Fellows proceeded to examine the other candidates, and elected Strother Ancrum Smith, B.A., of the College, as having acquitted himself best.

Mr Inge considered himself aggrieved by the election of a person who had not been educated at Coventry School, and on 31 March 1831 appealed to the Visitor. The Lord Chancellor, Lord Brougham, dismissed the petition, but ordered that the rejected candidate should be at liberty to present himself again for examination, and that the Master and Fellows should examine him apart from the other candidates. In case of his proving himself competent he was forthwith to be elected into the Frankland Fellowship.

Accordingly, 9 November 1831 was fixed for the examination, but Inge informed the Master and Fellows by letter (24 October 1831) that it was not his intention to give himself further trouble about the matter. The election of December 1830 was therefore held to stand good.

These proceedings show the danger of attaching bye-Fellowships to particular schools, without taking great care to insure that the standard attained by the candidates is really satisfactory. The electors should at least have power to postpone election until suitable candidates present themselves; the "endowment of mediocrity" has nothing at all to recommend it.

[1] See pp. 325 foll.

Colleges after a period of depression often recover with a bound; the reaction is both short and sharp. A few brilliant or strong characters take the work of reconstruction in hand, and find their task all the easier because of the contrast between their own efficiency and the futility of their predecessors. So it was at St Catharine's in the earlier years of the nineteenth century. Thomas Turton, Temple Chevallier and George Elwes Corrie were really sound men, who while they held the Tutorship threw themselves into their work, and attracted undergraduates by their careful attention to their duties and their sincere desire to be really and helpfully *in loco parentis*. There was for half a century a fine body of Fellows, among whom may be mentioned Thomas Jarrett, Henry Philpott and Henry Kuhff, while the Skerne Fellows included Edmund Yorke and Charles Hardwick. With such a Society failure was impossible at a time when personal influence was chiefly responsible for any increase in numbers. To learning and kindliness two of the Fellows added financial ability, powers of administration and attention to detail, qualities especially important in a College without a College Office or even a clerk. How Philpott and Corrie got through all their work without becoming dull drudges is a mystery, yet get through it they did, while retaining all the finer qualities of their characters. The result was that the number of freshmen rose rapidly; for 30 years before 1810 the average was 4, but for 30 years after 1810 it was 20. Philpott became Master in 1845.

This recovery of the College came to a fitting climax in 1847. In that year Queen Victoria, along with the Prince Consort, who was Chancellor of the University, visited Cambridge. Dr Philpott was then Vice-Chancellor, and to him fell the task of entertaining the Royal party. On the evening of 5 July the Queen and Prince Albert, along with a distinguished number of guests, dined in the College Hall. The Master was naturally proud of the honour that had come to him and the College, and he recorded the incident in the manuscript he presented to Bishop Browne. There is no need to describe here the Royal visit, for Browne prints Philpott's account in full.[1] The Duke of Wellington, who was one of those who accompanied the

[1] *St Catharine's College*, pp. 214, 215.

Queen, slept at the Master's Lodge, and there was long a tradition in the College that he "had it in command from the Queen to inform Dr Philpott that in no Commoner's house had her Majesty been made to feel so completely at ease".[1]

A Royal visit of such a character would make any College proud today, and the other Colleges, perhaps, a trifle jealous. The effect in the most snobbish period of the nineteenth century must have been very great indeed. It used to be a piece of College gossip that jealousy of the honour done to the smallest of Cambridge Societies played no inconsiderable part in the outcry that attended the election of Robinson to the Mastership fourteen years later, and made Cambridge inclined to believe the worst.

On 21 July 1855 an Order in Council directed that burials in the College Chapel should be discontinued altogether. Burials in the Ante-chapel were still allowed, but only under the most strict conditions. These were:

(1) Only in the case of the Master or of some member of the foundation dying within the precincts of the College were such burials to be permitted.

(2) In such case the body must be enclosed in an air-tight metallic coffin, and each coffin must be separately enclosed in brickwork and well cemented.

An inquiry on this occasion showed that from its consecration in 1704 to 1842 four persons had been buried in the Chapel. These were:

(1) Lady Dawes, wife of the Master, in 1705.

(2) Henry Moore, in 1729.

(3) Kenrick Prescot, in 1779.

(4) Susannah Eyre, in 1782.

"To these should be added, 1719, John Addenbrooke, whose stone is in the floor of the Ante-chapel, and Archbishop Sir William Dawes, who is believed to have been buried by the side of his wife at the east end of the Chapel. In

[1] *St Catharine's College*, p. 215.

Plate VI

The Rev. C. K. Robinson

1842 a vault was made in the Ante-chapel, and three persons have been buried in it, viz. 1842, Mr Burrell; 1845, Dr Procter; 1847, Mr Pine."[1]

Just before the Master resigned on becoming Bishop of Worcester the statutes of 1860 came into force. They did away with the bye-foundations, including that of Mrs Ramsden, and imposed a system of open Scholarships awarded by competitive examinations. An analysis of them is given on pp. 339 foll.

On 16 October 1861 Charles Kirkby Robinson was elected Master in the room of Henry Philpott. There were five voters:

Milner,[2]
Robinson,
Jameson,[3]
Crabtree,[4]
Hurst.[5]

The first three voted for Robinson, and the other two for Jameson.

Nobody now living can possibly speak with authority of the motives that influenced the Fellows voting on this occasion; their secrets were known only to themselves and to their friends.[6] But it so happens that one of these friends, who was elected Fellow in the room of Jameson, had inner knowledge of the affair, and felt very strongly about it. This was G. F. Browne, afterwards Bishop of Bristol. When he wrote his history of St Catharine's in 1902 his lips were sealed, but several years later he drew up for the College a letter, which

[1] *St Catharine's College*, p. 217.

[2] His vacant Fellowship was filled up 6 March 1871.

[3] Rector of Coton 14 June 1862, after the income had been increased on 13 June. His vacant Fellowship was filled 6 June 1863.

[4] Vacated Fellowship filled 17 March 1868.

[5] Vicar of Ridgewell 24 June 1862, after the income had been increased by College Order, as in the case of Coton, on 23 June. Vacant Fellowship filled 9 March 1865.

[6] Their public acts and declarations after the election are in an entirely different category. The historian is fully entitled to pass judgment upon these.

he intended to be used when the time for publishing it should arrive. This letter is here printed in full for the first time.

Statement of some points in connection with the election of CHARLES KIRKBY ROBINSON to the Mastership of St. Catharine's, and the hostile attitude of F. J. JAMESON who received two votes on that occasion,

By

George Forrest Browne, D.D., D.C.L., LL.D.,
Honorary Fellow and formerly Foundation Fellow of St. Catharine's College, lately Bishop of Bristol.

December 4th, 1916.

At a very pleasant dinner of the Society of St. Catharine's College, Cambridge, last year, the conversation in the Combination Room turned upon the election to the Mastership in 1861, on which I have said something in my "Recollections" at pages 117 to 121. A general desire was expressed that I should write a brief statement as near as might be like the account I then gave to those present, that it might be placed in the Library of the College for future reference.

It may be stated as a preface that after taking my degree in 1856 I was never in Cambridge between June 1857 and the early part of 1863, in which last year I was elected to a Fellowship and entered upon residence. I had been very much put out by the serious discredit of the controversy about the Mastership of the College, and had taken my name off the Boards of the College, my view being hostile to Robinson. On the ground of that hostility I had refused the offer of a Fellowship and lectureship, preferring to remain at Trinity College, Glenalmond. About three months later a second offer of a Fellowship came, and as I was then in a poor state of health I accepted it and went into residence. On my first night in Cambridge I walked till late at night on the grass plot with the Reverend E. W. Crabtree, an old school fellow and then Tutor of the College, hearing from him all the details of the election of the Master, and, as I told him in the end, having heard it, I saw a fair case for Dr. Robinson, to my great surprise.

It should be recorded that Jameson had been brought from Caius to be Tutor by Robinson's influence, and that Robinson was Bursar and knew the affairs of the College as no-one else did. Jameson supported Robinson for the Mastership on the ground that he owed to Robinson his position in the College, and that Robinson was the business man of the College. Both of them were prominent members of the Evangelical school in the University. Jameson was decidedly the more popular man of the two.

I give what Crabtree told me, as nearly as I can in his own words,

"Hurst and I (the two Junior Fellows) had discussed the election the night before. We had intended to vote for Robinson; but as the result of our discussion we determined to vote for Jameson. On the morning of the day of election, I went up to Barnwell Vicarage to fetch Robinson, who had left College and was living there, meaning to tell him of the change of our purpose. I put off till we got close to the College. When I stopped and told him, he fell back against the shutters, not yet opened, of the Porter's house. I shall never forget the sound of his back falling on the shutters. He couldn't speak. Then I said 'But you will be elected, for Jameson has said positively he means to vote for you; you vote for yourself, as the practice has always been at St. Catharine's: Milner the Senior Fellow is to vote for you, and that elects you'." Milner, it should be noted, had not been in residence. He was a double-second, two years senior to Robinson.

Crabtree told me he never opened the *Cambridge Chronicle* or the *Saturday Review* for many weeks after the controversy arose without fearing to find himself come down upon as the author of the process which elected Robinson. Robinson never told it. It never came out. If Crabtree had confessed to it, some at least would have taken a less severe view.

To proceed with Crabtree's story.

"We went to Jameson's rooms, and there found Milner, Jameson, and Hurst. As we left the room to go to the Chapel, Jameson said to Robinson 'I'm going to vote for you, as I have always said I should'. Robinson replied, 'You had much better not, Jameson.' In Chapel, Hurst voted for Jameson, then I voted for Jameson, then Jameson voted for Robinson, then Robinson voted for Robinson, then Milner voted for Robinson and declared him elected."

That ended Crabtree's story. It is evident that Milner, who had heard what took place in Jameson's rooms, could have adjourned the election if he thought there was anything not quite right.

My next informant was the Bishop of Worcester, Dr. Philpott, whose appointment to the Bishopric—he was consecrated March 25, 1861—had created the vacancy in the Mastership. He told me that his wife and he were in the Lodge—the Old Lodge of course—and he was watching the Chapel door to see who came out first. Robinson came first, and Philpott called to his wife, "Robinson's elected, but it's all right, Jameson has his arm round his neck".

It is matter of common knowledge that Robinson and Jameson walked about the town that day together, Jameson announcing that Robinson had made him

Tutor and between them they did mean to make the College go. Jameson was enthusiastic about it.

My next informant was Edward Perowne, then Tutor, afterwards Master, of Corpus Christi College, an intimate friend of Jameson and Robinson. I asked him, could he at all help me to ascertain the time and the cause of Jameson's change from extreme friendliness to hostility. He at once replied, "Do you know, no-one ever asked me that. It ought to have been asked long ago. I can tell you exactly." This was what he said.

"Jameson and I and someone else went out to Somersham that night to Dr. Pinnock, to dine and sleep. We sat rather late and went up to bed about midnight. There was a bright fire in my room, and Jameson came in and we sat over the fire talking about the election. I happened to remark 'It's so very nice for Robinson; he's to be married this month and instead of going to the Vicarage at Barnwell he takes his wife to the Lodge'. 'Married!', Jameson cried, 'he's deceived me!' From that moment, Jameson took absolutely against Robinson. Robinson went off next day to Scotland to be married, and in his absence a storm of hostility broke out."

"But", I asked, "had Robinson concealed his engagement to be married?"

"Certainly not. He had met Miss Stewart at Aldourie, and become engaged to her. He came back full of it. There never was so charming a woman, and so on; he was the happiest of men."

"But how was it that Jameson didn't know?"

"They were not specially intimate, and Robinson had left the College and gone to live in Barnwell. I don't suppose they practically ever met."

"Did any one but you know?"

"Oh yes, my brother Tom for instance, ask him."

Thomas Perowne, afterwards Archdeacon of Norwich, assured me in like manner that Robinson's engagement was fully known among his friends. I asked could he name some layman in the town?

"Certainly. Hough the Surgeon knew all about it."

I asked my old friend Mr. Hough. He assured me the engagement was quite common knowledge. Robinson talked about it freely among his intimates.

I was completely satisfied that Robinson—a secretive man by nature, as Jameson was by nature a rather gushing man—had not made any secret of his purpose of marriage. But I can well understand that it was a great shock to Jameson to learn that Robinson had intended to vacate his Fellowship by marriage immediately. This would have put him out of the running for the Mastership, in which case Jameson would naturally have been elected Master.

My last informant was that dear lady, Mrs. Robinson, herself.

"We had a delightful honeymoon, but Charlie kept saying, 'Why *doesn't* Jameson write?' At last we got to Risplith on our way to Cambridge (Risplith Manor, near Ripon, Robinson had inherited from his mother, Miss Kirkby). Among letters lying on the table was one on which Charlie pounced, 'here's the dear fellow's letter!' I put my arm round his neck and we walked into the garden to read it together. It was something of this kind, 'Sir, as things touching your honour are being said here, it would be well if you returned as soon as may be'." I cannot put on record her heart-broken words, repeated to me on more than one occasion. There was a blight on her life, staunch as she was on her husband's side.

It is known that Robinson asked Jameson if his view was that he should resign, and that Jameson would not take that view. It could not have been a satisfactory solution, whether the result of another election would have been in favour of Robinson or of Jameson. If Jameson had on the day of election protested that there was something wrong in the election, Robinson would have had an opportunity of considering what his course should be. But Jameson's action was exactly the opposite of that. For the Master to have resigned because one of the electors had learned—what other people knew—that he was engaged to be married, would have been childish.

I afterwards got it at first hand that Jameson never said they had agreed to cross votes.

The practice of each candidate voting for himself was due partly to the fact that the electors were so very few, five at the outside, and partly to the feeling that a man ought not to be a candidate if he did not regard himself as the right man, if one of the existing Fellows was to be chosen. Dr. Philpott voted for himself against Dr. Corrie, otherwise he would not have had "the vote of a majority of the Fellows present". There were only four electors present on that occasion.

G. F. BROWNE.

DR ROBINSON'S *own account of the election.*

(Sent by MR R. C. WILTON.)

The late election to the Mastership of St. Catharine's College.

During the six weeks in which I was absent from Cambridge, certain statements have gone abroad in reference to the late election to the Mastership of St. Catharine's College.

Whilst these rumours were in circulation, I was detained in the north of England by a very severe domestic affliction. Not being able to leave my father, who was then dying, I had no means of setting matters in a right light except by writing a few hurried letters to friends in Cambridge, when I had little time and still less inclination for such a task. Consequently those who gave currency to these rumours, had the advantage of impressing the public with erroneous views of the matter in question, and thus an unfavourable impression has been produced as to my own share in the election. I have no right to complain that these statements were circulated during my unavoidable absence at such a time. I only mention the cause of this absence to explain why, when I knew that these rumours were abroad, I did not at once return and contradict them on the spot.

The chief feature of the report current against me is this—that I was guilty of a breach of faith with Mr. Jameson, which I understood to mean, that after having promised either to vote for Mr. Jameson or at least not to vote for myself, on the condition that Mr. Jameson should vote for me, I first secured his vote and then voted for myself. This report was widely circulated in Cambridge and elsewhere. After some time had elapsed, the report was contradicted "on the best authority". It is needless therefore for me to assert that the report was entirely untrue, and that neither by word nor by implication, conditionally nor unconditionally, did I promise to vote for Mr. Jameson or not to vote for myself. The report in question may have arisen from a voluntary promise on my part to Mr. Jameson that I would not canvass the electors for their votes, and to this promise I adhered.

After careful consideration I submit the following as the true facts of the case:

(1) On the day before the election to the Mastership, i.e. on October 15th, Mr. Jameson called at my house. After some conversation on the subject, *I said to Mr. Jameson that he must vote for himself and that I should also do the same*; adding as a reason why we should take this course, that, since the election took place without any previous discussion, the only way in which each could signify his desire to have the office was to vote for himself.

Almost immediately after Mr. Jameson left my house, Mr. Bathurst, Rector of Birchanger, came in to luncheon. I told him all that had transpired. During my absence in the north, Mr. Bathurst wrote to Mr. Clayton on October 31st to this effect, that on reaching home, he commended to a third person the statement which I had made in reference to the conversation that passed between Mr. Jameson and myself. Both of them distinctly said that the substance of this conversation was (to use Mr. Bathurst's own words) that, "*Mr. Robinson had exhorted Mr. Jameson to vote for himself, saying he should do the same, as it would serve to shew that they were both candidates for the office and both prepared to undertake its responsibilities*". Of Mr. Bathurst's letter I knew nothing until November 28th. Then for the first time I find that we had already both expressed in writing the substance of the conversation that occurred between Mr. Jameson and myself. As both statements agree, first as to the *fact*, that I had told Mr. Jameson he must vote for himself, and that I should do the same, and secondly, as to the *reason*, added, that this would serve to shew we were both prepared to undertake the office, it is an evidence that this conversation actually took place and that therefore I gave Mr. Jameson due notice of my intention to vote for myself.

(2) Mr. Jameson left upon the minds of two of the Fellows the impression that the vote which he gave for me on the 16th October was bona fide and not complimentary.

On the morning of the election, Mr. Crabtree told me that I might have the Mastership if I pleased, as Mr. Jameson had made up his mind to vote for me.

This is a proof of the conviction which Mr. Crabtree entertained. He never could have suggested to me such a course, if he had not been fully convinced of Mr. Jameson's sincerity.

Mr. Milner (who breakfasted alone with Mr. Jameson on the morning of the election) was also convinced that Mr. Jameson by the announcement of his intention to vote for me, had expressed his desire to leave the decision in my hands. Mr. Milner's vote for me (given after the other votes had been recorded) could only be given on the understanding that I had not taken an unfair advantage of Mr. Jameson in the matter. But that this was his conviction is placed beyond doubt by a letter of the 20th, in which he says:

"I know from the reasons, which I will now mention, that you gave your vote with perfect honour. Because on the morning, before we went into the Chapel, when you came to Jameson's rooms where I was present, he acquainted you with the fact that both he and I intended to vote for you, *and as I believe expressed to you his wish that you should vote for yourself.*"

I cannot now remember the exact words in which Mr. Jameson expressed this desire that I should vote for myself. But whatever the words were, Mr. Jameson had distinctly conveyed to Mr. Milner the impression under which I acted—viz. that his vote was bona fide and not complimentary.

(3) When Mr. Jameson before the election declared his intention of voting for me, I requested him not to do so, and I repeated this request two or three times over. But the only answer I received was that he had made up his mind on the matter, with some remark the tenor of which was that I was not to consider him in the vote I gave.

Now this request of mine must have conveyed to Mr. Jameson the idea that I felt his vote to be of value. *If his vote was to preclude me from voting for myself, his promise to vote for me took away as much as it gave.* I designed not only to give Mr. Jameson an opportunity of reconsidering his determination but also to let him know that I looked upon his vote as sincere. As he still persisted in his determination, I considered that he practically threw upon me the responsibility of accepting or of refusing the Mastership, as I might think fit, and that he was prepared to acquiesce in any result to which my vote might lead.

(4) Mr. Jameson's conduct towards me after the election was inconsistent with a conviction on his part that I had taken an unfair advantage in the matter.

After the voting was over I went up to Mr. Jameson and in the presence of all the Fellows; I thanked him for what he had done, adding that I owed my election entirely to his generosity. Mr. Jameson received my thanks in the spirit in which they were offered, greeted me with very hearty congratulations, and walked with me out of the Chapel to the College gates, expressing kindly feelings at the result, and adding that he hoped I would not allow my joy at the result to be damped by considering that he had not himself been elected.

Mr. Jameson accompanied me to the Vice-Chancellor, signed the necessary College documents, allowed me to go to Norwich to be installed in the Canonry. He further signified his readiness to accept from me the office of President of the College, an office then at my disposal.

And during the few days which elapsed before I left Cambridge, he evinced no abatement in his expressions of friendship. And never once either by word, reserve or coldness of manner gave me to believe that I had misunderstood his vote. Up to the time when I received his letter, I was under the full impression that his vote was genuine and not a mere compliment.

If Mr. Jameson considered my conduct unfair, he was bound by every sense of honour and justice to tell me this as soon as the election was over, and not to convey as he did contrary impressions by accepting my hearty thanks, by cordial congratulations and by unchanged kindliness of manner. Such conduct seems to me inconsistent with the supposition that he thought I had acted a dishonourable part.

My own letter of thanks to him, which he received on October 19th, merely expressed in writing what I had already expressed in the College Chapel. I do not wish to say too much. But as the facts to draw forth opinion were the same on the day of the election as on the day when he answered my letter, I can only infer that his feelings and opinions must have undergone a very decided change.

(5) On the whole I distinctly, and after due reflection, make the following assertions:

That on the day before the election I told Mr. Jameson he must vote for himself and that I should do the same.

That two of the body of Fellows, beside myself, acted under the impression that Mr. Jameson's vote was bona fide and not complimentary.

That without any promise or condition implied or understood between us, Mr. Jameson recorded his vote for me.

That after the election Mr. Jameson did not question the fairness of the votes, but acquiesced in all, and treated me with a kindness and warmth of manner inconsistent with a conviction on his part that I had taken any improper advantage.

Finally, I can say with a clear conscience, that when Mr. Jameson left the refusal or acceptance of the Mastership in my hands, I accepted it with a firm conviction that his vote was sincere, and not given on the condition that I should return his vote or vote for another than myself.

It was not unnatural that Jameson had a grievance against Robinson. But it is surprising that he should through his friends appeal to the outside world to be the judge of his cause, thereby violating the rule—a statutory one until 1860[1]—not to disclose College secrets which if divulged might be to the detriment of the Society. It is even more surprising that the outside world took up his cause, discussed it with a malicious pleasure, pronounced judgment without full inside knowledge, and so dealt untold harm to a public institution. It is safe to say that nobody to-day would act as Jameson did, safer still to say that the University would not now lend an ear to any Fellow of a College who might so far forget his duty to remain silent about a domestic matter as to put personal feelings before the good name of the house he professed to serve. Nothing shows more clearly the change that has come over the University during the last hundred years than to imagine what would now take place if a Fellow of a College, thinking himself aggrieved, were to make a similar appeal to the University at large. Nobody would listen to him for a moment. That a war of pamphlets would follow is simply unthinkable. Yet a Fellow did in 1861 make such an appeal. He gained a wide and sympathetic hearing. A pamphlet-war ensued which lasted for years. So great is the gulf between then and now.

To write fairly of the period that came between Robinson's election and

[1] Jameson must have taken the oath required by the Statutes of Edward VI: "Secreta collegii in ejusdem collegii damnum aut praejudicium nemini revelabo." An aggrieved Fellow might appeal to the Visitor, but Jameson apparently never contemplated that step.

death is not easy; it is doubly difficult for one who was a Fellow at the end of these distressful years. The last member of that Society to survive cannot fail to have strong convictions, and even stronger suspicions, but they are all based upon subjective evidence, persuasive enough if it appeals to personal experience, but lacking in force when a reader with no inside knowledge is its critic and judge.

The scandal caused by the election was probably the greatest disaster that ever happened to any College in either University. But the disastrous consequences were not all manifest at once. There was no sudden drop in numbers, such as attended the quarrels about Procter's election at the beginning of the century. Had Robinson's tenure of office been short, the incident, like earlier scandals, might soon have been forgotten. But he was Master for nearly half a century, and his presence in Cambridge was a perpetual reminder of "Robinson's vote", and of the "man who voted for himself". Trevelyan's unfortunate reference to the election[1] in *Horace at the University of Athens* kept alive in the minds of the outside public an association between St Catharine's and dishonourable conduct. At last everybody knew the worst construction that had been placed upon the election, and believed it; nobody, on the other hand, knew anything else about either this election or the College whose Head had been condemned. In course of time the whole College began to suffer from an inferiority complex, a cloud which deepened and darkened until it became a dominating element in the lives of those who dwelt within its walls. Old members think first of this cloud when their undergraduate days are recalled. Only afterwards do they remember their friendships, their failures, or their triumphs.

[1] See the 1888 edition of *The Ladies in Parliament and other Pieces* by G. O. Trevelyan, p. 43 (footnote): "The Mastership of St. Catharine's fell vacant in 1861. The electors with whom the appointment lay were five in number, of whom two were candidates—Mr Robinson and Mr Jameson. Of the other three votes, Mr Jameson got two, and Mr Robinson one. Mr Jameson voted for Mr Robinson and Mr Robinson for himself, thus securing the Mastership. Through the cloud of pamphleteering and pasquinading which has been floating about intermittently ever since, one fact is discernible: that Mr Robinson continued to hold the Mastership after he had become aware that Mr Jameson was dissatisfied with the transaction."

Senior members, however, and juniors were not affected in the same way. The former, sharing in the disgrace of their Master, who was ostracised by University society, withdrew into their shell, and lived a life of their own amongst themselves and their friends. The result was a backwater of University life, which for many years produced interesting and amusing characters, but was barren of all contributions to the general good. The one exception was G. F. Browne, who for a long period not only served the University well, but was in the estimation of many the embodiment of it. The others, too conservative to join Browne, and too easy-going to mark out a path for themselves, sank deeper and deeper into a rut from which they were not shaken until the upheaval of 1914. The junior members, on the other hand, felt that on them alone depended the honour of their College. Most of them shouldered the burden manfully. A few, indeed, lacking in character, gave way, and by their carelessness brought the reputation of the College lower than ever, but the great majority proved desperately loyal, and made heroic efforts to uphold the honour of their predecessors both in study and in sport. It is this struggle that they remember as the outstanding feature of their undergraduate days.

But although during the Mastership of Robinson St Catharine's in many ways fell behind the rest of the University, there were nevertheless signs that the Society realised the need for domestic improvements. The way in which these were carried out may not commend itself to the artistic taste of everybody, yet they were all attempts to make residents happier and more comfortable.

In 1868 a bay was built into the south-east end of the Hall, in order to make easier the service at the Fellows' table, and the windows of Hall and Library were replaced by others in the Gothic style. As soon as the work was finished, artistic critics discovered an unsuspected beauty in the severe style of architecture that had disappeared under the hands of the workmen. In a similar way forty-five years later Cambridge awoke to the attractions of a three-sided court when the march of progress threatened to close it by building on the site of the grove.

In the next year there was a proposal to build new fives-courts, and very soon afterwards the purchase of a piece of property to the east of the present Fellows' Garden afforded junior members:

(*a*) a common room;

(*b*) a library;

(*c*) a swimming bath skilfully constructed in an old cellar, probably the first of its kind in a University College.

The new Master's Lodge was built in 1875–6. This has been described elsewhere, and it is sufficient to say here that the old Lodge, although commodious, was unsuited to the needs of a growing family. It was far better adapted to serve as a Fellows' Building, as it did until 1922, and at small cost it has been turned into undergraduates' rooms, with an excellent Junior Common Room on the ground floor and baths in the basement.

Some little time before 1880 began a movement to amalgamate King's College and St Catharine's. The latter had been founded by a Provost of the former. The two Colleges were adjacent; one needed more rooms, and the other was in a bad way and needed money. At least two Fellows of St Catharine's were in favour of the scheme, while G. F. Browne, although no longer a Fellow, supported it with enthusiasm. But the difficulties in the way were great; the position of the Master of St Catharine's in the proposed united College proved a fatal stumbling-block. On 20 April 1880 St Catharine's finally rejected the plan of amalgamation. At the time of the recent Commission the scheme was again revived, but never seriously proposed or discussed.

In 1882 new statutes came into force. Imposed by a Commission of which Philpott was Chairman and Browne Secretary, they nevertheless were rigid and difficult to administer, particularly in the matter of Fellowships and reelections thereto. They are printed, almost *in extenso*, on pp. 339 foll.

Members of the College whose undergraduate years coincided with the early nineties will remember how their depression was lightened by the news that J. N. Figgis had won the Prince Consort Prize (1892). Figgis was never

Plate VII

Dr C. H. W. Johns
from the portrait given by Mrs Johns

a Fellow, but to him was due more of the recovery of St Catharine's than is now generally recognised. He was the first to show by his record that St Catharine's was not without hope, and it is perhaps significant that he supervised F. M. Rushmore, who as the lieutenant of Johns and the first post-War Tutor contributed so much to the regeneration of the College.

The year 1892 saw the beginning of a fresh outburst of activity, the last before the great upheaval that began with the Mastership of Johns in 1909. The Tutors, Spratt and Southward, had just been appointed (the Master announced their appointment in May 1892) and they were young enough to see that something ought to be done to attract pupils, as the Master was sinking into a soured and embittered old age.

In 1893 the playing-field at Newnham was bought and laid out. Additions and improvements were subsequently made, which will be described in their proper place. The purchase money came mainly from the fund given by Mr Yorke, rather vaguely, for "educational purposes". Within the memory of the writer there have been some who regarded the transaction as a scandalous misuse of trust money; to-day few would fail to recognise that true education could not be promoted in a better way.

The improvement of the Chapel and the installation of the present organ[1] occupied the attention of the new Tutors from 1893 to 1895. Spratt, active in securing the playing-field, as a good cricketer would be, was equally eager to have a fine organ in the Chapel. He was himself an accomplished organist with a genuine love of the best church music; while his colleague, though a weak Tutor, was an admirable Chaplain and a really remarkable musician. The pair worked hard at collecting subscriptions, giving, as the rest of the Society gave, liberally from the profits of their office. The work proceeded rapidly during the year 1894.

The dinner after the re-opening of the Chapel, with its spontaneous tribute of gratitude and affection, has been called by one who knew and loved him

[1] At the time of writing the organ is being renovated by Messrs Harrison at a cost of over £3000.

"the apotheosis of Spratt". Certain it is that from this time he and his colleagues began gradually to sink into inefficiency. They had shot their bolt, and the success of their efforts was small; the Robinson cloud grew darker still. Neither the Bursar nor the Tutors had the character necessary for pioneers and reformers, and there was still alive in the College a strong feeling, which had been strengthened by the presence for nearly one hundred years of six Skerne Fellows with no duties, that a Fellowship was intended for the good of the individual Fellow, and not for the building up of a body of undergraduates, with all the sacrifice of one's own individuality that such a task demands if it is to be done thoroughly. So all three officers relaxed their efforts and followed their own bent. The Bursar retired to the country living of Little Shelford. Spratt gave himself up to his private coaching, and Southward devoted himself to music. For these occupations they were well qualified, but their proper work for the College suffered lamentably. Carr, who had been Tutor, buried himself in his parish on becoming Bursar, and spent but little of his time in St Catharine's. Spratt retained a lively interest in the Classics, but began to neglect undergraduates undistinguished in work or sport. He disliked, and did not respect, his partner in office, and never could be induced to collaborate with him except in their joint efforts for the Chapel. This lack of team spirit soon had serious consequences. Numbers began to fall off, and Southward yielded to the temptation of admitting less suitable candidates or even undesirable migrants. The business side of College administration did not keep pace with modern demands. Carr was a kindly landlord and scrupulously careful, but hopelessly conservative and out-of-date. Spratt proved a good Steward but a bad keeper of accounts. Southward, in charge of Tutorial money which, after the payment of Lecturers and other similar charges, was divided between the Tutors, had no business capacity, and was the last person to see when he was being imposed upon. The Master, a better business man than any one of the three, was sinking into a soured old age, and his protests against bad management became feebler and more futile. No wonder that the undergraduates suffered, while the number of first classes dropped to a minimum.

In this gloomy prospect there were two bright spots, cheerful enough, yet by their unimportance bringing into greater prominence the sad condition of the College in all respects that really mattered. One was Southward's success in fostering musical talent, the other was the influence, upon at least a portion of the College, of the powerful personality of Spratt.

The Chapel services were remarkably good. Here was one department in which both Tutors could and did co-operate. Southward trained a choir well, and Spratt played the organ with taste and skill. Visitors at the Sunday services were numerous, and the undergraduates themselves were eager to attend. It was the same with secular music; the concerts given by the Musical Society were some of the most popular in all the University.

No account of St Catharine's during the last century would be complete without some special mention of A. W. Spratt, a fascinating and interesting character. As a pure classical scholar, at any rate as a composer, he would be among the first five chosen by any competent judge to represent Cambridge scholarship at its best. The kindest-hearted of men, he would lavish more than he could afford upon anyone whom he happened to like. But there were few whom he did like, and the others he would treat with an almost incredible contempt which made them hate him. He veiled his soft heart in a rough severity ("protective colouring", it has been called) which made him a terror to all evil-doers. A stickler for etiquette, he proved a truly formidable Dean. Story after story, most of them authentic, used to be told of the terrifying effect of his gruff voice and fierce appearance.[1] But his friends, young and old, loved him, and found him at his Sunday dinners a lavish and charming host.

Yet this fascinating personality was worse than "a child in finance". He simply could not see why the Steward's fund should not help to pay for the

[1] Some sportive undergraduates, meeting in King's Parade an Italian with a performing bear, suggested that, if the latter went through his tricks on the lawn of St Catharine's, a rich reward might follow. Those who may remember Spratt will not be surprised to hear that a few minutes later a cowed attendant and a more cowed bear were making a hurried exit through the front gates. The writer, calling to pay his respects to Mrs Spratt, was told that importunate beggars had recently been troubling the College. One had annoyed the maids that afternoon, refusing to go away and inserting his foot to prevent the door being shut. "At last I fetched Billy, who spoke to him, and then he went." Spratt's acquaintances will know why.

new organ, and left old cheques payable to the Steward, uncashed, among the papers to be handed over to his successor.

Dr Johns, elected to succeed Robinson in 1909, had a task before him trying enough to break the strongest nerve. The obstacles to urgent reforms were old friends, all now "stricken in years", victims of circumstances and of a system as old as the College itself. When he finally did strike, he struck ruthlessly, but not without long and thoughtful consultations with his most trusted friends. During the first year of his Mastership he was often to be seen walking in the courts of Queens' in close conversation with Coates, a singularly lovable but severe Tutor of that college. They were planning, as Johns used to say afterwards, how a difficult situation could be met fairly, with full justice both to the future of St Catharine's and also to its old staff of Fellows. He could find no obvious solution, and at last appealed to the Visitor, who was not inclined to interfere. Finally, after calling in a London firm of accountants, he deposed all three officers by a magisterial ruling. Such an act was unconstitutional, but the offenders, if they may be called such, were too broken by age and anxiety to protest. Two of them died soon after, but not before the Master himself had retired from his position, worn out by continued worries and shortly to die as the result of his exertions on behalf of the College. His work for the College has a fitting memorial in Johns Building, a handsome range of chambers just completed (1936) with the help of a large and generous donation from Mrs Johns.

To describe the changes, structural, domestic and financial, of the last twenty-five years is not a difficult task, and they are recorded in their appropriate places in this narrative. But the true history of this period cannot be written yet; we are too near the events to estimate fairly their relative importance and the wisdom of the policy pursued from time to time by the Governing Body. Be the ultimate result, however, what it may, all the members of the Society have made their contribution to it. Union and agreement on all essentials have characterised both their deliberations and their actions. Consequently there have been no struggles between widely divergent views, and the responsibility does not lie on the shoulders of one or two individuals.

But although a just verdict is a task for posterity, it is safe to say that the

War Memorial in the Chapel

R. A. BARKER, M.C.
L. A. BARTLETT
G. BELCHER, M.C.
P. C. H. BIRD
A. E. BOULTBEE
E. BUCKLEY
R. C. CAIN, D.F.C.
B. CARTER
C. CARTWRIGHT
F. D. E. CAYLEY
G. M. CLARK
M. T. CLARKE
B. I. CONAN-DAVIES
H. V. CORBETT
H. G. DRIFFIELD
K. C. GILL, M.C.
E. T. GRAY
C. S. R. GRIFFITHS
A. L. GULLICK
R. P. HILL
H. HUGHES
J. A. B. JOLLEY
C. H. KIRKUS
H. V. LEE
F. G. LEMMEY
J. H. LEWIS
J. W. F. MCNAUGHT-DAVIS

ALVMNIS · S · KATERINAE
QVI · PRO · PATRIA
ANTE · DIEM · PERIERVNT
EIVSDEM · COLLEGII · ALVMNI
MONVMENTVM · EREXERVNT
HAVD · IMMEMORES
MDCCCCXIV—MDCCCCXVIII

J. W. MANN
W. C. MAYO
D. R. MILNER
G. MOORE
T. PHILLIPS
E. F. S. PREDDY
R. PRITCHARD
N. S. PUDUMJEE
J. H. R. RAWES
G. RIGBY, M.C.
W. S. ROSS
A. C. T. K. RYAN
W. F. SCOTT
W. E. SMART
D. G. SMITH, M.C.
F. E. G. SOUTHWELL
R. J. STOKES
W. SWIFT
J. J. TALL
R. THEOBALD, M.C.
E. F. UNWIN
L. S. WARD-PRICE
H. L. WATTS
F. R. WHITE
H. G. WILLIAMS
O. E. WORMALD

initiative in these changes came from Johns. A determined man, who combined an unbendable severity with a genial pleasantness of manner, he resolved that the old order must give way to the new, and found an apt lieutenant in Rushmore to carry out his views. The one planted and the other watered. And then, just at the right moment, came Drury. A saint, if ever there was one, he achieved during his short Mastership a task which it is certain that few men could have accomplished. He fostered in the College a spirit that had often been wanting in the past but was now absolutely essential for success. It is hard to put a name to it, but perhaps the least inadequate word to describe it is "faith". To a College still suffering from the inferiority complex caused by the long ostracism that followed "Robinson's vote", it was an invaluable asset to have at its head a man of real Christian courage, who never allowed anyone, from the President to the youngest Freshman, to forget that the destiny of St Catharine's depended, not on its past, but on the efforts of its present members. The incubus was thrown off, never to return.

Drury's influence was all the more important because his mentality differed so greatly from that of his predecessor. Johns, a profound scholar, aristocratic and exclusive, would have tried, had he lived, to make St Catharine's a Cambridge Balliol; he often expressed great contempt for what he called the "endowment of mediocrity". Such an ideal is no unworthy one, and the College has benefited from coming into close contact with a man who championed it with energy and courage. But Drury was of a far more catholic temper. While placing a high value on intellectual distinction, he held that the duty of a college was not only to attract it but to create it. In other words, he measured the efficiency of a college by the improvement in a man effected during his years of residence. Drury, moreover, laid rather more stress than Johns on the character-forming side of collegiate life, holding that the spiritual element in man is fundamental, and gives a meaning and value to all his other gifts.

The War of 1914–1918, during which the College lost the income accruing from the fees of undergraduates, while establishment expenses were by no means proportionately reduced, brought out clearly the defects in the old methods of conducting College business. The end of the War coincided with the retirement of the old financial officers, now very old men. The new officers were not unaware of the difficulties of their task, and set about it with some anxiety, especially as a University Commission was imminent. But they were helped by two strokes of good fortune. In the first place it was possible to make a fresh start, with modern methods of book-keeping. Secondly, the financial tension was quickly relieved. Agricultural prices rose, and by selling most of its farms and investing in gilt-edged securities the College nearly doubled its income from endowments. In addition, the number of undergraduates increased to an embarrassing extent, and rapidly reached that above which additional fees are very profitable. Instead of just paying its way, with Fellows' dividends varying from year to year but always below the maximum, the College was before long able to pay regularly a full dividend, and at the same time to add annually to its capital.

Several new Fellows were elected, larger revenues making it possible to increase the statutory number of six, and in this way the teaching power of the College was improved and fresh wisdom brought to its deliberations.

Soon after settling down to its post-War work the Society felt that it was necessary to obtain fresh statutes. Greater freedom was desirable in the election and re-election of Fellows, and recent events had shown the need for a system of superannuation. With the help of Mr J. J. Withers, afterwards Sir John Withers and Burgess of the University, new statutes were drawn up and passed through Parliament in 1921. This is the only time in its history that St Catharine's has made statutes entirely on its own initiative. Their main features are preserved in the statutes imposed a few years later by the University Commission.

Larger numbers meant more correspondence and book-keeping, and so there was established and developed that most important institution—the College Office. A College tutor should certainly at some early period in his career make out some of his pupils' bills, and a bursar is none the worse for having kept a ledger; but too much of this kind of work prevents an officer of a large institution from concentrating on his proper function, just as an architect cannot profitably be also bricklayer, plasterer and carpenter. St Catharine's had no clerical staff until 1919, and the old account books show

Plate IX

Dr T. W. Drury

all the defects and mistakes of the amateur. The historian is pleased that unimportant details are so often recorded in full, the ledger doing the work of a petty-cash book, for valuable information is thus added to his store of facts, but at the same time he is forced to admit that less detail and more business-like book-keeping would have been a great boon to the College. St Catharine's owes to the late F. M. Rushmore the foundation of its clerical department. As financial Tutor he laid down the principles which have since been faithfully followed, with the result that to-day much of the College business is carried on automatically and without friction, while the Office is the recognised if unofficial collector of complaints and mishaps, often clearing away petty annoyances before they have begun seriously to annoy.

To Mr Rushmore is also due in great part the regeneration of St Catharine's in the period after the War. It is difficult, perhaps impossible, to say now what was his greatest contribution to this rebirth, but posterity will probably say that he made the College more business-like. He brought order out of chaos in all departments of College life. After a short Mastership he died in 1933, and was succeeded by the Rev. H. J. Chaytor, the Senior Tutor, under whom the College is more flourishing than ever. Mr Rushmore's work is appreciated in the inscription to his memory in the Chapel, and he has a fitting tribute in the Rushmore Memorial Fund that is being collected as these few words about him are being written.

The post-War boom saw the revival of many College activities and the birth of many new ones. Societies, which always find a fertile soil in Colleges, sprang into existence, some of mushroom growth and doomed to perish as quickly as they were born, others founded on more secure foundations and therefore still enjoying a healthy existence. Of the latter perhaps the most typical and the most useful is the Shirley Society.[1] Founded in honour of the Catharine dramatist, it fosters and encourages all interests of a literary nature; comprehensive and wide in its scope it appeals to all classes of undergraduates and dons, none of whom find their tastes, if *litterae humaniores* move them at all, unprovided for or unsatisfied. Less catholic, but only less im-

[1] Into this gradually was absorbed the old Literary Society, intended to bring dons and undergraduates together to discuss literature. Smoking a churchwarden was compulsory at meetings.

portant in that it makes a more limited appeal, is the John Ray Society—Ray was our great botanist—the members of which meet to hear and discuss papers of a strictly scientific character. The Historical Society and the Classical Society cater for the special needs of men reading for these particular triposes.

The St Catharine's Society of old members, founded in the Mastership of Drury, is an invaluable link between the present and the past. Its annual dinners, now always taking place at Cambridge, are much appreciated by those who renew their youth by spending a few days in College. It publishes every year a *Magazine*, and a sign of its vitality is to be found in the Rushmore Memorial Fund, which is entirely due to the efforts of enthusiastic and loyal sons of St Catharine.

Before the War most of our men were either ordinands or intending schoolmasters, a large number of them reading for a pass degree. After the War both the subjects and the objects of study changed. Schoolmasters continued to be numerous, but the ordinands dwindled to a very small figure. Other careers—law, civil service, business, etc.—became increasingly popular, and the triposes now favoured were those of Mechanical Sciences, Natural Sciences, History, Modern Languages, Geography and English. Comparatively few took the ordinary degree. Recently the College has encouraged some of its more brilliant students to take part in exploring expeditions, where they have achieved a marked measure of success.

Determined efforts have been made to enlarge the Scholarship Fund. Bishop Drury himself gave the capital to provide an Exhibition for ordinands. A gift, supplemented by a legacy, from the Rev. Francis Knowles has added a new Scholarship, and the Rev. Canon Warren has founded another of £120 a year to be held, if a suitable applicant be forthcoming, by a boy from Oakham Grammar School. Choral Exhibitions of £30 a year are now offered, as well as an Organ Scholarship of much higher value, the holder of which trains the choir, now consisting entirely of Catharine men, and directs the other musical activities of the College. Wherever the Scholarship Fund fails to answer the calls made upon it, the Tutorial Fund comes to its aid, although of course the latter cannot bring up the amount available for Scholarships to what it should be in a college with a yearly entry of nearly one hundred. One

Plate X

Johns Memorial Tablet

Drury Memorial Tablet

Rushmore Memorial Tablet

of the most useful augmentations effected in this way is the addition made to the Exhibition founded by Arthur Phillips, a late Fellow, in memory of his Tutor, Ely Willcox Crabtree. The Crabtree Exhibitions are of the value of £30 to £40 a year, and are open to candidates who possess, in the words of the official prospectus, "in addition to such intellectual qualities as would enable them with diligence to gain a 2nd Class Honours Degree, qualities of initiative and leadership as indicated by their School record....Work done as a Prefect, as a member of the School athletic teams, and in connection with the School Magazine, Dramatic and Literary Societies, the O.T.C. etc., should be included. Only those boys whose pecuniary circumstances are such that an Exhibition is essential will be considered for these awards". The idea of these Exhibitions, which are not, as sometimes supposed, a mere endowment of athletics, was due to the insight of the late Master, F. M. Rushmore, who when Tutor had in his hands a great part of the post-War reconstruction.

The earliest records of the College contain but few references to the amusements and recreations of its junior members. The Bursar's accounts show items for "bonefires" on anniversaries, and the Tutors' bills have occasionally charges for "football"; beyond this there is little or nothing that bears on the pastimes of undergraduates. Of healthful and legitimate forms of exercise there was riding for the rich and walking for the poor, but serious athletics and organised games were all but unknown until the nineteenth century.

It is hard in these days, when opportunities for play and recreation are so many, to realise how dull and monotonous life was for the young not only at the University but everywhere. High spirits had no healthy outlet, and leisure was full of temptations. The result was that degrading amusements and dubious pastimes were always popular, in spite of the efforts of University authorities to suppress or ban them. Youthful energies refuse to be checked; they can only be directed, and three hundred years ago the channels waiting to receive them were mostly undesirable. Gaming, cock fights and "town-and-gown" riots were some of the least objectionable pursuits favoured by undergraduates.

One of the most valuable contributions to University life was the rapid growth of athletic games and sports in the reign of Queen Victoria. Charles Kingsley noticed it in *Alton Locke,* though his reference to Parker's Piece as the scene of University sport reminds us that he was unfamiliar with College playing-fields, which now hold an honoured place in College life along with the Chapel, the Hall and the Library.

Unfortunately the history of sport at St Catharine's is entirely a blank until the early "eighties". A tradition here, a chance reference there, a few faded photographs, are all that remain to remind us that the College played a not undistinguished part in the struggles on the river or in the field. In the first *Year-book and Register of St Catharine's College* (1902) Mr R. R. Conway tells how organisation was introduced into the chaotic condition into which the sports clubs of the College had drifted, and so made history possible. At first each club was an independent unit, with a separate subscription from each member. Here lay the possibility of confusion and possible bankruptcy. One club might be very expensive to run, and yet, although important, have but few members. "No less than five separate clubs, with a total annual subscription of £6. 15*s.* 0*d.* were, in our own College, on the look-out for members; one club prospered for a while at the expense of others, and some amount of ill-feeling was naturally caused."

After a long discussion, which bore good fruit in carefully drafted rules, the various clubs were in June 1888 amalgamated into one, and the total subscriptions were hereafter apportioned among the different branches of sport. The purchase of a playing-field by the College in 1893 brought the authorities into closer touch with the games of the undergraduates, and the succeeding years cemented this union. At the present day young and old co-operate in administering a large sum of money devoted to not the least important of College activities. The experience gained in directing financial concerns under sympathetic guidance is of great and lasting value to the officers of the clubs.

The playing-field was enlarged by the purchase in 1914 of a strip on the east side, and another addition, again on the east, was made in 1930. The Master and Fellows provided the money required for the first of these pieces of land, but the Amalgamated Clubs bought the latter and shouldered the

Plate XI

F. M. Rushmore
from the portrait given by Mrs Rushmore

burden of the squash courts built on it, while the pavilion at the north-west corner was paid for by subscriptions generously given by old members during the years 1907–1910. This pavilion has just (1936) been enlarged, and shower-baths have been added.

It is a new St Catharine's that has grown up since 1918. The old buildings have been made more comfortable, while the chambers recently erected are equipped with every possible convenience. The number of residents, which just before the War was about 120, has steadily risen to 300. Success after success has rewarded the efforts of the College to reassert itself. Intellectually there has been good progress during the last fifteen years; First Classes come in good numbers with occasionally a University prize. The record of sport is phenomenal. The inter-collegiate tests have given us the Rugby Cup several times, and boxing Blues are more than common. Association Football and Athletics are well to the fore, and other branches of sport show results of which the College may well be proud. St Catharine's, in short, has forgotten its dark past, and is looking forward, in confidence and faith, to a brilliant future.

PATRONAGE OF THE COLLEGE

The Rectory of Coton came to the College as a gift from the Founder. The conveyance is dated 22 November 1475. The commissioners of 1546, while mentioning the advowson of the Vicarage of Ridgewell as in the gift of the College, have nothing to say about Coton. The Lord Chancellor by an order dated 21 December 1795 decided that the cure of souls at Coton did not vacate a Fellowship, on the grounds (1) that the incumbent was only a chaplain or curate, the Master and Fellows being the Rectors; (2) that usage for 200 years had permitted the holding of the two offices at one and the same time.

The Vicarage of Ridgewell was bought on 4 March 1542 for £130, but was not formally conveyed until 6 December 1549, although the commissioners of 1546 describe it as belonging to the College. Lord Eldon on 13 August 1816 sanctioned the appropriation of £2712. 14*s*. 0*d*. Consols from the Patronage Fund for the augmentation of Ridgewell Vicarage, this sum having arisen from the revenues and estates of the old foundation.

The Rectories of Gimingham and Trunch were conveyed to the College on 7 October 1592. They were a gift from Mr John Duke, of Kelsale, Suffolk. On 7 May 1751 a petition was sent to the Bishop of Norwich, begging him to consolidate the two Rectories, and the petition was granted August 1751; the united livings were stated to be worth £210 a year. But on 3 June 1793 an Act of Parliament was passed for the separation of the two Rectories, and for the building of a parsonage house at Trunch on the next vacancy of the Rectory.[1] A house had been built at Gimingham in 1788; the one at Trunch was completed in 1832, the College contributing £600.

On 16 December 1791 a Patronage Fund was founded. An Order was made that the surplus of College stock arising from time to time should be invested in 3 per cent. Consols, and allowed to accumulate by adding the interest to the principal continually.

£120 was to be paid annually to the Rector of Coton after the next avoidance of the Rectory, and £150 annually to Ridgewell after the next avoidance.

[1] The Act cost £325. 17*s*. 1*d*.

Junior Combination Room

Senior Combination Room

These purposes effected, in case of the capital of the fund proving sufficient, ecclesiastical preferments were to be bought for the Fellows of Mrs Ramsden's foundation, such preferments to be more than twenty miles from Cambridge, while not more than £2500 was to be expended on any one of them.

At the time of the Order the 3 per cent. Consols already purchased amounted to £5424. 3*s.* 8*d.* It was allowed to accumulate under the name of the Patronage Fund until 1818, when the amount of stock was £12,225. 8*s.* 4*d.* Upon the occasion of the appeal of Wood and Burrell, the Lord Chancellor directed (15 September 1802) that the College should prepare a statement from what fund and estates the Patronage Fund had arisen, and to what purpose it was applicable and under what authority it was conceived to be applicable to such purpose. The Master in Chancery, Mr Campbell, approved of the plan in his report of 1807, but submitted to the Lord Chancellor the difficulty caused by Mrs Ramsden's Rule XXVII, which gives directions for the use of surplus funds from the Ramsden estates. In his final decree of 8 August 1807 the Lord Chancellor gave no directions about the Patronage Fund.

In the next year the College sought legal opinion from Mr John Bell, who decided that the fund could not consistently with Rule XXVII be used for purposes of ecclesiastical patronage, and dissuaded the College from applying to the Court of Chancery for any sanction.

The fund was afterwards applied to the rebuilding of the Bull Inn, for buying property in Silver Street and Queens' Lane, and for other general purposes.

This move of the College was sound in principle, and it was unfortunate that the will of Mrs Ramsden would not permit of it. One of the most crying needs of the College has always been a means of securing a rapid succession of Fellows. In the days when most of the Society were in orders no better method could be devised of securing this end than plenty of good College livings.

Mr Burrell, who all his life was a staunch supporter of sound College finance, willed that his own property should be given to the Patronage Fund, and on his death in 1843 the College received a net sum of £7662. 15*s.* 0*d.* This was allowed to accumulate until the Patronage Fund was able to purchase the advowsons of Marnhull (1873), Newent (1874) and Little Shelford (1879). The first two were sold at the time of the recent Commission, in order to provide capital for a pension scheme; the last is still owned by the College.

COLLEGE RETAINERS

Most Colleges gather round them a body of craftsmen and small traders who, without being actually on the staff of servants, nevertheless derive most of their livelihood from the College custom. Throughout the period covered by the record books copious evidence appears that the relations between employer and employed were usually[1] happy and even affectionate, especially so in the case of these irregular servants. An odd word or phrase, prettily out of keeping with its arid environment of business details, impresses forcibly yet favourably even the casual reader. One is almost compelled to believe that nicknames, with all the kindly feelings that they generally imply, are not unknown to the Bursar's accounts. It may perhaps be a mere coincidence that "Goody Sparks" provides sedge for lighting the Hall fire, but even a sceptic wavers when he reads that in the year 1626–7 the sum of ten pence was paid to "Vulcan ye Smith for ye Jacke dressing". In the eighteenth century the books of account begin to be more formal, as well as more condensed, but the accounts of the seventeenth century contain what we should call "petty cash" items which are picturesque and attractive. The Sparks, or Sparkes, family flourished in the two decades 1660–1680, and probably lived in a house adjoining, or near to, the College buildings, as the Sadler family certainly did a generation earlier. Goody Sparks was given "above wages" an extra sum in 1675–6 and in 1676–7, and in 1674–5 two and sixpence "for ye Lodgings". Shortly afterwards a Tutor charges D^{s} Norris "0 : 1 : 6" paid to "Sparks for sitting up wth him" when sick, and later "0 : 3 : 0" was paid, apparently to Sparks, for the same service. Sparks was paid "0 : 3 : 6" by the Tutor "for a cap", which he probably took over from a departing Bachelor of Arts. We find mention of this couple in 1684, when the Tutor notes: "pd old good

[1] The sole evidence for unpleasantness occurs in the Audit Book: "it appears also yt Christopher Green (who was ye Cooke ye first halfe yeare) and Joseph Spenet have receivd full satisfaction both for Commons and wages for this yeare ending Michaelmas 1656". This comes after a statement that the Brewer had refused, it is claimed unreasonably, to give a general acquittance.

Sparks 0–15–0"; "pd old G Sparks 0–9–6"; "paid widd Sparks 0–13–0"; with a final entry in 1685: "pd old G Sparks 0–9–6".

The Sadler family lived in what is often called "Sadler's house" in the Audit Book. The father did various work for the College, and received "00. 15. 06" in 1637–8 for help in the "sicknesse tyme". Six shillings were given him "in his sickness" during the year 1658–59, and in the same year ten shillings to "Sadler's daughter by Consent". Doubtless the old man had died in the interval.

A similar tale is told by a series of items in the Audits of a slightly later date, which are best given as they stand without any comment:

1677–8	To ye Skull for scouring	0.	1.	0
	To hir for cloaths	0.	2.	6.
	Sent Mary ye Skull w^{n} sick	0.	3.	0.
1678–9	To ye Skull for dishcloaths	00.	02.	06.
1681–2	Given Mary ye old Scull	0.	2.	6.
1683–4	To Mary ye old Scull	0.	2.	6.
	To Mary ye old Scull	0.	1.	0.
	To ye old sculls buriall	0.	10.	0.

COLLEGE CHARITIES

Colleges are legally and in fact charities, and from the first there must have been considerable sums of College money given away to worthy causes or to persons in distress, although the earliest recorded instances are in the Audit Books. When the relief of poverty was much less organised than it is to-day, and public authorities took little account of suffering and hardship, more calls came to the charitably-minded, while after the Reformation it fell to colleges and similar institutions to carry on the work hitherto performed by religious houses. Some payments are donations, like the one in the accounts for 1632–3 for the building of Pauls 6. 6. 8.

Other payments are merely extra wages, as when (1651–2) two shillings and six pence is the sum given "for Xtmas boxes to ye women". Occasionally it appears that the College subscribed to a more or less organised effort, but in the following list no mention is made of rates, taxes, and other obligatory payments, unless they happen to be in some way interesting or instructive.

The number of entries varies considerably in the different years. The reason may be in some cases the carelessness of the Bursar, for the accounts appear sometimes to be incomplete, while in others small payments are grouped together or even concealed in sums entered under other heads. But there can be no doubt that there were waves of charitable feeling. In particular, the second half of the seventeenth century is a period when kindly gratuities were numerous and, it is to be feared, somewhat indiscriminate. Dr Eachard seems to have been unable to resist a piteous appeal, and the Bursar of the day often notes, apparently with tacit disapproval and certainly disclaiming all responsibility, that such and such a sum was given "in my absence".

It will be necessary to give a full, though not a complete list of these alms, in order to illustrate the liberal interpretation put by the College on its duties as a charitable institution.

1625–6	To the blind scholler of St. Johns Colledge	0.	3.	0
	To a poore ffellow for a days work in ye garden, and filling ye vaulte in ye garden with earth	0.	1.	3
1626–7	Given ye blind scholler by ye Agreement of ye heads	0.	3.	0

		£	s.	d.
1627–8	To ye blind schollar of St. Johns	0.	3.	0
	To a schollar of ye palatinate taken by ye French on his way to England	0.	2.	0
1628–9	Given to poore people at sev: times	1.	7.	8½
1629–30	Given to severall poore people and towards the releife of ye visited in tyme of ye plague	4.	6.	9
1632–3	Given to the town of Newport burnt to the ground the breife of which Mr Buck brought and commended to us	1.	0.	0
1638–9	Given by the appointment of the Mr towards the repairing of Winterton Church in Norfolke	2.	0.	0
1641–2	payd for the two ffellows of Dublin Col: maintenance for the first halfe yeare, according to the rate of the Colledge in Consistorie	0.	15.	0
	To the towne poore in the plague time after the Colledge rate	1.	0.	0
1644–5	To the Butler's boy att Christmas	0.	1.	0
1645–6	To Holden for the visited one moneths rate for the poore	0.	1.	0
1648–9	A contribution to Strangewayes	0.	1.	6
	Given towards ye Cure of the distracted Batchelor of Arts of St. John's	0.	5.	0
1649–50	To a Grecian	0.	5.	0
	To ye poore for ye whole yeare	6.	0.	10
1650–1	given by consent to a poore schollar, pris'ner in towne	0.	6.	0
	Theologo Bohemiensi	0.	2.	0
1652–3	To a poore man in prison	0.	8.	0
	To a poore schollar	0.	2.	0
	To a poore minister	0.	1.	0
	To a Christian Jew	0.	2.	0
	To a poore woman and a poore man	0.	1.	6
	To a poore minister	0.	2.	6
	To a Russian	0.	1.	0
	To a poore minister	0.	5.	0
	To a poore woman	0.	1.	6
1654–5	To a distressed minister	0.	2.	6
1655–6	Towards building Pesthouses by Order of ye Consistory	0.	16.	0
1657–8	To a Norwegian by Order	0.	4.	0
1658–9	To Sadler in his sickness	0.	6.	0
	To Sadler's daughter by Consent	0.	10.	0
1659–60	Given by Mr Eachard in my absence	0.	5.	0

1660–1	Given to Mr Lisle once fellow of Kings Colledg	0.	5.	0
	To a poore distressed Travailer	0.	1.	0
	Given at another time in my absence by Mr Eachard	0.	7.	4
	To a poore Irish Gentlewoman	0.	2.	0
	To a poore blinde Gentlewoman	0.	5.	0
	As also to a poore Scholar	0.	2.	0
	Given to two poore Travailers	0.	2.	0
	To one Mr Fitch a distressed Minister	0.	3.	0
	To a company of seamen who had loste theire vesselle	0.	2.	0
	To Shagnussi an Irish Scholar by consent	0.	8.	0
	To Spinosa an Italian by consent	0.	8.	0
	Given to Mr Hawkins newly returnd from banishnt	0.	5.	0
	Given by Mr Bruning to a converted Jew	0.	10.	0
	Given by him to Rhodocranacis ye Grecian Alchymist	0.	16.	0
1661–2	To a poore man newly come from Algeirs	0.	1.	0
	To Amodeus by Consent	0.	2.	6
	Given by Mr Eachard to peticioners in my absence in Michaelmas term	0.	10.	6
	To ye Lithuanian Protestants by Order of ye Consistory	0.	15.	0
	To Abendana for his booke by ye Master	1.	10.	0
	To a carpenter of St. Andrew's Parish fallen lame	0.	2.	0
	To Lieftenant Collonel Duncan	0.	2.	6
	To one Capn Roan recom̃ended by Mr Thomas Buck	0.	5.	0
	To Mr Sclavergni a Polonian Scholar recom̃ended	0.	5.	0
	To one Mr Grey once Fellow-Com̃oner of Trinity Colledg	0.	5.	0
1662–3	To 2 poore men Travailing Northward	0.	1.	0
	Given by Mr Eachard to Peticioners in my absence in Michaelmas Term	0.	13.	6
1663–4	To Monsieur Adams a Lithuanian recom̃ended by ye Vice-Chancellor	0.	5.	0
	To Samareus an Hungarian by consent	0.	5.	0
1664–5	To Abendana for his yeares pension	2.	0.	0
	Given by Mr Eachard in my absence in Trinity Term	0.	5.	6
1667–8	Lieftenant Coll. Ryly recom̃ended from ye General	0.	7.	6
	To a poore woman	0.	0.	6
	Given by Mr Eachard to an Ipswich Stationer	0.	10.	0
1668–9	By Mr Eachard to an Hungarian	0.	5.	0
	By him to a Seaman	0.	0.	6

		£	s.	d.
1668–9	By him to a Norfolk Minister	0.	5.	0
	by Mr Eachard to a Minister	0.	2.	6
	Given by Mr Eachard to 3 widdows	0.	3.	0
	Given by Mr Eachard to one of Chesterton	0.	2.	6
	By him to a divine Recom̄ended	0.	4.	0
1669–70	To Abendana by Order	1.	0.	0
	Given by Mr Eachard in my absence			
	To one Recom̄ended	0.	10.	0
	To an Algeirs prisoner	0.	2.	6
	To 2 Turky women	0.	2.	0
	To another	0.	1.	0
1670–1	To a Dominican friar	0.	10.	0
	To a German	0.	5.	0
	Given to Oxford fire	0.	16.	0
1675–6	To Abendana	0.	10.	0
	To an Archbishop	1.	0.	0
	To a Transylvanian	0.	4.	0
1676–7	To 3 polonians	0.	9.	0
	To a Schoolemaster	0.	5.	0
	To old Battee	0.	5.	0
	To ye Hungarians Briefe	2.	0.	0
1677–8	Sent Mary ye Scull wn sick	0.	3.	0
1678–9	To redeem a Captive	1.	0.	0
	To a Traveller	0.	1.	0
	To Fabricius Heydleburgh Professor	0.	15.	0
	To a Scotch Gentleman	0.	2.	6
	By myself to travellers and others in small sums	0.	10.	10
1679–80	To Prisoners Seamen Souldiers and other petitioners	0.	17.	0
	To a Polonian	0.	5.	0
	To a Rhoetian Traveller	0.	1.	0
	To a Fire at Dereham in Norfolk by ye Mr.	1.	10.	0
1680–1	To 2 Shipwrackt Dutchmen	0.	1.	6
	To James Gowre A seaman Shipwrackt	0.	2.	0
	Given by the Master to Petitioners	0.	17.	6
	To Lieutenant Dowse A Petit.	0.	4.	0
	To a Converted Turke	0.	2.	6
1681–2	To Two Decayed Souldiers	0.	2.	0
	To Prisoners in ye Tolboth	0.	2.	6

1682–3	Prisoners, widdows soldiers & other Petitioners	1.	1.	0
	To a Polonian	0.	10.	0
	To Newmarket after the fire there	2.	10.	0
1683–4	To a Polonian recom̃ended by ye King	0.	10.	0
	To Ely fire recommended by ye Heads	1.	1.	6
	To a widow	0.	0.	6
	To captive seamen	0.	1.	0
	To 2 souldiers widowes	0.	0.	4
	To a petitioner from Kent for fire	0.	1.	0
	To a poor widow to bind out her son apprentice	0.	2.	6
	By Mr Gouge in my absence			
	To ye old sculls buriall	0.	10.	0
	To 3 Tangier souldiers	0.	1.	0
1684–5	Giv'n at times to soldiers seamen Widdows Forreigners & other petitioners	3.	8.	0
1685–6	Given to the Brief for French Protestants	5.	0.	0
	To one Campion a broken Tradesman of this Towne	0.	5.	0
	To Wm Bradwell formerly a workeman in ye new building	0.	2.	6
	To a French Protestant & to a French Count	0.	5.	6
	To Mr Jenkins a Clergyman a great sufferer by the Western Rebells	0.	5.	0
	To sufferers by fire at Sawson	0.	5.	0
	at Trumpington	0.	2.	6
	at Exne	0.	2.	6
1688–9	Given by the Master to charitable uses	2.	18.	6
	To people burnt out at Barton	0.	2.	0
1689–90	Binding a poor boy apprentice	0.	2.	6
	To a prisoner a Widdow	0.	1.	0
	To a man in ye Isle of Ely ruined by water	0.	5.	0
	To a poor housekeeper	0.	2.	6
	To Capt. Crow recommended of Coll. Cutts	0.	2.	6
	Given to people ruined by fire	0.	4.	6
1691–2	Given to ye ransom of two gentlemen in Tunis	0.	5.	0
1693–4	To a labourer of ye colledge faln sick	0.	0.	6
1694–5	Given to Stretham fire	2.	0.	0
1696–7	To Mr Parker formerly of Imannuel Coll. in great difficulty	0.	15.	0
	To a poor blind maid under Cure	0.	1.	0
1698–9	fire at Ickleton	1.	2.	0

After this year for a considerable period few or no charities are recorded in the accounts. Perhaps the College authorities wished to economise, owing to the heavy drain on their resources caused by the new building-scheme carried out by Dr Eachard, whose death occurred on 7 July 1697. Possibly too there now occurred a reaction from the eager generosity (often at other people's expense) of the late Master. By 1728, however, credit balances were piling up, and in the year 1743–4 the sum of five guineas is given to the Vice-Chancellor for the Society for the Propagation of the Gospel. It is noteworthy, and regrettable, that these balances were in part due to vacant Fellowships and vacant Scholarships. On the other hand, the Fellows did not fail to refresh themselves on the following occasions:

1744–5	Spent in ye Combination on receiving ye News of Mrs Ramsden's Legacy	0.	6.	0
1745–6	April 25 Spent on receiving ye News of ye Dukes Victory at Culloden...over ye Rebels	0.	11.	0
1746–7	April 16 Anniversary of ye Battle of Culloden	0.	5.	0
	On receiving ye news of Admiral Anson's Victory at sea	0.	5.	0

In the same year the stream of charity began to flow afresh. For we find:

	Given to ye sufferers by loss of Cattle at Cottenham	1.	1.	0
1747–8	Giv'n to Hattley who broke his arm in whitewashing ye Combin.	1.	1.	0
	Giv'n to Evangelista Palermo Convert from Popery	1.	1.	0
	Allow'd ye Porter...Coals	1.	10.	0
1748–9	Givn to Mrs Ivatt on ye account of her Loss of Cattle	1.	1.	0
1755–6	To the University of Dobritzon in Hungary	2.	2.	0
1756–7	To bricklayer on laying ye Foundation of the New Building July 1st	1.	1.	0
1757–8	A clergyman's Widow in Distress	2.	2.	0
1759–60	To the British Forces in Germany	6.	6.	0
1762–3	To the Colleges in America	3.	3.	0
1764–5	To Ale given to Persons assisting in extinguishing the Fire at Barton	4.	4.	0

One would think that the ale was plentiful enough to extinguish the fire. Later the items in the Bursar's accounts are often grouped together, and the picturesque details, so characteristic of the seventeenth-century accounts, are fewer, but there are no general headings, such as "donations" or "gifts".

1782–3	Paid for a Member of the College in Distress	31.	17.	0
1784–5	To the sufferers by Fire at Biggleswade	3.	3.	0
	To Do. at Chesterford	1.	1.	0
1787–8	To Petitioning Parliamt. for the Abolition of the Slave-Trade	2.	2.	0
	To the Sufferers by Fire at Foxton	3.	3.	0
	To Widow Fairchild in Distress	1.	1.	0
1788–9	To the poor Sufferers by Fire at Ikleton	2.	2.	0
1796–7	Gave to the Widows of the Seamen kill'd in the engagemt with the Dutch Fleet off the Texel	4.	4.	0
1797–8	As a voluntary contribution to Governmt	100.	0.	0
	To Mr Salmon's Children	2.	2.	0
1807–8	An aged & distressed Clergyman incapable of doing Duty	5.	0.	0
1812–13	Subscription for relief of Russians	26.	5.	0
1821–2	For the relief of the distressed Irish	10.	10.	0
	Widow & 10 chn. of the Revd. Th. Halwen a late Member of this College	10.	0.	0
	Widow & 9 chn. of the Revd. Postlethwaite	5.	5.	0
1826–7	Clergyman's Widow and 10 children	10.	10.	0
1829–30	The Widow and Children of the Revd. Abbott a late Member of this College	21.	0.	0
1830–1	The Sufferers by Fire at Willingham	5.	0.	0
1831–2	The Widow of the late undertenant at Braintree being in great distress	10.	0.	0
1832–3	for the Relief of the Irish Clergy	25.	0.	0
1837–8	Society for building Churches in London	105.	0.	0
	to a Poor man at Coton	1.	0.	0
1840–1	to the Rev Johnson in illness	5.	0.	0

After this the charitable payments are subscriptions of the modern type, e.g. £100 "for a Cemetery at Cambridge" in 1844–5.

VARIOUS

There are given here a few items that cannot find a place elsewhere.

Insurance appears first in the accounts for 1803–4; the premium was greatly increased in 1812–13. "News" appears as an item in 1766–7, and "The Star" and "Camb. Chron." were bought in 1799–1800. Gas first appears in the accounts for 1825–6. It cannot be discovered when the College adopted town drainage and town water. It was probably in the 'sixties in both cases. Electric light in the Chapel and Hall was pre-War. The extension to the whole College took place in 1919.

The portraits acquired since G. F. Browne drew up his list are:

Bishop Philpott
Dr Johns
Bishop Drury
Mr F. M. Rushmore
Bishop G. F. Browne
Sir Norman Moore
Dr Robinson (print)

There are three stained-glass windows in the Chapel:

(1) given by Alfred Pretor in memory of his mother, 1899;
(2) given by the Rev. A. O. M. Jay in memory of his father, 1913;
(3) War-Memorial window, 1923.

Chapter III

BIOGRAPHICAL

Only distinguished members of the College, and no living persons, are included in this list.

ADDENBROOKE, JOHN. There were three of this name, one who entered in 1671, the second, was the founder of the Cambridge hospital, and a third (B.A. 1711–12, M.A. 1714–15, Fellow 1716). Only the second is deserving of a place here. He was admitted a Pensioner 13 December 1697 and was a Scholar 1702–4, being elected Fellow in 1704. He took the degree of Doctor of Physic 1710–11, and disappears from the list of Fellows 1711–12. A pioneer of the science school at Cambridge, he left his books and cabinet to St Catharine's. The great hospital is his best and greatest memorial. An interesting point in his career is that prior to 1860 he is the only Fellow to take the medical course at Cambridge. The Founder permitted his Fellows to study (for a degree) only philosophy and sacred theology; the Edwardian statutes added "the Arts", not till 1860 was it strictly legal for a Fellow to study medicine. It is perhaps significant that Addenbrooke ceased to be a Fellow in the year following his taking the degree of M.D. There is an unpublished life of this Addenbrooke by Dr A. W. Langford, which was submitted as a thesis for the Cambridge M.D. An instalment from it appears in the St Catharine's Society *Magazine* for 1935.

ARROWSMITH, JOHN, graduated at St John's in 1619. He became Fellow of St Catharine's in 1623 and vacated his Fellowship in 1631. Regius Professor of Divinity and Master of St John's in 1644, he became Master of Trinity in 1653. He died in 1659. A staunch Puritan and an able divine.

BACON, NATHANIEL, of Friston Hall, Suffolk, entered Fellow Commoner in 1660. He settled as a colonist in Virginia, and espoused the cause of those settlers who suffered from the ravages of the Indians. Considering that the Governor was slack, he begged for a commission. Failing to get one, he fought against the Indians as a volunteer. Arrested for this, he apologised and was granted a commission, which was not signed. Hearing that he was about to be arrested again, he made war on the Governor, gaining many successes, but died of dysentery 26 October 1676. There is a sympathetic account of this "Virginian Hampden" in Browne, pp. 126–128.

BAINBRIGGE, REGINALD, was a native of Westmorland and a Fellow of the College; he was Proctor in 1516. He held a number of ecclesiastical appointments, being Rector of Downham and of Stambourne, Vicar of Bricklesea and of Steeple Bumpstead, Prebendary of Wells and Rector of Great Oakley. Master of St Catharine's from 1529 to 1547.

BALDERSTONE, RICHARD, was Master from 1506 to 1507. His serving the office of Proctor in 1501 is the earliest evidence that St Catharine's was acknowledged as a constituent part of the University. He was Rector of Coton in 1505.

BANCROFT, THOMAS, was at St Catharine's with Shirley. Like the latter he was a poet of some note, who composed chiefly epigrams and other short pieces. He died about 1660.

BECKETT, HENRY FREDERICK, B.A. 1840, was ordained in 1840, and after holding curacies at Aston, near Birmingham, and elsewhere set out in May 1867 to found a brotherhood in South Africa. He was the first canon of Bloemfontein (installed 8 September 1867). He died in 1885. "He did a great work, and the work he began, and the Mission he founded, is still a monument to his memory." [Letter from the Rev. Brother Carmichael, St Augustine's Priory, Modderpoort, O.F.S.] Beckett was one of many who have done pioneer work abroad but "have left no memorial" except that of their lives.

BLACKALL (BLACKHALL), OFFSPRING, entered as a Pensioner in 1670. He was elected in 1679 to a Fellowship, which he vacated in 1687. He was presented in 1708 to the bishopric of Exeter, and proved very active in promoting schools for poor people.

BLACKBURNE, FRANCIS, admitted 1722, was elected Conduct Fellow in 1728. Archdeacon of Cleveland in 1750, he proved to be latitudinarian, and scarcely an adherent of the Church of England. He urged in his book, *The*

Confessional, that the clergy ought to be required to profess only a belief in the Bible as the word of God. He was the leading spirit in the attempt (1771–2) to persuade Parliament to introduce legislation to free the clergy from the obligation to subscribe to the Thirty-nine Articles. He died in 1787.

BOND, JOHN, born 1612, was the son of an influential Parliamentarian, Dennis Bond. Entered 1628, B.A. 1631, Fellow 1634. In 1643 he became a member of the Assembly of Divines, and in 1645 succeeded to the Mastership of the Savoy. In the next year, when the Fellows of Trinity Hall had chosen Dr King as their Master, Parliament compelled them to elect Bond instead. Vice-chancellor in 1658, he lost his preferments at the Restoration and retired to the family seat in Dorsetshire, where he died in 1676.

BONNELL, JAMES (1653–1699), who entered in 1668, is interesting to all members of St Catharine's as the correspondent of Strype, his cousin and friend. He was a man of singular and sincere piety, "of whom the College may well be proud" (Browne). Much of his life was spent in Ireland as Accountant-General. He won a name for himself in this office, but wished to be ordained. He tried to find a substitute whom he could trust; failing in this he remained at his post. "He gave one-eighth of his income to the poor, and his probity was so highly esteemed that the fortunes of many orphans were committed to his care." (*D.N.B.*) His *Life* has been published by the Religious Tract Society.

BOYD CARPENTER, WILLIAM, was born in 1841 and took the B.A. degree in 1864. Ordained in the same year he rose rapidly in the Church until he was consecrated Bishop of Ripon, 25 July 1884. D.D. Cambridge 1884, hon. D.C.L. Oxford 1889, hon. D.D. Glasgow 1901. Honorary Fellow of St Catharine's 1887. A great favourite with Queen Victoria, he was appointed her Chaplain in 1883, "but his appointment to the See of Ripon was entirely the doing of Mr Gladstone. To the rest of the world he is known as quite unrivalled in his power of delivering, without note of any kind, long sermons and addresses, closely reasoned, most aptly illustrated, with unfaltering precision, and with a charm of manner which leaves in his hearers no sense of the flight of time" (Browne). For his sermon preached before the House of Commons on the occasion of the Jubilee of 1887 he received the thanks of the

House. He was the author of many religious and devotional works, including *Thoughts on Prayer*, 1871, *Narcissus*, 1879, *Witness of the Heart to Christ* (Hulsean Lectures), 1879, *My Bible*, 1884, *Permanent Elements of Religion* (Bampton Lectures), 1889, *Popular History of the Church of England*, 1900.

BRADFORD, JOHN, was born at Blackley, near Manchester, about 1515, and was educated at the Grammar School. In early adult life he was, according to his own view, addicted to vanities, but, converted by a sermon of Latimer's, he turned from frivolity to a serious life. Entering Catharine Hall in 1548 he was soon granted the degree of M.A. by a special Grace of the Senate, as a man of mature age and approved life, who for many years had been diligently employed in the study of literature and the Holy Scriptures. Very shortly afterwards he was elected Fellow of Pembroke Hall, owing to his influence with his friend Ridley, Bishop of Rochester and Master of Pembroke. In 1551 as Prebendary of St Paul's he made his mark by preaching against heresy and errors. Very soon after Queen Mary's accession he was brought before the Privy Council and committed to the Tower, where his companion was Dr Sandys, the late Master of St Catharine's. Finally he was burnt at Smithfield on 1 July 1555. See Browne's *St Catharine's College*, pp. 52–54 and C. R. Haines in the St Catharine's Society *Magazine* for September 1932.

BROWNE, GEORGE FORREST, graduated B.A. in 1856. He was Fellow from 1863 to 1865. Many times Proctor, he was also secretary to the Local Examinations Syndicate from 1870 to 1892 and to the University Commission of 1877–1881. Disney Professor of Archaeology from 1887 to 1892, he became Canon of St Paul's in 1891, Bishop of Stepney in 1895, and Bishop of Bristol in 1897. He was the author of many antiquarian and ecclesiastical books, and published in 1902 *St Catharine's College*. He died in 1930.

BROWNRIGGE, RALPH (1592–1659), was a Pembroke man who became Rector of Barley,[1] near Royston, and was elected to the Mastership in 1635, an office which he held until 1645, when, having preached a sermon before the University in favour of the Royalists, he was deprived. While Master he held high ecclesiastical preferment, and was appointed Bishop of Exeter in

[1] There is a monument to his wife in Barley church.

1641. He retired to Sonning in Berkshire, and in 1658, about a year before his death, went to live with the benchers of the Middle and Inner Temples. His sermons there were popular, but Browne says "they are immensely long, very full of matter, very keen in looking into all possible meanings of words of Scripture, very difficult reading". Brownrigge was highly praised by Fuller, who knew him personally, and by Lloyd in his *Memoires*. As Praevaricator or Jocoserius he delighted King James I on his visit to Cambridge by "luxuriancy of wit consistent with innocency".

BUCK (BUCKE), THOMAS, was elected Fellow 16 March 1615. He was one of the truest and most loyal sons of St Catharine, and an appreciation of his work as the business man of the College is given on pp. 13, 14.

BURRELL, CHARLES WILLIAM, was elected Fellow 3 April 1787. A brave and vigorous adherent of Procter when St Catharine's awoke out of its eighteenth-century lethargy, he supported the scheme of a Patronage Fund, at that period the only means available to secure the early retirement of Fellows, and to obviate in some way the dangerous consequences of greed and senile decay. When legal difficulties arose that rendered unworkable the original scheme, Burrell resolved that his own property should be devoted to this purpose. He died in 1843, and the net value of his estate was £7662. 15*s*. 0*d*. From the sum left to accumulate were purchased, forty years later, the livings of Marnhull and Newent.

CAESAR, SIR CHARLES, of Bennington, Herts, was one of the many of the Caesar family who entered the College as Fellow Commoners between 1667 and 1701. He bought much of the plate that went towards rebuilding the College. See pp. 248, 386.

CALAMY, BENJAMIN, entered as Pensioner in 1663, and from 1666 to 1674 was a most successful Tutor. He left the College in 1674, and, after various ecclesiastical preferments, became Canon of St Paul's in 1685. Calamy never recovered from the execution of his friend Henry Cornish on a charge of conspiracy. He died 7 January 1686.

CAPELL, EDWARD, entered St Catharine's about 1730. He published a ten-volume edition of Shakespeare in 1768 and a three-volume edition later, the last volume appearing in 1783, two years after his death. Two other members of the Capell family had entered St Catharine's in 1638. Edward Capell presented most of his valuable library to Trinity College.

CAPON, WILLIAM, graduated B.A. in 1499, and is fifteenth on the list of Fellows. He was Proctor in 1509, and Master of Jesus College in 1516. After holding various offices (he was Chaplain to Wolsey, Dean of Ipswich, Vicar of Barkway, Prebendary of Wells, Archdeacon of Anglesey, etc.) he resigned his Mastership in 1546 and died in 1550.

CARR, EDWIN TREVOR SEPTIMUS, entered Christ's as a Scholar in 1858. Graduating as eighth Classic in 1862, he became Fellow of St Catharine's in the same year. He was Tutor 1862–1892, and then retired to Little Shelford Rectory, where he died in 1929, after being Bursar for several years.

CHEVALLIER, TEMPLE, was a Pembroke man who played an important part in the revival of the College during the early part of the nineteenth century. A contemporary of Corrie, second Wrangler when Corrie was eighteenth (1817), Chevallier was also a distinguished classical scholar. Appointed Fellow and Tutor of St Catharine's soon after taking his degree, he was Hulsean Lecturer in 1826 and 1827. In 1835 he became Professor of Mathematics at Durham, and in 1841 Professor of Astronomy. He was made sub-warden of Durham University in 1846, and Canon of Durham in 1865. Interested in the natural sciences, he was one of the chief supporters of the movement that ended in the foundation of the Newcastle College of Science in 1871.

CORRIE, GEORGE ELWES (1792–1885), entered 1813, B.A. 1817, Norrisian Professor 1838, Master of Jesus College 1849–1885. Corrie was a very successful and popular Tutor, as is clear from the many letters addressed to him by his pupils and now in the possession of the College. Browne tells some delightful stories of his humour (*St Catharine's College*, pp. 221–3). When he became Master of Jesus College a number of old pupils established in St Catharine's a divinity prize as a memorial of their respect and affection, contributing £166. 6*s*. 4*d*. for that purpose. Corrie wrote much on theology and ecclesiastical history.

Cosyn, Edmund, was Master from 1554 to 1559. He was chosen in obedience to a letter, dated 13 January 1554, from Stephen Gardiner, the Chancellor, commanding the President and Fellows to choose "Mr Cosyn, a man for his wisdom and honest behaviour very meet for that Room", in place of Dr Sandys, who by reason of his marriage "contrary to the Ecclesiastical Laws and your Statutes" had made the office void. Fellow of King's since 1537, and one of the original Fellows of Trinity in 1546, Cosyn held many ecclesiastical appointments, chiefly in Norfolk. He was Vice-Chancellor in 1558, when a Grace was passed allowing him to be admitted to his office "in his own house, and there to take the oath and receive the Seal and the Keys, in the presence of Doctors Younge and Bullocke, the Proctors, Mr Hansop and Mr Hewater, by reason that on account of ill-health he dares not come forth".

When Elizabeth came to the throne he resigned his Mastership, his Vice-Chancellorship and his ecclesiastical appointments, and then retired to Caius. The Matriculation Book of that College says that "Edmund Cousen, born in Bedfordshire, 50 years of age, formerly Praefectus of St Catharine's Hall, was admitted into our College, November 20, 1561. He was assigned the first upper cubicle, and paid 7*s.* 4*d.* for his matriculation." Dr Venn says that he was still at Caius in August 1564. For some time after 1568 he lived abroad, being suspect on account of his religion. The date of his death is uncertain, perhaps 1576.

Cragge, John, is among the Bachelors of Arts in the Registry list of 1558. The business man of the College during the latter part of the sixteenth century, he appears to have initiated several interesting innovations in College policy and methods of finance. He built a "gallery", pulled down in 1611 to make room for the Claypoole Building.

Cromwell, Oliver, second son of the Protector, entered the College as a Pensioner in 1641. In 1642 he became a cornet in Lord St John's troop of horse, a unit of the Earl of Essex's army, in which his father was captain. He died of small-pox at Newport Pagnell in March 1644, at the age of twenty-one.

Plate XIII

Sir John Cutts

CROSSE, THOMAS, was Master from 1719 to 1736. Browne calls him a "useful man to the College and to the University". He gave to the College a property on the south-east side of the new buildings—the nucleus of Sherlock Court. As Vice-Chancellor in 1720 he laid the foundation of the Senate House—an ordeal to a timid man of Crosse's temperament.

CUTTS, SIR JOHN, entered Fellow Commoner in 1676, at the age of fifteen. A fearless soldier, he was also a man of literary tastes and scarcely deserves the sneer of Dean Swift:

"brave and brainless as the sword he wears".

He fought at the Boyne (1690), Steinkirk (1692), Namur (1695) where he was nicknamed "Salamander", Venloo (1702) and Blenheim (1704), where he was third in command.

DAWES, SIR WILLIAM, entered as a Fellow Commoner in 1689. Although under thirty he was elected Master by a royal dispensation in 1697, and proved an admirable Head. He was Vice-Chancellor in 1698, when he was only twenty-six. Bishop of Chester in 1707/8, he became Archbishop of York in 1713. Tory and High Church, he was not popular with everybody, but he won high praise from many critics, while he was considered the best preacher of his time. Cole praises him for his neat handwriting, the excellence of which is manifest in the College records. He died in 1724, aged fifty-three. There is a memorial to his wife in the Ante-chapel.

DEALTRY, THOMAS, the son of poor parents, matriculated in 1825, when he was thirty-one. He took a high degree in Law, was ordained, and worked for a time at Cambridge. In 1829 he went out to India, became Archdeacon of Calcutta in 1835 and was consecrated Bishop of Madras in 1849. He died in 1861.

DEALTRY, WILLIAM, entered St Catharine's in 1792. Migrating to Trinity, he was second Wrangler, second Smith's Prizeman and Fellow of Trinity.

DRURY, THOMAS WORTLEY, was a Christ's man who was ordained in 1871. He had a distinguished career as Principal of Ridley Hall, Bishop of Sodor and Man, and Bishop of Ripon. In 1920, when he was seventy-three years of age and living in retirement, he became the last Master to hold a canonry at Norwich. He exercised an invaluable influence on all sides of College life, not so much by what he actually did as by the spiritual force with which he inspired all those with whom he came into contact. There is an appreciation of his work for St Catharine's in *The Cambridge Review* for 19 February 1926, the year of his death.

DYKES, JOHN BACCHUS, 1823–1876, entered St Catharine's in 1843. He graduated in 1847, and helped to found the University Musical Society. He was a famous writer of Church music.

EACHARD, JOHN, was Master from 1675 to 1697, after a most successful Tutorship. He continued his tutorial duties after becoming Master. Under his vigorous leadership the rebuilding of the College, already begun by Lightfoot, was completed with the exception of the Chapel. A dull man and a casual manager of money affairs, he nevertheless performed a great service for the College. His first literary work was an examination of Mr Hobbes' *State of Nature*, published in 1672, his most famous was *Grounds and Occasions of the Contempt of the Clergy*. He was Vice-Chancellor in 1679 and 1695. His work, and his collection of letters, are fully illustrated by the extracts from his note-books printed in this volume.

ELLIS, JOHN, was pre-elected Fellow in 1631. Another Fellow of the same name was pre-elected in 1634. It was apparently the former who in 1647 published *Vindiciae Catholicae* in favour of Presbytery.

FIGGIS, JOHN NEVILLE, graduated B.A. in 1888. Deserting mathematics for history, he took a first in the Historical Tripos of 1889 and was Lightfoot Scholar (1890), Whewell Scholar (1891), and winner of the Prince Consort Prize (1892). After a period of work in Cambridge, during which he was sub-editor of Lord Acton's *Cambridge Modern History*, he was Rector of Marnhull 1901–1907. He published much valuable work in English and Church History and at last joined the Community of the Resurrection, Mirfield. Old members of the College remember his stimulating teaching. He was never a Fellow, but was elected to an Honorary Fellowship in 1909. He died in 1919.

FOSTER, WILLIAM, matriculated Sizar 14 March 1589. He became Vicar of Ridgewell in 1598, and D.D. by Royal Letters in 1617. In 1633 he became Bishop of Sodor and Man, but died in 1634. Browne has "Forster."

FURMARY, JOHN, was a Fellow, not otherwise noteworthy, who had a serious dispute with the Master (Hound), who declared his Fellowship vacant because of illegal absence. The case was a notorious one from 1580 to 1582. See p. 85.

GARNETT, HUGH, of Lonsdale in Lancashire, was Fellow in 1509 and dead by 1526. "He is the first Fellow who is recorded as a benefactor. His gifts comprised his lands, messuages, and moveable goods in Coton and elsewhere, a book for the Chapel, a silver piceum (piece of plate) of the value of four nobles (13*s.* 4*d.*, evidently a handsome piece) and 40*s.* in money. He was the prompt first-fruits of the Fellowship founded in 1503 by Richard Nelson, with preference to natives of Lonsdale." (G. F. Browne.)

GOODWIN, CHARLES WYCLIFFE, brother of Harvey Goodwin, Bishop of Carlisle, was a scholar of catholic tastes. Hebraist, botanist, geologist, with a sound knowledge of Coptic, Anglo-Saxon and German, he wrote on music and law, but was mainly interested in Egyptology. He made many contributions to the Cambridge Antiquarian Society. He lost his Fellowship in 1847 by not obeying the statute that there must always be three Fellows in Holy Orders, and that if the number of such Fellows fell short, the senior lay Fellow must take orders within a year. Goodwin maintained that as the statute ran *a Collegii emolumentis recedat*, without the addition of *et pro non-socio habeatur*, as in another statute, he regained his Fellowship by taking orders, merely losing his stipend from 10 November 1847 to 9 January 1848, the period during which the statute was not fulfilled. This appeal struck the Visitor (Lord Cottenham) as ingenious, but he decided that the Fellowship was vacant. Goodwin finally took up law, and in 1865 became Assistant-Judge at Shanghai. He returned to England in 1876 and died two years later.

GOODWIN, THOMAS (1600–1679), was educated at Christ's (B.A. 1616) and became a Fellow of St Catharine's 21 March 1619. In 1649 he became chaplain to the Council of State, and was for a long time a favourite of

Oliver Cromwell. He was made President of Magdalen College, Oxford, in 1650, and in the *Spectator* (no. 494) is an account of a terrifying interview with a would-be undergraduate, in which the latter was asked if he were ready to die. A dull, gloomy but able man, he wrote sermons and theological disquisitions published in twelve large octavo volumes. There is a good account of him by C. R. Haines in the St Catharine's Society *Magazine* for 1935.

GREENE, THOMAS, was Master from 1507 to 1529. He was our first Vice-Chancellor (1523) and in 1514 helped to settle the cycle for the appointment of Proctors. A range of chambers facing Queens' Lane was named after him.

HAGGERSTONE, CUTHBERT, was a Fellow of St Catharine's at the time of the dispute about the Proctorship in 1542. It was alleged that Edwin Sandys, Fellow of St John's, had given Haggerstone £2. 13*s.* 4*d.* to induce him to resign from his Proctorship.

HAINES, CHARLES REGINALD, graduated 14th Classic in 1880. After a distinguished academic career he held assistant masterships at Dover College and Uppingham School. A distinguished author and translator, he received the degree of D.D. in 1930 and died in 1935.

HARDWICK, CHARLES, entered St Catharine's in 1840, was first Senior Optime in 1844 and was elected Skerne Fellow in 1845, holding this position until his death in 1859. An historian and antiquarian, with a fondness for Church antiquities, he edited or published many works dealing with this subject, and in 1850 was elected Christian Advocate on Hulse's Foundation, an office converted by the 1860 Statutes into the Hulsean Professor of Divinity. In this capacity he wrote *Christ and other Masters*. He was also the author of a History of the Articles. He became Chaplain to the College and a member of the first Council of the Senate. In 1859 he was made Archdeacon of Ely, but died in the same year as the result of an accident in the Pyrenees. He showed to the undergraduates of his period "a pleasant courtesy, not the less acceptable to young men because rather prim" (Browne).

HEY, JOHN, entered Pensioner 1750–1, graduated eighth Wrangler 1755, elected conduct Fellow in 1757 and became Tutor of Sidney Sussex in 1760. He was the first Norrisian Professor of Divinity (1780), being re-elected in 1785 and 1790. He died in 1815.

HICKMAN, HENRY, after graduating at St Catharine's, migrated to Magdalen, Oxford, in 1647, of which college he was made a Fellow by the Parliamentary Visitors. At the Restoration he was ejected and then went to live at Leyden. He was a keen controversialist in favour of Nonconformity, combating among others Scrivener and Ellis, both members of his old College.

HILLS, JOHN, was Master from 1607 to 1626. Born at Fulbourn, he was buried at Horseheath. His Mastership was not a happy one, as he was at variance with the Fellows both in domestic and in political matters.

HOADLY, BENJAMIN (1676–1761), was one of the most celebrated of the many ecclesiastics educated at St Catharine's. Third Wrangler 1696, Fellow 1697, Tutor 1699, Bishop of Bangor 1716, Bishop of Hereford 1721, Bishop of Salisbury 1723, Bishop of Winchester 1734—such were the main incidents in a varied career. In 1717 he preached a sermon the name of which was the *Nature of the Kingdom or Church of Christ*. This was answered by the Provost of Eton, and thus began the famous Bangorian controversy. Into this all varieties of Churchmen and Latitudinarians were drawn, and an attack was made by Hoadly on Sherlock.

HOADLY, JOHN, the younger brother of Benjamin, graduated at St Catharine's in 1697. After work in Norwich Grammar School and as Archdeacon of Salisbury he became in 1727 Bishop of Leighlin and Innis, and Archbishop of Dublin in 1729. He died in 1746, after giving excellent service to his adopted country and showing himself a much more attractive man than his more famous brother.

HOUND (HOWND), EDMUND, was never a Fellow of St Catharine's, but his Mastership covered the period 1577–1598. He was admitted Fellow Commoner at Caius on 14 June 1568, and passed from this College to our Mastership. After stormy quarrels with the Fellows, in which the historian is often in doubt on which side, if either, justice lay, he became Rector of Symondsbury in Dorset, where he died in 1597/8. He left the College a legacy of £100.

HUBBARD, EDWARD, was Master from 1736 to 1741. On 4 July 1719 his Fellowship was declared vacant because he had brought no certificate of taking the oath to the King, but two days later he was re-elected. He was Vice-Chancellor in 1739. Cole knew him well, and calls him a "worthy and amiable character, mild, placid and serene". A modest and retiring man, he never married. He was buried in Norwich Cathedral, and left the College a legacy of £40.

HUTCHINSON, FRANCIS, entered St Catharine's in 1678 and died in 1739. Ordained in 1680, he became Bishop of Down and Connor in 1721. He was a voluminous author, publishing, besides sermons, at least nineteen other works.

JARRETT, THOMAS (1805–1882), graduated as thirty-fourth Wrangler in 1827 and was seventh in the Classical Tripos. After being Fellow and Classical Lecturer for a few years, he was presented to the College living of Trunch, where he died in 1882. A very skilful linguist, he was at different periods of his life Professor of Arabic and Regius Professor of Hebrew, which latter office was then united to a canonry at Ely. His really remarkable powers were dissipated by his versatility and lack of concentration. He was a benefactor of the College, leaving to it all his library.

JEFFERY, JOHN, graduated in 1668; (a second John Jeffery became Fellow in 1704). He worked in Norwich at St Peter Mancroft, and Tillotson, Archbishop of Canterbury, made him Archdeacon of Norwich in 1694, by virtue of the old right by which any Archbishop could name one cleric to be provided for by any bishop whom he had consecrated. Jeffery was a friend of his fellow-townsman, Sir Thomas Browne, and died in 1720.

JOHNS, CLAUDE HERMANN WALTER, was Master from 1909 to 1920. He had been a Fellow of Queens', and at the time of his election was Fellow of Jesus. A mathematician by education, he was an Assyriologist by inclination, and was in the front rank of scholars in this study. To him fell the task of wakening the College out of the stupor into which it had sunk after the Robinson episode. The strain proved too great; he broke down and died in 1920.

KNIGHT, HENRY JOSEPH CORBETT, graduated as tenth Classic in 1882. After a very distinguished academic career he was Tutor of Selwyn College (1885–1895). From 1895 to 1901 he was Rector of Marnhull, and then became Fellow of Corpus Christi and Principal of the Clergy Training School. Afterwards he was Bishop of Gibraltar, and died in 1920.

KNOWLES, JOHN, was in 1627 elected Fellow from Magdalene, and had as his colleagues a famous body of divines. He had a stormy career, chiefly owing to his Puritan opinions. An opponent of Laud, after reprimands and threats, he was finally deprived of his licence. He went in 1639 to New England, but was debarred from preaching on the ground that he would neither wear a surplice nor use the Book of Common Prayer. On his return, when he found forty-seven of his old St Catharine's pupils either members of Parliament or members of the Assembly of Divines, he was made Lecturer in Bristol Cathedral, where he aroused much opposition among the Quakers. At the Restoration he lost this appointment, and subsequently under the Act of Uniformity a lectureship at All Hallows the Great. He showed his humanity and courage by his services during the great plague of 1665. He died in 1685.

LENG, JOHN (1665–1727), having joined the College as Sizar in 1682, became Fellow in 1688 and Bishop of Norwich in 1723. He died of smallpox in 1727. He was an excellent scholar and a popular Tutor, preaching the sermon at the consecration of the Chapel. He published editions of the *Clouds* and *Plutus* of Aristophanes in 1695, and of Terence in 1701. He also published fourteen of his sermons.

LIGHTFOOT, JOHN, was Master from 1650 to 1675. He entered Christ's in 1617, and was considered the best orator of his generation. In 1642 he became a member of the Assembly of Divines, and in 1643 Rector of Much Munden, Herts, which he loved greatly. He was Vice-Chancellor in 1654–5, but "begged to be excused". He began the rebuilding of the College in 1673.

Philpott had a poor opinion of his fitness for the Mastership—perhaps because of his studious character and love of his country living—but when he offered at the Restoration to retire in favour of his extruded predecessor the Fellows, only one of whom was left of the intruded Fellows of 1650, met and re-elected him. Lightfoot was author of *Horae Hebraicae*, dedicated to students of Catharine Hall (*Catharinenses mei*) and, in whole or in part, of many other learned works.

LOTHIAN, JOHN, was elected Fellow by Royal Mandate of James I on 30 March 1622, on the same day as Jeremiah Gray and Andrew Perne. He was senior Fellow when the curious incident occurred, in which he was himself deeply involved, that resulted ultimately in the admission of Dr Brownrigge to the Mastership in 1635. As a Scotsman he naturally wished his countryman, Crichton, Public Orator, to secure the Mastership, but adopted secretive and dubious methods, which were unsuccessful, in order to realise his wish.

LUMBY, JOSEPH RAWSON, was a Magdalene man who graduated in 1858, obtaining a First in the Classical Tripos. A man of most varied accomplishments, he became Professorial Fellow in 1881, having been elected Norrisian Professor of Divinity in 1879. He was elected Lady Margaret Professor of Divinity in 1892. He was one of the Revisers of the Old Testament Version, and did much work for the Master of the Rolls. "On one occasion he was suddenly asked in the Combination Room, 'Lumby, what's the price of a second-hand wooden-leg?' 'Ten-and-six. Brass-tipped, twelve-and-six.' The inquirer went to the hospital the next day to test the accuracy of the answer, and was told it was curious he should ask the question, for Dr Lumby had only a few days before got one for an old parishioner.

"Physically, Dr Lumby was a man of remarkable power of muscle. He could do almost what he liked with pokers, breaking them if they would break, and winding them round his arm if they would not." (G. F. Browne.)

MAPLETT, JOHN, of Bury in Suffolk, published a book in black letter on natural history as a means of discovering God. This was in 1559. He was the sixty-third Fellow of the College. Another Maplett, Edward, also of Suffolk, was seventy-fourth Fellow.

MASKELYNE, NEVIL, entered St Catharine's in 1749, but migrated to Trinity. Seventh Wrangler in 1754 and Fellow of Trinity in 1757, he became Astronomer-Royal in 1765. He died in 1811.

MEY, JOHN, was Master from 1559 to 1577. His brother, William Mey, was one of the Commissioners of Edward VI. John was Vice-Chancellor in 1569 and became Canon of Ely in 1564. In 1577 (29 September) he became Bishop of Carlisle, in which office he died, 1598.

MILLS (MILLES), DANIEL, intruded Commonwealth Fellow 1650–1656. He left a register, carried on by other members of the College, giving e.g. lists of Masters and Fellows, with brief characterisations of the former, written in Latin, with the admissions for a few years down to his own time. This is a useful book, but scarcely worthy of the enthusiastic praise bestowed upon it by Browne. Excerpts from the descriptions of the Masters are given on pp. xiii and xiv.

MILNER, JOSEPH, Second Chancellor's Medalist in 1766, became a schoolmaster when he failed to get a Fellowship, and helped his brother Isaac (the Milners were very poor) to come up to Cambridge in 1770, where he was Senior Wrangler and ultimately President of Queens'. He published many works, including a *Church History*.

MOORE, EDWARD, Fellow and Priest of the Chantry of William Myles, obtained in 1537 leave of absence to hold his Fellowship and Chantry "for three years or four at most" while he studied abroad.

MOORE, SIR NORMAN, resided 1865–8. M.D. 1876; Hon. LL.D. (Cambridge) 1920. He was Harveian Orator, 1901; Physician to St Bartholomew's Hospital, London, and Lecturer on the Principles and Practice of Medicine; Representative of Royal College of Physicians in General Medical Council. Author: *Pathological Anatomy of Disease*, 1889; *Distribution and Duration of Visceral New Growths*, 1889; *History of Medicine as illustrated in English Literature*, 1903; *The Presidents of the Royal Medical and Chirurgical Society, 1805–1905*; *Life of Charles Waterton*, 1870; translations of Windisches' *Irish Grammar*; *The Loss of the Crown of Loeghaire*, Text and translation; many lives in *National Dictionary of Biography*; *Fitzpatrick Lectures on History of Medicine*. He died 30 Nov. 1922.

MOULE, HANDLEY CARR GLYN, was Professorial Fellow from 1899 to 1901. He had a distinguished career at Trinity and as Principal of Ridley Hall before becoming Norrisian Professor in 1899. He published many works on religious subjects, became Bishop of Durham and Honorary Fellow of St Catharine's in 1901, and died in 1920.

NATARES (NATERES), EDMUND, eighteenth on the list of Fellows, was B.A. in 1500, M.A. in 1502, Proctor in 1506 and Master of Clare from 1514 to 1530, being Vice-Chancellor in 1517, 1520, 1525, and 1526. He died in 1549.

OVERALL, JOHN, entered St John's in 1575, and became scholar of Trinity in 1578 and Fellow in 1581. In 1596 he became senior Fellow of Trinity and Regius Professor of Divinity. He was elected Master of St Catharine's in 1598 and Dean of St Paul's in 1602. He took part in the Hampton Court Conference, and the section on the Sacraments added to the Church Catechism stands now practically as Overall left it. He resigned the Mastership in 1607, and in 1611 took part in the revision of the English translation of the Old Testament. In 1614 he was appointed Bishop of Coventry and Lichfield, and in 1618 Bishop of Norwich. A few months afterwards he died.

PAIN, ARTHUR WELLESLEY, took his degree in 1866, but, after serving as a curate in Suffolk, went to New South Wales. In 1902 he became the first Bishop of Gippsland.

PHILPOTT, HENRY (1807–1892), entered 1825. Senior Wrangler and fourteenth Classic 1829, Master 1845–61, Vice-Chancellor 1846, 1856, 1857, Chairman of the Cambridge University Commission 1878, Bishop of Worcester 1861. A fine scholar, an able administrator with phenomenal powers of work, and an attractive personality, Philpott was perhaps the greatest man St Catharine's has produced. The historian of the College is bound to be biased in his favour, as most of the spade-work necessary for a history was done by Philpott and left carefully arranged and catalogued.

PRESCOT, KENRICK, was Master from 1741 to 1779. Vice-Chancellor in 1744, he was one of those mediocre personalities who seem to do more harm than good to all those with whom they come into contact. Certain it is that the decline of the College roughly coincided with the beginning of his Mastership.

PROCTER, JOSEPH, was third Wrangler and second Smith's Prizeman in 1783. Master 1799–1845. Vice-Chancellor in 1801 and in 1825, he saw the beginning of the revival which culminated in the rule of Corrie and Philpott. G. F. Browne tells two good stories about Procter—stories such as were often told during the so-called "years of idleness", 1700–1850. (See his *St Catharine's College*, p. 209.)

RAY, JOHN, entered St Catharine's in 1644. In 1646 he migrated to Trinity, preached as a layman the funeral sermon of Arrowsmith, a former Catharine man, then Master of Trinity, and was ordained in 1660. He became a celebrated naturalist.

ROBINSON, CHARLES KIRKBY, entered St Catharine's in 1845. Scholar in 1846, twenty-second Wrangler in 1849, and Fellow and Tutor in 1850, he was elected Master at the disastrous election of 1861. He was a kindly and efficient worker, but his tenure of office can only be regarded as a tragedy. He died in 1909.

ROBINSON, RALPH, took his B.A. in 1638. He took Presbyterian orders in 1642, but protested against the execution of Charles I. His death took place in 1655.

ROCHE, RICHARD, was, if we exclude Woodlark, the first Master of St Catharine's. He was a Fellow of King's, but we know little else about him. He was Master from 1475 to 1480.

ROKEBY, SIR THOMAS, was a member of the celebrated Yorkshire family, and entered in 1646, graduating in 1650. Fellow in this year, he retained his Fellowship for nine months only, and then concentrated on his legal studies. William III made him in 1689 one of the twelve judges of Common Pleas, and granted him a knighthood. In 1695 he was transferred to the King's Bench, and died in 1699.

RUSHMORE, FREDERICK MARGETSON (1867–1933), was the first lay Master, 1927–1933. He graduated with a Second Class in the History Tripos of 1898, and was for many years a most successful assistant master at the Perse School. In 1907 he was elected to a Fellowship at St Catharine's, and during his Tutorship after the War the College began to make the most memorable recovery in its history. A College man rather than a University man, he was nevertheless Proctor several times after 1908, and served the town of Cambridge as Councillor, Alderman and Justice of the Peace. There is an appreciation of him in *The Times* for 19 June 1933.

RUST, GEORGE, graduated from St Catharine's as Senior Wrangler in 1647 and was Fellow of Christ's from 1649 to 1659. Like Jeremy Taylor he was a native of Cambridge, and was persuaded by him to go to Ireland. On Taylor's death in 1667 he preached his funeral sermon and succeeded him as Bishop of Dromore.

SANDYS, EDWIN, was Master from 1547 to 1554. A strange and interesting character, who on occasion did not hesitate to have recourse to his dagger, he nevertheless appears to have had little influence upon the College history. He became Bishop of London in 1570 and Archbishop of York in 1576. His life, as given in the *Dictionary of National Biography*, makes interesting reading, and G. F. Browne has selected the most attractive episodes in his *St Catharine's College*, pp. 58–60, 66–71, 82–4. These episodes, however, concern the character of Sandys rather than his influence upon College life.

SCRIVENER, MATTHEW, was never a Fellow, but as Vicar of Haslingfield was in close touch with the College and its doings. A worthy and always loyal son of St Catharine's, he was the first to urge the rebuilding of the College carried out by Lightfoot and Eachard. Both the latter and Loggan agree in assigning to him this honour. He gave not only counsel but also his substance. He died in 1688, leaving £50 to the University Library to buy chains for securing the books already there or to buy new ones; £50 towards the new Chapel; lands to pay 20 marks (£13. 6*s*. 8*d*.) to the proposed Frankland Fellowship, and 50 shillings a year towards improving the Gostlin feast. The residue of his lands was to increase the income "to be expended about the

Chapel of the said College by repairing, adorning it, or promoting the more solemn worship of God".

Browne very cleverly suggests that Scrivener attended in 1679 the "ill-dressed" Gostlin dinner that provoked the criticism made by the mild Bonnell, and was afterwards informed by the Bursar that the College gave the best meal possible with the available funds.

SHERLOCK, THOMAS, was Master from 1714 to 1719, and was the first Master to be Canon of Norwich Cathedral. He was a rich man, owning much property in the town of Birmingham, and a large sum came to the College from Sherlock to endow the Library, in his time a more important part of the College than it is to-day. He had a most distinguished career, succeeding Hoadly as Bishop of Bangor in 1728, and becoming Bishop of London in 1748. His great failing (if it be a failing) was ambition; he and his family appear to have been grasping even to selfishness. He died in 1761.

SHIRLEY, JAMES, the dramatist, was born in 1596. He took orders, and was for a time Master of the Grammar School at St Albans. Afterwards he became a Roman Catholic, and devoted himself to the production of plays. He wrote many dramas, which, although popular for a time, are now regarded as poor stuff. He was the composer of a magnificent lyric, the foundation and sole source of his fame.

SIBBES (SIBBS) RICHARD (1577–1635), a native of Tostock in Suffolk, was not a Catharine man but a Fellow of St John's. He won golden opinions everywhere, and was Master of St Catharine's from 1626 to 1635. Fuller says (*Worthies*, II, 343) that he found St Catharine's in a mean condition, and left it replenished with scholars, beautified with buildings and better endowed with revenues. He was twice offered the Provostship of Trinity College, Dublin, but remained faithful to Cambridge. He became Preacher of Gray's Inn in 1617 and held this office with the Mastership of St Catharine's, in spite of its requiring residence. A supporter of Puritanism at home and Protestantism[1] abroad, he incurred the enmity of Laud, and was saved only through his powerful friends and connections. He left in his will the sum of £100 to

[1] See p. 167 (Charities) for help given to people of the Palatinate.

found a Scholarship of four pounds per annum, naming his kinsman, John Sibbes, as the first holder of it. No trace can be found of any accounts in which this benefaction appears. See p. 25. His published works have been edited in seven volumes, with a memoir, by the Rev. A. B. Grosart (Edinburgh, 1862).

SLADER, JOHN, was elected Fellow in 1650. He was the only one of the intruded Fellows left to give at the Restoration a welcome to the late intruded Master (Lightfoot) when the latter offered to resign in favour of the Master extruded in 1645.

SOUTHWARD, WALTER THOMAS, graduated as sixteenth Classic in 1875. Fellow of St Catharine's (1876), Chaplain and Dean (1884), Tutor (1892), Proctor (1889, 1898), he was an amiable man who deserved better success than fell to his lot. He was an excellent musician, and brought the Chapel services to a high degree of efficiency. He died in 1920.

SPRATT, ALBERT WILLIAM (1842–1920), took a First Class in the Classical Tripos of 1864. Elected Fellow in 1865, he served the College as Dean, Steward, and Bursar, finally becoming senior Tutor in 1892. He was a famous classical scholar and coach, his favourite author being Thucydides, whose work he knew practically by heart. There is a very sympathetic notice of Spratt (and of E. T. S. Carr) by R. R. Conway in the St Catharine's Society *Magazine* for 1932.

SPURSTOW, WILLIAM, was Master from 1645–1650. He was son of the William Spurstow who left the College £100 to provide £5 a year for one poor scholar of the College. He was one of the five writers who in 1641 published *An Humble Remonstrance* by "Smectymnuus". An original member of the Assembly of Divines (1643), he was one of the commissioners appointed to treat with Charles I in the Isle of Wight. Refusing, however, to take the "engagement", he was deprived of his Mastership. He became a Royal chaplain on the Restoration, but, not accepting the Act of Uniformity, he resigned his preferments.

STRONG, WILLIAM, was pre-elected Fellow on 10 December 1631. In 1634 the Vice-Chancellor suspended him from all his degrees, and banished him from the University, for contumacy. On 31 December 1645 he was appointed to the Westminster Assembly. Five years later he became Pastor to a congregation of Independents. Buried in Westminster Abbey 4 July 1654, his remains were disinterred at the Restoration and thrown into a pit in St Margaret's churchyard.

STRYPE, JOHN (1643–1737), came up from St Paul's School first to Jesus (1662) and soon after to St Catharine's. He was ordained, and in 1711 obtained the sinecure rectory of West Tarring. He is best known for his biographies of Cranmer, Sir Thomas Smith, Grindal, Parker, Whitgift and Aylmer, and for the two great works *Annals of the Reformation* and *Ecclesiastical Memorials*. There is a most valuable collection of letters written to him at various times (Camb. Univ. Libr. Add. MSS.), to which this history owes much.

SWINBURNE (SWYNBURNE), ROBERT, was twenty-second on the list of Fellows. Proctor in 1529, Priest of the Chantry of William Myles in 1525, he became Master of Pembroke in 1534 and Rector of Tilney in 1537. He died in 1540.

TAPTON, JOHN, was appointed Master by Woodlark himself in 1480, although only an M.A. and without a degree in Divinity, as the statutes required. Woodlark thus dispensed with one of his own statutes, a right he had reserved for himself. Tapton was Master until 1487, but we do not know when he died. He held ecclesiastical positions at Sleaford, St Asaph, York, Liddington and St Paul's.

THOMAS, JOHN, took his B.A. in 1713. He became Dean of Peterborough in 1740, Bishop of Lincoln in 1744 and of Salisbury in 1761.

TURTON, THOMAS, entered Queens' in 1801. Elected scholar of St Catharine's in 1803, he was Senior Wrangler in 1805. Tutor of St Catharine's in 1807, he became Lucasian Professor of Mathematics in 1822 and Regius Professor of Divinity in 1827, Dean of Peterborough in 1830 and Dean of Westminster in 1842. From 1845 to 1864 he was Bishop of Ely. An eager controversialist, he was also a writer of church music, some of which is still used.

TYLSON, ROGER, twenty-sixth on the list of Fellows, was one of the twelve Cambridge men appointed in 1530 to meet twelve Oxford men to examine English books containing "pestiferous doctrine".

WARDALL, JOHN, one of the two original Fellows, was Master before 20 November 1487 and ceased to be such before 7 July 1506.

WOODLARK (WODELARKE), ROBERT, Provost of King's from 1452. He was the Founder, and is sometimes called the first Master, of St Catharine's. The chief incidents in his life are given on pp. 44–47.

WOORTS, WILLIAM, entered in 1694, graduating as Wrangler in 1698. He was a benefactor to both town and University, giving a fund for repairing roadways round Cambridge, and also one known as the "Worts Fund", which is for the encouragement of research by Cambridge men abroad. His name is familiar to townsmen because of "Worts Causeway".

WOTTON, WILLIAM (13 August 1666–13 February 1726), was an "infant prodigy", who made a mark for himself without being a really distinguished man. He was admitted by Eachard in April 1676 when not yet ten years old. In 1682 he was elected to a Fellowship at St John's. He was elected F.R.S. in 1687, and received his D.D. from Archbishop Tenison in 1707. In 1694 he published his *Reflections upon Ancient and Modern Learning*. The friend of Bentley, he was celebrated for wide learning rather than for exact scholarship. His best work is perhaps *A History of Rome from the death of Pius to that of Severus Alexander*, published in 1701. Wotton died and was buried at Buxted, near Uckfield in Sussex. (Browne, pp. 161–163 and C. R. Haines in the St Catharine's Society *Magazine*, 1934.)

WYLLEBORDE, JAMES, entered as Fellow Commoner (a Bachelor of Arts) in 1473. Afterwards Fellow.

YATES, LOWTHER, was Master 1779–1799. There was a great deal of discussion about his election, on the ground that undue influence had been exercised in favour of Mr Gardner. A discussion at the Lodge of Trinity Hall brought to light the fact that at the first scrutiny two Fellows voted for Mr Gardner, two for Dr Hallifax, Mr Yates for himself and Mr Prescot for himself. Then "they departed from the Chapel, breakfasted together, were sensible that if they persisted the election would go to the Crown, and an alien would be made choice of, who, it was easy to foresee". The Fellows thereupon elected Mr Yates. Yates was perhaps the last of the easy-going dons who lent a certain stolid dignity to the St Catharine's of the eighteenth century. It is typical of the times that he is best known because of a distich, neither witty nor elegant, hurled at him by his nephew from a window in King's Parade as Yates walked to the University Church in trousers instead of the regulation breeches and stockings:

"Gadzoons, Gadzoons,
Lowther Yates in pantaloons!"

YORKE, EDMUND, was elected a Skerne Fellow in 1810. He left the College in 1813. Dying in 1872, he bequeathed money to found the Yorke University Prize, and also a considerable sum to the College "for educational purposes". Legal disputes had to be settled before the money actually came to the College, but ultimately there was enough to buy the playing-field at Newnham and to augment the Scholarship Fund.

FOUNDATION FELLOWS OF THE COLLEGE

1473–1650

Date of Election	*Fellow*
1473, Nov. 26	Welde, Peter
1473, Nov. 26	Wardall, John[1]
—	Wylleborde, James
—	Bacton, Edmund
—	Cok, John
—	Redborne, John
—	Wall, Richard
—	Redman, Walter
—	Burton, Edward
[Name occurs in title deeds 6 Nov. 1498–1 May 1501.]	
—	Wode, William
[Name occurs in title deeds 15 Nov. 1498–1 May 1501.]	
[Proctor 1501.]	Balderstone, Richard[1]
—	Lyster, Lawrence
—	Widder, Roger
—	Garnett, Hugh
—	Capon, William[2]
—	Greyndale, John
—	Sherpe, Thomas
—	Natares, Edmund[3]
—	Kyghtley, John
[Presented to rectory of Coton 11 June 1507.]	
—	Bainbrigge, Reginald[1]
—	Twyer, Nicholas
—	Swinburne, Robert[4]
—	Beriff, Edmund
—	Artwycke, Edward
—	Shafto, Ninian[5]
—	Tylson, Roger
—	Masterman, Robert
—	Bainbrigge, Geoffry
—	Moore, Edward
[Fellow in 1534 and 1537.]	
—	Wilson, James
—	Mackareth, William
—	Barker, John
—	Walles, John
—	Crosier, John
[Fellow on 6 July 1543.]	
—	Haggerstone, Cuthbert
—	Cowper, Robert
[Fellow on 6 July 1543.]	
—	Snell, Robert
[Fellow on 6 July 1543.]	
—	Blande, Christopher
[Fellow on 6 July 1543.]	
—	Buskell, Giles
—	Coney, William
[Proctor 1556.]	Glyn, Hugh
—	Layfeld, Edward
—	Blande, Leonard

[1] Afterwards Master.
[2] Master of Jesus 1516–1546.
[3] Master of Clare 1514–1530.
[4] Master of Pembroke 1534–1537.
[5] One of the first admitted Fellows of St John's.

Foundation Fellows of the College

Date of Election	*Fellow*
—	Taylor, James
—	Degge, Thomas
—	Carter, William
—	Jenkins, Thomas
—	Baxter, John
—	Grendall or Crednall, Nicholas
—	Calvert, Michael
[Members of College in 1558.]	Chatburn, George
	Madock, John
	Monson, Marmaduke
	Cowlton, Ralph
	Dorington, Francis
	Cragge, John
—	Pryse, John
—	Walker, George
—	Mason, Richard
—	Ferfax, Thomas
—	Greenwood, John
—	Maplett, John
—	Kempe, John
[Signed petition against new University Statutes 6 May 1572.]	Lawrence, John
	Messinger, Edmund
	Stanton, William
—	Hobbes, John
—	Jernegan, Henry
1573, April	Furmary, John
—	Cansfield, Robert
—	Holden, John
—	Frankling, Edward
—	Maplett, Edward
—	Longworth, Adam

Date of Election	*Fellow*
1580, Dec.	Foxe, John
—	Forster, William
—	Rider, Richard
—	Hills, John[1]
—	Anderson, William
—	Moone, William
—	Forby, John
—	Cragge, Christopher
1592, July	Foster, William[2]
—	Sill, Miles
—	Kilborne, William
?1606	Bridges, Richard
—	Hollingworth, James
—	Knowles, John
—	Barwick, William
—	Fuller, William[3]
—	Wilson, Thomas [?]
1607, Nov. 5	Coppinger, Ambrose
1609, Mar. 10	Steward, Rowland
1609, June 21	Wilson, Thomas [?]
1611, Oct. 26	Alyngton, Hugh
1611, Dec. 18	Whattaft, Brian
1614, Oct. 20	Horsman, Thomas
1615, Mar. 16	Buck, Thomas
1615, June 22	Rayment, Thomas
1616, June 6	Parker, George
1616, June 22	Drake, Michael
1617, Sept. 8	Best, Paul
1618, Dec. 18	Taylor, Robert
1619, Mar. 21	Goodwin, Thomas
1622, Mar. 30	Gray, Jeremiah
1622, Mar. 30	Perne, Andrew
1622, Mar. 30	Lothian, John
1623, April 10	Meres, Robert

[1] Master 1607–1626.
[2] Bishop of Man.
[3] Dean of Ely 1636, Dean of Durham 1645.

Date of Election	Fellow
1623, April 10	Arrowsmith, John[1]
1627, July 9	Knowles, John
1630, Jan. 7	Spurstow, William[2]
1631, Dec. 10	Strong, William[3]
1631, Dec. 15	Ellis, John
1633–4	Coulson, John
1634, Aug. 30	Lynford, Samuel
1634, Dec. 17	Ellis, John, Junr.
1634, Dec. 17	Bond, John[4]
1637, Mar. 12	Duckfield, Daniel
1637, Aug. 4	Brooke, Samuel
1638, Jan. 24	Blake, William
1638, April 27	Spurstow, Joseph
1643, Sept. 1	Savage, John
1643, Sept. 1	Waite, Joseph
1648, Sept. 8	Thexton, Robert
1649, Oct. 30	Hutchinson, William

Brooke, Blake, Savage, Waite, Thexton and Hutchinson received stipends up to Mich. 1650 and no longer. Six new Fellows began to receive stipends at Christmas 1650.

1650–1932

At Michaelmas 1650 the stipends of all the then existing Fellows ceased—no stipends at all were paid between Michaelmas and Christmas 1650—and at Christmas 1650 the stipends of six new Fellows commenced.

—	Milles, Daniel
—	Duckfield, John
—	Barker, George
—	Green, William
—	Slader, John
—	Rokeby, Thomas
1652	Dowson, Ralph
1655	Fullwood, Gervase
1656/7	Lathum, Thomas
1657, Sept. 15	Brunning, Samuel
1658, July 9	Eachard, John[5]
1658–1659	Everard, Hugh
1661–1662	Paget, Thomas
1668–1669	Calamy, Benjamin
1671–1672	Shaw, Nathaniel
1672–1673	Fisher, Peter
1674–1675	Smythe, Charles
1675–1676	Gouge, Nicholas
1676–1677	Golty, Richard
1678–1679	Calamy, James
1678–1679	Blackall, Offspring[6]
1680–1681	Warren, John
1680–1681	Braddock, John
1681–1682	Muston, Thomas

[1] Master of St John's 1644, Master of Trinity 1653, Regius Professor of Divinity 1644–1656.

[2] Master 1645–1650.

[3] Deprived of his degree and expelled the University for contumacy, 1634.

[4] Master of Trinity Hall 1646–1660.

[5] Master 1675–1697.

[6] Bishop of Exeter 1708.

Foundation Fellows of the College

Date of Election	*Fellow*	*Date of Election*	*Fellow*
1684–1685	Langley, Francis	1727, April 7	Patrick, Symon
1685–1686	Buddle, Adam[1]	1731, Jan. 15	Hanmer, Humphry[9]
1686–1687	Phillips, William[1]	1733, Nov. 6	Bunbury, William
1686–1687	Lea, Samuel	1736, Oct. 19	Eyre, Venn
1688, Sept. 13	Leng, John[2]	1736, Oct. 19	Pemberton, Henry
1691, Oct. 16	Bower, John	1736, Oct. 19	Fountayne, John
1691, Oct. 16	Bence, Alexander	1737, Dec. 3	Wilson, Christopher[10]
1692, Nov. 9	Western, William	1739, April 29	Stebbing, Henry
1692, Nov. 9	Candler, John	1740, Nov. 15	Smith, William
1695, Dec. 24	Tilson, Thomas	1741, Dec. 31	Butts, Eyton
1697/8, Jan. 10	Hoadly, Benjamin[3]	1741, Dec. 31	Thorpe, Joseph
1698, Aug. 12	Sherlock, Thomas[4]	1742, Nov. 20	Dalton, William
1701, July 2	Clotterbooke, Richard	1745, April 20	Chester, Peter
1701, Oct. 13	Newcomen, Stephen	1745, Oct. 18	Burrough, Henry
1704, Mar. 25	Addenbrooke, John[5]	1748, May 12	Hirst, John
1704, Mar. 25	Jeffery, John	1751, May 2	Pemberton, Christopher
1704, Mar. 25	Crosse, Thomas	1753, Jan. 25	Yates, Lowther[11]
1706/7, Feb. 5	Halfhyde, Edmund	1753, Jan. 25	Bradbury, William
1710, Oct. 19	Sparrow, Joseph	1759, May 15	Kerrick, Walter
1710, Oct. 19	Stebbing, Henry	1759, Dec. 7	Cullum, John
1712, Nov. 21	Gouge, Nicholas	1762, April 26	Catlow, Joseph
1715, Oct. 24	Jordan, John	1763, May 11	Gardner, Philip
1716, Sept. 3	Addenbrooke, John[6]	1767, Nov. 11	Prescot, Charles
1718, Feb. 3	Hubbard, Edward[7]	1774, Nov. 22	Waterhouse, Joshua
1719, Oct. 26	Blackall, Theophilus	1775, Nov. 11	Johnson, Thomas
1723, Nov. 6	Pegge, Nathaniel	1779, Nov. 9	Wood, Joshua
1724, Oct. 22	Thurston, Thomas	1781, Mar. 31	Atkinson, William
1726, Nov. 9	Prescot, Kenrick[8]	1783, April 26	Procter, Joseph

[1] Non-jurors whose Fellowships were declared vacant 16 Oct. 1691.

[2] Bishop of Norwich 1723.

[3] Bishop of Bangor 1716, Hereford 1721, Salisbury 1723, Winchester 1734.

[4] Master 1714–1719. [5] M.D. 1710–11. [6] Dean of Lichfield 1745.

[7] Master 1736–1741. [8] Master 1741–1779.

[9] Hanmer, born in Wales, was thought to be ineligible under the statutes. Mr Samuel Gatward gave his opinion that 27 Henry VIII ch. 26 granted persons born in Wales the rights of other King's subjects. [10] Bishop of Bristol. [11] Master 1779–1799.

Date of Election	*Fellow*
1787, April 3	Burrell, Charles William
1789, July 7 and 1790, March 1	Goodwin, Francis
1803, Dec. 27	Howes, George
1803, Dec. 27	Starkie, Thomas[1]
1804, April 28	Joynes, Richard
1808, Dec. 2	Turton, Thomas[2]
1817, May 6	Corrie, George Elwes[3]
1820, Nov. 3	Chevallier, Temple
1820, Nov. 3	Durham, Thomas
1824, Dec. 28	Rusby, Samuel Stones
1825, Dec. 14	Gedge, Sydney
1828, Oct. 22	Blakelock, Ralph
1828, Oct. 22	Jarrett, Thomas
1829, April 6	Philpott, Henry[4]
1831, Dec. 13	Kuhff, Henry
1840, Feb. 10	Goodwin, Charles Wycliffe
1842, Dec. 13	Procter, Francis
1846, Mar. 27	Pine, John Rose
1847, April 3	Purton, John Smyth
1847, Oct. 21	Hopkins, William Bonner
1848, Mar. 31	Milner, Joseph
1850, Feb. 14	Coopland, George William
1850, April 22	Robinson, Charles Kirkby[5]
1855, May 31	Jameson, Francis James
1860, June 27	Crabtree, Ely Willcox
1860, Nov. 12	Hurst, Francis Thomas
1862, Aug. 26	Carr, Edwin Trevor Septimus

Date of Election	*Fellow*
1863, June 6	Browne, George Forrest[6]
1865, March 9	Spratt, Albert William
1866, April 20	Phillips, Arthur
1868, Mar. 17	Kimm, William Frederick
1871, Mar. 6	Bell, John Thomas
1871, April 22	Pretor, Alfred
1874, Mar. 20	Lumby, Joseph Rawson
1876, Feb. 24	Southward, Walter Thom
1879, May 30	Turnbull, William Percival
1890, Nov. 18	Lay, Charles Johnson
1899, May 1	Moule, Handley Carr Gl (Norrisian Professor)
1907, Mar. 19	Rushmore, Frederick Margetson[7]
1908, Nov. 19	Jones, William Henry Samu
1909, Oct. 19	Biffen, Rowland Harry
1919, Oct. 9	Chaytor, Henry John[8]
1919, Oct. 17	Newman, Leslie Frank
1919, Oct. 17	Portway, Donald
1920, Feb. 27	Withers, John James
1925, Nov. 28	Steers, James Alfred
1926, July 3	Henn, Thomas Rice
1930, June 24	Waddams, Christopher Douglas
1930, June 24	Rich, Edwin Ernest
1932, Dec. 3	Hodson, Thomas Callan
1932, Dec. 3	Williams, Robert Allan

[1] Downing Professor of Law 1823.
[2] Bishop of Ely 1845.
[3] Norrisian Professor 1838, Master of Jesus 1849.
[4] Master 1845–1861.
[5] Master 1861–1909.
[6] Bishop of Bristol 1897.
[7] Master 1927–1933.
[8] Master 1933.

CONDUCT FELLOWS

Date of Election	Fellow
1701, July 2	Pupplett, Robert
1710, Oct. 19	Gouge, Nicholas
1712, Nov. 21	Jordan, John
1717/8, Feb. 3	Pyke, William
1720, Mar. 25	Pegge, Nathaniel
1723, Nov. 6	Rayner, Thomas[1]
1724, Oct. 22	Prescot, Kenrick
1726, Nov. 9	Cross, Richard
1728, Feb. 27	Blackburne, Francis
1729, Nov. 4	Hubbard, Henry[2]
1733, Feb. 13	Maule, George
1740, Nov. 15	Kippey, John
1757, Feb. 10	Hey, John[3]
1762, April 26	Gardner, Philip
1770, Oct. 13	Perkins, John
1774, May 9	Waterhouse, Joshua
1774, Dec. 13	Johnson, Thomas
1775, Nov. 11	Wood, Joshua
1787, April 3	Goodwin, Francis
1801, April 23	Pearce, Harry

FRANKLAND FELLOWS

1711, April 30	Palmer, John
1721/2, Mar. 16	Craner, John
1728, April 4	Denham, Edmund
1784, April 24	Twigger, Joseph
1792, June 6	Edmonds, John
1799, Dec. 19	Hewitt, John Dyer
1803, Feb. 8	Allott, James
1815, Dec. 12	Procter, William
1830, Dec. 16	Smith, Strother Ancrum

Frankland Scholar

The only Election recorded in the Conclusion Book is of John Brooke, from Tamworth School (10 Nov. 1733).

[1] Was never admitted.

[2] Migrated to Emmanuel. Lady Margaret Preacher 1752, Registrary 1758–1778.

[3] Migrated to Sidney Sussex. Norrisian Professor.

SKERNE FELLOWS

Date of Election	*Fellow*
1772, Nov. 10	Dobson, Samuel
1772, Nov. 10	Dawson, Francis
1772, Nov. 10	Lawson, Marmaduke
1772, Nov. 10	Eamonson, William
1772, Nov. 10	Wilsford, John
1772, Nov. 10	Blackburne, Francis
1775, April 11	Ingham, Benjamin
1776, April 2	Cowper, Thomas
1777, April 22	Grenside, Ralph
1781, May 29	Clapham, Christopher
1782, April 30	Wood, Richard
1785, Mar. 15	Coates, John
1787, June 17	Atkinson, William
1789, Jan. 13	Gresham, John
1794, April 22	Foster, Richard
1795, April 6	Hucks, Joseph
1799, Feb. 5	Jenkinson, William
1800, Nov. 5	Ponsonby, John
1806, Nov. 18	Turton, Thomas
1807, Aug. 11	Verelst, William
1808, Feb. 16	Geldart, James William
1809, Jan. 3	Gee, Robert
1809, Nov. 7	Geldart, Richard John
1810, May 22	Harrison, Charles
1810, Nov. 13	Yorke, Edmund
1811, Aug. 20	Maynard, David Jefferson
1818, Nov. 10	Tyson, Edwin Colman
1821, May 29	Holroyd, John
1822, July 3	Glendall, John William
1823, Mar. 18	Hildyard, Robert Charles
1831, Dec. 13	Harrison, William Hopkins[1]
1832, April 10	Forster, Francis
1832, Aug. 21	Maddison, George
1835, June 9	Marsden, William Dalabene
1839, Nov. 19	Sharpe, William Robert
1842, April 12	Windemann, George Francis R.
1844, Nov. 26	Parr, William Henry
1845, May 6	Hardwick, Charles
1847, Mar. 23	Ogle, William
1849, Nov. 14	Baxter, Thomas Preston Nowell
1854, May 31	Morley, George Bentley

HONORARY FELLOWS

ESTABLISHED BY THE STATUTES OF 1882

Date of Election	Fellow
1887, June 3	Philpott, Henry Carpenter, William Boyd Browne, George Forrest
1896, Nov. 9	Trevor, Sir Charles Cecil
1901, Nov. 5	Moule, Handley Carr Glyn
1909, Oct. 25	Moore, Sir Norman
1909, Oct. 25	Figgis, John Neville
1922, Oct. 21	Coulton, George Gordon
1923, April 28	Searle, Sir Malcolm William
1925, May 9	Schuster, Sir Claud
1934, June 18	Carr, Charles Lisle

[1] Was not admitted, not being a complete B.A. at the time of his election.

Chapter IV

FINANCE

OF the pre-Reformation benefactions that do not found Fellowships, those for the Bible Clerk and the Butler have already been noticed in Chapter II, but there remain several others, intended either for the extension or maintenance of the buildings, or in some cases for general purposes. But, like all pre-Reformation endowments, they are bargains rather than gifts; prayers for the dead are as it were bought, and arrangements made to insure as far as possible that the terms of the composition shall be carried out. The donors use the phrase *in puram eleemosynam* without appearing to realise the discrepancy between their words and their actions.

The grant of a Royal Charter in 1475 enabled St Catharine's to acquire and to sell property, and on 22 November 1475 Woodlark conveyed to the Master and Fellows all the property he had acquired on the Mill Street front, together with all his lands etc. in Cambridge, Grantchester, Barton and Coton, the Manor of Coton and the advowson of the church there, and the reversion of lands and tenements in Over. Nearly two months before the Royal Charter was received, the College seal was (quite illegally) affixed to an agreement with the executors, Henry Hardman and William Twheyts, of William Cotte and Clement Denston. The latter gave £40 towards completing the Chapel and Library, and the Master and Fellows agree to celebrate yearly an obit day with Mass of requiem. "And though we cannot make a fair recompense, yet in part at least we can repay, and so with prayful and joyful minds we make a contribution from our spiritual goods." This was the second benefaction to the College. The first was that of Lady Joan Barnardiston, who gave towards the original building 100 marks, upon consideration that one Fellow in priest's orders should pray hereafter for the safety of her soul.

Probably no legal deed went with this gift, but the Founder gives it a special paragraph at the end of his statutes.[1]

On 12 April 1480 William Bassett, Rector of Bennington in the county of Lincoln, conveyed to the Master and Fellows all his lands, tenements etc. in Stoke-by-Clare, Whixol and Kedington in the county of Suffolk, except a certain tenement in Stoke. A week later the College leased all this property to William Bassett for the term of his natural life at a peppercorn rent. On 15 September of the same year the Master and Fellows sealed a composition whereby in consideration of this gift they undertake to keep an obit day, and also to appoint a Fellow of the College in priest's orders to pray and celebrate for the souls of the said William Bassett, and of his parents and benefactors, and to preach, or cause to be preached, yearly two sermons, one at Glapthorne in Northamptonshire, and the other at Godirstoke (Cotterstock) in the same county. The Fellow is to receive an annual stipend of four pounds, and for presence at the obit the Master is to receive 12 pence, and each Fellow 8 pence.

Then in October 1480 the Master and Fellows convey back to William Bassett the said lands, and give up all their right and title to them.[2]

On 20 November 1487 was sealed an agreement between the Master and Fellows and William Bassett. It recites that the said William Bassett had conveyed by deed, dated 10 December 2 Richard III (1484), to the Master and Fellows *in liberam, puram et perpetuam eleemosynam*, a tenement at Babraham in the county of Cambridge called the Tabert, with the lands etc. thereto belonging. The Master and Fellows make the same covenants with William Bassett, in consideration of this gift, as were made in the indenture of 15 September 1480, except that the priest appointed to officiate is to receive

[1] "Statuimus quod perpetuis temporibus futuris sit unus sacerdos socius hujus collegii, qui specialiter oret et celebret pro anima dominae Johannae de Barnston, quae dedit ad primum edificium hujus collegii centum marcas sub tali conditione, quod haberet perpetuis temporibus futuris sacerdotem socium hujus collegii specialiter orantem pro salute animae suae et suorum benefactorum, qui quidem sacerdos assignetur per magistrum hujus collegii pro tempore existentem."

[2] *Register*, I, 24–7.

13 shillings and 4 pence for his sermons, in addition to the four pounds, yearly salary.[1]

The Bassett benefaction, with its many changes, must have caused considerable trouble. We have an indication of this in a deed (11 February 1493/4) whereby Thomas Pollard, of Stoke-by-Clare, the executor of William Bassett, releases John Wardall, Master of St Catharine's, John Redborne, Fellow, and others from their bond for £24 to the said William Bassett; and also releases the said John Wardall and the Fellows of the College from all actions, real and personal, which he may have against them on account of any bond, covenant or promise, except only an exhibition of a certain sum for six years.

The most important endowments given during the fifty years immediately following the opening of the College are those for the endowment of Fellowships; during this period no Scholarships are founded, although provision is made for a Bible Clerk and a (student) Butler. At the opening only two Fellows "entered commons", while Woodlark's statutes established "three or more". The Edwardian statutes speak of "six or more or less", and six has been the recognised number of Fellows on the old Foundation, with the exception of a short period (1860–82), down to the present day.

In the interval between the Founder's statutes and those of Edward VI four Fellowships were founded, and it is curious that the composition constituting the last of them speaks of "four Fellows now being of duty and accustomed in the said Hall". We should have expected, not four, but five. Perhaps one Fellowship was vacant when the deed was drawn up.

The details of the Bassett composition (1487) have already been given; the other three are dated respectively 1503, 1506 and 1515.

[1] *Register*, I, 16. This deed has been erased in the Register by dark lines drawn across it. But the Commissioners of Henry VIII mention the Bassett foundation, and charge against it £4. 11*s*. 8*d*. (i.e. salary £4. 0*s*. 0*d*.; one sermon 6*s*. 8*d*.; exequies, Master and 6 Fellows 5*s*. 0*d*.). This erasure is surely misplaced; the deed to be erased was that conveying property at Stoke-by-Clare.

Under date 20 August 1503 the Master and Fellows agree, in return for £100 received from Richard Nelson, to allow him to nominate on the feast of St John the Baptist, 1505, a scholar in priest's orders, born in Londisdale or at least in the diocese of York, to be a Fellow of the College, receiving an annual stipend of £4 from the College property in Cambridge, Coton, Over, Babraham and Barton. The second and subsequent elections are to be made by the Master and Fellows from candidates fulfilling similar conditions. There is to be a solemn requiem Mass on the death of Richard Nelson, while the Fellow elected is to pray and celebrate for the soul of Richard Nelson, his parents and their benefactors. Failure to fulfil these terms involves forfeiture, with a fine, to St Michael's College, the latter engaging to hand over forfeiture and fine to the Master and Brothers of the House of St John the Evangelist, to be spent in works of charity for the health of the soul of Richard Nelson, his parents and benefactors, according to the discretion of the Master of St Michael's, of the Master of Clare and of the Master of the House or College of St John the Evangelist.[1]

On 20 August 1506 a Fellowship was founded by William Stockdale and three others. The said four persons conveyed to the College a tenement at Layer Breton in Essex, a tenement at Barton and a tenement at Whitwell, with lands belonging to each. The deed gives the first nomination to Robert Sympson (Symson), one of the four benefactors, and the Fellow is to receive £4 yearly. The donors are to be regarded as benefactors of the College, and the Society is to pray for their souls and keep an obit day yearly on 23 July. In this case it is King's College that is set to keep a watch on St Catharine's, and Jesus College and Peterhouse are to see that King's performs its duty. The forfeit money is to be spent on "good and healthful works, namely in celebrating Masses, in relieving poor scholars, in mending broken roads, in alms-giving and in other good uses...to the praise of Almighty God and the prosperous health of the aforesaid souls".[2]

The last foundation Fellowship to be founded is the subject of a quadripartite indenture, dated 20 February 1515, between:

[1] *Register*, I, 53. [2] See *Register*, I, 34.

(1) The Master and Fellows.

(2) The Master and Brethren of the House or Hospital of St Thomas the Martyr of Acon in Westcheap, London.

(3) John Mylbourn, alderman and draper of London, and Joan his wife.

(4) The Master and Wardens of the Fellowship or Mystery of the Drapers of the City of London.

The terms of the trust are best understood from a few sentences taken out of the deed itself.

"The said John Mylbourn and Joan his wife have...well and truly paid...unto the aforesaid Master and Fellows...the sum of one hundred and twenty-four pounds sterling for the purchasing and buying of lands and tenements to the clear yearly value of ten marks sterling above all charges and reprises to the use of the said Hall;...the said Master and Fellows...grant, and them and their successors by this indenture bind, that they...shall provide and have in their said Hall or place one Fellow over and above the number of four Fellows now being of duty and accustomed to the said Hall. Which one Fellow so to be provided there perpetually to continue as a Fellow of the same place shall be an honest priest of good name, fame and conversation, and a Master of Arts and student in Divinity... the same Fellow over and above the said four pounds in money shall have, take and perceive for evermore in the said place at the charges of the said house his Diriges, his chamber and all other emoluments, profits, commodities and advantages in as large a manner as the other Fellows of the said Hall have, and shall have, take and perceive. Which Fellow shall be a Fellow of the said Hall, and shall ever be called the Fellow or Scholar of John Chester of London, draper, and a scholar to the augmentation and increase of the scholars of the said Hall."

The deed goes on to state that the Fellow, on the Sunday next after Trinity, shall preach in the church of St Thomas of Acon, when he is to pray specially by name for the soul of John Chester, and for John and Joan Mylbourn, "six shillings and eight pence over and above the said yearly four pounds, his Diriges, emoluments and profits". The Master and Fellows are to keep a yearly obit day, receiving five shillings therefor, and John and Joan Mylbourn are to have the first nomination.

The Master and Brethren of St Thomas are to recover £200 from St Catharine's if the conditions be not fulfilled, and after paying £20 to the

Drapers are to dispose of the residue "in deeds and alms of charity, as by their conscience and discretions they shall seem most to the pleasure of God".

On 26 September 1544, when the Mercers' Company had purchased the church of the College of Acon, an agreement was made with that Company that a sermon be preached in the Mercers' church in Cheapside yearly on Good Friday, the College to pay its Fellow six shillings and eight pence and his travelling expenses.

On page 27 of Browne's *St Catharine's College* is a paragraph which, though correct in substance, needs correcting in certain respects. "This was the gift of the house", he writes,

"which those who remember Cambridge twenty years ago or more [i.e. 1880] used to know as the house of Mr. Cory the grocer, projecting boldly into Trumpington Street on the north side of the Bull Inn. It was given by Isabella Caunterbury, the Founder's sister, August 13, 1479. John Caunterbury, her deceased husband, had been clerk of the works at King's, and this was their residence. When King's College pulled the house down, there was still preserved in it some handsome woodwork of the later middle of the fifteenth century, especially a settle of Caunterbury's time, marked with his initials, and no doubt made by the workmen under his orders at King's. This gift of Caunterbury's house was in itself of importance, and it was made of still more importance by the fact that among the considerable property which came to the College from the founder, after the conveyance of the foundation land, was a large and important tenement behind it called Fordham's Place. On this latter site the secret meetings were held before the Reformation which caused it to be nicknamed 'Germany', its real name having by that time been changed to 'The White Horse'. The relatively few Reformers at St. Catharine's had a safe entrance to it by a back way. The College most unfortunately sold these very important sites no long time after they came into possession."

The tenement given by Isabella Caunterbury on 13 August 1479 was in the parish of the Holy Sepulchre, and was sold to Nicholas Gryme for £60 on 28 June 1502.[1] This could not have been the house of the Caunterburys, which was conveyed (23 December 1498) to the Master and Fellows from Robert Bryan, sole survivor of Robert Woodlark and others, and already conveyed

[1] *Register*, I, 14 and 48.

by the College (28 March 1498) to William Myles. This is said to be in the parish of St Benedict and to have been lately occupied by John Caunterbury. On 4 April 1509 a reversion of this property together with 38 a. 1 r. of land in the towns and fields of Coton, Cambridge, Burgh and Dullingham, was conveyed to eight persons, three of whom were Fellows, by Catharine Myles, widow, late wife of William Myles, on certain conditions. Within one month after the decease of the said Catharine Myles and Thomas Gery, the Master and Fellows are to appoint one Fellow of the College in priest's orders to say Mass daily for the souls of William Myles, Catharine Myles and all their benefactors' souls. Every vacancy in the office is to be filled up within twelve days. When the number of feoffees is reduced by death to two, they are to convey the property to seven other persons, four to be named by the Master and Fellows of Catharine Hall and three by the Master and Fellows of Corpus Christi.

The first appointment to this office was made 13 September 1525, when Robert Swinburne was granted the chantry or service of William Myles and Catharine his wife, for so long a time as he shall continue to be Fellow of the College and not beneficed. The Master and Fellows agree to pay him £4 yearly, if the houses and lands given by Catharine Myles produce so much, if not, then to give him all that they do produce.[1] It thus appears that the College at this time came into possession of the property mentioned in the indenture of 4 April 1509.

On 26 June 1556 the College conveyed to John Mere for £100 three tenements in St Bene't's parish. There are two copies of the conveyance in the Register,[2] one in Latin and the other in English. The English document describes the three tenements as the White Horse, the Corn House (?), and a third, builded and set betwixt them both. The English deed also contains a covenant to discharge the said John Mere of and from all manner of bondages, services, saying and singing of Mass for the souls of William Myles, Catharine Myles, and the souls of all their benefactors, and all other chargeable covenants contained in certain indentures tripartite made between the said Catharine Myles, St Catharine's College and Bene't College, 4 April, 24 Henry VII.

[1] *Register*, I, 22. [2] *Register*, II, 82.

On 14 October 1504 the College seal was put to the composition of Hugh Pemberton, late citizen and alderman of the city of London.

In consideration of the gift of 200 marks paid to the Master and Fellows by his executors, Catharine Pemberton, his widow, and Robert Pemberton, clerk, to be disposed of to the wealth and profit of the College and to the pleasure of God and the blessed virgin St Catharine; as well as of other benefits to the said College by the said Catharine and Robert afore this time; the Master and Fellows bind themselves to celebrate a Mass daily in the College Chapel while the world shall endure, every day except Shere Thursday, Good Friday and Easter Even, for the souls of the said Hugh Pemberton, of all his children, of the father and mother of the said Hugh and his wife, and their benefactors and for all Christian souls, and also for the prosperity and welfare of the said Catharine and Robert while living and for their souls, when dead.

Also to cause a sermon to be said by a graduate, either M.A. or of higher degree, on the Sunday next before 7 September, or on 7 September if it be a Sunday, yearly in the church of St Martin Ottewiche in the ward of Bishopsgate, London; the said graduate in his sermon to exhort the people present to pray for the afore-mentioned souls;

Also to keep an obit day, with service, in the said church, yearly on 7 September and to distribute then and there as follows 15*s.* 5*d.*, viz.:

to the parson of the church 12d.
to his deputy, if he be absent, 8d.
to every priest conduct, present and helping, 4d.
to the parish clerk 8d.
for 4 tapers of wax, each weighing 6 lbs and
for 4 candlesticks 20d.
to the Master of Merchant Tailors, if present, 20d.
to every warden of the craft, present, 12d.
to the clerk of the Master's clothing of the
said craft 8d.
to the bedell of the same clothing 4d.
the remainder to be distributed by the parson and
churchwardens among the poor of the parish.[1]

[1] *Register*, 1, 56.

The commissioners of King Henry VIII state the sum to be paid for the sermon 6*s*. 8*d*. and for the distribution 15*s*. 10*d*., but the deed clearly states 15 shillings and 5 pence.

On 26 October 1505 the College seal was put to the composition of William Taylard, Esq. of Duddyngton, in the county of Huntingdon.

The deed recites that the executors of the said William Taylard, viz. his widow Elizabeth Taylard and his sons William Taylard, clerk, and John Taylard, had paid to the Master and Fellows £100, which the said William Taylard had given them for the purpose, to be expended by the Master and Fellows at their discretion in building, repairing and maintaining the College, or in bearing other charges of the College; in consideration whereof the Master and Fellows agree with the said executors to keep an obit day, with services, on the Vigil of the Transfiguration yearly for ever for the said William Taylard and for each of his said executors, when dead, in the chapel of the College, and to distribute upon every such day the sum of 13*s*. 4*d*., viz.:

to the Master, or his deputy, if present	20d.
to every clerk Bibliotist	4d.
for additional commons for a feast	3/4d.
the remainder to be divided equally among the Fellows present.	

Also every week, when the Mass for the founder is celebrated, to cause the officiating priest to pray for the soul of the said William Taylard and for the soul of each of his executors, when dead.[1]

A document of great historical interest is in the College Register, dated 20 March 1513.[2] It is an inventory of all lands and houses belonging to the College at this time. In addition to what was conveyed to the Society by the Founder on 22 November 1475, this document mentions the following properties as purchased by him.

In Cambridge:

(1) Licence to build on the wall on the south side of the College ground. This was bought of Andrew Dockett, President of Queens' College, 27 August 1477.

[1] *Register*, I, 18. [2] P. 119.

(2) A tenement called Fordham Place, bought of Hugh Tapton in 1454 or 1455. This was sold to William Myles in 1498, but its return was certain because of the composition of 1509. It was also known as the White Horse.

(3) A tenement called Corn House (?) in St Bene't's parish (1459).

In Coton. A parcel of land near the Pond, 20 feet in width and in length equal to the breadth of a croft called Willcroft. Bought of John Fynn 1461.

In Whitwell and Barton. 2 a. 12 r. of arable land bought of Elena Fynn, 7 February 1476.

No mention is made in this inventory of John Rasour's tenement, nor of the tenement given by Isabella Caunterbury, as this had been sold in 1502. The College is described as built on two tenements in St Edward's and St Botolph's parishes, and the Library on the tenement to the north of them. The tenement to the south, bought of the chantry of St Clement, is called Wodhows, i.e. Woodhouse.

Besides the lands given by William Bassett (1487), by the founders of Robert Sympson's Fellowship (1506), and by the composition of Catharine Myles in 1509, the College possessed other lands, doubtless bought at different times with money given under the compositions of Nelson, Pemberton and Taylard, together with the proceeds of the sales in 1498 and 1502. These lands were apparently bought during the Mastership of Thomas Greene, and were as follows:

In Coton. Parcels of land, 13 acres bought 14 March 1509, 4 acres 3 roods (4 April 1511), 6 acres (28 June 1507), 7 acres 3 roods (23 October 1507), 5 acres (23 February 1508), and $1\frac{1}{2}$ acres, along with a tenement and croft (24 March 1511).

In Whitwell and Comberton. A tenement and croft of 1 acre (20 November 1507), a grove of $1\frac{1}{2}$ acres (26 October 1507), 6 acres (10 February 1508), 3 acres $1\frac{1}{2}$ roods (24 October 1508).

In Harlton. 16 acres 3 roods (10 May 1507).

In Fulbourn. 20 acres $\frac{1}{2}$ rood, together with a tenement and a messuage and croft (20 May 1507).

In Wilbraham. A close called Talmage near the Mill (4 July 1507).

In Paxton. A tenement (20 October 1510).

Mention is also made of 1 acre in Whitwell, for which 4*d*. a year is to be paid.

There is a sign that the revenues of the College were growing in the letters patent granted 15 February 1513 to the Master and Fellows to hold lands, tenements and revenues to the value of ten pounds a year notwithstanding the Statutes of Mortmain.[1] Edward the fourth, when he made a similar grant, had proved a veritable Shylock,[2] but in this case there was no fine or fee.

On 16 January 1515 Elizabeth Southwell and William Wotton, executors of Sir Robert Southwell, conveyed to the Master and Fellows all their right in the manor and lands, late John Fynn's, of Coton, Barton and Whitwell.

By an indenture made 4 November 1509 Sir Robert Southwell bargained to sell to Thomas Greene, Master of the College, and others, all the lands, late John Fynn's, in Coton, Barton, Whitwell, Grantchester and Cambridge, for £100 then paid to the said Robert Southwell, together with £50 to be paid on 8 November 1514 in St Paul's Church, London, and other £50 to be paid 8 November 1515.

In March 1515 Edward Plegg and Rowland Loft, heirs of John Fynn, clerk, by two separate deeds convey to the Master and Fellows all the lands, late John Fynn's, lying dispersedly in the town and fields of Grantchester. In an indenture made 22 September 1514 the said Edward Plegg, Rowland Loft, and Joan his wife, bargain to sell the said lands, late John Fynn's, to the Master and Fellows for the sum of thirty pounds.

On 6 May 1516 Richard Fletcher and Thomas Wright convey to the Master and Fellows certain lands etc. at Biggleswade.[3]

At this time occurs the first recorded instance of money being borrowed by the College from a private individual, a practice that became very common later on. On 5 May 1516 the Master and Fellows give a bond to Thomas Greene, the Master, for the payment of twenty pounds on the next Michaelmas day.[4] This bond was doubtless for money lent in order to enable the College to complete some of its purchases, or to extend or improve its buildings.

On 29 April 1517 the College seal was put to an indenture obliging the Master and Fellows to observe an obit day, with services, on 8 June in every

[1] *Register*, I, 21. [2] See p. 50. [3] *Register*, I, 79. [4] *Register*, I, 90.

year for the souls of Thomas and Agnes Greene, for the good state of the said Master while living and for his soul when dead, and for the souls of their benefactors; a distribution of 3*s.* 4*d.* is to be made on the occasion, namely:

for the Master if present	6^d
for each Fellow present	4^d
for the Bibliotista	2^d

The residue is to be spent on increase of commons on the day.

The consideration was the gift by the Master, Dr Thomas Greene, of ten pounds to the use of the College towards erecting four new chambers on the south side of the College.[1]

On 5 August 1523 the College seal was put to an indenture of agreement with Alice Lupsett, widow and executrix of Thomas Lupsett, goldsmith of London.

The indenture recites that the said Alice Lupsett, in compliance with the last will and testament of her husband, had given to the Master and Fellows ten pounds to the use of the College for the building, repair, maintenance and other charges of the College.

The Master and Fellows, in consideration of the said gift, agree to keep an obit day with services yearly for 20 years for the souls of the said Thomas Lupsett, and of Thomas Bowden, priest.[2]

On 12 October 1524 Hugh Garnett, clerk, conveys to the Master and Fellows for the use and profit of the College, a messuage in Paxton Parva between a tenement of the same College on the north and a tenement of William Neve on the other side and abutting eastward in the King's way in the town of Paxton Parva.[3]

On 1 April 1526 the College seal was put to an indenture of agreement with Hugh Garnett, clerk.

The indenture recites that the said Hugh Garnett had given to the Master and Fellows for the use of the College certain lands at Paxton Parva in the county of Huntingdon and at Coton in the county of Cambridge and also

[1] *Register*, I, 64. [2] *Register*, I, 32. [3] *Title-deeds Paxton*, 46.

certain "bona mobilia"; and that in consideration of such gift the Master and Fellows agreed to keep an obit day with services yearly for the souls of George Garnett and Agnes his wife, the parents of the said Hugh Garnett, for the good estate of the said Hugh Garnett while living and for his soul when dead, and for the souls of all his benefactors.

The Master and Fellows also agree to distribute 3*s.* 4*d.* on every such anniversary, viz. to the Master, if present, 6*d.*, to each Fellow, present, 4*d.*, to the Bibliotista 2*d.*, and the residue, if any, for the increase of the commons of the Master and Fellows.[1]

On 24 June 1527 the College gave a receipt to Sir Edmund Bidyngfield and Robert Bonam, Esq., executors of the will of Sir John Marney, late of Layer Marney in the county of Essex, for twenty marks left by the said Sir John Marney in a legacy for the use of the College. Perhaps this gift was due to the influence of Robert Sympson, a great benefactor, who was Rector of Layer Marney from 1488 to 1530.

On 20 December 1538 the churchwardens of St Clement's Church in Cambridge conveyed to the Master and Fellows the quit rent of eight shillings a year, payable out of a tenement bought by the Founder at Michaelmas 1472, for part of the site of the College. The purchase money was £6. 13*s.* 4*d.*

At about this date the stream of benefactions ceases. Probably everybody was suffering from the financial depression, and the uncertainties of the time discouraged those who had still money to give. But the last two pre-Reformation benefactions are both of interest, but in different ways.

The first, that of Robert Sympson, besides giving much information incidentally, shows how uncomfortable early college buildings were. To us it seems unthinkable that "light and heat" should not be a first charge upon the revenues of any institution, but in mediaeval days comfort was considered incompatible with serious study, and this view lived long and died hard. Not so many years ago baths were thought to be subversive of the Spartan habits that ought to prevail among undergraduates. Sympson thought that eight

[1] *Register*, I, 31.

shillings a year should be spent on fuel to be burnt in the Hall, or else in the "Parlour",[1] timidly adding "at the discretion of the Master, or in his absence of the President, with a majority of the Fellows present", i.e. at a meal or meeting.

The second composition contains nothing but the purchase of a requiem Mass and obit. The College is not treated as an educational institution, but as a chantry or collegiate church. It is to perform religious services; in return it receives twenty marks to produce the thirteen and four pence necessary to pay for them. That is an end of the matter.

We add here a brief analysis of the compositions.

The College seal on 14 December 1530 was put to a deed obliging the Master and Fellows to say the psalm *de profundis* with the accustomed suffrages for the souls of Robert Sympson, clerk, and of his parents and benefactors, whenever they are required to dispute or to "keep problems" (*observare problemata*) in the College Chapel.

The consideration for this obligation was the gift of eight pounds by the said Robert Sympson to the Master and Fellows for the use of the College, viz. to buy fuel[2] yearly to the value of eight shillings for burning in the hall or parlour of the College.[3]

On 31 January 1536 the College seal was put to an indenture obliging the Master and Fellows to keep an obit day with services, for the Right Worshipful Master Robert Shurton, D.D., Dean of Stoke-by-Clare in the county of Suffolk, and to pray therein for the souls of the said Robert Shurton and his father and mother and for all Christian souls.

The consideration for this obligation was the gift by the said Robert Shurton to the Master and Fellows of twenty marks to be expended, within four years, in the purchase of land to the value of 13*s.* 4*d.* a year or to so much

[1] The old name for what was later styled the Combination Room.

[2] The accounts of the seventeenth century often mention sedge to be used as a fire-lighter, e.g. 1644–5 "sedge to kindle the Hall fire 0. 4. 0". The usual fuel was turf, 1637–8 "turfs for the Hall 0. 2. 0". On special occasions wood was burnt, e.g. 21 April 1634 "to Margaret Gill for 4 fagots for the Hall on Easter day 0. 0. 4".

[3] *Register*, I, 32.

value as can be got for the money; the land, when purchased, to be put in mortmain.

The Master and Fellows bind themselves to distribute on every such obit day to the Master, if present, two shillings; to each Fellow, if present, one shilling; to the Bible Clerk, if present, four pence; to the Butler, if present, four pence.[1]

On 26 September 1544 the College of Acon having been dissolved and the Mercers' Company having purchased its church, an indenture was made this day between the Master and Fellows of the College, the Master, Wardens and company of the Mercers, Joan Mylbourn (widow of John Mylbourn) and the Drapers' Company, whereby the College covenanted to cause one of their Fellows once a year to make a sermon in the said church, then called Mercers' church in Cheapside, London, for ever; the day being altered from the Sunday next after Trinity Sunday to Good Friday: the College to pay the Fellow 6*s*. 8*d*. for his costs in coming to London, under the same penalties as are mentioned in the indenture of February 1515.

There is no copy of this deed in the College Register; but the particulars were supplied to the College in 1854 by Mr John Smith, Chaplain to the Mercers' Company.

The middle of the sixteenth century was a period of financial depression, which was felt in Cambridge as acutely as elsewhere. Disturbance and dislocation followed, giving rise, at least equally with the religious changes of the day, to repeated interference with the University at the hands of the Sovereign.

An excellent picture of the distress at Cambridge can be seen in the famous sermon of Thomas Lever, Fellow of St John's, delivered 14 December 1550.[2] In it he says:

"There be divers there which rise daily about four or five of the clock in the morning, and from five till six of the clock use common prayer....And from six till ten of the clock use ever either private study or common lectures. At ten of the clock they go to dinner, whereas they be content with a penny piece of beef

[1] *Register*, I, 68.

[2] See Strype, *Ecclesiastical Memorials*, II, 259.

among four, having a few pottage made of the broth of the same beef, with salt and oatmeal, and nothing else. After this slender diet, they be either teaching or learning until five of the clock in the evening; whenas they have a supper not much better than their dinner. Immediately after which they go either to reasoning in problems, or to some other study until it be nine or ten of the clock. And there being without fires, are fain to walk, or run up and down half an hour, to get a heat on their feet when they go to bed." A little before this Lever speaks of "two hundred students of divinity, many very well learned...which be now gone home: and many young toward scholars, and old fatherly doctors. One hundred also of another sort, having rich friends or being beneficed men, did live of themselves in hostels and inns, be either gone away or else fain to creep into colleges."[1]

The records of St Catharine's show clear signs of the financial crisis. In 1543 they increased, without statutory authority, the income of the Master and of each Fellow by twenty shillings, the old stipends being now inadequate. They also changed their financial policy; they sold tenements near the College and bought agricultural property. Thus on 26 June 1556 the Master and Fellows conveyed to John Mere, M.A. and Bedell, three tenements (the White Horse, the Corn House, and another "betwixt them both") for £100, discharging the purchaser from all services for the souls of William and Catharine Myles. On 8 September the same John Mere bought two tenements in St Botolph's parish (the White Swan, bought in 1516, and Appleyard's) for £50.[2] Apparently this sacrifice of a large portion of the island site did not yield enough for the purpose that the Fellows had in mind, for on 10 May 1557 they sold to William Cole the lands they had on 6 May 1516 bought at Biggleswade from Richard Fletcher and Thomas Wright. On the same day as the Biggleswade property was sold the College bought at Chesterton King's Meadow (3 acres), 44 acres of arable land, right of pasture for 80 sheep, a close and 18½ acres of land called Bassam's, Turke meadow and a willow bank for £100. The vendor was Richard Brakyn, from whom on 16 December 1556 the College had bought for £150 two other Chesterton properties, Green End Close and Long Close. Letters patent had to be obtained from Philip and Mary[3] in both cases as authority for the conveyance.

[1] Then, as now, living in colleges was cheaper than in lodgings.

[2] *Register*, II, 83.

[3] The lands were abbey lands.

The fines paid were 22*s.* 8*d.* and 17*s.* 10*d.* respectively, while in both cases the seal cost 20*s.* 4*d.* and the execution 8*d.*[1]

In the report of the Commissioners of King Henry VIII the revenues of the College were given as follows:

Cambridge. Average net rents of tenements, cottages and gardens	£8.	2.	1
Coton. Net rents and profits	20.	5.	8½
Barton. Net rents	7.	13.	4
Grantchester. Net rents	.	3.	4
Harlton. Net rents		14.	3
Over. Net rents	3.	16.	2
Wilbraham. Net rents		8.	6
Fulbourn. Net rents	1.	17.	1
Biggleswade. Net rents	2.	15.	9½
Paxton. Net rents	1.	12.	3
Layer Breton. Net rents	3.	6.	8
Ridgewell Rectory etc.	5.	3.	4
	55.	18.	6

The gross rents were £66. 2*s.* 6½*d.*

There follows (modernised) a most important College Order:

"Memorandum that it was decreed the 28 day of September anno domini 1560 by the whole consent of the Master and the Fellows of this College that the pigeons of the said College should be sold unto the commons for 4 pence a dozen and not above and also if the Master or any of the Fellows would buy of the same for their own use in the College they should pay 6 pence a dozen and not above and the rest to be sold for the most advantage. All the profit of the which dove house to be divided quarterly amongst the Master and Fellows of this College.[2]

Item it was agreed the day and year above written by the said consent that the Steward of this College for the time being shall not lend any of the

[1] Bassam's Close was the subject of a curious dispute between landlord and tenant a few years later. See p. 84 and Browne, pp. 78–80.

[2] This is the first instance in our records of the practice of declaring a supplementary "dividend" to fixed stipends.

College money without a real occasion and that with expressed consent of the Master and the most part of the Fellows.

Item it was likewise decreed the same time that the Steward of the College for the time being shall make his final account yearly at the feast of St Michael the Archangel and bring in within a month after all such sums of money as shall be behind or unpaid in pain of forfeiting his whole year's stipend allowed for his Stewardship and shall otherwise also satisfy the College according to the Master and most part of the Fellows' discretion.

And furthermore the said Steward shall quarterly make his account before the Master or President and two other of the senior Fellows at choice (?) present of such sums of money as he hath paid out the same quarter."[1]

There are several indications that during the last forty years of the sixteenth century the College was making efforts to manage its finances better.

(1) There is this College Order of 28 September 1560 forbidding the Steward (i.e. the Bursar) to lend money without the sanction of the Master and Fellows, and requiring quarterly accounts of his payments.

(2) College bailiffs were appointed in order to keep the Steward in touch with the tenants and to secure prompt payment of rents. See p. 224.

(3) Power of attorney is often granted to competent persons to conduct difficult or intricate pieces of College business. John Betts, for instance, a Bachelor of Laws, was on 14 January 1576 appointed syndic or proctor of the College, to appear for them in any court or cause and to act in their name and behalf.[2] Other instances are recorded or referred to in deeds of 1574, 1580, 1581, 1582, 1591, and 1592.

One of these (20 July 1582) gave John Cragge, M.A., Fellow of the College, and evidently the Steward, power of attorney to collect rents etc. from the College estates for three years. A similar power was again granted for three years in 1587. Two of the other instances raise the question of "squatter's right", and illustrate a practice which the College has employed quite recently. A piece of property may for some reason be ownerless, unclaimed, and possibly falling into disrepair and becoming a public nuisance.

[1] *Register*, A. For an example of the audit here ordered see pp. 391–399.

[2] *Register*, II, 132.

An interested person may occupy it, and take the chance of his action being challenged in a court of law.

On 24 April 1580 the College sealed a letter of attorney to John Cragge and Lancelot Flower "to enter into that our manor of Godstone" in the parish of Reigate in the county of Surrey and into all the lands etc. belonging to it, "to our use to claim and the possession thereof to our use to take, and having possession thereof or of any parcel thereof then to seal a certain writing containing the form and words of a demise made in our names to John Stevens of the city of London, citizen and tallow chandler of London, of the aforesaid premises with their appurtenances for the term of five years from the feast of Easter last past" and "then in our place, right and name to deliver the same to the said John Stevens as our deed".[1]

There is no trace anywhere else of the College having any interest either in this property or in the one referred to in the letters of attorney granted (9 December 1581) to Adam Longworth, Master of Arts and Fellow of the College, to enter into and take possession of all their lands, tenements and hereditaments, commonly called Chater and Hewley, in the parishes of Hurst and Cuckfield, Sussex, and to seal a demise thereof made in the name of the College to William Hound, of Broadwater, Sussex, gentlemen, for five years from next Easter, and to deliver the same to him.[2]

No arrangements are made in the Founder's statutes for the management of College property and the care of its finances. In the absence of any positive evidence we may assume that at first the Master, in his capacity as *custos* or Keeper, carried out Bursarial duties, received income and controlled expenditure. But the development of the College[3] would require before long the appointment of a financial officer, and there is a College Order, dated 6 July 1543, directing that in every year one of the Fellows in rotation should hold both the office of Collector of Rents and that of priest of the Chantry of

[1] *Register*, I, 70.

[2] *Register*, II, 104. Was William Hound a relative of the Master? If so, the sequence of events becomes clearer.

[3] It was the policy of the College during the sixteenth century to sell house property and to buy farms.

William Myles, and render his account in the week before or in the week after the Feast of St Catharine, his extra salary to be forty shillings.[1] This Order was confirmed by the Edwardian statutes of 1549, which provide for a *senescallus seu receptor*. His duties are to receive the revenues of the College, to carry out repairs, to buy the necessary materials for the same, and to render account annually to the Master and Fellows. His salary is to be forty shillings.

The same statutes insist on an inventory of College possessions being kept in the "Tower or Treasury". This is to be checked every year by the Fellows near the Feast of St Catharine. It is possible, in fact probable, that Woodlark's omission to legislate for the business side of College life had led to confusion or actual loss. The *senescallus* soon had a Bailiff to assist him, and two appointments to the post are recorded in the Register.[2] Clearly the Steward's duties were not easy, and the College Order of 1543, whereby the Fellows became Steward in rotation, distributed a burden rather than a prize.

The Steward is often called the Bursar in the accounts of the early seventeenth century, and the latter name gradually prevailed over the other. By a College Order of 11 December 1792 the two offices were separated,[3] and in the accounts of 1799–1800 the Steward's stipend is given as ten pounds. The duties of the two offices are not specified, but they were probably much as they are to-day for each officer.

The stipends fixed by the Founder's statutes were for the Master five pounds and for each Fellow four pounds a year, payable quarterly. Neither Master nor Fellows were debarred from receiving some pay from other sources. The chief additions to income, excluding ecclesiastical preferment,

[1] *Register*, I, 118. As the priest received a stipend of £4, the total income of the Bursar would be £4+£4+£2=£10.

[2] Under date 10 August 1572 Francis Cooper of Barnwell is appointed Bailiff of the College during pleasure at an annual fee of 20 shillings (*Register*, II, 100). On 15 November 1596 the College Seal was put to a deed appointing John Baniker (Banister ?), of the town of Cambridge, bricklayer, Bailiff of the College, during pleasure, to ask, levy, receive and recover all rents etc. due to the College in Cambridge, Chesterton, Whitwell, Coton, Barton and Grantchester for an annual salary of 5 shillings (II, 120).

[3] The Order does not say this in so many words, but for the first time a Steward is appointed as well as a Bursar.

seem to have been derived from attendance at prayers for the dead or at Masses, along with fees for preaching sermons.

In Isabella Caunterbury's composition (1479) the Master receives 20 pence for attendance and each Fellow 12 pence. In William Bassett's composition (1487) the Master receives *pro exequiis et missa* 12 pence and each Fellow 8 pence; the preacher of two sermons receives 13 shillings and 4 pence, or at least 10 shillings. In Taylard's composition (1505) the amounts are 20 pence for the Master and a residue to be divided equally among the Fellows.

Under the Sympson foundation (1506) the Master receives 8 pence and each Fellow 4 pence. Under the deed for the foundation of a Bible Clerkship (1506) the Master gets 12 pence and each Fellow 8 pence. The deed of the foundation of the John Chester Fellowship (1515) gives 6 shillings and 8 pence for a sermon and 5 shillings to be divided among the Master and Fellows.

The composition of Hugh Garnett (1526) gives 6 pence to the Master and 4 pence to each Fellow.

Under the composition of Robert Shurton (1536), "at the Dirige and mass the said Master, being there present, to have two shillings, and every one of the Fellows, being present, twelve pence, the bible clerk four pence, being also present, and the butler four pence".

At the Reformation most "extras" ceased, and there are not wanting signs that the Master and Fellows foresaw the coming loss. Perhaps for this reason, though possibly because of a fall in the value of money, the College Order of 6 July 1543 raised the stipend of the Master to six pounds and that of a Fellow to five pounds. In so ordering the Master and Fellows were doubtless acting *ultra vires*, but the change was afterwards legalised. The fact is that, with certain exceptions, payments ought not to be fixed by statute, as money is constantly changing in value, and a statute is of a permanent nature.

By the time our Audit books begin (1622) the stipends have again increased. They appear there as £7 and £5. 13*s*. 4*d*., and a loose paper of accounts, of a slightly earlier date, informs us that the additional sums were for *commemorationes*. The stipends as thus fixed appear in the books until they were abolished by the first Victorian Commission.

The Edwardian statutes fixed the stipend of the President and of the Steward. As these statutes remained in force for over three hundred years, the stipends for these officers were sometimes (quite irregularly) varied by a

College Order. In the accounts of the seventeenth century there often appears an item of £1. 2*s.* 0*d.* called the "gift to the Steward".

In the year 1671–2 it was decided that the surplusage of the Cook's and Lecturer's wages should "be divided between the Steward, Deane and Lecturer: and so to continue till there be need of restoring it to the College". The stipends of Dean, Lecturer and Librarian were not statutory, and the College had a perfect right to vary them from time to time. Here are two entries.

1628–9	Praelectori	0. 6. 8
	Bibliothecae custodi	0. 6. 8

On two occasions during the second half of the sixteenth century the College granted a kind of pension to its legal advisers. On 15 October 1577 an annuity of ten shillings for ten years was given to Robert Shute, Recorder of the town of Cambridge, for good and faithful counsel given by him to the College and to be given henceforth. The money was to be paid out of the revenues of the Manor of Coton, and power was given to Mr Shute to distrain upon the lands of the Manor in default of payment. This Mr Shute lived at Oakington, was sworn Recorder of Cambridge 1 March 1559, and was afterwards a Baron of the Exchequer.[1] Again, on 28 April 1582 an annual rent of ten shillings was granted to Edward Ellis of Gray's Inn during his natural life for counsel given and to be given to the College in all causes and matters which concerned it.[2] We know nothing of the details, but on the face of it the grants seem to be of the nature of retaining fees. One likes to think, however, that the College was showing a praiseworthy desire to reward faithful service, and also that it was not acting *ultra vires* in doing so in this particular way.

There is some evidence that Fellows acquired a kind of right to certain sets of rooms, of which they received the "income". The question is rendered a little uncertain by the ambiguity of the term "income", which occasionally means a kind of allowance for improvements and the like carried out at the Fellow's own expense. Thus in the accounts for 1680–1 we find:

Incomes allowed Mr Sparrow	2. 8. 8
Ds Angier	1. 6. 8

[1] Cooper, *Annals*, II, 147 and *Register*, I, 128.

[2] *Register*, II, 104.

There is some doubt about the meaning of the following:

1623–4 For allowance to Mr Lothian and Mr Arrowsmith for their losse in ye Income of ye Chamber next ye New entry when it was taken downe 0. 12. 0

1648–9 Allowed Mr Lynford for ye Income of the middle study in the furthest chamb^{r} of ye Cloister building 4. 2. 6

We may compare an entry in the Order Book under date 21 November 1722:

> I do hereby give ye Income of ye Chamber in our College of Katherine Hall up two pair of Stairs on ye South side adjoining to ye Gatehouse to ye use of our said College.
>
> Witness my hand
>
> Tho: Crosse Master.

The audit for 1729–30 contains an item of £9 received from Mr Prescott as income for his chamber "given to the Coll by Dr Crosse".

Again, it was agreed on 8 April 1724 that "Mr Pegge's Income to the Chambers up one pair of stairs next the Bull Gate-House be Ten Pounds, Six Pounds of it to be paid by giving up his Right to the Income of his other Room the other Four Pounds to be paid in Money".

The attitude of the College towards rooms and the right to them was very different in its earlier days from what it is to-day. This is plain from a curious lease granted (24 April 1577) to Marmaduke Monson, sometime Fellow of the College. There had previously been a fire, by which certain chambers had been destroyed. Monson and his friends contributed to the rebuilding. In consideration of this generosity, the College authorities now seal a lease of "one chamber, being above and over a chamber which Mr Edward Croft, Pensioner[1] of the College hath, being also betwixt the Queens' College little orchard of the South end and a chamber which Mr John Furmarie, Fellow of the College, is in of the north end; with one little bedchamber and one study in the south end of the chamber and one other little study in the north end of the chamber; with one upper chamber also,

[1] At this date a Pensioner at St Catharine's was what was afterwards called a Fellow Commoner.

having a study in the south end of that chamber and one little coal house in the north end thereof".

The lease was for 21 years, if Mr Monson should live so long, and the rent was to be 20 shillings a year. The Master and Fellows undertake all necessary repairs, and to allow ingress and egress at such times as the statutes permit their gates to stand open. There is no clause against sub-letting.

The fixing of stipends by statute, and the continued fall in the value of money, led to the custom of declaring at the annual audit a supplementary "dividend". The practice was of course prevalent throughout the University, and apparently established itself in the first half of the seventeenth century,[1] when the number of undergraduates was large, and colleges flourished. The earlier Catharine records are silent about this reasonable but illegal means of supplementing an inadequate income; indeed a careful reader might go through the first Audit Book without even a suspicion that there was as yet such a thing as a "dividend". So we cannot say for certain when the Society of St Catharine's began to follow the prevailing practice, but Dr Philpott seems to have been convinced that it was in the year 1684,[2] for he has left in manuscript calculations of dividends from that year to 1853.[3]

The principle behind the custom of dividends is that the Master and Fellows were entitled to divide among themselves certain revenues not specifically allocated for other purposes. Nobody seems to have advocated the wisdom of letting these surpluses accumulate to form a reserve for expansion purposes, or for meeting the hardships of a "rainy day". Perhaps it was felt that with the fall in the value of money the rainy day was already come.

It may be of some interest to set out the various items that went to form a dividend at St Catharine's. First we have what is called "corn money". This term arose from a result of the Act 18 Eliz. ch. 6, entitled "An Act for Maintenance of the Colleges in the Universities and of Winchester and Eaton".

[1] The first hint of the practice at St Catharine's is the quarterly division of the profits of the dove-house in 1560. See p. 221.

[2] This may possibly be the year of the first regular dividend, but windfalls, such as fines and "corn money", must have been divided up long before.

[3] See p. 389.

This Act, to secure an adequate supply of food for Colleges, ordered that of the reserved rents under any lease, one third should in future be paid in wheat or malt, wheat to be reckoned at 6*s.* 8*d.*, malt at 5*s.* a quarter. The wheat and malt, or its value in money in Cambridge Market at the time, were to be used solely for the relief of the commons and diet of the College. This section enabled the College, after carrying to College Stock the reserved rents due before the Act (£59. 19*s.* 1*d.*), to divide among themselves the difference between these reserved rents and the actual rents received, which latter were often enhanced by the increased value of wheat and malt. In this way "corn money" came to be carried to a dividend account. The other items were certain small rents (e.g. that of the Porter's House after the Ramsden alterations), fines, degree fees, scholars' absence, and profits on beer, bread and coal. Coal profits do not appear until 1731. Bread profits disappear in 1807, beer profits in 1843, scholars' absence in 1852.

As a specimen we may take the Dividend Account for the whole year to Michaelmas 1792.

Corn money:			
491. 6. 8¼ less 59. 19. 1 =	£431.	7.	7¼
Degrees	28.	14.	8
Profits of bread and beer	29.	3.	6
Scholars' absence	22.	17.	0
Rent for Porter's House and a tenement called the Three Horse Shoes allowed by the Court of Chancery	10.	1.	7
	522.	4.	4¼
To the Master and six Fellows each	74.	12.	0½

There was also a dividend from coal (£5. 16*s.* 10*d.*) and from a fine £5. 4*s.* 3*d.*

The College records of the second half of the eighteenth century include some which throw light on the system of land tenure whereby the tenant held a lease at a very low rent, and then during the course of the lease, usually at the end of seven years, came to the landlord and offered to pay a "fine"[1] for an extension of the existing lease. At the best it was a clumsy method of adjusting rent to agricultural values, and in course of time gave way to the system of rack-rent. At the period mentioned above the College was evidently getting dissatisfied with "beneficial" leases, as they were called, and wished to bring them to an end. But a difficulty lay in the way. Rents went to College Stock, that is to say to the ordinary expenses of running the College, but fines went to swell dividends. The ingenious plan was adopted of letting a lease run out, but borrowing from a College fund the fine that would have been paid had it been renewed. It was thus possible to get the best of both worlds.

On 15 May 1773 it was decided to let the lease run out of Over Manor, seven years of which had expired at Michaelmas 1772. It was agreed to borrow from the Chapel Fund free of interest £94. 0*s*. 8*d*. to pay the fine then due to the Master and Fellows, such sums to be repaid out of the profits arising from the estate as soon as may be. On the same day an order was made to borrow from the Chapel Fund £113. 2*s*. 4*d*. to pay the fine due to the Master and Fellows for Ridgewell Parsonage.

By a subsequent order (22 December 1773) these sums were commuted to £132. 2*s*. 4*d*. for Ridgewell Parsonage and £95. 9*s*. 9*d*. for Over Manor.

Similar orders were made to borrow from the Chapel Fund on the same conditions.

22 November 1774	£24. 0. 0	for the fine of Coton land.
26 November 1776	£35. 3. 0	for Barton.
13 May 1777	£99. 6. 0 £61. 8. 6	For Coton Lordship land.

No other orders were made, but as the time arrived to renew the several leases the money to pay the fines due to the Master and Fellows was taken out of the Chapel Fund until Michaelmas 1788.

In this way the leases of Over Manor, Ridgewell Parsonage, Chesterton, Coton, Barton Farm and Wilbraham were run out. The sums borrowed from

[1] Colleges generally had a formula, according to which (with modifications when necessary) a fine was fixed.

the Chapel Fund for this purpose amounted altogether to £988. 3*s*. 3*d*., no part of which was ever repaid by the Master and Fellows when the land came into rack-rent.

At Michaelmas 1798 there was a debt against the Chapel Fund of £397. 8*s*. 8*d*., which was cancelled, but the College accounts at that time are too confused to show how this was effected.

At Michaelmas 1797 the Master and Fellows borrowed from the College Stock £170. 7*s*. 5*d*. for the fine of Whitwell land without interest, and from time to time other sums which enabled them profitably to run out the leases of Whitwell, Paxton, Over tenement, Layer Breton, Burrough and Dullingham, Harlton, Fulbourn, and Barton tenement. This last borrowing extended over the years 1797–1811, and all the money borrowed was repaid by instalments as soon as the lands came into rack-rent.

The Tutors divided among themselves the tuition fees of their pupils. The tutorial system was older than the College, but the College records of tutorial matters begin with the first Admission Book (1642), and financial details are wanting before the first volume of pupils' accounts (1676). We can however be sure that Tutors were appointed, not at a College Meeting, but by the Master himself, as the Lord Chancellor stated this to be the tradition of the College in his judgment given on 15 September 1802. The fees paid to the College by members *in statu pupillari* seem to have been controlled chiefly, if not altogether, by the Tutors or senior Tutor, with presumably the tacit consent of the Society or at least of the Master. The Tutor appears to have collected all dues payable by a pupil to the College or the University, but apart from this the College did not interfere, leaving the Tutor to settle matters with tradesmen, parents and his fellow-Tutors. The accounts, accordingly, of the Tutors are for the most part meagre scrap-books, disorderly and incomplete, although those of the late eighteenth century show greater care and regularity. One item in an account to Michaelmas 1695 may be taken as typical of tutorial accountancy:

"Rec^{d} of him I think 10. 0. 0."

So it is impossible to ascertain accurately how much was due to a Tutor, how much he lost by negligence, or how much he remitted to deserving pupils out of pity or generosity. On the other hand, most of the dues appear to be moderate; in fact mere numbers do not seem to have been considered a financial advantage, except to the Tutors. The tutorial fees during the seventeenth century were usually these:

10 shillings a quarter for a Sizar;
20 shillings a quarter for a Pensioner;
40 shillings a quarter for a Fellow Commoner;
80 shillings a quarter for a Nobleman.

Caution money was usually £3 or £5. As each Tutor had charge of a number of pupils which varied from about five to about fifty,[1] it is clear that a Tutorship was a lucrative post, much better paid than the Bursarship or Deanery.

A reader of the College records, familiar with modern terminology, might easily be misled by the use of the word "scholar". When we say to-day that a man is "a Scholar of his College" we mean that he has a rank awarded to him for his superior attainments. To this rank an emolument is attached, but the holder may keep his title and forgo the pecuniary reward. The Exhibitioner has a similar but inferior rank, while Pensioners hold no superior position and receive no emolument.

But in the oldest records *scholares* or "scholars" means simply "students". It is true that one early Latin deed, dated 29 April 1517, speaks of "socii sive scholares", which is obscure, but seems to be a piece of legal phrascology. The rules for College exercises require all *scholares* to attend Holy Communion on certain stated days. An old register claims to contain a list "omnium Scholarium cuiuscunque ordinis et conditionis", and the Bible Clerk is to be "discretus scolaris". The list of members of the College in 1558, preserved in the University Registry, recognises no *scholares*, dividing undergraduates into *pensionarii* and *discipuli*, while the Tutor's and Bursar's books have usually the grades of *commensales* (Fellow Commoners, who dined at the Fellows'

[1] Eachard had about 46 in 1666, Calamy about 38 in 1670, and Gouge about 24 in 1680.

table), Pensioners and Sizars, although "Scholarships" and "Exhibitions" are known early in the seventeenth century. In the early books of the Steward the commons, or charges for food, are divided into "Fellows' Commons" and "Scholars' Commons". In the deeds of the seventeenth century endowing the College with the means of helping students, the term "scholar" implies no rank. A typical extract is the following, taken from the will of Mrs Julian Stafford, which is dated 21 June 1627: "five pounds a year to four poor scholars[1] of St Catharine's Hall in the University of Cambridge, that shall study divinity and carry themselves soberly and religiously".

The terms "Scholarship" and "Exhibition", between which it is hard to draw a distinction in early records, are often used in them but imply no status, only an endowment of study. Into these were elected either Pensioners or Sizars, generally in at least their second year of residence, who after election retained, if they were Sizars, their old style, but are sometimes called, not "Scholars", but "Scholars of the House". "Scholars" is used in its modern meaning in a College resolution passed in October 1716, to the effect that Scholars of the standing of B.A. were to reside for at least thirteen weeks in the year.[2]

The College records[3] are thus fairly consistent until comparatively modern times in attaching no special rank to the terms "Scholar" and "Exhibitioner". Indeed it is very remarkable that no official record of Scholars (with the exception of the Skerne Scholars) has ever been kept at St Catharine's, nor is there any ceremony of admission. When the College is described from outside, the junior students are styled during the sixteenth century thus:

1558 8 *discipuli* (with perhaps some *pensionarii*);
1564 7 *scholares*;
1573 *bibliorum lector*, 3 *inferiores ministri*, 21 *pensionarii*.

[1] They would be called "Mrs Stafford's scholars", from which style the modern sense of "Scholar" comes by natural and easy stages.

[2] See p. 113.

[3] The first Admission Book grades entrants into Pensioners, Sizars, Fellow Commoners and Noblemen. There is not a single entry of "admitted Scholar".

In the seventeenth century we find:

1621 8 scholars with students;
1651 10 scholars, 9 exhibitioners and other students;
1672 18 scholars, 9 exhibitioners and other students.

The conclusion appears to be that the technical meaning of "Scholar" came into use very gradually, and that St Catharine's adopted it rather late. Outsiders therefore might use it of St Catharine's students when the College authorities themselves employed a different terminology.

For the first fifty years from the foundation gifts and bequests had as their object the enlargement of the College or the establishment of new Fellowships. After the Reformation there came for a time but few fresh endowments. Perhaps the College became unpopular; perhaps times were hard, and the public uncertain as to the best way of encouraging education and research. Be this as it may, there was a lull, and when endowments again become numerous, the donors are mainly anxious to found Scholarships.

At first there were two Fellowships, but others were added in 1478, 1503, 1506 and 1515, and six has been the number of foundation Fellowships ever since, although bye-Fellowships were founded in 1691, 1695 and 1743. On the other hand, there were, unless the offices of Bible Clerk and Butler come under this category, no Scholarships before 1587, after which there followed in quick succession others in 1610, 1613, 1626, 1627, 1631, 1633, 1646, 1674, 1691, 1695 and 1743. These two sequences of dates are eloquent testimony to the change from Woodlark's ideal of a learned and religious Society served by a few Sizars to the modern ideal of a body of young students served and educated by teaching Fellows.

The first Scholarship was the result of a bequest made by John Cholmeley in a will dated 12 December 1587. The testator was a Londoner, and the scholar was always to be a Londoner also, maintained by fifty shillings a year chargeable upon the Golden Ball, a house in the Old Bailey, the payments to begin five years after the marriage of his mother or within a year after death, whichever shall happen first. The mother died about two years after the date of the will. John's brother William, to whom letters of administration had been granted, sold the house for £300 to one Fonnes without making any mention of its liability to the charge of the annuity. William Cholmeley by his will, 30 November 1641, left £37 to the inheritors of the Golden Ball, as a recompense for the payment of the annuity, having himself paid the fifty shillings a year as long as he lived. Presumably he wished the Scholarship to remain connected with the Golden Ball, for a much simpler transaction would have been to leave the money directly to the College. Perhaps he distrusted the ability of the Society to make sound investments, or suspected that they would not invest the endowment at all. But the owner of the Golden Ball never paid the annuity, and the College sued Samuel Fonnes, the son of the purchaser, in the Court of Chancery (Michaelmas Term 1654). Successful in their suit the Master and Fellows continued to receive no annuity, and on 5 March 1661 took steps to enforce payment and to recover arrears. The Bursar's accounts contain items showing that law proceedings were tried, but in vain.

In 1658 one payment (law expenses) 1. 3. 0
In 1659 one payment 1. 11. 8
In 1661 three payments 0. 1. 2, 0. 10. 0 and 0. 10. 0
In 1662 one payment 0. 10. 0
In 1663 four payments 0. 2. 0, 1. 0. 0, 0. 8. 6 and 0. 7. 0

The College continued to pay the Scholarship up to 1665, after which time it was discontinued.

William Cholmeley's executors were Dr Ralph Brownrigge, Master of St Catharine's, Robert Skerne, and Jasper Cholmeley. The second of these became attached to the College, either because of the injustice it had suffered, or because the lovable character of Brownrigge attracted him. By his will he founded in 1662 eight Scholarships, and doubtless influenced indirectly his great-niece Mrs Ramsden to make her splendid benefaction in the next century.

Cholmeley's scholars were bound to be Londoners, and the practice of tying a Scholarship to a particular town, district or school was common at this period, as also was that of reserving the right to nominate. The modern system of open competitive examinations requires an elaborate organisation of education that did not come into existence until comparatively recent times, and there was operant in the sixteenth and seventeenth centuries a strong feeling, in fact an assumption, that Scholarships were not an honour but a charity,[1] and that the givers of a charitable endowment had the right to nominate the recipient. But times and circumstances changed, and the framers of the 1860 statutes required that no regard be taken, in the election of scholars, of either birthplace or school, but that merit alone should count.[2] A reason often put forward in favour of close Scholarships has less force now than when urged fifty years ago by G. F. Browne. A provincial grammar school, it was said, cannot provide the expert teaching and coaching necessary to equip the budding genius for a struggle with a skilfully prepared candidate from the great public schools, and therefore many deserving candidates are unable to come up to the University except through a close Scholarship. But a levelling tendency has long been at work among the teaching staffs of various types of schools; means tests are now often imposed, which give the emolument of a Scholarship to the "hopeful poor scholar" and only the honour to the brilliant rich student. Moreover, close Exhibitions are to-day becoming, if not more popular, at least more tolerated.

The choice of suitable candidates for Scholarships is now made on carefully devised, scientific principles; three hundred years ago it was a more personal matter, and charity usually began at home. The difference must be borne in mind in appreciating the early deeds governing all such endowments.

On 4 July 1610 Mrs Rosamond Payne, a Devonshire lady, left the sum of £100 for the maintenance of two scholars[3] in Catharine Hall. Each scholar was to receive five marks (£3. 6*s*. 8*d*.) annually, and was to be called Mrs Payne's scholar in Catharine Hall in Cambridge. The capital was invested in the block

[1] Poverty rather than learning or ability was the chief qualification for these early Scholarships. They were to be given to "poor scholars", or to "honest hopeful poor scholars".

[2] "Sed in electione non ulla ratio cuivis habeatur vel loci ubi natus vel scholae ubi literis institutus fuerit: eligantur...qui...vel in studiis academicis praestantiam exhibuerint vel in examinatione in hanc rem a magistro et sociis instituta laudem meruerint."

[3] From this point "scholar" not "Scholar" is printed wherever from the original documents it appears that the word is not used to denote a special rank. This special rank seems to have been generally given after the Ramsden foundation.

Plate XIV

Dr John Gostlin

of chambers erected shortly afterwards and called after the donor Rosamond Payne's Building.

On 14 March 1610 probate was granted of the will of John Duke, of Kelsale, Suffolk, bequeathing to the College his books, writings and the residue of his goods "for the maintenance of most godly students in divinity abiding in the College". The date of the will is 2 October 1604.

On 31 December 1613 Sir John Claypoole or Cleypoole, of Northborrow in the county of Northampton, gave by deed to the Master and Fellows the sum of £120 "for and toward the edifying and erecting of certain lodgings and chambers in the said College or Hall commonly called the New Buildings". The College agreed out of the rent of the said lodgings and chambers continually hereafter to maintain two scholars, who should be called Sir John Claypoole's scholars, allowing them £5. *6s.* *8d.* a year, equally to be divided between them, as the said rent of the chambers. If the rent did not amount to this sum, then the scholars were to have no more or further allowance than the rent of the chambers—an awkward arrangement for the scholars, as they could never be sure of the value of their Scholarship. The Master and Fellows agreed to accept the nominee of Sir John Claypoole from time to time, namely one scholar for the one half of the said allowance, if they should "find him fit and capable thereof, and not against the statute of the University, nor the customs, statute and privilege of the said College or Hall of St Catharine aforesaid". This £120 nearly paid for the Claypoole Building put up by John Atkinson in 1611.

The will (9 October 1626) of John Gostlin, who left the Bull Inn to the Master and Fellows, stipulates that there are to be founded six Scholarships in his name, each scholar to receive out of the rents of the said Bull Inn four pounds yearly. No conditions are added.

Mrs Julian Stafford, wife of Alexander Stafford, of High Holborn in the county of Middlesex, by her will (21 June 1627) gives the reversion of an estate at Harlow in Essex, after the death of her husband and herself, to certain trustees, to pay for ever yearly, out of the rents and profits of the same, twenty pounds to be equally distributed, namely "five pounds a year to four poor scholars of St Catharine's Hall...that shall study divinity and carry themselves soberly and religiously, to be nominated and appointed by the

Master....And my mind and will is, that the said five pounds be continued yearly to every such scholar...until the scholar or scholars take the degree of Master of Arts, or depart from the said Hall and continue his absence from the same for the space of a quarter of a year or more without the licence of the Master."

The College papers and books do not contain any account of payments to these scholars till 1689, though it is certain that scholars were appointed much earlier than this. Thus in the third volume of the College Register, p. 112, is a copy of a receipt given by the College for five pounds paid to it on account of a like sum which Mr Lynford had in his hands for Mrs Stafford's Exhibitions; but Mr Lynford ceased to be a Fellow in 1648.

Thomas Hobbes, in his will dated 21 February 1631, recites that he has granted the lease of his estate at Braintree on trust to his nephew, Henry Lawrence, and his cousins, Peter Pheasant and Richard Bellingham, to be disposed of in various ways.

"And the like sum of five pounds yearly from and after my decease shall be for ever at the days aforesaid bestowed for the maintenance of a Catechising Lecture, which I have begun in Catharine Hall in Cambridge, so long as by the Master of the said house for the time being and my said friends trusted with the said lease or their assigns shall be thought fit....And all the rest of the said rents and profits to be for and towards the maintenance of two or three honest hopeful poor scholars, students in the University of Cambridge, namely in Catharine Hall and Emmanuel College, or one of them, being also of sober and Christian conversation. And I will that the sons of godly poor ministers, painful in the work of the Lord, shall be especially respected before others; and that a priority of respect in selection of the said scholars shall be had to Catharine Hall, if any such shall be there to be had and elected, especially so long as my worthy friend Doctor Sibbs shall continue master of the said Hall....And my will is that during the said lease as well the said lecturer as the said scholars shall from time to time be chosen by them that have the interest of that lease, and by and with the consent of the master of such one of the said College or Hall for the time being, where the election shall be made."

On 21 October 1646 the College seal was put to an indenture between the Master and Fellows and Henry Spurstow, citizen and merchant, executor of William Spurstow, late father of William Spurstow, then Master of the College. The indenture recites that the said William Spurstow, the elder, had bequeathed £100 to be laid out for the relief and maintenance of one poor scholar in the College, and that the Master and Fellows had received from the executor the said £100 to be laid out in purchasing land or rent of inheritance for the maintenance of the said scholar. The Master and Fellows covenant to pay five pounds a year to a scholar in the College, who shall be called Mr Spurstow's scholar, and during the natural life of the Master, William Spurstow, be chosen from time to time by the said William Spurstow.[1]

The next foundation of Scholarships was made by a member of the family that befriended the College in its early days. Dame Elizabeth Barnardiston had endowed the office or Sizarship of Butler in 1514, and in 1633 Lady Katharine Barnardiston founded three new Scholarships. The value of each was not a fixed sum, but a share of certain rents. The details of the endowment are best understood by a quotation from Lady Barnardiston's will, which is dated 25 February 1633.

"The whole yearly rents and profits, that shall be raised and made out of the said land so to be purchased with the said four hundred pounds as aforesaid, and for which the same land shall be letten, shall from time to time for ever be disbursed and paid...unto three such poor scholars of the said society of Katharine Hall, whose parents are not well able to bring them up and to maintain them in the University, and whose sufficiency in learning and honest condition of life and conversation shall be approved and allowed of by the aforesaid Master and Fellows ...or by the greater number of them. And my will likewise is that, if any of mine own poor kindred shall be brought up in learning and be admitted into the said society of Katharine Hall, and that they be of sufficient learning and honest life and conversation",

then such are to be chosen into all or such of the Scholarships as shall be vacant. Failing these, a poor student, one only, from the parish of Witham, in the county of Essex, "where my dwelling now is", being admitted into the said Society of Katharine Hall, and of sufficient learning and honest conversation, shall be elected before any other into one of the Scholarships. In the fault of any such scholars in the Society akin to Lady Barnardiston, then, if there shall happen to be any poor scholar in the said Society of Katharine Hall, who were formerly educated in Christ's Hospital, such poor

[1] *Register*, III, 65.

scholars, being of honest conversation and sufficient of learning, shall be elected into the two other of the aforesaid three Scholarships. Should a vacancy occur when no such person is available, then any Barnardiston, if suitably qualified and a member of Katharine Hall, shall be elected into a Scholarship. Failing all other, the Master and Fellows are to elect as scholar or scholars such as they or the greater number of them shall out of their religious care think most fit. The Scholarships are to be tenable for seven years or until the scholar is qualified to take the degree of Master of Arts.

This will seems to lay stress upon candidates being already members of the College before they become eligible. An examination of the few records possessed by the College of Scholarship elections shows that usually, though not always, men were chosen who had already resided for a time, and that scholars in receipt of a small Scholarship were often promoted to one of higher value. Such a system has obvious disadvantages, but we must remember that it was not easy in the seventeenth century to test a candidate previous to admission. Even at the present day, with all the elaborate machinery at the disposal of electors, mistakes often occur, and it is deemed right to review elections every year in the light of the results of University examinations.

The Skerne Scholarships were the result of the will of Robert Skerne of Fockerby in Yorkshire. It is dated 16 November 1661, and leaves lands at Adlingfleet and Whitgift for the maintenance of three scholars, the first nomination to be made by Skerne himself, subsequent nominations by the Master and Fellows. By a codicil dated 5 October 1662 the Scholarships are increased to four, and the testator goes on to say that "I do further will and appoint that my executors out of my personal estate shall lay out so much money for the purchase of lands of inheritance for ever, as shall maintain four scholarships, and shall settle the said lands upon the Master and Fellows of St Catharine Hall aforesaid and their successors for ever". The executors purchased land to the value of £736. 16*s*. 8*d*., which was conveyed to the Master of the College and other trustees on 24 December 1663.

The first year of the great rebuilding saw another instance of capital being invested in chambers, the income therefrom to go to the support of poor students. On 4 July 1674 an indenture was sealed between the Master and

Fellows and John Cartwright of Aynho in the county of Northampton. The deed recites that the said John Cartwright "willing to encourage virtue and learning in the said Hall", has paid to the Bursar £200 to be employed in the building of chambers in the College "for the improvement and bettering the revenue of the said society". In consideration thereof the Master and Fellows agree to pay £12 a year to such one, two or three poor scholars in the said Hall, as shall be nominated from time to time by John Cartwright and his heirs by writing under his or their hands and seals. The Scholarships are to be tenable for eight years.

The Master and Fellows are to give notice in writing of every vacancy, within a month, to Mr Cartwright or his heirs, or to leave such notice for him or them at his dwelling-house in Aynho. If at any time there be no scholar, so nominated, in the College, the stipends are to be kept until Mr Cartwright or his heirs direct the money to be paid to some poor scholar or scholars to be sent by him or them to the College. The indenture is endorsed with a memorandum:

> "Thomas Cartwright, Esquire, heir and grandson of John Cartwright, upon the request of the Master and Fellows of Catharine Hall, did at or before the seventh day of February 1692, give fifty pounds more for the easier payment of the twelve pounds per annum to his poor scholars.
>
> John Eachard.
> Sam. Lea."

John Cartwright valued highly the right to nominate in perpetuity. Two years later than the indenture a scheme was put forward by the Governors of King Edward's School, Birmingham, whereby the school was to send to the College seven scholars and two Fellows. To supplement the grant from Birmingham Mr Brokesby, the chief master, gained the consent of Sir Thomas Barnardiston to the use of Scholarships established at Catharine Hall by Sir Thomas's ancestors, and a similar favour was asked of John Cartwright by the Master, Eachard. The reply was curt and decisive.

Worthy Sir,

I received your letter of 29 September. I desire to be excused from parting with the nomination to the scholarships in Catharine Hall (lately settled) out of myself and family to Birmingham, a free school having been erected here in the place where I dwell, by my late dear mother.

I remain,
Your humble servant,

Aynho 4 Oct: 1676. Jo. Cartwright.

This is the proper place to describe the efforts of the indefatigable Brokesby and the equally energetic Eachard to bring about a lasting connection between the school and St Catharine's.[1] It introduces us to the important question of bye-Fellowships. It was the demand of the College that the new Fellowships should be of this nature that wrecked the proposal.

Eachard was firmly convinced that it was a wise plan to bind the College to certain schools by the system of close Scholarships and Fellowships. One of his memoranda says:

"There being 30 Scholarships belonging to Catharine Hall in Cambridge, and not any one of them determined to any particular school or county in England, the Master and Fellows of the said College by the consent of the founders or executors to the founders of the scholarships are advised to settle ten of the best upon five eminent schools in the nation, namely Paul's, Merchant Taylors, Eton, Ipswich and Bury, provided that the Governors of the said schools shall be pleased to settle Scholarships of like value upon such Scholars of their own as shall be sent to Catharine Hall. They may settle to the value of 4, 5 or 6 pounds per annum upon each of their Scholars, we having no Scholarships that are greater. We have already determined two to Eton and two to Merchant Taylors, and are ready to do the like to the rest of the Schools."

The object in view was twofold, to secure students of greater intellectual ability and to increase the value of the existing Scholarships, which had fallen with the change in the value of money.

The proposal of the Governors of King Edward's was bound to be welcomed by Eachard. A member of the Corporation of Birmingham and the chief schoolmaster visited St Catharine's,[2] bringing with them the letter which

[1] The matter has been discussed, and the evidence given in full, in *The Records of King Edward's School Birmingham*, vol. III (Dugdale Society's Publication, 1933) by W. F. Carter and E. A. B. Barnard.

[2] There is a reference to this visit in the Bursar's accounts for 1675–6, which contain an entry: Wine for Birmingham Governors 0. 10. 0

contained a brief outline of the suggested scheme. One is tempted to think that Samuel Frankland, native of Tamworth, schoolmaster of Coventry and benefactor of the College, who is mentioned in a letter (1 May 1676) written by Brokesby to Eachard after the meeting in Cambridge, was the prime mover in the whole matter. For a time all went well; apparently, before the scheme was settled, two Exhibitioners from Birmingham came into residence at Michaelmas 1676.

In 1677 a draft agreement was drawn up, the chief articles being as given below.

The sum of £70 per annum is to be expended by the Governors of King Edward's:

(1) In the maintenance of two Exhibitions of £5 each to be settled on Catharine Hall, Cambridge, to increase two out of seven Scholarships which the Hall promises to fix upon scholars from Birmingham School, making each £10 per annum.

(2) In establishing at the College two Fellowships of £30 per annum, one to commence at Lady Day 1681, the other at Lady Day 1682, confined to scholars from Birmingham School.

Alternatively:

(3) In the establishment of seven Scholarships of £10 yearly, tenable by scholars of Birmingham School at any College in either University.

(4) No Fellow is to enjoy his Fellowship for more than ten years, and within two years after taking his degree of M.A. shall be obliged to take orders.

(5) No scholar is to enjoy his Scholarship for more than seven years, or after he has taken his degree of M.A.

Towards the end is a clause in brackets, containing carefully worded proposals for regulating the status of the Birmingham Fellows.

Presently we find Brokesby strongly objecting to certain of the proposals; in a letter dated 8 December 1677 he protests that the Birmingham Fellows are left "mere nominal tanquams, void of votes in election of your fellows: though ours are left wholly to the election of you and yours", and expresses regret that the cause of this inferiority, the founder's statutes and the oath to observe them,[1] had not been explained earlier. The result will be, he fears, that the Scholarships will be made open to any College in either University. "If this come to pass, you must blame your founder, and not us, no more than we dare you, who it seems are tied up from enlarging your College, and permitting any to incorporate with you, only while I presume to remember you, how in your own lodgings, when the ridiculous state of tanquam fellow was discussed, I told you that we would have full fellows or none." The writer goes on to say that the provision about entering holy orders is unfair, "unless it shall be added: except they shall profess law, or physic: for as we maintain our scholars so it seems equal to me that they should be at liberty to choose their profession".

A few years later (February 1680–1) Brokesby wrote again, urging that certain "vehement" objections to the scheme were being made in Birmingham.

(1) The Scholarships proposed were too small to be of real help to poor boys.

(2) It was unwise to bury all their Scholarships in one small college, where the hopes of preferment were inconsiderable.

Brokesby is not quite so fiery in this letter as he was when he objected to "tanquam Fellows", and suggests various means of meeting these difficulties, even going so far as to promise conditionally £600 to Catharine Hall out of his private means, and £400 more for the benefit of Birmingham scholars.

"The practical result of all their negotiations was that four exhibitioners—Baldwin, Milner, Grove, and While—went up from Birmingham to Catharine Hall, of whom Milner and While certainly proceeded to the degree of M.A.; Milner also becoming a Fellow, and the School contributing to his fellowship these amounts—in 1681/2 £15, in 1682/3 £30, in 1683/4 £30, in 1684/5 £30, and in 1685/6 £30. And on the 13th of October 1685 the New Charter Governors decided to withdraw from whatever agreement subsisted between the two Foundations."[2]

[1] The College at this time was not governed by the Founder's statutes, but by those of Edward the Sixth, while the number of foundation Fellows is nowhere limited to six. The statutes say "sint sex socii sive plures sive pauciores iuxta rationem proventuum et reddituum dictae domus". The Founder's supposed regulation seems to have been an excuse to secure for the College "advanced studentships" instead of full Fellows.

[2] Carter and Barnard, *op. cit.* p. xxii.

Plate XV

Queens' Lane and the 1634 Building
(about 1840)

Finance

The following account of the financing of the rebuilding is taken from MS. notes of Dr Philpott. These are given as far as possible verbatim, as he had access to documents since lost. This remark applies to all that follows down to p. 261.

On 23 February 1673/4 the rebuilding of the College was commenced. Dr Lightfoot, the Master, contributed £38 and exerted himself to procure contributions from other persons. The Fellows also did the same and large sums were obtained.

After Dr Lightfoot's death, 6 December 1675, the new Master, John Eachard, used the most indefatigable diligence in procuring contributions and carrying on the work, the success of which may be said to be mainly due to him.

1. The sum expended from 23 February 1673/4 to 17 February 1676/7 was £3103. 16*s.* 0*d.* During this time the College Hall and Combination Room and the room over it were finished.

2. The sum expended from 17 February 1676/7 to 20 January 1678/9 was £1524. 4*s.* 6*d.* During this time there is a notice in the accounts of "Chambers pulled down". There are also charges for payments to Sir W. Jones and to the secretary and servants for "the King's letter about Queens' College garden".

It then appears that the west side of the College square and the Master's Lodge were built in 1677 and 1678.

Large sums of money were paid for interest on money borrowed.

3. The sum expended from 20 January 1678/9 to 18 November 1681 was £1101. 18*s.* 2*d.*

The accounts show considerable payments for upholstery and furniture for the Master's Lodge.

4. The sum expended from 18 November 1681 to 26 February 1683/4 was £1292. 19*s.* 5*d.*

The accounts show a charge of £1. 10*s.* 8*d.* for "lease of ground in the street of the town", and another charge of £22. 11*s.* 1*d.* to the carpenter for rails in the street. No copy of this lease was entered into the Register, but an additional rent of 6*s.* 8*d.* a year for the ground began to be paid from Michaelmas 1680, the former rent of one shilling continuing to be paid under the lease of August 1629. In the Bursar's accounts the rent of 6*s.* 8*d.* a year is said to be for the ground where the pales stand. Still larger sums are charged for interest on money borrowed.

5. The sum expended from 26 February 1683/4 to 29 September 1687 was £1924. 0*s.* 6*d.*, making the whole sum spent from the commencement of the work (23 February 1673/4) to Michaelmas 1687, £8946. 18*s.* 7*d.*

After Michaelmas 1687 the work seems to have ceased till 1694; the sums paid during the interval (excepting about £100 for more furniture for the Master's Lodge) being almost entirely for interest on money borrowed. In 1694 and 1695 the work was proceeded with; the sum expended from Michaelmas 1687 to St Thomas' Day 1695 was £1673. 13*s.* 4*d.*

In a memorandum dated 29 September 1687, Dr Eachard states that what was saved out of Bachelors' feasts and Fellows' feasts, and what was given by the Master and Fellows out of their fines for leases, was allowed towards interest money, entertainment of benefactors, horse journeys and such like extraordinary expenses above what is entered into the accounts. That the plate, likewise, that was taken out of the treasury, was sold and applied to the same purposes. There were three several parcels:

1.	£76.	0.	0
2.	44.	6.	3
3.	76.	19.	9
	£197.	6.	0

Loggan in his *Cantabrigia Illustrata* (1688) gives a plan of what the College was intended to be when finished, but the plan was never carried out. He says that Mr Scrivener first suggested the rebuilding of the College.

On 16 December 1676 Cornelius Archer conveyed to Dr Eachard a tenement in St Botolph's parish in the High Street with the appurtenances for £210. Dr Eachard mortgaged it to William Baron for £200, 18 December 1687. The tenement is always called the White Swan in the College books; the rent of it (£14) was always carried to the College stock, and the interest of the mortgage, together with the taxes and repairs, were also charged to the College stock. The mortgage was paid off by the College 26 October 1719, the Master, Dr Sherlock, having given the College £200 for the

TRANSLATION OF THE INSCRIPTION UNDER LOGGAN

Robert Wodelarke, born in Northumberland, S.T.P., the third Provost of King's College and Chancellor of this University, having first obtained permission from Edward IV, founded this House A.D. 1475 and wished it to be named College or Hall of St Catharine the Virgin, in which he established one Master and three Fellows only. But by the generosity of excellent benefactors three other Fellows have been added, as well as thirty Scholars and Exhibitioners. Among which benefactors there are to be specially recorded and always piously remembered: Isabella Canterbury, sister of the founder; William Taylor; Robert Sympson; Hugh Pemberton; John Chester; John Duke; Robert Skerne; John Cartwright; John Gostlyn, Master of Gonville and Caius College and Regius Professor of Medicine. There are other men who have shown marked generosity to this Hall, who have built at their own charges the House which you see, in the place of a hovel, very small, of poor materials, and tumbledown from the very beginning. Of these only the most generous are here recorded, namely, Thomas Barnardiston; John Rouse; John Fagg; Charles Blois, Bart.; Charles Caesar, Kt.; William Spence; Edward Pickering; Robert Spurston; Thomas Bedingfield; Peter Pheasant; Thomas and John Knyvet; and a man always to be held in honour, the Reverend Matthew Scrivener, a most learned and worthy member of this College, who was not only the first to promote the present new buildings, but in honour of God gave and consecrated a very large estate especially for the use of the Chapel about to be built. This is not the place to enumerate all the learned and famous men who have passed through this small House; it will be enough to mention and set forth certain excellent Masters only, viz. Edwin Sandys, Archbishop of Canterbury; John Mey, Bishop of Carlisle; John Overall, a most learned man, Regius Professor of Theology, Bishop of Lichfield, afterwards of Norwich; Ralph Brownrigge, Bishop of Exeter; and, quite recently, John Lightfoot, S.T.P., a man of universal learning and an excellent scholar in Oriental languages. This picture does not show the remains and ruins of the old College buildings (a sight too ugly to appear as a picture among the other Colleges of this University), but only the buildings recently set up, as well as those which, to-day only planned, in a short time will be actually constructed. For the intention is that Patrons of Letters may see what kind of a work this of theirs will be at last when finished, which, carried solely by their own generosity to the present point, now remains to be completed.

Plate XVI

Loggan's St Catharine's (1688)

purpose. In 1766, when the White Swan was pulled down to make way for Mrs Ramsden's new building, the Court of Chancery ordered that £252 (18 years' purchase) should be secured to the College stock in the Barton farm, as a compensation for the loss, with interest at 4 per cent. per annum.

In the conveyance, 1 April, 13 James I (1615), from William Archer to Cornelius Archer, the tenement is said to abut on the High Street to the east, and to lie between the tenement of Thomas Hobson on the north and a tenement formerly Robert Jenkinson's on the south. Also in the conveyance 14 July, 22 Eliz. (1580), from Nicholas Wilson to William Archer, the tenement is said to lie between a tenement, lately belonging to the Master and Fellows of Corpus Christi College, but now to Helen Hobson, widow, on the north and a tenement of Robert Jenkinson on the south; our head abuts on the High Street to the east and the other head on a "stabulum cum solario" belonging to St Catharine's Hall towards the west. This description helps to prove incidentally the purchase of the ground to the north of the White Swan by the College in 1637.

On 2 May 1687 the College seal was put to the following bonds: To Peter Fisher, Rector of Bennington, Herts, for £210 to be paid 3 May 1688. Dr Sherlock adds a memorandum (5 July 1709) that Dr Fisher said he had then no claim on the College.

To Thomas Smith, of Layham, Suffolk, for £210 to be paid 3 May 1688. Dr Eachard paid £100 at Midsummer 1691, and Dr Sherlock writes a memorandum 26 July 1709 that Mr Smith then made no claim.

To Thomas Sayer, of Huntingdon, surgeon, for £318 to be paid 3 May 1688. The interest was 6 per cent.

To Thomas Gate, of Cambridge, cook, for £210 to be paid 3 May 1688. £100 was paid 23 April 1695, and £100 was paid 11 October 1726.

To Henry Argill, of London, painter and stainer, for £318 to be paid 3 May 1688. The interest was 6 per cent. £100 was paid in August 1688.[1]

In the Bursar's accounts for the year to Michaelmas 1681 is a charge for "the upholsterer's bill for chairs, carpets, curtains and for scholars chambers in the whole year. £18. 7. 3." Similar charges occur in other years and show that the rooms of the scholars at that time were furnished by the College.

[1] For these bonds see *Register*, III, 173–175.

On 25 September 1688 the College seal was put to a bond to Richard Gardner, of Cransford, Suffolk, gentleman, for £315 to be paid 26 September 1689. £100 was paid 20 March 1689/90 and a memorandum signed by J. Addenbrooke states that £50, and all interest due to Lady Day 1710, was paid 15 June 1710. The rest was paid to Mrs Pells, formerly his wife, Lady Day 1720.[1]

On 22 November 1688 the College seal was put to a deed of bargain and sale to Sir Charles Caesar, of Bennington, Herts, knight, of sundry tankards and pieces of plate, weighing altogether 402 ounces, in satisfaction and discharge of £100, part of a debt of £200, which the College owed him for money borrowed of him and expended about the new buildings. Dr Sherlock writes a memorandum (5 July 1709) stating that Mr Caesar made no claim on the College at that time on account of this bond; but that he urged a claim on another bond, originally given to Mr Estcourt, and which he had paid off. There is no account of such a bond in the College Register, and it was probably a security for which Dr Eachard alone was personally liable. In consideration of this claim, Mr Caesar refused to pay the contributions to which he was liable on the first and third funds. It was said to be a bond for £200.[2]

First Fund

On 1 May 1695 the College seal was put to an indenture tripartite between the Master and Fellows of the first part;

> Dr Henry James, President of Queens',
> Dr Wm. Cooke, Fellow of Jesus and Chancellor of Ely,
> Susannah Crouch, of London, spinster,
> Elizabeth Morgan, of London, spinster,
> Richard Gardner (Dr Eachard's brother-in-law),
> William Fuller, Clerk,
> Uriah Taylor (formerly Sir Chas. Caesar's cook),
> Hugh Martin (Esquire Bedell),

of the second part; and

[1] *Register*, III, 175.

[2] *Register*, III, 176.

*John, Lord Cutts,	*Offspring Blackall, Clerk,
*Sir Thos. Rookby,	*Henry Gore, Esq.,
*Sir Thos. Barnardiston, Bart.,	Sir Thomas Willoughby, Bart.,
*Sir John Rous, Bart.,	*Sir Nicholas Garrard, Bart.,
*Dr Peter Fisher,	John Durnall, Sergeant at Law,
*Charles Caesar, Esq.,	Sir Thos. Roberts, Bart.,
*Thomas Cartwright, Esq.,	John Bence, Esq.,
James Selby, Esq.,	Robert Kempe, Esq.,
*Samuel Western, Esq.,	*Thos. Blunt, Esq.,
*James Calamy, Clerk,	*George Nodes, Junr., Esq.,

of the third part.

The indenture recites that:

Dr James, Elizabeth Morgan, Dr Cooke, Richard Gardner,	}	had paid £50 each,
William Fuller, Uriah Taylor, Hugh Martin,	}	had paid £100 each,

to the Master and Fellows "for or towards the building of a new chapel and the finishing of other buildings in the College". In consideration of which the Master and Fellows covenant to pay:

Dr James,	£5 a year, during his life.
Dr Cooke,	ditto.
Susannah Crouch,	ditto.
Elizabeth Morgan,	ditto.
Richard Gardner,	ditto.
William Fuller,	£5 a year during the life of his son William Fuller.
Uriah Taylor,	£10 a year during his life.
Hugh Martin,	£10 a year during the joint lives of him and of his wife Mary and after the death of either, then £5 a year during the life of the survivor.

Each of the parties, named as of the third part (they having all been formerly members of the College and being willing to contribute towards the enabling the Master and Fellows to pay the said annuities), agrees to contribute during his life (if the annuitant live so long) £5 a year to the Master and Fellows; provided, however, that when any one or more of the annuitants die, 5*s.* shall be deducted from every half year's payment for and in respect of every £5 annuity that shall so cease and determine.

Of the contributors named in the deed only fourteen executed it, being those which are marked with a cross; the other names, it appears, were inserted without the consent of the parties, in the hope that they might be willing.

The annuities ceased as follows:

Dr James died 5 March 1716/7.
Dr Cooke died 24 October 1707.
Susannah Crouch died 10 April 1729.
Elizabeth Morgan was paid up to Michaelmas 1732.
Richard Gardner died 16 January 1696/7.
William Fuller's annuity was paid to Michaelmas 1738.

Of the contributors, Lord Cutts and Sir Thomas Barnardiston paid nothing. Mr Cartwright refused to pay more than one year, but all the others paid well, particularly Sir John Rous, Dr Fisher, Mr Calamy, Blackall, Bishop of Exeter, Mr Blunt (afterwards Sir Thomas Pope Blunt).

Second Fund

On 1 May 1695 the College seal was put to an indenture quinquipartite between the Master and Fellows of the first part;

Dr John Covel, Master of Christ's,
Dr W. Stanley, Master of Corpus Christi,
Dr Peter Fisher,
Isaac Newton (Professor of Maths.),
John Pern (Esquire Bedell),
Anne Gardner, the younger, spinster,
Christopher Gardner,
Richard Gardner, the younger,
Lawrence Eachard, Clerk,
Christopher Eachard, Clerk,
Moses Holwey, Clerk,
William Worts (Esquire Bedell),
Edward Bartlett and Jane his wife,
Elizabeth Henley of London,

of the second part;

Sir William Dawes, Bart.,
*George Barnardiston,
*John Jeffery, Archdeacon of Norwich,
*Thomas Twistleton, Clerk,
John Brame,
Robert Jennay,
Thomas Titson, Clerk,
William Milner, Clerk,

*George Raymond,
*John Reynolds,
*John Candler, Clerk,
*Thomas Eachard, Clerk,
Henry Hoar,
Samuel Elgeley, Clerk,
*William Grove, Clerk,
*John Turton, Clerk,
Joseph Powell, Clerk,
Thomas Pagett, D.D.,
Samuel Bradford, Clerk,
Thomas Muston, Clerk,
*Richard Morton, M.D.,
Thomas Smith,
*John Sansom, Jnr.,
Robert Goodwin,
Samuel Stephenson,
Edward Russell, Clerk,
Humphrey Whyle, Clerk,
Daniel Algar,
*Robert Dimsdale, surgeon,
Abraham Chaplin, Clerk,
John Braddock, Clerk,

of the third part;

*Samuel Lea, *John Leng, *John Bower, *William Western, Alexander Bence, } Masters of Arts and Fellows of the College,

of the fourth part;

Dr John Balderston, Master of Emmanuel,
Dr Wm. Cooke, of Jesus College,
Dr Thos. Smoult, of St John's College,

of the fifth part.

The indenture recites that:

Dr Covel, Dr Stanley, Mr Newton, Mr Pern, Anne Gardner, Christopher Gardner, Richard Gardner, Mr Worts, Edward Bartlett, Elizabeth Henley, } had paid £25 each,

Dr Fisher, Lawrence Eachard, Christopher Eachard, } had paid £50 each,

and Moses Holwey had paid £100 to the Master and Fellows "for or towards the building of a new chapel and the finishing of other buildings in the College".

In consideration whereof the Master and Fellows covenant to pay:

Dr Covel,	50*s*. a year during his life.
Dr Stanley,	ditto.
Dr Fisher,	50*s*. a year during the life of Sarah Osborne and 50*s*. a year during the life of Hannah Fisher.
Mr Newton,	50*s*. a year during his life.
Mr Pern,	ditto.
Anne Gardner, Junr.,	ditto.
Christopher Gardner,	ditto.
Richard Gardner,	ditto.
Lawrence Eachard,	ditto and 50*s*. a year during the life of his wife Anne.
Christopher Eachard,	50*s*. a year during his life and 50*s*. a year during the life of his wife Frances.
Moses Holwey,	£5 a year during his life. 50*s*. a year during the life of Stephen Holwey, and 50*s*. a year during the life of Rebecca the wife of the said Stephen Holwey.
Mr Worts,	50*s*. a year during the life of his wife, Mary.
Jane Bartlett,	50*s*. a year during her life.
Elizabeth Henley,	ditto.

Each of the parties of the third part (being willing to contribute towards the enabling the Master and Fellows to pay the said annuities) covenants to pay the said during his life (if the annuitants live so long) 50*s*. a year to the Master and Fellows; deducting, however, from every half-yearly payment, 2*s*. 6*d*. for every 50*s*. annuity which shall appear to cease by the death of the annuitant.

Each of the persons, named as of the fourth part, i.e. the Fellows of the College, being likewise willing to contribute to enable the Master and Fellows to pay the said annuities, covenants to pay to the persons, named as of the fifth part, as trustees for the Master and Fellows, 50*s*. a year during his life (if the annuitant lives so long), deducting, however, 2*s*. 6*d*. for every 50*s*. annuity that shall determine by the death of the annuitant.

Only twelve of the persons, named as of the third part, executed the deed, namely, those whose names are marked with a cross, and of the Fellows' names, as of the fourth part, Mr Bence did not execute the deed.

Of the annuitants: Dr Covel executed a release to the Master and Fellows (10 July 1714) of all arrears and all future payments; they giving a bond at the same time to pay £25 to his executors after his decease. The money was paid to the executors between Michaelmas 1722 and Michaelmas 1723. Dr Stanley executed a release of the annuity and of all arrears due to him (29 March 1712) "in consideration of the poor Estate of the College". Sir Isaac Newton executed a release of his annuity and all arrears 4 May 1714. Mr Pern executed a similar release 21 April 1714. None of the above four ever received any payment.

Anne Gardner, Junr., died 1 April 1698.
Christopher Gardner was paid only £2. 10. 0.
Richard Gardner, Junr., was paid as late as Michaelmas 1748.
Lawrence Eachard died April 1714.
Anne Eachard died August 1721.
Christopher Eachard died 29 November 1706.
Frances Eachard died 1725.
Moses Holwey died 1701.
Stephen Holwey died 1707.
Rebecca Holwey died 1713.
Mary Worts died 1705.
Jane Bartlett died 1712.
Elizabeth Henley died February 1714/5.

Dr Fisher had only received £20 at Midsummer 1722, and probably never received any more.

Of the contributors the four Fellows paid regularly and more than they were bound to.

Thos. Eachard, William Grove, John Turton,	paid nothing,	Archdeacon Jeffery, Mr Twistleton, Dr Dimsdale,	paid long and well.

The other six paid more or less, leaving considerable arrears.

Third Fund

On 28 September 1695 the College seal was put to an indenture tripartite between the Master and Fellows of the first part;

Jane Hussey, of St. Giles in the Fields, Middlesex, spinster,
Peter Fisher, D.D.,
George Oxenden, LL.D., Master of Trinity Hall,
Christopher Eachard, Clerk,
Richard Gardner,

of the second part;

*John, Lord Cutts,
*Sir Wm. Dawes, Bart.,
Sir Thomas Roberts, Bart.,
Sir Thomas Willoughby, Bart.,
Sir Richard Bonnet, Bart.,
Sir Thomas Brograve, Bart.,
John Darnall, Sergeant at Law,
*Charles Caesar,
John Middleton,
Jane Selby,
Robert Kempe,
*Thomas Clarke,
Hugh Martin,
*Moses Holwey, Clerk,
*Thomas Tilson, Clerk,
*Uriah Taylor,

of the third part.

The deed recited that

Jane Hussey had paid £300,
Dr Fisher, Christopher Eachard, Dr Oxenden, Richard Gardner, had paid £50 each,

to the Master and Fellows "for and towards the building of a new chapel and the finishing of other buildings in the College and for augmenting the Mastership and Scholarships of the College".

In consideration of which the Master and Fellows agree to pay:

Jane Hussey:
£10 a year during the life of William Balle;
£10 a year during the life of Brian Broughton;
£10 a year during the life of Thomas Broughton;

Peter Fisher, £5 a year during the life of his wife Elizabeth;
George Oxenden, £5 a year during the life of his wife Elizabeth;
Christopher Eachard, £5 a year during his life;
Richard Gardner, £5 a year during the life of his wife Anne.

The persons, named as of the third part, having all been formerly members of the College or had relation thereunto and being willing to contribute towards the better enabling the Master and Fellows to pay the said annuities, agree to pay £5 each yearly during his life to the Master and Fellows for that purpose.

Only seven of the persons, named as contributors, executed the deed; the names of the others having been for the most part inserted without their consent. The names of those who executed the deed are marked with a cross.

Dr Oxenden had not paid his £50 on 1 January 1696/7, and he never demanded anything as due to him by way of annuity; so that it seems certain that no money was ever paid by him.

Of the other annuitants: Jane Hussey executed a release to the Master and Fellows, 20 May 1714 (William Balle, her nephew, being then dead, and only two lives remaining), on the payment of £150, £100 of which was contributed by Sir Wm. Dawes, then Archbishop of York. There were some arrears due to him when she executed the release. Dr Fisher never received anything. Christopher Eachard died 29 November 1706. Anne Gardner, afterwards Pells, was paid to Lady Day 1741.

Of the contributors:

Lord Cutts paid nothing,
Sir W. Dawes,
Mr Tilson,
Mr Holwey,
and Uriah Taylor (for Alexander Bence) } paid long and well.

Mr Clarke (afterwards Sir Thomas Clarke) was released from his obligation by the College under seal. He paid £12. 10*s*. 0*d*., and then Sir W. Dawes (Archbishop of York) paid for him till Mrs Hussey's release, 20 May 1714.

Mr Caesar paid nothing because of a debt which the College owed him. Sir W. Dawes continued paying till Lady Day 1723; he died 30 April 1724.

The accounts of the new building, in Dr Eachard's handwriting, show that up to St Thomas' Day 1695:

Sum expended	£10,620. 11. 11
Sums received from various benefactors	8,972. 14. 2
Paid out more than received	1,647. 17. 9

The receipts here mentioned do not include Mrs Hussey's payment of £300, Dr Fisher's payment of £50, Dr Oxenden's payment (if ever made) of £50, on account of the third fund, but do include the money laid down on the first and second funds, and £100 of the third fund.

Also the sums expended on account of the purchase of Guilden Morden, £189. 1*s*. 0*d*., which were paid out of the monies of the third fund, do not appear among the expenses.

The following list contains the names of the contributors who gave £20 or upwards (including the three funds) towards the rebuilding of the College 1673–1704:

Sir Charles Caesar, of Bennington, Herts	£250.	0.	0
Mr Thos. Daynes, of Gunthorpe, Norfolk, besides £70 given later	203.	10.	0
Mr John Cartwright	200.	0.	0
Mr John Slader, Fellow of the College (the College paying his sister Mary Newport £5 a year for life)	200.	0.	0
Dr Daniel Milles, Fellow of the College	159.	0.	0
Sir John Rous, of Henham	145.	0.	0
Duke of Somerset, Chancellor of University	100.	0.	0
Mr John Owen, Southgate, Edmonton	100.	0.	0
Mr Peter Pheasant	100.	0.	0
Mr William Spence (by Dr Lightfoot)	100.	0.	0
Mr Matthew Scrivener, of Haslingfield	95.	0.	0
Mr Samuel Frankland, for chambers for 2 scholars	60.	0.	0
John, Lord Cutts	50.	0.	0
Alderman Spurstow, of London	50.	0.	0
Lady Williamson, Hales, Norfolk	50.	0.	0
Madame Maresco, London	50.	0.	0
Sir Thomas Barnardiston, Bart.	50.	0.	0
Mr Thomas Cartwright, added to his grandfather's settlement	50.	0.	0
Sir John Fagge	45.	0.	0
Capt. John Knyvett	40.	7.	6
Mr Thos. Gouge	40.	0.	0
Mr Thos. Bidingfield, Dursham Hall, Suffolk	40.	0.	0
Lady Wendy, of Haslingfield	40.	0.	0
Dr John Lightfoot, Master of the College	38.	0.	0
Mr Thos. Firmin, London	36.	0.	0
Dr John Gostlin, Caius College	34.	6.	0
Isaac Bootby, Esq.	33.	0.	0
Mr Robert Cook, Norfolk	30.	0.	0
Dr Thos. Paget, Fellow of the College	30.	0.	0
Dr Clench, London	26.	16.	6

Sir Charles Blois	£25.	0.	0
Mr James Calamy	25.	0.	0
Mr Paul, of Cornhill, London	25.	0.	0
Mr Everard, Fellow of the College	20.	0.	0
Mr John Blomfield, Suffolk	20.	0.	0
Mr Bryan, Cambridge	20.	0.	0
Mr John Buck, Esquire Bedell	20.	0.	0
Mr Robert Thexton, Fellow of the College	20.	0.	0
Mr Nathaniel Haws, Christ's Hospital	20.	0.	0
Sir Wm. Wiseman, Rivenhall, Essex	20.	0.	0
Sir Walter St. John	20.	0.	0
Sir Thos. Fitch, London	20.	0.	0
Mrs Tuckerey, widow of Dr Spurstow	20.	0.	0
Sir Thomas Slater, Cambridge	20.	0.	0
Bishop of Norwich, Dr Reynolds	20.	0.	0
Mr James Leigh, Fellow of Christ's	20.	0.	0
Mr Richard Golty	20.	0.	0
Mr Edmund Jenny	20.	15.	0
Sergeant Rawlinson, Gray's Inn	21.	10.	0
Mr Robert Harvey, Stockdon, Warwickshire	24.	0.	0
Mr John Sayer, Westly, Cambs	22.	0.	0
Mr Edward Pickering, Swavesey	20.	0.	0
Mr Jennison, Northamptonshire	20.	0.	0
Sir John Brograve	21.	10.	0
Duke of Albemarle	20.	0.	0
Crewe, Bishop of Durham	20.	7.	6
Sir Gervase Elwes	20.	0.	0
Sir George Downing, Cambs	20.	0.	0
Madam Cartwright	20.	0.	0
Sir Thos. Willoughby	20.	0.	0
Sir Thos. Cooke, London	20.	0.	0
Mr William Blomfield	20.	0.	0
Mr Robert Baxter	20.	0.	0
Archbishop Sancroft	20.	0.	0
Lord Clare, afterwards Duke of Newcastle	20.	0.	0
Sir Thos. Rokeby, formerly Fellow	20.	0.	0
Dr Spencer, Dean of Ely	20.	0.	0
Alderman Aske, of London	20.	0.	0

Sir Isaac Newton was among those who lent money to the College on annuity, for which he and others eventually gave a release. A large number of members of the Mercers' Company also contributed to the rebuilding of the College.

Mr Daynes made the condition (14 September 1677) that £100 should be paid back to him if at the next vacancy of the livings of Gimingham and Trunch the College appointed an incumbent whom he or Sir Nevil Catelin disapproved.

After Dr Eachard's death the new building was necessarily stopped for a time, in consequence of the large debts which had been incurred and the want of funds. It afterwards advanced slowly, and the following sums are entered in the Audit book as having been spent from time to time upon it:

After the account to Michaelmas		1702	£247.	13.	8
(Chapel account)	,,	1706	856.	2.	9
		1708	48.	14.	4
		1709	113.	7.	8
		1711	220.	5.	2
		1714	142.	18.	2

Besides the special contributors to the Chapel fund, there was a legacy from Mr Addye of £100, a donation from Mr Daynes of £50, the Master (Sir W. Dawes) contributed the profits of his Mastership for three years, the Fellows gave up their fines, and sold plate to the value of £108. 10*s.* 2*d.*; the profits of vacant Fellowships, the payments of Bachelors for feasts and of Fellow Commoners for plate, were also added to the fund.

Dr Eachard died 7 July 1697. At that time it appeared that the College had the following debts, incurred on account of the new building:

To Mr Argyle	£200	Bond given in King James' time 1687
To Mr Gardner	200	
To Mr Yates	100	
To the builder	300	
To Mr Reynolds	200	
To Dr Gower	50	
To Mr Caesar or Mr Estcourt	200	
	£1250	

There were also many debts, incurred on the same account, to which Dr Eachard's estate only was liable. Among them:

This debt was paid by the College in 1715 together with £83 for interest. See Bursar's account for 1715.	To his brother Gardner	£150
	To Mrs Game	100
	To Mr Standish	100
	To Sir John Duke	50
	To Mr Holman	50
	To Mr Wright	153

He likewise owed the University a balance of £950. 17*s.* 5$\frac{1}{4}$*d.*

There is a memorandum in Dr Eachard's handwriting dated "London, 29 March 1697", in which he states that "since he was Master, besides all his own revenues, which he was always ready to fling in, and besides what has been allowed and placed to account towards horses, journies, feasting Benefactors &c. out of bachelor's feasts, Fellow's feasts, fines, plate sold, and the like, he has spent, as it is granted, the sum of 2 or 3 hundred pounds".

He also reckons up liabilities, which he thinks that the College ought to pay, amounting to £1000, and for which he suggests that a Fellowship, if need be, may be sunk, and £100 worth of plate sold. He suggests, also, that each of the six Fellows should undertake to beg, of such chiefly as have been of the College, £100 apiece; and that the Master should engage for £200.

He reckons up also other liabilities (including the debt to the University, which he states at £500) incurred on account of the College, for which he is personally impunible, and which he considers to amount in the whole to about £1000. To defray these charges, he states his willingness to give £1000, to be paid out of the produce of his share in the lease of an estate at Yarmouth (which share he reckons to be worth £700), out of his estate at Bramfield, and out of his personal estate. But, he says, "I would have the University paid first, because their money was made use of for the paying of College debts and carrying on the building in the time of my Vice-Chancellorship".

There is another memorandum dated 4 June 1697, in which Dr Eachard states "about this time there may be owing to workmen for this last year's work about £300; how that may be probably paid may be seen in my little pocket book with a red string. The Company of the Mercers and merchants in London, especially such as have been formerly benefactors, if duly applied to, may finish the inside of the chapel."

The memorandums in the said little book show that Dr Eachard was contemplating the foundation of another fund, to raise £1000 "towards a new Chapel and the augmentation of the Mastership and twelve scholarships". He records the names of persons who had promised contributions to the amount of £600. The contributors were to receive annuities at the rate of 10 per cent.

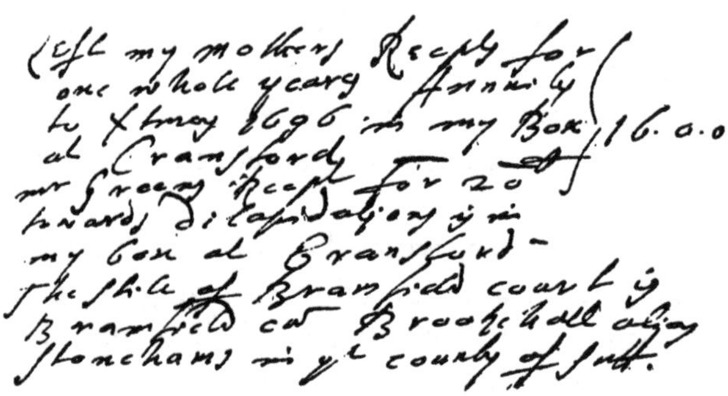
Left my mothers Receipt for one whole years Annuity to Xtmas 1696 in my Box at Cransford 16.0.0
Mr Greens Receipt for 20 l towards dilapidations in my Box at Cransford—
The title of Bramfield court in Bramfield cal Brookhall alias Stonchams in ye county of Suff.

Memorandum of Dr Eachard

At the time of Dr Eachard's death the balance due by him to the University was £950. 17*s.* 5¼*d.* In part payment of this debt he left to the University his share in the lease of an estate at Yarmouth granted by the Dean and Chapter of Norwich to himself and other members of his family. The University gave a power of Attorney, 15 November 1698, to certain syndics, twelve in number, to sell and convey to any purchaser the right and interest so vested in it, or to deal with it in any other way, as might seem best to them. The syndics eventually sold the interest of the University in the lease to Dr James, Regius Prof. of Divinity and President of Queens' College, for four hundred pounds, 22 November 1705.

The University, then, seems to have lost more than £500 by Dr Eachard.

Chapel

Fellows' Garden

Soon after Dr Eachard's death, July 1697,[1] a paper was printed, stating the embarrassed state of the finances of the College, the building being still far from finished and the College burdened with a very large debt, and soliciting contributions "as well towards the discharging the said debt as carrying on the said Chapel".

Various contributions were made for finishing the Chapel, amounting in all to £764. 14*s.* 6*d.*, including a legacy of £300 from Mrs Cartwright, a donation of £10 from the Bishop of Ely, and fines for leases given up by the Master and Fellows to the amount of £116. 10*s.* 0*d.* The sum spent on the Chapel after Dr Eachard's death was £835. 6*s.* 8*d.* The wainscoting was executed by John Austin at a charge of £350. The carver, Francis Woodward, received £110. 15*s.* 0*d.*

The Chapel, being at length finished, was consecrated by the Bishop of Ely, Simon Patrick, 1 September 1704. In the deed of consecration the Chapel is stated to be, within the walls, in length from east to west 72 feet, in breadth from north to south 26½ feet. The proceedings and form of consecration are in a MS. book in the handwriting of Mr Leng, afterwards Bishop of Norwich.

"In the next month (August 1704), I was desired to consecrate a new Chapel built in Catharine Hall, Cambridge. Accordingly I considered of a form wherein to do it and upon the 1st of September went thither, accompanied with the heads of several colleges and other worthy persons, dedicated it to the worship and service of God, to which it was set apart, with prayers and a sermon and the Holy Communion. The Master of the College, Sir William Dawes, and the Fellows desired the form of consecration might be printed, with the sermon preached by Mr Leng, a worthy Fellow of that College. Unto which I consented and both were printed at Cambridge a little after."[2]

The accounts of Eachard illustrate some of the ways whereby the College raised money when in need. It never sold land in order to be able to put up

[1] There is a memorandum made by the Master, Sir W. Dawes, 2 January 1698/9, in the College order book, of his expenditure for the College, in which the following entry appears: "For printing 100 of College cases 12s."

[2] Bp Patrick, *Autobiography*, Oxford, 1839, p. 187.

buildings,[1] but it was quite ready to sell its plate. Money was often borrowed, sometimes without interest, sometimes with interest and at other times in return for a life annuity. The lenders were members of the College, friends or even speculators. The security was excellent and the investors' capital did not depreciate, while the rate of interest, if interest was demanded, was good. The practice of borrowing goes back to the early years of the sixteenth century, for on 5 May 1516 the College gave a bond to Thomas Greene, the Master, for £20. Another instance is the bond given on 3 February 1623/4 to Dr Thomas Wilson for £20 lent to the College "out of the love and affection which he beareth to our said College". The money was to be repaid on 2 February in the next year. Thomas Buck at about the same date frequently lent the College money. On 5 March 1792 the Rev. John Stevenson lent £500 at 4½ per cent., and on 23 January 1809 John Dickon of Norton lent £300 at "lawful interest". As late as 1844 £2000 was repaid to the Master of Jesus. These are but a few instances out of very many.

It is perhaps significant that the first time St Catharine's had a banking account was in 1845—the year in which Philpott became Master.[2]

Giving an annuity for a sum down was a more risky business for a small College with limited resources. A College is not justified in turning itself into an insurance company, and transactions of this nature were practically confined to the Eachard régime. The College might have been hard hit had it not been for the generosity of many annuitants, who, when they could afford it, granted a release.

At a meeting of the Master and Fellows of St Catharine's Hall held on the 24 March 1683, it was unanimously agreed that henceforth no Tutor was to hold over payment to the Bursar of Steward's bills incurred by his pupils for more than six weeks after the College quarter ended, or five weeks after receiving such bills. If the bill was not paid within that time, the Bursar was to put out of commons and sizings the pupils of the Tutor concerned, and

[1] The College seems to have been very unwilling, at least after the middle of the sixteenth century, to alienate any of its houses or land.

[2] This information is due to the kindness of Mr E. Mellish Clark, who took great trouble to discover the facts. The College first invested in Stocks 5 April 1786.

not to re-admit them until the accounts had been paid. The Bursar having done this, the Master and Fellows guaranteed payment to him in the event of the Tutor's death or failure to pay before the end of the second quarter. If, however, the Bursar neglected to enforce these regulations, then the whole matter was to be regarded as his own debt; the Master and Fellows would accept no responsibility for previous bills, nor would they safeguard him in the future. The Bursar was to render to each Tutor the quarter's bill within seven days after the end of that quarter; if ten days expired without this being done (unless for some reason approved by the Master and Fellows), he was to forfeit five pounds to the College, and five pounds for each succeeding week until the bills were settled. If, however, he had a valid excuse, then the term of the College security and the time prescribed to the Tutor for payment were to be increased proportionately. For the Quarter ended 20 March 1683, the Bursar was allowed until 3 April to make up his and the Tutors' bills for payment by 15 May. No person, either Fellow Commoner or Pensioner, was to reside in College unless the Master or one of the Fellows accepted responsibility for his Steward's bills. At the end of each quarter Tutors were to inform the Bursar which of their pupils were in arrears, the Bursar to put into force the above rules until the Tutor certified that the bill had been paid or that he had caution money to cover it.

Matthew Scrivener, Vicar of Haslingfield, in his will dated 4 March 1687, besides leaving £50 towards erecting a new chapel and fifty shillings towards the Gostlin feast,[1] directed that out of the rent of his lands at Bruisyard, which also he left to the College, there should be set aside "twenty marks yearly for an augmentation of the salary arising from the said Mr Franklin's gift".[2] This gift was for the foundation of a new Fellowship, and one of a peculiar character.

[1] The will says: "I understanding that the sum assigned by him for that purpose falleth short in these days of what may be necessary to that end." Bonnell notes jocularly what a poor affair this feast was in 1679. See p. 69.

[2] Scrivener directs that the twenty marks, along with the residual profits of the estate after the charges on it have been met, are to be "committed to the treasury". Great uncertainty exists as to the source and use of the money placed in the Treasury. It was

"Franklin" was "Samuel Frankland, Master of Arts and of the city of Coventry head-schoolmaster", who by a will dated 21 July 1691 left a messuage with lands at Cubbington, near Leamington in the county of Warwick, for two purposes. The first was "the maintenance of one Fellow, to be sent to the said Hall out of the free Grammar School in Coventry, to which Mr Matthew Scrivener hath by his last will and testament annexed twenty marks per annum for ever, the which, with a convenient chamber for which as may appear by the instrument under the seal of the College now in my hands I have paid sixty pounds, will make a handsome provision for the Frankland Fellowship". The other was that "ten pounds a year out of the lands and personal estate before devised shall be for and towards the maintenance of one scholar, to be sent to the said Hall out of the free Grammar School in Tamworth, the parish of my nativity, to which the College hath promised a chamber gratis". The testator goes on to say that if his real and personal estate should fall short of the £600, then the Fellow from Coventry is to have full twenty pounds per annum, and the shortage is to be borne by the scholar from Tamworth School.[1]

The terms of the Frankland bequest were probably not dictated, but the result of much discussion between the College and the benefactor—Scrivener in fact, a Catharine man although not a Fellow, knew of them in 1687. So we may assume that the College wished to try the experiment of bye-Fellowships.[2] A College Order (19 October 1710), which also deals with the

rarely brought to account, and seems to have been under the special control of the Master. Perhaps cash balances not wanted immediately for use or investment were placed there to meet unexpected calls. In the year 1657–8 £61 was taken from the Treasury for extraordinary repairs. In pre-banking days expedients of this kind were perhaps not only expedient but necessary.

[1] The electors are the Master and Fellows, but they are to have a careful regard to the recommendation of the Mayor and Aldermen of Coventry in the case of the Fellow, and to that of the minister and schoolmaster of Tamworth in the case of the Scholar.

[2] A letter from Eachard to Frankland in the possession of the Corporation of Coventry, dated 26 July 1683, says: "The Fellows with myself have lately considered it, and are of opinion it will be every whit as convenient for the College (though heretofore we were of another mind)...to give...two Scholarships of ten pounds apiece instead of a Fellowship."

Holwey Fellowship of 1695, outlines the method of electing the new Fellow and the position he held in the College. The latter was evidently no better than that of a senior scholar.

"Ordered, that Mr Crosse shall, within a month from this present nineteenth of October, go to Coventry, and examine the boys in the upper Form of the great School there, and enquire of the Master of the said School, concerning the tempers and moral behaviour of the said boys, and after having so done, shall appoint one or more of them whom he in his judgment shall think most proper, to come to the College, in order to undergo the examination of the Master and Fellows, and to have one of the said Scholars nominated and elected by them into Mr Frankland's Fellowship.

Ordered, that the ground-Chamber, on the right hand, betwixt the Butteries and the Gatehouse, be the chamber of the said Fellowship."

[2 November 1711; "Ordered, upon reconsidering that matter, that the chamber up one pair of stairs, next the Combination Room, in the new building, be the chamber of the Coventry Fellow."]

"Ordered, that the Fellow who shall be from time to time in the said Fellowship, shall, during his being an undergraduate, be under the same regulations with the undergraduate pensioners of this College with regard to tuition, exercise, commons, seat in Hall and Chapel and all other things; excepting that he shall wear a gown of the sort commonly called Bull's gowns, and a square cap without a tuft."

The Holwey Fellow was of much higher rank. The same Order says "that the Fellow who shall be, from time to time, in Mr Holwey's Fellowship, shall take place among the Fellows of the old foundation according to his seniority as Fellow, and shall have his place in Chapel and Hall accordingly".

This endowment is the subject of a tripartite indenture, dated 3 August 1695, between Sir John Rous of Henham in the county of Suffolk, the Master and Fellows, and Moses Holwey, "now or late of Michaelstow in the county of Cornwall, clerk". In consideration of £800 paid to him by Mr Holwey, £350 from the Master and Fellows, with five shillings from certain trustees, to surrender the lease of the rectory of Guilden Morden, granted to him by the Bishop of Ely for three lives.

The trustees are required to pay £8 yearly to the Steward for raising fines beforehand to be paid to the Lord Bishop of Ely for renewing any lease or leases. £26 annually is to be given to a Fellow of the College, "who shall constantly do the office of a chaplain or Conduct,[1] and who shall go under the name of the Conduct Fellow,...which Fellow the said Master and Fellows...agree shall from time to time have the advantage of keeping the library of Catharine Hall aforesaid, and shall also have a chamber furnished in the said College rent free".

There are also to be maintained in the College two scholars taken from Eton and Merchant Taylors' respectively, who are to receive £6 annually from the Holwey trust and £6 annually from the revenues of the College applicable to Scholarships.[2]

The sum of £4 is to be expended every year on a feast in commemoration of Matthew Scrivener, "the Chapel's great benefactor", £3 at the Fellows' table, and £1 at the rest of the tables, "at which feast the Vicar of Morden for the time being is to come, if able; and the said Master is to give him yearly forty shillings; on which feast day the Master for the time being is to preach a sermon in the Chapel". The residue after all charges have been met is to be given to the Master.

Relatives of Moses Holwey are to be preferred for both the Fellowship and the Scholarships. Failing these, a scholar late of Eton is to have a preference, "if any such there be in the said College capable"; failing such a scholar, then a scholar late of Merchant Taylors' is to be preferred, "if any be in the College capable".

22 Oct. 1725

Ordered by the unanimous Consent of the Master & Fellows then resident in the University, that Fifty Shillings a piece be paid Annually to Two poor Scholars, that study God's Word & live sober & honest Lives according to the Direction of the Lady Moyer in her last Will & Testament, wherein She bequeathed the Sum of One Hundred Pounds to be distributed to that Purpose; the Exhibitions to commence from Mich^mas^. last.

The payments referred to in this Order were made irregularly to Michaelmas 1762 and then ceased altogether. An interesting and instructive Order of

[1] "Conductus," that is "hired", or having special duties to perform as a condition of the Fellowship.

[2] It should be noticed that the nominal value of a Scholarship is steadily increasing.

18 December 1730 gives "£5 out of Lady Moyer's Benefaction to Radcliffe our Chapel Clerk, there being no poor Scholars qualified".

The Bursar's accounts for 1744–5 contain an entry for wine in the Combination on receiving the news of Mrs Ramsden's legacy. The Fellows might well be pardoned for celebrating an event which they knew was important, but really has turned out to be of greater consequence than any other event in the history of the College. Without the increased endowments from her benefaction the College could scarcely have held its own during the next century and a half, in which values fell so seriously that revenues sufficient in 1770 for 18 Fellows proved inadequate for six, and Scholarships shrank in a corresponding degree.

Mary Ramsden was a daughter of Robert Robinson, of Fockerby in Yorkshire, and the great-niece of Robert Skerne whose benefaction of Scholarships has already been noticed. Her brother, Thomas Robinson, died in 1709, and her elder sister Elizabeth, who married the Reverend Henry Brearey, Rector of Boxworth near Cambridge, died childless in 1719. So Mary was left sole heiress of Fockerby. William Ramsden, her husband, was son of John Ramsden of Norton, not far from Doncaster, and of Catharine, a daughter of John Dawney, Viscount Downe. He died childless in 1717, six years after his marriage, and his father died six months later. The death of the latter may have been hastened by the action of his daughter-in-law, who had him arrested for refusing to grant possession of the Manor of Norton, with lands in Norton and its neighbourhood, which by a marriage settlement was to be Mary Ramsden's for life in the event of her husband's dying. In 1736 Mary Ramsden bought the reversion of the Norton property and additional lands at Fockerby, Adlingfleet and Haldenby. The deaths of relatives gave Mrs Ramsden lands at Linton-on-Wharfe and Burrowby, first for life, then absolutely.

So all the Robinson property came to Mrs Ramsden either for life or absolutely. Everything that she owned absolutely she left to the College by a will dated 3 November 1743, "and I would have it observed", she says, "that the estate I give is all my own, that I had no part of it from my husband". She appears to have had little love for the Ramsden family.

The will of Mrs Ramsden caused some litigation. She died on 5 April 1745, and in the Michaelmas Term 1746 an information was filed by the Attorney-General, at the relation of the Master and Fellows, against the Honourable Christopher Dawney, Edward Simpson, and John Audley, the executors and trustees of Mrs Ramsden, Henry Smith her heir at law, and the trustees of the York Infirmary, praying that the said executors and trustees might come to an account for the personal and trust estates of Mrs Ramsden, and might be decreed to perform the trusts of the will and codicils. An information was also filed (25 November 1746) by the Attorney-General, at the relation of the poor boys and girls in Fockerby, Norton, Linton and Adlingfleet and of Mrs Ramsden's tenant cottagers against the same executors and the Master and Fellows of the College, praying that the legacies to the relatees might be decreed and that the interest might be applied for their benefit. A supplemental information was filed (Easter Term 1750) at the relation of the Master and Fellows against the Archbishop of York, who after the death of Dr Audley had succeeded him in the trust of Mrs Ramsden's will.

As a result of these informations the Lord Chancellor made an order, declaring that the will and codicils of Mrs Ramsden were well proved and ought to be established. Also that the legacies to the York Infirmary and to the poor boys and girls and to the tenants were good legacies to charge her personal estate, and ought to be paid in the first place after the debts and funeral expenses, and that the principal of the said legacies should be placed out at interest in the names of the trustees, and the interest applied to the benefit of the objects of the charities. Also, that, after all the debts and legacies were paid and the annuitants dead and the houses and grounds purchased for erecting the new buildings, the trustees should convey the freehold estate and surrender the copyhold estate and assign what should remain of the personal estate to the Master and Fellows for ever. On 16 July 1757, the trustees of the York Infirmary having declined to accept the legacy of £200 bequeathed by Mrs Ramsden, the Lord Chancellor made an order, declaring the legacy not accepted, and directing the money to be applied in the same manner as the rest of the personal estate. On 21 November 1766 an order of the Court of Chancery was made directing that the estates should be conveyed to the Master and Fellows, chargeable with an annuity of £20 to Mrs Anne Frank.

Plate XVIII

Mrs Ramsden's monument in Adlingfleet Church

It was also directed that the sum of £693 should be secured to the Master and Fellows on the farm at Barton, according to the report of the Master in Chancery 7 July 1766. In August 1767 the Honourable Christopher Dawney, sole survivor of the trustees under Mrs Ramsden's will, with the consent of the Archbishop of York, conveyed to the Master and Fellows Mrs Ramsden's estate, he himself covenanting to stand seized of the copyholds in trust for the Master and Fellows, according to the will. At the same time a deed of trust was executed, securing to the Master and Fellows the sum of £693 as agreed.

In order to understand the matter of the £693 we must remember that the Ramsden trust was a separate unit in the College finances, while in order to house and accommodate Ramsden Fellows and scholars certain possessions belonging to the corporate revenues of the College had to be either abandoned or handed over to the new trust. On 7 July 1766 the Master in Chancery reported to the Lord Chancellor that the Master and Fellows, having pulled down several houses and buildings of their own possessions to make room for Mrs Ramsden's new buildings, ought to be reimbursed to the amount of £693, and that he approved of the proposal that the same should be charged on the land recently acquired at Barton and upon Mrs Ramsden's other estates at 4 per cent. interest. The valuation was:

	Annual value	
White Swann	£14	£252
Sadler's House	4	72
Triplow's House	5	90
Young's House	5. 10. 0	99
Porter's House	—	180

The Ramsden bequest brought about some disputes with the town authorities as to the rates and taxes the College was legally bound to pay. On 19 April 1769 in the Court of King's Bench Joseph Thorpe, Fellow, brought an action against the collectors of land tax for the parish of St Benedict for seizing a horse belonging to him in the College stables then recently erected on the site of houses lately removed. The houses when standing had been subject to rates and taxes, but the plaintiff contended that as the houses had been removed and their site added to the College ground there was no liability to land tax, as a clause in the Land Tax Acts exempted the sites of Colleges. Judgment was given for the defendants, with costs £94. 10*s*. 0*d*. After this verdict the parish officers of St Botolph assessed the College for land tax at £55 a year for the site of the houses removed to make way for the Ramsden building, £55 being the amount of the original assessment on the houses. Part of this had been added to the College court, while another part had been added to the Master's garden, and on yet another part the Butler's and Porter's houses were built, the rest being left open as an area in front of the College and planted with trees. The College had (19 August 1760) obtained the opinion of the then Solicitor-General, Mr Yorke, who advised that, as no part of the site of the houses had been added to the site of the College at the time when the then last Land Tax Act was passed, the proviso in the Act that exempted the sites of Colleges did not extend to any part of the land in question; but that, if the Land Tax Acts which should be passed after the addition of the ground to the site of the College should contain the same proviso, the ground would be exempt from Land Tax. He considered that the Butler's and Porter's houses, then proposed to be erected, would in the same case also be exempt from Land Tax as being really a part of the College.

The annual Land Tax passed afterwards did contain the same proviso, as well as the act 38 George III, ch. 60, which made the Land Tax perpetual. Both the St Botolph's Land Tax and that of St Bene't's were redeemed 27 July 1801. So it would appear that the College continued to pay the tax.

Then came the question of the Poor Rate. The parish officers assessed the College at the same sum of £55. The College refused to pay, and an order was obtained from the Justices of the Peace for Mr Gardner, the Bursar, to appear and show cause why he refused payment. The Bursar did not attend the summons, whereupon the officers obtained a distress warrant upon the goods and chattels of the College or of two College servants, the Butler and Porter.[1] The warrant was executed 20 April 1770, and in the Butler's house some of his private property, a silver cream jug and some silver spoons, were seized. On 8 November were seized a silver watch, chairs, tables and glasses,

[1] It is clear that by this time there was a servant to act as Porter. "Porter's place" appears in the Tutor's accounts as late as 1743, and so undergraduate porters ceased between 1743 and 1770.

all belonging to the Porter. Six months later the College took legal advice in connection with these distraints, and the opinion given was that both were clearly wrong, as being levied on the goods of persons not assessed, but that no action for damages could be sustained, as too long a time had in each case elapsed since the trespass. The College authorities were advised to wait until the distress was repeated and then bring an action without delay. The Court of Quarter Sessions in Cambridge confirmed (16 July 1772) the assessment at £55 per annum, which was amended to £51. 15*s.* 0*d.* later, the assessment for the new buildings (£3. 5*s.* 0*d.*) being omitted "as the buildings were not then occupied". An end was reached on 6 June 1774, when the Court of King's Bench amended and confirmed the order of the Cambridge Court of Quarter Sessions, and decided that the Butler and Porter should be assessed to Poor Rate, each in his own name, for their houses, and that the Master and Fellows should be rated for the additions to the Master's garden and College court, and for the area in front of the College. This is a classical case, and has been quoted as an authority to prove that a corporation seized of lands in fee for their own profit are liable in their corporate capacity to be rated to the poor.

The object of the Ramsden benefaction was to provide rooms and maintenance for six new Fellows and ten new scholars. Whether Mrs Ramsden wanted her Fellows to have equal rights with the foundation Fellows, it is impossible to say for certain; one of her "Rules and Orders" seems to suggest that she had discussed the matter with the College authorities. Actually they were all bye-Fellows, with no vote in College matters and none of the special privileges (i.e. a dividend) of full Fellows. Apart from this they were well provided for. They each had rent-free chambers and a stipend of £52 a year. The Ramsden scholars had a set of rooms rent-free, just as the Fellows had, and a stipend of £15 clear a year. The dividend of a full Fellow at this time was in an ordinary year about £33, while his stipend was £5. 13*s.* 4*d.*

The first six Ramsden Fellows were elected on 10 November 1772, notice being given of the election of ten scholars, the examination to be held on 24 November. Only two, however, were elected; five more were elected in 1773, one in 1775, one in 1776 and one in 1778.

Under powers of the Land Tax Redemption Acts, the College conveyed to Edward Prime on 23 April 1801 all their land at Barrington for the sum of £1400. With this money three per cent. reduced Consols were purchased and applied to the redemption of Land Tax in the following way:

	Tax			Stock paid		
Ridgewell	£10	0	0	£366	13	4
Cambridge						
St. Benet's	9	0	0	330	0	0
St Botolph's	11	16	0	432	13	4
St Giles'		8	0	14	13	4
Chesterton	7	5	0	265	16	8
Coton	18	16	0	689	6	8
Paxton Parva	2	0	0	73	6	8
Therfield	2	18	0	106	6	8
	62	3	0	2278	16	8

The balance, amounting to £16. 5*s.* 0*d.*, was applied to pay part of the redemption of the Land Tax on land at Luddington.

On 11 June 1805 the Burrowby land was sold for the same purpose. This sale appears to have been agreed to some six years before, as the last rent to account is in 1799. The money was spent as follows:

	Tax			Consol. stock used		
Fockerby	£18	8	5	£675	8	8
Adlingfleet, Haldenby, Whitgift	6	16	1	249	9	9
Luddington	1	14	8	47	6	11
				16	5	0[1]
Garthorpe	4	9	3	109	2	2
				54	11	2

In the accounts for 1817–18 we find £160 allowed for the augmentation of the vicarage of Ridgewell, Mr Joynes the Vicar having given £240. In 1820–1 £200 was advanced, in 1821–2 £100, in 1822–3 £200, and in 1824–5 the College contributed £18. 19*s.* 3*d.* towards the expenses of purchasing

[1] Balance of proceeds of the Barrington sale.

Plate XIX

Johns Building

land for the improvement of the vicarage. Among the receipts we find £40. 13*s*. 9*d*. from the Vicar in 1820–1, £81. 7*s*. 6*d*. in 1821–2, £81. 7*s*. 6*d*. in 1822–3 and £76. 11*s*. 3*d*. in 1823–4.

On 2 April 1828 a contract was signed for the rebuilding of the Bull Inn. The contract was for £4825. The sum actually expended was:

Bennett (contractor)	£7282	19	3
Clerk of the Works	99	17	4
Walter (architect)	300	5	4
	7683	1	11

Towards the close of Robinson's Mastership rumours spread abroad that valuable seams of coal lay under the College property at Norton. As Lords of the Manor of Norton, the Master and Fellows had always assumed that, in accordance with the terms of the Norton Inclosure Act of 1814, they owned the minerals under the commons and waste grounds within the Manor. On 10 May 1912, in the High Court of Justice, Chancery Division, Mr Justice Neville gave judgment establishing the title of the College to the ownership of the manorial minerals in the suit of St Catharine's College *v*. Greensmith. This action was brought in consequence of the announcement of a sale by public auction of certain land in Norton Common owned by Mr Greensmith, which sale was stated to include the minerals under the land. The College considered itself bound to contest any such claim. Subsequently in the same Court a similar action was brought by the College against the Dowager Countess of Rosse and Mr J. B. Cooke-Yarborough, with a similar result. On 22 October 1915 the Master of the Rolls and Lords Justices Bankes and Warrington, in the Court of Appeal, confirmed this decision of the High Court. So far so good, but a set-back was to follow.

On 26 July 1917, in the actions College *v*. Rosse, Mr Cooke-Yarborough and others, Frank's Trustees *v*. the College, it was held by Mr Justice Sargant that the College, although owning the minerals, is not entitled to sink pits or to let down the surface of the land by working the mines. This decision was confirmed on 22 March 1918 in the Court of Appeal by Mr Justice Swinfen Eady, Lord Justice Bankes and Mr Justice Eve.

The final blow fell on 27 January 1919, when, in the action Frank's Trustees and others *v.* the College, Lords Findlay, Dunedin, Shaw, Atkinson and Sumner decided in the House of Lords against the College as to its ownership of the manorial minerals, and consequently its claim as to mining rights failed.

The result of the litigation is that the College failed to establish its title to the Norton manorial minerals; but as Lady Rosse, Mr Cooke-Yarborough and Mr Greensmith did not appeal to the House of Lords, they are bound by the judgment of Mr Justice Neville and the Court of Appeal, and to the minerals under the lands of these persons the title of the College holds good. The total area affected is 374 acres out of 784 acres.

The judgment of the House of Lords not only deprived the College of the ownership of the minerals which had been granted by the High Court and the Court of Appeal; it confirmed the decision of the same courts that the College had no surface rights. Consequently it was necessary to make terms with those landlords whose claim to minerals had failed because they did not appeal to the House of Lords.

So when a lease was made with the Askern Colliery Company to work the coal, the royalties from the Common coal were halved with these landowners, while the royalties derived from coal under land the freehold of which belonged to the College, as the rights of the College had never been a matter of dispute, were to go to the College alone.

The total cost of these proceedings was about £10,000. This money had to be found before the College recovered from the financial strain of the War period, and caused some temporary inconvenience.

The profits from coal have up to the present not been great, but there are possibilities of a larger income from this source in the near future. As the Norton estate was bequeathed by Mrs Ramsden, the profits are credited to the Ramsden Trust, from which the Open Scholarship Fund derives a great part of its income.

After the war of 1914–1918 the policy was adopted of selling land and buying stocks and shares. Much of the College land was thus sold, and the Bursar of the time drew up a statement which is reproduced on pp. 401–404. This policy is still being carried out, but along with stocks and shares suitable house property is being acquired.

Main Court (facing East) about 1840

The old Grove, 65 and 66 Trumpington Street
and the Bull Hotel

Finance

The period 1919–1936 has seen a complete reorganisation of the College finances and several new benefactions. The present is, strictly speaking, the proper place to describe these, but they are so integral a part of the modern rebirth of the College that they are included in the account of that happy event in this history. But two benefactions must be recorded here. A generous gift from the widow of Dr Johns, the prime mover in the attack on the old régime, has made possible the erection of the splendid range of buildings on the site of Sherlock Building. Mr John Hornby, who was a Scholar from 1886 to 1889, recently left £4700, subject to two annuities, no special object being mentioned in the will. The money was paid over in 1935.

PART II

MATERIALS

I. AUTHORITIES

THE material for a history of St Catharine's College is to be found for the most part in the Muniment Room, or Treasury, as it, and its predecessor in the original College buildings, are styled in the old records. This is at the south-west corner of the staircase now known as Old Lodge, and although separated from it to-day formed a part of it when the Master resided there, who as Keeper had direct access to the store-place of the College archives and of the College chest and valuables. The room is suited to its purpose, and the documents are well preserved. A few of them, including the charter of Edward IV, have been transferred to the Library in order that they may be more easily shown to visitors.

Several past Fellows have seriously studied the muniments. One of them, Daniel Milles, Fellow from 1650 to 1656, made out lists of Masters and Fellows, giving short descriptions of the Masters down to Dr Brownrigge. Of all these workers none can be compared to Dr Henry Philpott, Master from 1845 to 1861. In the latter year he published through the Cambridge University Press forty-seven historical documents, while the manuscript notes he made for a College history formed the chief material used by the late Bishop G. F. Browne for his well-known work, *St Catharine's College*.

In 1930 Mr E. A. B. Barnard made a complete catalogue of the College documents, a copy of which has been deposited in the Cambridge University Library. In general, these documents are of the usual type—legal deeds, letters, books of account, admission registers, and so on. One manuscript, however, needs special mention. This is the *Memoriale Nigrum*, so named from the colour of its binding,[1] which contains, in the Founder's own writing, short descriptions of his possessions, the last being the College itself. From it is derived almost entirely our knowledge of the circumstances in which the College was founded. Of the other records the following are the most important to the historian.

[1] The binding to-day is of a dark chocolate colour. It is, however, impossible to say whether the black has faded or whether a new binding has superseded the old black one.

Authorities

The Audit Books begin with the year Michaelmas 1622–3. But although there are no audited accounts surviving of previous years, much may be inferred from the items in this and in subsequent years. The proverbial conservatism of Colleges is plainly to be seen in the method of keeping accounts. The same items appear regularly for nearly two hundred years after 1622, and it is a legitimate conclusion to infer that they did not originate in that year, unless, indeed, evidence is produced that they actually did so.

It is difficult to exaggerate the historical value of these accounts. Not only are the entries themselves of great interest, but the picturesque details often give much information to those who have learned to read between the lines.

The earlier accounts are in a mixture of Latin and English. Latin disappears from the accounts of 1762–3.

The accounts of the Steward also begin with the year 1622. At this date the Bursar was also Steward. The books of account are very roughly kept, being at first little better than scrap-books intended for the use of the Steward only; they were not audited until the year 1919.

The pupils' accounts were kept by the Tutor, and like accounts of the Steward were not audited until 1919. The first volume in the series is not a Tutor's book, but a scrap-book made by Dr Eachard. The earliest entries in the second volume are not dated, but refer to one Norris, who was admitted in 1672. Later entries are usually dated, after a time invariably so, but until the middle of the eighteenth century little care was given to the accounts, which appear to be intended for the Tutor's eye only. Before the year 1918–1919, although the College fixed what the various fees should be, the financial relations between Tutor and pupil were by tradition regarded as a purely personal matter. There is a serious gap in these records for nearly half a century after Eachard's death.

The Admission Books[1] begin with the year 1642. At first scrappy to a degree, they become more illuminating, as well as neater, as time goes on.

[1] The first of the Admission Books, with entries from 1642 to 1818, is probably the one mentioned by the Bursar in his accounts for 1638–9:

For a Colledg booke to put in the names of the Admitted   00. 08. 00

Authorities

What is to-day called the Order Book was at first called the Conclusion Book; it contains the important resolutions of the Master and Fellows. In the first volume the minutes range from 1640 to 1721, but there are also inventories from 1637 to 1706 and, from 1638 to 1661, the names of "Schollars of the house".

It is significant that all these books begin in the seventeenth century, all, except the Tutor's, in the first half of it. It was then that the number of students greatly increased, and it became necessary to keep records in a more business-like way than before.

The Register, the later volumes of which are called Lease Books, contains copies of important legal documents, along with certain other matters, such as presentations to livings, which in later times were entered into the Order Book, or, in some cases during the last twenty years, on the minutes of College meetings. In the first volume are lists of Masters, Fellows, Bible Clerks and donations to the College, together with a catalogue of books presented by the Founder and others. The earliest entry is a copy of a receipt, in an early sixteenth-century hand, given by the Founder under the date 28 June 1475. The last date mentioned in this volume is 1592. Owing to the scarcity of other records, the first volume of the Register is the chief evidence for the history of the College during the first hundred years of its existence.

Letters, with the exception of business correspondence of the last hundred years, are unfortunately few. There are some concerned with the disputes in the Society at the beginning of the nineteenth century, but nearly all the others were written to or by Eachard, and refer to tutorial matters, the new buildings, and the business of his Vice-Chancellorship.

Historians may like to know that a typed transcript of the *Memoriale Nigrum* is in the Cambridge University Library. A facsimile of a few lines is given on p. 364.

PRINTED AUTHORITIES

1574 John Caius, *Historiae Cantebrigiensis Academiae ab urbe condita.*

1634 Thomas Fuller, *History of the University of Cambridge.*

1651 G. Langbaine, *Foundation of the University of Cambridge.*

1672 John Ivory, *The Foundation of the University of Cambridge.*

1753 Edmund Carter, *The History of the University of Cambridge.*

1814 George Dyer, *History of the University and Colleges of Cambridge. University of Cambridge.*

1838 John Lamb, *A Collection of Letters, Statutes and other Documents from the MS. Library of Corpus Christi College.*

1842 Charles Henry Cooper, *Annals of Cambridge*, 5 vols.

1861 Henry Philpott, *Documents relating to St Catharine's College in the University of Cambridge.*

1873 James Bass Mullinger, *The University of Cambridge from the earliest times to the Royal Injunctions of* 1535. [Followed by two other volumes in 1884 and 1911.]

1902 G. F. Browne, *St Catharine's College.*

Dr H. Philpott

MUNIMENT ROOM

Bundle

I/1 Coton, Barton, and Whitwell, co. Cambridge. "No. I."

(A) 1424–1514. (14.)

(B) *temp*. Henry VI–Henry VII; etc. (19.) These documents are numbered "1000–1019". They are not arranged in chronological order.

I/2 Coton, Barton, and Whitwell, co. Cambridge. "No. II."

(A) Undated (20)–1323. (17.) Nos. 15, 16 and 34 missing.

(B) 1294–1418. (32.) No. 44 missing.

(C) 1420–1498. (53.) Nos. 77, 94, 98 and 99 missing.

I/3 "Burrough and Dullingham etc. (exchanged for Brinkley) Title Deeds etc."

(A) 1464–1508. (4.)

(B) 1634 and later. Various Terriers and Maps. (10.)

I/4 "Chesterton Title Deeds."
1556–7. (14.)

I/5 "Coton etc. Title Deeds."
Undated (21)–1428. (79.)

I/6 "Coton etc. Title Deeds."

(A) 1428–1439. (30.)

(B) 1440–1455. (30.)

I/7 "Coton Title Deeds."

(A) *temp*. Henry VII–Edward VI etc. (31.) Not arranged in chronological order.

(B) 1450–1460. (36.)

Bundle

I/8 "Fulbourn Title Deeds."
1422–1506. (6.)

I/9 "Grantchester etc. Title Deeds."
Undated (11)–1514. (38.)

I/10 "Harlton Title Deeds."
Undated (3)–1506. (43.)

I/11 "Layer Breton Title Deeds."
1307–1505. (23.)

I/12 "Over Title Deeds."
Undated (1)–1477. (34.)

II/1 "Paxton Parva Title Deeds."
Undated (7)–1524. (39.)

II/2 "Ridgewell: Rectory and Vicarage Title Deeds."
1295–1549. (21.)

"Licences of Alienation from the Crown, for the sale of the Impropriate Rectory of Ridgewell and the Advowson of the Vicarage." No. 6 has a perfect impression of the Seal of the Prior and Convent of Stoke by Clare, co. Suffolk. Also:

1542. Feb. 27. Licence from Henry VIII to Edward Elryngton. This deed has a perfect impression of a Great Seal of Henry VIII.

1549. Nov. 16. Licence from Edward VI to Dr Bainbrigge. This deed has a perfect impression of the Great Seal of Edward VI.

Authorities

Bundle

II/3 "Cambridge No. 1. Title Deeds. St Edward, St Bene't, and St Botolph."

1308–1578. (39.)

III/1 "Adlingfleet, Fockerby and Whitgift, No. 2. Skerne's Scholarships, Fockerby School and other Charities of Mr Skerne."

1627–1681. (15.) No. 40 has a perfect impression of the Great Seal of the Commonwealth.

VI/1 "Cambridge No. 2. The White Swan and the Three Horse Shoes Title Deeds."

1559–1730. (Nos. 1–18. There are actually 20 deeds.)

1788. July 12. One deed.

VII/1 "Cambridge No. 3. Houses bought for Mrs Ramsden's Building in 1754. Title Deeds."

1623–1754. (35.)

VII/2 "Cambridge No. 4. Houses bought of Queens' College for Mrs Ramsden's Building in 1757. Title Deeds and Deeds of Trust."

1754–1767. (5.)

VII/3 "Cambridge No. 5. Title Deeds etc."

1753–1821.

"Silver Street Printing Office. Bought from Stevenson and others." (10.)

VIII/1 "Barrington Title Deeds. 1–50 etc."

Undated (6)–1648. (44.)

Bundle

1729 etc. Terriers of Property at Barrington. (3.)

1648; 1708; 1776. Copy of Court Baron. (5.)

X/1 (B) 1697–1729. "20 Papers respecting the New Building and the Funds." Dr Eachard and others.

MS. List of contents of parcel.

X/2 1549. Nov. 14. (In box.) "A License of Mortmayn for 20£. 3 Edw. 6th to Master and Fellows of the College or Hall of St Katherine...." Bears a perfect impression of the Great Seal of Edward VI.

1556. Nov. 29. "A lycence of Alyenacon frome Richard Braken to the Mr and ffelowes of Saint kateryns hall in Cambrydge." Land at Chesterton. Bears the Great Seal of Philip and Mary.

X/4 1509. July 20. "A plenary pardon to the Mr and fellows of Cath: Hall...."

A Great Seal of Henry VIII attached.

X/6 1756. Apr. 14. "Master and ffellows of Katherine Hall in Cambridge. Licence in Mortmain...." Great Seal of George II attached.

XII/1 1736–1875. Deeds and documents relating to freehold premises in Silver Street, Cambridge, purchased of Messrs Jones and

Bundle

Rowton by the Rev. Charles Kirkby Robinson, D.D. and the Rev. E. T. S. Carr in 1875. (16.)

XII/4 1879. Oct. 11. The trustees for sale under the will of the late Mr William Fitch, to St Catharine's College. Bargain and sale of hereditaments and premises situate at Ridgewell, co. Essex. (14 deeds 1759–1882.)

XII/7 1806–1893. Deeds and writings relating to land at Nether Whitacre, co. Warwick, purchased of the Rt. Hon. C. B. Adderley. (13.)

XIII/3 1841–1894. Title deeds relating to a freehold messuage, 69 Trumpington Street, Cambridge, purchased of Mr Frank Tomson. (19.)

XIII/6 1729–1836. Lease etc. of premises in the parish of St Botolph. President and Fellows of Queens' College to the University and to St Catharine's Hall. (5.)

XIV/4 1691–1823. Correspondence etc. *re* the Coventry Scholarship etc.; Letters *re* the election of Mr Edmonds in 1792. (20.)

XIV/10 1794. April. Disputed election of Richard Foster to a Ramsden Fellowship. (3.)

XVIII/4 1658–1702. Gimingham and Trunch, co. Norfolk. Documents, Letters, etc. relating to the College Advowson. Letters from Robert Thexton to Dr Eachard and others.

c. 1650. Petition of inhabitants of Trunch.

1793. Acts.

Manuscript Book, Reference to a map of Gimingham and Trunch. (70.)

XVIII/6 1762–1847. Therfield, co. Hertford.

Account Book.

1806–1893. Miscellaneous Papers. Congeston, co. Leicester.

1758. June 23. Extracts from Dr Thomas Sherlock's Will.

c. 1760. Rules and Orders for the Library Keeper of Catharine Hall Library on the foundation of Bishop Sherlock.

Sherlock Bequest; Fellowship, etc. (35.)

XIX/2 (A) 1867–75. Cambridge. Property in Silver Street. Abstract of Title. Draft Conveyances, etc. (12.)

(B) 1860. Bruisyard, co. Suffolk. Abstract of Title of Earl of Stradbroke.

1687. March 4. Extract from Will of Matthew Scrivener.

c. 1860. Miscellaneous Papers and Plan. (6.)

(C) *c.* 1862. Stafford benefaction. Miscellaneous Papers. (20.)

Bundle

(D) *c.* 1874. Attorney-General *v.* St Catharine's College. (20.)

(E) 1867. Papers *re* Thomas Tomson deceased. (16.)

(F) *c.* 1868. Property at Impington, Chesterton and Histon. (6.)

XIX/5 1535–1801. "Old Deeds relating to a Freehold Estate in Trumpington Street, Cambridge, purchased of Mr Charles Balls by St Catharine's College."

1838. Agreement.

1874. Draft of Conveyance, etc. (32.)

XX/5 1578. Papers respecting the suit *v.* Richard Anger Esq., of Coton. *c.* 1576. (20). [Bound in covers, now loose.]

XX/6 1781–1838. Master and Fellows of Jesus College, Cambridge, and David Bradwell and others. Property in St Andrew's Street, Cambridge. (25.)

XXI/1 1831. Frankland Fellowship. Papers relating to Mr Inge's Appeal.

1841. Petition of the College to Chancery. (50.)

XXI/7 1801–7. Petition of Dr Procter, D.D., Master of St Catharine's Hall, and Charles William Burrell, M.A., President. (19.)

XXII/4 1604–1770. Coton. "Four Pound and Forty Shillings land." (20.)

Bundle

XXVI/1 1813–20. In Chancery. Gresham and others *v.* Master and Fellows of St Catharine's College. Briefs, etc. (13.)

XXXI/1 1848. St Catharine's Hall. Petition; Revised Statutes; Admissions; Affidavits; etc. (35.)

XXXI/2 ? 1675–1680–1. "Proposed Agreement for the Foundation of Seven Scholarships and two Fellowships for Scholars from Birmingham School."

XXXI/4 1316–1809. Miscellaneous. (25.) These documents have been found dispersed amongst various bundles. Two of them are undated.

XL/1 1634–1806. "Royal Letters dispensing with the College Statutes":

I. 1634. Aug. 7. Charles I.

II. 1664. Dec. 9. Charles II.

III. 1678. Jan. 7. Charles II.

IV. 1691. Oct. 7. William III and Mary.

V. 1697. Aug. 2. William III.

VI. 1806. Nov. 5. George III.

XL/2 1557. Apr. 5. "Chesterton." A Licence of Mortmain. Bears the Great Seal, decaying, of Philip and Mary.

XL/3 1513. Feb. 15. A Licence of Mortmain for £10. Great Seal, damaged, of Henry VIII.

XL/5 1704. Sep. 1. Act, signed by Symon, Bishop of Ely, of Consecration of Chapel.

Bundle

XL/6 1704. Sep. 1. Form of Consecration of Chapel. MS.

XL/7 1467–78. "The Several Instruments[1] and Writings by which Dr Wodelarke conveyed His Property to the Masters and Fellows of his College and their Successors in perpetuity."

II Book of Transcripts.

III *c.* 1848. Transcripts in the handwriting of Dr Henry Philpott.

1542. "Disputes about the Proctorship between Edwin Sandes of St Catharine's Hall and Matthew Stokys of King's College."

IV 1580–2. "Proceedings in an appeal of John Furmary to the Vice-Chancellor against the Sentence of the Master, Edmund Hound, which deprived him of his Fellowship."

V 1582–3. "Proceedings in the University Courts in an action against the Master and Fellows for cutting and felling Timber on a Farm at Chesterton which they had demised on lease for 40 years."

VI 1592. July 19. "Proceedings of the Master, Dr Hound, against Four of the Fellows in the Vice-Chancellor's Court."

VII 1592–3. "Proceedings in an appeal to the Vice-Chancellor for Robert Cansfield against a Sentence of deprivation of his Fellowship."

VIII 1597. "Proceedings upon the Election of a Master after the death of Dr Edmund Hound."

IX 1635. "Proceedings in the Election of a Master upon the death of Dr Sibbs...."

X 1698–1705. "Proceedings respecting Dr Eachard's Estate mortgaged to the University...."

XI *c.* 1697. Original printed Appeal for funds for new Chapel—headed "The State of St Katharine's Hall in Cambridge". [The College Order Book has a memorandum by Sir William Dawes, 2 Jan. 1699, "for printing 100 of College cases—12s". The above is evidently one of them.]

XII "The Stipends paid to the Master and Fellows from the College Stock...under the Statutes of 1860 these Stipends are discontinued. H. P. [Henry Philpott]."

XXXII/3 1623. "The Inventory of such goods as are in the M^r's Lodging of St Katherine hall that appertaine to the said College."

1782–1860. Inventories, etc. of College Plate. (30.)

[1] At least one of these documents bears the reputed seal of Dr Woodlark.

Bundle

XXXII/8 1688–1864. 66 Trumpington Street, Cambridge (J. Knightley). Copies of documents etc., and deeds. (25.)

[The property known as 65 and 66 Trumpington Street is now the site of Hobson's Building, erected in 1930.]

XXXII/10 1891. 69 Trumpington Street, Cambridge. Title Deeds. (3.)

XXXII/12 1803–71. 69 and 70 Trumpington Street, Cambridge. Deeds, etc. (two packets). (14.)

XXXIII/3 1888. Correspondence between W. J. Atkinson and Rev. Dr Procter. (25.)

XXXIII/7 1861. Pamphlets, etc. relating to Dr Robinson's Election to the Mastership of St Catharine's College. (12.)

XXXV/1 *c.* 1820–1922. Norton (co. York) Estate and Minerals. Askern Coal Co.: Thompson and others *v.* Master and Fellows of St Catharine's College: correspondence, printed papers, plans, etc., etc. (300.)

XXXVI/1 1730–1847. St Catharine's College, Cases and Opinions. (13.)

1855. Discontinuance of Burials in the College Chapel. Order, etc. (3.)

1927. Suspension of Election to Mastership pending passing of Act of Parliament, with power also to elect a layman. (1.)

1906–26. Bull Hotel, Cambridge. Correspondence and counterparts of lease. (5.)

1798–1807. Lawyers' Bills. (7.)

1926–7. Agreement and Act, St Catharine's College and the Dean and Chapter of Norwich Cathedral. Separation of a Canonship or Prebend in Norwich Cathedral from the Mastership of St Catharine's College, and other matters relating thereto. (2.)

XXXVI/7 1913. St Catharine's College. Book of plans of proposed new buildings.

XXXVI/13 Parcel of eleven old documents:

(1) 1493. Feb. 11. Receipt from Thomas Pollard, of Stoke-by-Clare, the executor of William Bassett.

1505. April 3. A Chalice pawned for £5 to the President of Catharine's Hall by the Prioress of Swaffham Bulbeck.

1511. March 26. Affidavit respecting false assertions of Nicholas Glosse.

1574. June 22. Revocation of a Letter of Attorney granted by the Master and Fellows to W. Spyres of Chesterton (2 Nov. 1573) authorising him to re-

Bundle

ject Richard Fanne and others and take possession of land at Chesterton. College seal attached.

XXXVII/4 1614. Sir John Claypoole's Scholarships.

1674. John Cartwright's Scholarships.

1718. Appointment of a scholar by Thomas Cartwright.

1847. List made by Dr Philpott of Papers in the Registrary's Office, connected with Catharine Hall.

1632–1748. List of Admissions in the Manor Court of Crowle to lands in Luddington and Garthorpe, co. Lincoln. (8.)

1691. Mr Frankland's will.

1687. Mr Scrivener's will.

— Mr Hobbes' will.

1746. Information filed by the Poor Boys and Girls of Fockerby, etc.

c. 1700. College Statutes, MS. written by Sir William Dawes, and having a list of Masters continued till 1779.

XXXVII/5 1831. Papers connected with an appeal to the Visitor of the College respecting the election of a Frankland Fellow. (13.)

— MS. copy of Statutes.

1848. Affidavit of Rev. Elwes Corrie, D.D.

1848–9. *In re* Catharine Hall, Cambridge. *Ex parte* Goodwin (printed petition).

1848–9. "Contents of Card Board Box", found in Master's Lodge. This is a list made by Dr Philpott. The "Contents" have now been put into the general collection in the Muniment Room.

— List of Benefactors made by Dr Philpott.

XVIII. Miscellaneous Papers:

(Addendum) 1611–1833. Accounts, Receipts, Bonds, etc.

Receipts by William Gostlin for rent of Black Bull Inn, Cambridge (1631–33); Receipts by Alice Holmes, brewress (1627–39); Receipt by Dr John Lightfoot, Master 1650–75; Sundry accounts of Dr Eachard, Master 1675–97; Correspondence of John Holwey with Sir William Dawes (Master 1697–1714) in 1699. (106.)

1577–1838. Correspondence and Sundry Papers.

Appointment by Dr John Lightfoot of deputy to act as Vice-Chancellor during his absence (1654–5); Letter, dated 27 June 1697, from Rev. William Clarke, formerly Rector of St Margaret's, Westminster, and now Vicar of Eye, co. Suffolk, to Dr Eachard. (13.)

LONDON COLLECTIONS, ETC.

WITH A FEW EXTRACTS MADE BY

MR E. A. B. BARNARD

British Museum. Add. MSS. 5813/254.

From Cole's notes:

"Account of Dr Eachard, M^r of St Catharine's Hall.

"The following Account of Dr John Eachard I transcribed from a MS. wrote by and left to me by Zach. Grey of Ampthill in May, 1759. It is a small Thing which he has prepared for the Press entituled Maxims, Sayings, Descriptions and Characters, extracted from a Book entitled, Grounds and Occasions of the Contempt of the Clergy etc., and the other Writings of the late Reverend, learned and witty Divine Dr John Eachard, Master of Catherine Hall, in Cambridge. With Historical and Explanatory Notes and similar Passages, from the fanatical Teachers and Writers in the Time of the Grand Rebellion and Usurpation.

"Dr John Eachard, an English Divine of great Learning and Wit in the 17th Century, was of a good Family in the County of Suffolk; and having been instructed in Gramar Learning was sent to Katherine Hall in the Univ. of Cambr. where he took the Degree of A.B. in 1656, and A.M. in 1660.

"In the year 1670 he published, without his Name, a Book, intitled, *The Grounds and Occasions of the Contempt of the Clergy and Religion enquired into*: which he ascribes in a great Measure to a wrong Method of Education, or the Poverty of some of the inferior Clergy. As to the first, he proves at the beginning of this Tract, The wrong Method of Education in some Country Schools in his Time and the Folly of such Parents as devoted their Children of the worst Constitution in Body, and the weaker Abilities, to the Service of the Church....Dr Eachard's Enquiry etc. was soon answered by an anonymous writer in a Tract intitled An Answer to a Letter of Enquiry into the Grounds and Occasions of the Contempt of the Clergy. London, 1671, in 12°. And Mr Barnabas Oley, a very worthy Divine of the Established Church, in his Preface to Mr George Herbert's Country Parson, his Character and Rule of holy Life and by several other Writers...."

London Collections, etc.

British Museum. Add. MSS. 5831/158.

Cole writes the following note after a copy of a letter from Thomas Sherlock, then Bishop of Salisbury, dated 5 April 1729, and modernised:

"There is no direction to this letter, but the subject shows sufficiently to whom it was addressed. The Bishop's hand at that time was very plain and legible; he wrote worse since; and now, 1759, June 4, I suppose can hardly sign his name; though his senses are as perfect, witness his last charge, and other late performances, as ever, with a very crazed and impotent body, and his tongue hanging out of his mouth, and slabbering like a child: so that he is a spectacle of concern and pity to those who know his great worth and greater abilities; and at the same time a mortifying picture of the vanity of great parts and accomplishments, which the greater they are, often terminate in the weakest: as witness the Duke of Marlborough, Dean Swift, and many others too tedious to mention."

British Museum. Add. MSS. 5841/17.

From Cole's notes:

"In the Cambridge Chronicle of Sept. 1, 1764, is this Article.

'Anecdote relating to the 2 late Bps. Hoadley and Sherlock.'

"These 2 Prelates were both of Catharine Hall in Cambridge, and, as I believe, both of the same Year, and Pupils of Mr Bower, a learned Scotchman. When they were Freshmen, they were called to Lectures in Tully's offices. One Day Hoadley performed so well as to receive a Compliment from his Tutor. As they were coming away from the Tutor's Chamber, Sherlock, who was probably a little nettled, called out, 'Ben, you have made good Use of L'Estrange's Translation to Day!' 'No, Tom,' replied Hoadley, 'I have it not, and I forgot to send the Bed-maker to borrow yours, which I am told is the only one in the College.' So early did the Emulation between these 2 great men commence."

British Museum. Add. MSS. 5813/f. 375b.

1769. Catharine Hall subscribed £5. 5*s*. o*d*. to the "making and maintaining the Turnpike Road from Cambridge to Ely".

British Museum. Add. MSS. 22911/f. 166.

"Master,

Pray send me a copy of your Statutes and I'll send them to the profess[rs] and will state the case to him myself, which I think is the most regular method according to your Statutes. *I intend to come to your College next Tuesday*. I had promised Mr

Edmundson a Congregation for that day for a Doctor of St John's. He will hear next post from him. If the Congregation holds, *it must be three in the afternoon* before I come to you: *if not, I would choose to be earlier of which you shall have regular notice tomorrow night.* For the meantime you may let *the fellows know the day, and that they shall be duly acquainted with the hour.* I desire we may be in a warm room.

Your most humble Servant

Tho. Sherlock."

Jan. 27th 1714.

[Addressed: "To the Revd the Master of the College These."

Endorsed: "Mr Vicechancr

Jan. 27. 1714/5

publish'd to ye Fellowes the same day."]

f. 168: (No date.)

"Master

Pray send me word what place in your College you agree on, for us to hear your Cause on Friday, and then you shall have the Citation.

Your humble Servant

Tho. Sherlock."

[This letter is addressed as above.]

British Museum. Harleian MSS.

The only reference in this Collection is:

7034. ff. 1–40. Collectiones ex Regro. Coll. sive Aulae S. Catherinae.

f. 42. Inscription upon monument of Lady Frances Dawes, "copied by Doctor Cross now Master of the College".

f. 47. Inscription upon Dr Eachard's monument, "copied by Dr Cross, Vice-Chancellor".

British Museum. Sloane MSS.

The only reference in this Collection is contained in:

4840. 48.

The foundation of the University of Cambridge, by Gerard Langborne.

This note is very short and refers to the small quarto publication of 1651, which is not to be found in the British Museum. The corresponding Oxford pamphlet is there.

London Collections, etc.

British Museum. Add. MSS.

St Catharine's Hall

(i) Memoranda concerning, 5866/f. 220b.

From Cole's notes:

St Catharine's Hall.

Collectiones et Registro Aulae Sc̄ae Catharina. Mr Baker's MSS. Vol. 7, p. 1.
Particulars concerning Catharine Hall. id. Vol. 27, No. 2, p. 39.
A Fellowship founded in St Katharine's Hall, 1515, by Mag^r Wm Stockdale, Eliz. Hermanson, Robert Symson and others. *v.* my MS. Collections, Vol. 42, p. 35.

In the Cambridge Chronicle of October 17, 1772, was this Paragraph:

"The M^r and Fellows of Catharine Hall have given Notice, the Tuesday 10 Nov. next to be fixed for the Election of 6 Gentlemen into the Fellowships of Mrs Ramsden's Foundation. The Candidates may belong to any College in the University, and to pass an Examination on 3 Nov."

"It is very extraordinary that the Vice-Chancellor, who was appointed by Foundation, to be an Examiner, is deprived of his Privilege, it being worded that the first Tuesday in November is to be the Election Day: now that happens on the day in the year when there is no Vice-Chancellor: the old one going out of office and the new one not being chose or put into Function till Nov. 4.

"Mrs Ramsden was sister to Mr Breary, Rector of Boxworth in this County, where she used to be often with her brother, who determined her benefactions to St Catharine's Hall.

"Dr Sherlock ordered his Librarian to be chosen by the Masters of St John's, Clare Hall, and Orator, out of dislike to Dr Prescot.

"A° 1714. 3 June. An Act for taking away Mortuaries in the 4 Welsh Dioceses, and giving a recompence to the Bp;s thereof and for confirming several L^rs Patents granted to her Majesty for perpetually annexing a Prebend of Gloucester to the Mastership of Pembroke Coll. in O. and a Prebend of Rochester to the Provostship of Oriel Coll. in O., and a Prebend of Norwich to the Mastership of Catharine Hall in Cambridge. Journals of the House of Commons, Vol. 17, p. 663, *penes me*.

"In a Book of com̄on Accounts belonging to Dr James, Master of Queen's College, in my Possession 1778, is this Entry:

"July 9, 1694. Paid to Dr Eachard Master of St Katharine's Hall towards building their new Chapel, 50 li. for which I am to receive £5 yearly during my Life from the said College, viz. 50s. every Halfe yeare, and the first 50s. to be paid at the Feast of S[t] John next, and so on etc. The said D[r] has promised that in Case I die within 2 yeares he will pay to any poor Relation such as I, or any Executor shall name, ten Pounds. Mr Lea, Fellow of the College, and the Master are engaged to see good Security given for the payment of 5 li yearely.

"Dr James made a good Bargain here, for he had the Annuity 22 years not dying till 1716, so that he got double his Money. *v.* my Vol. 18, p. 97, and Vol. A. C. M. p. 314 B.

"Sept. 1. 1704. Consecration of Kath. Hall new Chapel. Dr James's Act. Book. p.m.

"The Mercers Company have been good benefactors to this College, which sends a Preacher to them on Good Friday to their Chapel, where in 1688 Mr Strype, as having been formerly of the College preached and took notice of their Benefaction and his Education. Stow's Survey, by Strype. Vol. 2, p. 56, which see under Article *John Strype* in Vol. S/12.

"John Sayer, B.D., Fellow of Queen's, elected Master, 1736. *v.* my Vol. 48, p. 273."

(ii) Congratulatory letters to different persons, 1707–1727.

5858/f. 389, etc.

(*a*) Dr Leng, with coat-of-arms, 1723.

(*b*) Bishop Blackhall, with coat-of-arms, 1707.

(*c*) Sir William Dawes, 1713.

(*d*) Lord Harcourt, "upon the Grant of a Prebend of Norwich to their Mastership, drawn up by Dr Sherlock, Dean of Chichester and M[r] of Kath. Hall". Copied (by Dr H.) out of a Letter to Dr Sherlock to the College, dated May 4, 1714.

(*e*) Dr Sherlock „ „ 1727.

Beneath this Cole has written:

"There are no Gratulations to the 2 Hoadleys, perhaps the Society judiciously thought none were due.

"Bp. Sherlock was a great Man, but an arbitrary one. He gave me a *Living*, but I soon found that more civility and obsequiousness would be expected than was in my Nature to give: so I gave up all my future Prospects of great Ecclesiastical Preferment, for more liberty and less constraint; for which I was not made."

(iii) List of the Masters, Fellows, Scholars, etc. and of Bishops educated there, with the arms of the Hall. 5851/f. 149 etc.:

f. 149. Arms of Woodlark. St Catharine's Hall (8 spokes in wheel); College impaling Prescot; ? Sherlock.

f. 150. List of Masters, with prefatory note by Cole.

f. 151. Bishops [13] educated in St Catharine's Hall.

ff. 152–6. A list[1] of the Fellows [184] of St Catharine's Hall. [With date and provenance.]

f. 157. A list[1] of the Conduct Fellows [11] of St Catharine's Hall. [With date and provenance.]

(iv) Abstract of two indentures relative to the building of the new chapel and the lands given for that purpose by Mr Scrivener. 5819/f. 96b.

(v) Sherlock. (Thomas.) Bishop successively of Bangor, Salisbury and London. List of works published in his controversy with Bishop Hoadly concerning the Test Act. 6216/f. 34.

(vi) Memoranda relating to the University of Cambridge, with notes by W. Cole. 5822/f. 2367.

........Arms. St Catharine's College impaling Sherlock.

Note by Cole on a MS. book "relating to University Matters, sent to me by the Vice-Chancellor, Dr Yates, Master of St Catharine's Hall, October 5, 1780... compiled by Dr Sherlock, then Master of Catharine Hall...Bp. Sherlock, my most learned Patron...."

(vii) Correspondence with W. Cole respecting the living of Hornsey. 5808/f. 81.

(viii) Letters of Dr Grey, 5 April 1739. 5831/f. 158. In a note Cole describes Sherlock's pitiful physical condition in 1757.

(ix) Queries issued by Bishop Thomas Sherlock at his visitation of the diocese of London. 5808/f. 83b.

(x) Letter to Bishop Thomas Sherlock from J. Parke, 1731. 6210/f. 81.

(xi) Letter of thanks from Catharine Hall to Lord Harcourt, drawn up by Bishop Thomas Sherlock. 5858/f. 395.

[1] This list has been copied and collated with the list in the College Muniment Room, Jan. 1935.

(xii) Congratulatory epistle from Catharine Hall to Bishop Thomas Sherlock, 1727; with his arms. 5858/f. 396.

(xiii) Docquet of a grant to Bishop Thomas Sherlock of the office of Master of the Temple, 1705. 5808/f. 84b.

(xiv) Anecdote relating to Bishops Hoadly and Sherlock. 5841/f. 17. (See p. 291.)

(xv) Sir William Dawes, Archbishop of York. Letters to Rev. Mr Burton, 1718–1722. 5831/f. 144.

(xvi) Congratulatory epistle to Dawes, from Catharine Hall, with his arms, and a biographical note by W. Cole. 5858/f. 393.

(xvii) Edward Hubbard, Master of Catharine Hall, Cambridge. Considerations on the nature and value of College leases, with his arms. 5852/f. 108.

(xviii) Kenrick Prescot, Master of Catharine Hall. Letter to him from W. Cole, 1773. 5844/f. 73.

Epitaph for his children. 6402/f. 118.

His arms. 5851/f. 149.

(xix) John Lightfoot, D.D., Master of Catharine Hall. Letters to Dr S. Clarke, 1662, 1667. 22905/ff. 52, 64, 68.

(xx) Ralph Brownrigge, Bishop of Exeter, Letter to, from Sir William Dewes, 1643. Latin. 22916/f. 1.

(xxi) Sir William Dawes, 3rd Baronet, of Putney. Archbishop of York. Letter to Dr Warley, 1714. 22997/f. 125.

(xxii) Thomas Sherlock, Dean of Chichester, and Bishop of Bangor, Salisbury, and London.

Letters to Dr J. Covel, 1714. 22911/ff. 166, 168.

Letters to Dr Crosse, 1722. 22908/ff. 132, 136.

Signatures, 1728–38. 22910/f. 280.

Petition to, from J. Stevens, *c.* 1745. 29599/f. 350.

(xxiii) Thomas Crosse, D.D., Master of St Catharine's College, Cambridge and Vice-Chancellor. Letters to, from E. Lang, and others, 1721–22. 22908/ff. 111, 126–40.

Mr Lang's letter is dated from Pembroke Hall, Feb. 9, 1721, and is addressed:

These
For the Rev[d] D[r] Crosse att
Mr Crosse's a Tobacconist in
Bishops-gate Street w[th]in the Gate
London.

British Museum. Add. MSS. 5858/f. 389 *et sqq*.

Beneath the letter to Dawes, Cole has written:

"See his Article in my Athenae Cantabrigienses, D. p. 69.

"See his Life in the *Biographia Britannica*, Edit. 1, Vol. 3, p. 1630, by which it appears that the Bp. of York's Interest with the Queen was the Occasion of the Prebend of Norwich being annexed to the Mastership of St Catharine's Hall.

"I once heard Bp. Gooch, in his vexation at some ill Behaviour which he conceived to have met with from Dr Prescot about the Time of his being presented by the Chapter to the Great Church at Yarmouth, say, That the Prebend did the College more Harm than Good, as it made the Masters negligent of their Duty. His Brother-in-Law, Sherlock, I dare say, did not think so, on his first Appointment to it, and Bp. Gooch himself, before he attained the mitre, would not probably have thought so. But so different are People in an humble Station from what they are when Lords in Parliament."

Cole MSS. Vol. 14:

Sherlock, Thomas, much correspondence with the Duke of Newcastle, 1733–61.

Vol. 16. Catharine Hall. Suit *v*. Dawney, 1752. 36066/f. 1.
Case relating to taxation of buildings, 1769. 36204/f. 441.

Ditto Sherlock, Thomas, much correspondence with the first Lord Hardwicke, 1738–58.
Letter to Abp. Herring, 1749. 35598/f. 382.
Seal, 1758. CX, 90

Authorities

Public Record Office. S.P. Dom. Jas. I X^{a}.

1604.

Dec. 20? f. 77. [Transcript.]

The certificate of Katrine hall. All of our company are conformable to ye orders of ye churche of England and do vse the rites and ceremonies appoynted in the booke of com̄on prayer in time of divine seruice, wth all suche habits as are required by ye canons now inioyning suche things.

The ministers in our house be these. Mr Cragg. Mr Moone. Mr Sill. Mr Hollingsworth. Mr Knowles.

Mr Cragg was admitted into holy orders at Buckden 18° Septemb. āo don̄i 1557.

Mr Moone was admitted into ye sayd holy orders at Buckden 18° Octobris āo don̄i 1603.

Mr Sill was admitted vnto ye sayd orders at Buckden 7° Junij āo don̄i 1601.

Mr Hollingsworth and Mr Knowles have not there orders in ye colledge now presently, but haue them in there owne parishes and wilbe redy to shew them vpon any warninge yf they haue a sufficient time alloted vnto them.

Mr Sill and Mr Hollingsworthe are bothe of them bachilers in diuinity and licensed preachers by ye Vniversity.

Mr Sill was licensed 17° Decemb. 1602.

Mr Hollingsworthe was licensed 16° Decemb. 1604.

Mr Cragg, Mr Moone, and Mr Knowles are not licensed preachers as yet, nether do they vse to preache in any place except y^{t} be wthin there owne ꝑper cures

Willm Moone ꝑ president.

Somerset House.

Prerogative Court of Canterbury Indexes.

[No will of Robert Woodlark or of John Eachard.]

Mr Barnard examined all the following wills to which reference is made in the printed indexes, but there is nothing in any of them of interest to the College:

Vol. I. Nil.

II. 1519. Midilton, Leonarde, St Katrynes Hall, Cambridge; Schape, Westmerland. 20 Ayliffe.

1492. Tapton, John, Clerk, Leicester or Rutland; [? Master of Catharine hall, Cambridge]; Stoke-juxta-Clare, co. Suffolk. 30 Dogett.

1488. Bassett, Sir William, Clerk, Stoke-juxta-Clare, co. Suffolk. 21 Milles.

Testator leaves a book to the College Chapel.

III. Nil.

IV. 1586. Anderson, William, Mr of Arts, and fellow of St Katherine's hall in Cambridge; Chesterton, Cambs. 56 Windsor.

V. Nil.

VI. 1626. Hilles, John, D.D. and Mr of St Katherin Colledge, Cambridge, Archdeacon of Lincoln, of Fulborne, co. Cambs. 148 Hele.

Somerset House. P.C.C. 256 Cheslyn.

Thomas Sherlock, Lord Bishop of London (A wealthy man, definitely evidenced by his will). All freehold messuages etc. in Birmingham to my wife, and after her decease to my nephew, Sir Thomas Gooch, and then to my worthy friends the Hon. Edward Weston Esq. and the Rev. Dr John Fountayne,[1] Dean of York and their heirs.

Property at Bilesley, co. Warwick; and Upwell, co. Norfolk; parsonage at Aldin, co. Sussex:

"Item I give and devise my lands, tenements and hereditaments at Therfield, co. Hertford, commonly known by the name of farm pastures, to the master and fellows of Catherine Hall, in Cambridge" for ever....But nevertheless upon trust to pay and apply the clear rents and profits thereof from time to time as an addition to the Scholarship usually given to the said Master's sizar for the time being. And whereas there is a growth of young timber upon the estate my meaning is not that the scholar for the time being should have any advantage of it but that the Master and Fellows should dispose of the timber and apply the profits thereof to the necessary repairs of the College.

Item I give and devise my lands, tenements and hereditaments at Congeston in the County of Leicester to the said Master and fellows of Catherine Hall...to found a scholarship to go with the Library Keepers place which Library Keeper shall be chosen by the Master and Fellows and shall have £20 a year allowed him out of the rents of the said lands, and the remainder of the rent shall be applied to purchase new books for the said library.

And my will is that the said scholarship shall be given to some scholar who is of two years standing or more in the said College who has given proof of his sobriety and industry, who shall be subject to such rules as shall be appointed by the Master and Fellows.

[1] Cf. G. F. Browne, *St Catharine's College*, p. 197.

And my will is that an account of the produce of the estate and the disposition of the money arising from the rents thereof be annually entered into a Register Book kept for that purpose and called the Library Accounts.

Property in Hill S[t], Berkeley Square.

Widow of testator is to have "all coins and medals that shall be in any of my houses...and all my plate, jewels, clocks, watches, pictures, linen and household goods, and all my coaches and horses".

Trunk at M[r] Hoares, the bankers—to widow.

To Master and Fellows of Catherine Hall my library of books excepting such books either English or French that my wife shall choose for herself.

Wife, Sir Thomas Gooch and D[r] John Fountayne, executors.

There are several codicils, one of which contains this proviso:

"I do earnestly request that the King's Professor of Divinity and the Master of S[t] John's College at Cambridge and the Master of Catherine Hall...will be so good as to accept that trust, [*re* Library Keeper] in consideration wherof I do hereby appoint them electors of the person to be library keeper."

They are empowered to make rules and statutes relating to the office of Library Keeper; they are not confined in their choice, but can choose the keeper out of the University at large; but the appointed keeper must be admitted a member of Catherine Hall, in consideration of which he is to have an extra £5 per annum for a convenient room for the library keeper's place.

Anyone under the degree of M.A. can be elected, and shall continue keeper for 8 years. If he dies or resigns, his successor is to be elected within 3 months.

If the electors neglect to choose a successor, then the Provost of King's is asked to make the appointment for that turn only.

The remainder of the rents at Congeston are for the repairs of the library to keep the room sweet and clean and in keeping up and painting the iron rails[1] as often as they shall want it.

Another codicil contains the bequest of £4 p.a. to be paid to the Master and Fellows for the rent of a chamber which must be allowed to the said library keeper.

[1] *Op. cit.* p. 187.

Sherlock evidently made one or two of his codicils in his own handwriting—for a manservant testifies to his handwriting after his death.

Probate: 28 July 1761.

Public Record Office. S.P. For. and Dom. (Vol. XXI, Pt. I, p. 140).

1546. Cambridge: The University....

The list[1] of the houses with the onus or necessary expenditure of each is as follows:

...College or hall of St Katharine. 59 li. 14s. 6d.

S.P. For. and Dom. (Letters and Papers, Hen. VIII, Vol. I, Pt. I, p. 438, (3)m 19):

Thomas Grene S.T.B. master and the fellows of St Katharine's in Cambridge, 30 July, 1509–10.

They come in the lists of persons receiving the King's general pardon. "Every possible variation of name and designation of the parties is given, but no reason for the pardon is specified" (*op. cit.* p. 203).

S.P. Dom. Addenda (Vol. I, Pt. I, pp. 105, 109):

"The book of the view, valuation and tax of the University of Cambridge" consisting of 21 leaves of paper, unfortunately very much mutilated, with lists for the most part very illegible, both of graduated and *scholastici* arranged under the different colleges...:

f. 14. Catharine Hall [Aula divae Caterinae]. Two or three names quite illegible. Artium professores. Twelve or thirteen names almost totally illegible: Ric. Sutton and John Roberdy....

Birmingham Reference Library.

During Mr Barnard's examination of the Sherlock documents in this library he came across the following note in the *Birmingham Weekly Post*, 12 July 1913:

"Dr Thomas Sherlock, Lord Bishop of London.

"Queen Mary in 1555 granted the manor of Birmingham to Thomas Murrow [Marrow], in whose family it remained for nearly two centuries, when from the main line failing it became the property of four co-heiresses, who disposed of the

[1] *Op. cit.* p. 187.

private estate in the manor to Thomas Sherlock, Bishop of London, it then amounted to about £400 per annum. In 1790 the annual rent increased to £2,400. In 1746 the manor itself was sold to Thomas Archer, of Umberslade, for £1,700.

"The Bishop's name is perpetuated in Sherlock Street, and through this ecclesiastic the Gooch family of Benacre Hall, Suffolk, came to be large landowners in our city...."

This note is accompanied by a reproduction of an engraving of the Bishop: "The Right Rev[d] Dr Tho[s] Sherlock Late Lord Bishop of London."

II. LETTERS

The records of St Catharine's, rich in legal documents, are poor in letters; but among the papers left by Eachard are a number of letters written to him in or about 1680, which, with a few to be found in the Baumgartner Manuscripts,[1] throw a clear if not brilliant light upon the inner life of the College.

Here is a communication sent to Eachard on 23 April 1680 by J. Votier:[2]

"I never heard of the letter I sent a quarter of a year since: I did then desire an account, yet am not in capacity to pay at present....His carriage hath been ill. Let the milliners etc be forbidden to trust him: he hath clothes enough for a quarter of a year, or 2 months. Take him off from Tobacco, he hath forced it on himself, he neglecteth his study, would run after wenches: I hope you will laugh him out of these things. Task him well for his book: If a strict hand be not kept over him he will do but little. Let not him know of this my writing. I will endeavour to get money, as soon as I can, when I know my charge: I desire care be used in casting up the accounts, and that the profit of his scholarship may be allowed.

J. VOTIER

I have given my son much good counsel, but he very much slighteth it. Watch him for speaking untruths to which he is so prone: as also to chop and change his clothes so, as to cut and alter them to my great detriment: if he be not more moderate, I cannot hold. I hope yourself will do what you can in these things, for my comfort, and my child's good."

There is a modern ring about much of this fussy letter, and the writer's anxiety lest the Master should be at fault with his arithmetic, a reminder that in 1680 there was no College Office, is a delightful piece of unconscious impertinence.

On 29 May 1680 H. Gore wrote as follows:

"I have received my son's quarterly bills from Michaelmas to Lady day, which in truth I cannot but apprehend most extravagant, especially in the moneys given to him, and what is laid out in Books,[3] the latter of which since he came to the

[1] In the Cambridge University Library.

[2] Eachard, *Letters*, 37.

[3] The accounts dealing with these items are extant. The "Given him's" amount to £2. 10*s*. 0*d*. and the sums "laid out in Books" total £6. 10*s*. 11*d*. The bill from Michaelmas to Christmas amounts to £15. 3*s*. 4*d*., that from Christmas to Lady Day to £6. 4*s*. 9*d*.

College hath been six pounds eleven shillings. I entreat you Sir to (?) no more upon those accounts and to make some observations how he spends both his time and his money, for I have much reason to fear it is not employd as I expect: he is a younger brother amongst many children and at this rate I cannot maintain him.... When he went last from home which was after Candlemas, he carried with him six or seven pounds....I observe him much given to gaming. I wish that way hath not consumed it; pardon me Sir if I give you this trouble, since it proceeds from the high concern I have for a child to prevent him in ill courses before a habit becomes incurable.

Sir your obliged affectionate friend
to serve you
H. GORE."[1]

Shortly after this Gore's son fell ill, and in a letter under date 12 July 1680 his father asks that he may be sent home for a change with books, "that he may not go backward in his learning".[2]

Votier's son was evidently a source of anxiety, for about this date his father writes: "he hath a mind to be a lawyer now. I wish he would grow fixed."[3] And a little later:

"My son I cannot persuade to study; what the matter is, I cannot tell: He saith Duck hath his clothes, but Duck hath been at Kellshall but no clothes come....I earnestly crave time: for I have lately been much damnified."[4]

The qualifications expected of an undergraduate are thus set down by Sam. Golty in a letter dated "Ipswich 14 March 1680":

"As for Major, I am informed that by his own stock and a little help from his mother, he will be able to answer the charges of the College and University.—As to his qualifications, I think he is not in love now, for his mistress is married, he is formal enough, walks trim and brisk, and manages a cane gracefully—and I hope he will wear a gown as well, and may be brought to understand it is his business and interest, to lie close to books, and it is thought that he will too."[5]

There is something attractive in the two letters[6] from Roger Wilbraham. In the first he offers to give money instead of plate when his son, a Fellow

[1] Eachard, *Letters*, 47. [2] *op. cit.* 59. [3] *op. cit.* 60.

[4] Eachard, *Letters*, 64. Was this Duck related to Mr Duke of Kelsale, who was a great benefactor of St Catharine's? [5] *op. cit.* 101.

[6] Eachard, *Letters*, 63 and 98.

Commoner, leaves the College, and acknowledges "civilities...which had put me many times to the Blush, but that my Complexion in that did befriend me". In the second he answers the suggestion that his son should learn French and music,[1] and asks that he should learn to dance, "both to better his carriage and to exercise his limbs".

An interesting side-light on Fellow Commoners occurs in a letter from George Barker, dated 13 April 1681, who says:

"Many are admitted Fellow-commoners who neither are scholars nor are ever like to be....I told him that it was not usual for Masters of Colleges to meddle with pupils, but you...keeping some Fellow-Commoners after you were Master, I thought you might be prevailed with to entertain his son."[2]

The Strype Correspondence gives us more of the undergraduate point of view. The earliest letters are those of Strype to his mother. The son writes on 27 October 1663:

"You must not think much of so large a bill as you have received, it being my first quarter at this College: you write me that I should leave my French Master: you may be sure I did not intend to throw away more than 20 shillings about him: I have now done with him: for he useth to teach two months for 20 shillings and then leaveth them pretty well entered into the language. I have learned thus long of him, and now have left him. I am able to write letters, or to understand in a book, but not so well spoken: for that must come by use."

Remarkable progress, this, in two months, and equally remarkable insight into the way in which a language is learned.

"Here in this college hath died a lad whom I loved better than any since I came to Cambridge; some say of the spotted fever, which I think proved false; every one in the College, as also his acquaintance in Town, had gloves and ribbons: he was buried very nobly. The small pox and those fevers are very much about Town; so that it is dangerous being here."

"I was fain to pay for the carriage of the money; he [the carrier] had 1^{s}. 4^{d} for it: which I was loath to part with I had so little:...my scholarship comes but to 18 shillings a quarter."[3]

[1] For the study of "extras", particularly of French, at this period see p. 103.

[2] Eachard, *Letters*, 108. Eachard, as the College records show, retained his Tutorship after he became Master.

[3] B. 7, *S.C.* vol. IV, pt. i, no. 9 (Add. 7).

An interesting commentary on this account of a College funeral is to be found in the first book of Tutor's accounts, fol. 71, where is given the account for one quarter[1] of D^{s} Millington,[2] a Scholar:

Arrears to Mr Cal.	1. 15: 3
Given him by Mr Cal:	2. 0: 0
Coals	00: 2: 0:
Milliner	0: 6: 0
Cook's bill	0: 12: 9:
Steward's bill:	5. 8. 10
Shoemaker	0: 8. 4
Bedmaker	0: 3: 0:
Taylor	0: 14: 1:
For gloves, ribbons, wine, confectioner's bill, and other funeral charges	15: 12: 10
....	
Coffin	9. 6

There are two other letters from Strype to his mother.[3] In the former, dated 16 Aug. 1664 from "St Kath. Hall", he complains of his laundress that "besides her losing my linen, and washing dirtily, she hath also grossly abused me and one or two others, but when all comes to all hath worst of all abused and befooled herself: and all for a trifle, and most unjustly". The third letter was written from Katharine Hall on Saturday evening, 17 June 1665:

"I am unsatisfied", says Strype, "very much, if I cannot hear from you once a week, whilst times are so troublesome and the place and air you live in so dangerous and infective....I cannot but imagine you now begin to be a little fearful of the plague. The report goes that no less than 60 were buried Thursday evening of the disease. I hope by this time, you are convinced it is the best way. Change your habitation for the country....The next Monday or Tuesday come sennight I expect to be Bachelor of Arts, so that you will but supply me with some money. I have enquired, and understand that it will stand me in £8 the cheapest way."

[1] The quarter is not stated, the year being apparently 1678.

[2] The name of this Millington is not in the Admission Book, nor yet in *Alumni Cantabrigienses*.

[3] Nos. 10 and 11 in the same vol. of correspondence.

We have in the same collection two letters from that attractive person, James Bonnell, a cousin of Strype, who entered St Catharine's in 1668. He revisited Cambridge in 1679, and on 17 November writes to Strype that he went to St Catharine's, but

"by ill fortune it proved Gosling day and M[r] Blackal preached; I came when he had done; and was taken up in company all the time, at a long dinner of ill dressed meat (under the rose) and a formality of being served by gowned waiting-men, little dirty pawed sizars, with greasy old fashioned glasses, and trenchers that would hold no sauce; but this only for merriment between you and I: the end of the College next Queens' is finished, and the gate is plain next the street; but very handsome of the inside; they talk of going on, but whether next Spring or no, I can't tell; you will know before this I suppose that Dr Eachard is Vice-Chancellor".[1]

From a letter dated 9 February 1684 we gather, with a surprise and a shock, that the restoration period was marred by a scandal, but what it was is not known:

"I am sorry for the discredit of Kath: Hall. There was a young man Tutor to Sir H. Willoughby; I know not whether you mean him. 'Tis strange things should turn so, for Dr Lightfoot did not reside, yet the College was not debauched. But if the fellows, or any of them, are debauched, there is no help. I wonder that J. Calamy is melancholy; for I thought he would have married and been brisk".[2]

Another St Catharine's man, Samuel Crisp, writes a letter on 25 June 1694 that reflects humorously on the rather grasping character of the Eachard family:

"The Eachards abound with us, and have some of them 3 or 4 parishes each, so that a stranger not long since travelling that road and enquiring the ministers' names as he proceeded in his journey and hearing nothing but Eachard, Eachard, Eachard, thought we had here a distinct tribe of that name and that all the country had been Eachard".[3]

[1] B. 1, *S.C.* 1, i, 41.
[2] B. 1, *S.C.* 1, i, 53.
[3] B. 1, *S.C.* 1, i, 132.

St Catharine's College, Cambridge. Vol. XL/13.

Transcripts of certain letters written to Dr Eachard during the period 1676–1696.

12. *Newmarket*

March 12. [16]79.

Sir,

I hope my Brother Love and M[r] Sheldrake have been with you, and satisfied you that I am the same man I was when I spake with you on Ash Wednesday. Some of my reasons are private, and I cannot, without inconvenience, let you know them. I assure you they are reasons and not excuses. However, you have in that prevailed with me, for I will take my degree in your year, if none offer to stop me, which I entreat you, by all the true friendship that has been betwixt us, to prevent. Thus far I will offer. I will give you a sermon if you need it, but would take it as a favour never to appear at all, unless I should take occasion after a clerum, or so, to treat my good friends in Cambridge with something more palatable than my Latin: for I would, once more, be glad to see them together. If any man is willing to keep the Act but is not very able or willing to bear the charge, I will bear what share you shall judge convenient. And, indeed, I think it reasonable that they who take the degree and not the pains, do, among them, bear much of the charge of them that do, unless they be rich men. I again entreat you to favour and facilitate my business as much as you can when M[r] Sheldrake shall have again offered it to you, and to believe that I would have granted you your request at first asking, if I could have done it; and that I can no more do it than I can run with the racehorses. I am

Your most faithful friend and servant

T. TENISON.

[*Archbishop of Canterbury.*]

[A later note in pencil written in the margin of this letter says: "Archb[p] Tenison proceeded to his D.D. Degree, 1680, so that his letter refers to that degree."]

13.

Rev. Sir,

I humbly & heartily thank you for your great love and kindness and pains shewed to me and son both in the University & in the country when you were last with us. Will hath received the books you sent me, for which I stand your debtor, but your brothers could neither of them tell me their prices, which if they could I should have returned with thankfulness the money to you. Sir, above this, I have a request to you, wherein you will further oblige me. 'Tis this. Since God hath taken away my dear wife, and both my sons need not the services either of mother or nurse, and the little comfort I have in my public ministry in this place where I am now seated, though it be rated in the King's books £22 for the first fruits, I am therefore resolved, if the Lord will, to put myself into a monastery & to live a collegiate life. I cannot expect it in your learned Society; it is an honour above expression of thanks you have done my son, in what your intentions are when time shall serve, as your brother Laur[ence] was pleased to tell me: for which kindness my authority, prayers, and endeavours shall be used to render him meek, & when you shall require him, I shall present him to you & your Society. That wherein I desire your favour to me is, that if upon your commendation any college will give me a fellowship, I shall thank you, & serve that Society with all obedience, modesty, & industry according to the laws of it. This is that I desire of you: & with my hearty love to Mr Gouge & Mr Blackall & rest I know not, I rest

Sir

Your most affectionate friend
& humble servant, H. WOTTON.

March 16. 1679.

[Endorsement:
"These for the Right Worshipful & Reverend D[r] Eachard Vice-chancellor of Cambridge, at his lodgings in Katharine Hall, in Cambridge."]

34.

Sir,

A very good friend of mine intends to admit a young gentleman in one of your colleges. Before he came to me he had been advised to Bennet [College], and since that by some one (I know not who) dissuaded from that house. He desired me to inform him about Bennet College. I am utterly a stranger there, and therefore beg the favour of you to give me your thoughts of that house, and of the most careful Tutors there. My friend designs no preferment from the University, and indeed designs nothing but a virtuous education of a very hopeful young gentleman, and therefore is perfectly indifferent of what college he be, and whether he be Pensioner or Fellow-Commoner. I desire your answer by the next post. You may write your thoughts freely to me, for no man living shall know whom I have consulted. You may be very confident that I have and can have no other design but the securing a very pregnant youth in his morals. And you may be certain that I will make no other use of your letter than by it to give my advice sincerely. I am,

Sir, your most faithful
servant

April 14, 1680. RICHARD KIDDER

I beg your answer with the first.

[Richard Kidder, afterwards Bishop of Bath and Wells.]

[Endorsement:
"These for the Reverend John Echard, D.D. and Vice-Chancellor of the University of Cambridge."]

40.

Right Worshipful

I sent you a letter 3 weeks or a month since about the ordering of my son & some of his faults, which I suppose you received. I hope, as he groweth older, he will grow wiser. I desire he may be kept from expenses extravagant; about Midsummer I think to have him home again. He telleth me it is your mind that he go out a [?Midsummer man], but I do not approve of it. I would have him going to and coming from Cambridge till he be Master in Arts, & would have him to be kept close to his book. I would not have him increase charges for books without your approbation or his tutor's: he will need nothing till Midsummer, unless it be a pair of shoes. If he be not restrained in many things it will be for his hurt. And if you see he mend, then be pleased to countenance him. If you received the letter above mentioned, I shall not need to say more: pardon the boldness of giving you this trouble. No more, but that I am

your most humble servant,

3 May [16]86. J. VOTIER.

Communicate not to him that I write of these things. I would not have my son do anything about a degree, or coming home without your or other order.

66.

Park. 3 *Aug.* [16]80
near Newtown in Montgomery-shire. Salop post.

Honoured Sir

Your tenant Cadwalader causes me to trouble you at this time about the small tithes of Manynys, which the vicar saith you have bestowed upon him, and so detains them, and which are worth £7 annually. Your farmer would know whether a priest's word be sufficient or cause of contempt, and I pray let him or myself receive satisfaction therein. If the former he must expect allowance from your justice. Had I known early enough of your this year presiding in the affairs of the University, I would have attempted under your influence some Degree in order to be a fat abbot or prior when the northern nations are reduced, for then common law must be subservient.

I shall shortly be for Denbighshire and then enquire fully into your former commands and be further ready [to] execute whatever you shall lay upon

Your most affectionate friend
and humble servant

M. Pryce.

96.

London,
December 17 [16]80

Dear Sir

I am desired by a friend, whom I know you will easily gratify, to do him a favour.

Mr Millington of Magdalene College has a promise of being chaplain to Sir William Temple in his designed embassy into Spain. He has been introduced by a friend and accepted by the Ambassador, but is advised to strengthen his interest in and reputation at the embassy to get some testimonial or character of them from some men well known in the University which may be advantageous to him.

He tells me he preached at Newmarket last year upon your request and that you told him he was also recommended to that duty by others of the Heads to you. His request and mine in his name is to desire you to give him a fair character such as you may think fit of your own personal knowledge of him and what his general fame in the University is as to manners and other accomplishments.

I ought not to say more to you in it but leave it to your own justice and friendship, for I know you think him to be a learned, virtuous and accomplished person, and I wish the University had more such that might be justly so recommended to a person so discerning and distinguishing as Sir W. Temple. He intends this only *ad corroborandum* for he is promised the employ yet desires it may not at present take Aese (?).

If you please to direct your sense of him in a letter to me in Plow Yard, Fetter Lane, by the first opportunity, such as may contain nothing else but what relates to him, you will oblige him much, and I am by all old friendship

Dear Sir,

Your ever obliged and affectionate
humble servant

PH. FOWKE.

Mr M. has a recommendation from Mr Proran (?) and desires yours what you think fit on Monday if it be possible.

If you please to have our Master's hand who is Mr Millington's great friend.

98.

Honoured Sir,

I know you will not blame me to have a longing desire to receive an account of my son's behaviour and proficiency from yourself, to whose care and oversight I betrusted him, but remembering you told me you could not for the present intend him, nor take that account of him which otherwise you would, I imputed the disappointment of not hearing from you to your many avocations and multiplicity of business. And having had a letter from Mr Gouge which gave me hopes that my son's proficiency would answer my desires, I saw no reason to entertain any impressions to the contrary, specially being my son hath held a constant correspondence with me by letters, and therein hath acquitted himself of what I gave him in charge at parting.

You are pleased to intimate in your letter that you design when the holidays were over he should learn French and after that Music, the latter (as less pertinent) I could wish might be deferred for one half year at least, till he be better acquainted with Aristotle.

And if it may be with your approbation, I will have him immediately to enter himself for a month or six weeks to learn to dance, both to better his carriage and to exercise his limbs, in hopes it may be a means to shake off that lazy distemper of the jaundice which stole upon him unawares, and will be apt to return upon him if not prevented by due ordering himself, and exercise.

I have given him a hint that the best expedient to prolong his stay in Cambridge (if he desire it) will be to contract his expenses into as narrow a compass as may consist with his credit and mine, having admitted him in quality of a gentleman, and therefore as to that shall say no more, hoping if you find him tractable under your inspection, I shall find him dutiful and advisable when I see time to recall him.

In the interim your grave counsel and admonition (as occasion may serve) will not a little advantage him, being young and inexperienced, and no less oblige

Your humble and most faithful servant

REGINALD WILBRAHAM.

I beg the favour that when you see your friend, and my old acquaintance, Mr Scrivener, you would please to give him my service.

8 Jan. 1680/1

101.

Ipswich
March 14 1680/1

Sir,

After the tender of mine and Captain Sparow's thanks for your account of Mr Wright, I am ordered to crave your further assistance towards his placing here. He signified (in a letter to his friend at London about a month since) a purpose of being at Cambridge about this time. If you will please to treat with him, you may assure him there hath not been such an inviting opportunity for a physician to plant here since I knew the town, so that I am very confident a prudent and well accomplished person will fall into practice enough.

If he hath any incline here, you may please to encourage his coming over to see the place first, or if his occasions will not give him that leave, some person shall wait upon him from hence, if you will but favour us with a notice of his being with you.

Sir, if this should not succeed, I have been thinking of Mr Robinson of the same college—if you conceive he may be gained. For this case will not bear delays, neither will there be such probable advantage if this Spring be lost, as appears now.

Sir, as for Major, I am informed that by his own stock, and a little help from his mother, he will be able to answer the charges of the College and University.

As to his qualifications, I think he is not in love now, for his mistress is married, he is formal enough, walks trim and brisk, and manages a cane gracefully—and I hope he will wear a gown as well, and may be brought to understand it his business and interest to lie close to books, and it is thought that he will too.

Sir, my most humble service to yourself, Mr Gouge, Mr Warren and all friends.

I am Sir,
Your faithful servant,
SAM. GOLTY.

105.

Reverend Sir,

You may please to remember that about four or five years since I gave you forty shillings towards the rebuilding of our college.

I protest I do not tell you this to upbraid you with it, but merely out of hopes that the remembrance of it may move you to an action as far more meritorious than it is, as living bodies are more valuable than dead walls.

I confess ingenuously I did not do it out of any affection to your religion, nor do I expect anything from you upon the like account, but I gave it partly out of gratitude, having had my education there and partly for colleagueship sake, and old acquaintance with yourself.

Now the business I have to propose to you is this. There are a great many people of my persuasion in the North (as there are likewise in the South) who have suffered and do suffer a great deal for their conscience' sake amongst which I thank God I have had my share, though hitherto I have made shift to keep myself out of the gaol.

It is true we are charged with I know not what most damnable plots, the truth whereof will be seen at the Last Day, when the great Knower of hearts shall bring all hidden things to light. In the meantime we must be patient and say our prayers. Now, Sir, if you can find in your heart out of your generous disposition to give anything towards the relief of such as suffer on this account, I will assure you I will not take one farthing of it to myself more than yourself shall determine, and the rest shall be faithfully disposed on where there is real need by

Your most affectionate friend and
servant
ROBERT VINTNER

March 27th 1681.

Reverend Sir, I have no certain abode, God knows, but Mrs Greenhill, who lives but at Sawston, and brings you this, can convey anything safe to me by her sister who lives at York.

[In Dr Eachard's handwriting:]

Mr Robert Vintner at Mr Thomas Shephard's at Sizar near Kendal in Westmorland.

Sir, I remember that many years ago you gave forty shillings towards the re-building of the College, which to return to you is not in my power, though all the Fellows should consent to it. Had you given it to me or to me and those that are now Fellows you might then have had some other answer from, Sir, Yours

Jo. Eachard.

[This Robert Vintner was admitted to the Master of Arts Degree in the ordinary way in 1667. See *Graduati Cantab.*]

108.

Sir,

Mr Peirse of Lazenby, brother to that gentleman who was my pupil and late a benefactor to your New buildings, is about to send his eldest son abroad, and desires him for the University, particularly for your College, if he receive encouragement from you herein.

The young gentleman is turned of sixteen, so that it is time to dispose of him some way, especially considering that he hath no inclination to go any longer to school. But that which makes his father somewhat in suspense whether to send him unto the University or no, is because he is exceeding raw as to school learning, and (which is worse) he little cares for his book.

The truth is when he was young, being sickly, he was indulged too much liberty and not held to his book so strictly as was requisite, by which means he was cast far behind, so that despairing to overtake his contemporaries, he grew careless of endeavouring it. Upon this account for his learning he is unfit for the University, and by reason of his averseness from reading he is like to make no great proficiency in his studies, and moreover it is to be feared that if he should take little pleasure in conversing with books he may lie under strong temptation to sort himself with idle company, so as to be led by them into those extravagances and debaucheries which somewhere are too much in fashion, and this is the more to be feared forasmuch as he seems to be of a loving and complying temper.

As to all this I tell Mr Peirse that many are admitted Fellow Commoners who neither are scholars nor are ever like to be, and that though no great matter be to be expected from one in his circumstances (being like to have a considerable estate) as to improvement in learning whatever helps he have, yet by a straight looking on such books as may be recommended to him, and hearing his tutor's lectures with the exercises performed in the College and University, and conversing continually with men of parts and learning and of sober life he may insensibly advantage himself both as to solid knowledge and to good manners and as to a prudent behaviour.

And as for temptations he may meet with as many and great elsewhere (at London and in travels etc.) and may, if so inclined, yield to them without being so much as observed by any who have either love to him or concern for him, though he should run into never so high extravagances. Whereas being at the University under the eye and ear of a prudent and careful tutor he will neither dare to outray much, nor if he durst can he outray long without being discovered, let him be never so much inclined and tempted thus to do.

Upon such considerations as these Mr Peirse was resolved to send his son up to you, if you will be pleased to take the charge of him. I told him that it was not usual for Masters of Colleges to meddle with pupils, but you having had several Fellow-Commoners while you were Fellow and keeping some Fellow-Commoners after you were master, I thought you might be prevailed with to entertain his son, which if you were pleased to do he might confidently rely on your care.

As for Mr Slader, I know he takes no pupils, and besides he hath several occasions to be abroad, which made me not to mention him.

I desire you would let me know your thoughts and intentions as to this gentleman by the first post, for his father purposes to dispose of him one way or other as speedily as may be.

My best respects to yourself and Mr Slader

I am Sir,

Your affectionate friend

GEO. BARKER.

Danbywisk near North Alverton
April 12 1681.

115.

Trinity College,
October 13, 1679.

Sir,

The person from whom you receive this is so very little known to you that I fear the bare name at the bottom, without some other remarkable circumstance, will scarcely call anything of him to your remembrance, so that before I go any farther it may not be inconvenient to tell you that I am that person whom you lately were pleased to honour so far, as, upon Sir Charles Caesar's and Mr Harvy's recommendation of me, to visit the Senior Fellows of Trinity College on my behalf, a favour, I assure you, so great in my esteem that, though I very much fear how this presumption of mine in writing to so great a person as yourself may be taken by you, I think it far more pardonable to trouble you with a few lines than to omit my duty of returning you the humblest of my acknowledgements for your great goodness.

Perhaps by this time you may have heard something of the management of our election, but because I question whether such kind of businesses are commonly taken notice of by those of your rank, it may be convenient to tell you that out of twenty-five candidates four were chosen, all out of the upper year, and I myself that had the misfortune to be the last of the election was necessarily thrown out. But that which is the chief part of my present business is that in all probability I am likely to have another hit to try my fortune, at which time I hope my present ill-fortune may not deter you from using your interest once more in my behalf, for here as in most other places little is to be done without something in that nature, and I am very sensible that no man's is greater in Trinity College than yours.

Sir, I am the most ambitious of your favour,
and your most humble, faithful, and obedient
servant,

STEPHEN SKYNNER.

[This Mr Skynner seems by the *Graduati Cantabrig*. to have been Fellow of Trinity. Commenced B.A. 1678. M.A. 1682.]

119.

Honoured Sir,

My present circumstances under which the Divine Providence hath been pleased to cast me, put me upon entreating a favour from yourself and the University, with respect to the time of my exercises, which I was to have performed this approaching term.

It hath pleased God lately to take from me a good wife, whom I buried the beginning of September, the due and deserved respects to whom make me at present choose to determine myself to a retired solitariness. And my family left destitute thereby of one whose discretion prudently managed the whole concern thereof doth especially at this time need my presence and care.

It being here also a very unhealthful season, and three of my five children at this present sick, I who am now solely charged with them am for that cause the more determined to my house, and the less able to resolve on any certain time this term, when I may presume it prudent for me to be absent from them.

If therefore upon these reasons yourself shall please to propose and the University to grant me the favour, which I should not otherwise have asked, to defer my exercises which remain to be performed until the next term, which will end in March, it will be esteemed a great kindness to him who is

Your assured and obliged friend and servant

WILL. FFALKNER.

Lynn Regis
Oct. 8, 1680.

121.

I am mighty glad to hear the Stationers have given up their printing house to the University upon so easy terms, and that every particular member of our body have so rightly and so justly considered the only thing to put this design of erecting a new press on a sure and firm foundation by their unanimous vote of five hundred pounds for a continual dead stock to be employed only for the use of our new Printing House, independent of our public chest.

It will be the middle of the next month before I shall be in London, where I shall be glad to discourse both you and Dr Bentley further in this affair.

I am,

Your very humble servant,

SOMERSET.

Petworth,
October 30, 1696.

103.

Canterbury. March 19th (*17th?*) 1680/1

Honoured Sir.

My Lord Bishop of London sent me but two days ago a letter he received of you the 12th of November last, in answer to one of his Lordship wherein he desired of your worship a favour in my behalf, to wit that I might be admitted ad eundem. Sir, I took not long ago my degree of Doctor in Divinity in the University of Leyden; as for that of Master of Arts I have it these two and twenty years; but as for my diploma of Master of Arts I lost it nine years ago and above with many other papers of greater concernment to me; but Reverend Sir, I shewed it thirteen years ago to the Secretary of the Lord Bishop of Salisbury, who accordingly styled me Master of Arts in my orders, which I may produce if you think fit: If this will do I shall wait upon your Worships as soon as possible, to receive with thankfulness the favour I beg; unless you would be pleased to grant it me by a Proxy, for to speak freely I have for the present but little time to spare, having to manage the most important affairs of our Church by reason of my being Receiver General for this year besides my ordinary occupations.

This inclosed letter which was written whilst your Worship was yet Vice-Chancellor begs that same favour of you; you will find it somewhat old, for though I did sent it you, the very next day after it was written, a friend of mine whom it was directed to, kept it a good while and afterwards sent it back to me for reasons which I am yet ignorant of. Honoured Sir, if you are pleased to honour me with an answer pray direct it to Dr Le Feuers in the Pall Mall next door to the Scotch Arms, London, and he will take the care to send it to me to Canterbury, but before I make an end give me leave to put you again in rembrance [*sic*] of my humble suit to be admitted by a proxy. I am

Honoured Sir

your most humble servant—

Jo: Max: de L'Angle:

[What would a modern Registrary say to this request—*ad eundem*, no diploma and a proxy? Yet the degree was given! See *Alumni Cantabrigienses*.]

106.

These For the Reverend Dr Eachard
Cambridge.
post pd. 4d.
Honoured Sir

I received a letter from my Cousin Mr Wright of St John's & did design him an answer but that his occasions drew him unexpectedly from the College, & therefore I rather chose to give you the trouble of a letter than keep you and the other gentleman in suspense. I had received some letters not long before from Dr Goodall of London upon the same account, wherein he acquainted me with Dr Deyns his death, recommended the place to me for its air and situation, which I know to be pleasant, and that Dr Deyns's friends would so far endeavour my interest in practice there that he did believe it might be worth £150 or £200 per annum, as my acquaintance & length of time might raise it; by the Doctor's letters I could not discover that thêre was any certain & yearly allowance for a physician's reward in having some regard to the poor as is at Boston and some other places, nor that the gentry of the town made any certain and yearly allowance for their own families, if not visited with extraordinary sickness, as they make me here; I am not so fixed here but that to my advantage if certainly so I would remove, but according to Dr Goodall's estimate the value of the practice there amounts to no more or but little more than I have here nor can I promise myself by his letter that the growing practice of the country may amount to more than what I may probably in as short a compass of time expect here, nor do I suppose the practice to be much easier.

I am at so great a distance that I have not probably a true prospect of the place & cannot therefore give a determinate answer but if the account I have received of it corresponds with the truth I should blame myself to think of a removal. If I see it through false optics I should be gladly rectified and consider of it.

I most humbly beg your pardon for this great trouble I now give you & am

Your most humble and obliged Servant

Peterborough, March 28th [16]81 JO: WRIGHT

for The Reverend Dr Eachard Master of Katherine-hall in Cambridge
these humbly.
Leave this with the postmaster in Royston
pt. pd. rd peterbro

[In this letter there appears to be a most interesting anticipation of "panel" patients.]

[Reproduction not modernised]

To his Grace, the Duke
of Monmouth, Chancellor
of the University of
Cambridge.

Nov. 10th 1679

Cath: Hall Camb.

May it please your Grace

Although all the preferment I enjoy in the University is wholly owing to your Grace's singular favour, by preventing once a Mandate designed for y[e] Mastership of our Colledge; yet to make it my businesse now to acknowledge such a particular obligation to your Grace (w[ch] I can never sufficiently doe) would be to betray the privilege and honour of this addresse: the occasion hereof, my Lord, beeing no other than, taking y[e] customary confidence of such as have gon before me in y[e] office of Vicechancell[rs], to assure y[r] Grace of all readinesse and faithfullnesse to receive and obey y[r] Grace's commands. I know not, my Lord, how far this must travaile to arrive at y[r] Grace's hands; but wee all hope here y[t] in a little time our addresses may have a shorter journey: *for though your Grace has left us under the most certain and honourable protection of my Lord of Canterbury (w[ch] with y[r] Grace's pardon, I have thought fitt to own to his Grace)*# yet wee have been so long accustomed to y[r] Grace's peculiar sort of favours, and constant successe in all our applications, y[t] I am sure I have publick authority to wish and pray for your Grace's continuall health, and perpetuall prosperity.

And then nothing can make our University more safe and happy but y[r] Grace's return.

I am,
My Lord,
y[r] Grace's
most humble, most faithfull
and most obedient servant

John Eachard.

118.

Reverend Sir,

I had yr letter with ye inclosed & gave yrs to his Grace, who will be most glad upon any opportunity to doe you, & ye University ye best service He can. But in this to his Grace ye Duke of Monmouth our Chancelor my Lord desires you would change all that wch is markt with a black led pen [printed in italic] & instead of those words begiñing (for though) to put in these or somewt to this purpose wch He leaves to yr prudence (*for ye mean time we humbly beg y[t] when your Grace hath occasion next to write to His Majesty you would make it yr Request to Him y[t] during yr absence He would be pleased for Yr sake Graciously to receive such addresses as shall be made to Him in our behalfe by any of our friends about the Court*) so you may goe on *Yet wee have* etc. My Lord thinks it not convenient to be so particularly namd, tho' He shall as readily undertake any thing for yr service as if he were. I wish you heartily much joy of yr new Office all at present from

Lambeth. Nov. 15—79.

Yr most faithfull Serv[t]

114.

Westminster,
November 29th, 1679.

Sir,

After you had delivered your letter to my care, I inquired for an opportunity of sending it, but the Duke of Monmouth returning to his lodgings here on Friday morning, I had an unexpected opportunity of delivering it this day to his Grace himself. Having no secretary with him, he commanded me to return you this answer, that he was not unmindful of his trust from the University when he went away, but spoke to his Majesty for the Archbishop of Canterbury to patronize the University in his absence; and when I told his Grace what application had been made by the Archbishop for preventing Mandates upon the voidance of the Mastership of St. John's, he commanded me to wait upon the Archbishop to thank him, and further to desire him to continue his care of the University, being doubtful whether he should stay in England, having been denied to kiss his Majesty's hand, and commanded to return with what convenient speed he could. Under these heavy circumstances you may excuse him from not writing his own hand, which otherwise he had done, and not employed that of

Your very humble servant,

J. SAMUEL GARDINER.

For the Reverend Dr. John Eachard,
Vice-Chancellor of the University of Cambridge.

117.

London,
November 3rd.

Sir,

Though I know how ticklish a point it is to touch upon Degrees: yet I could not refuse Dr. de L'Angle any reasonable address in his behalf. He is a person very deserving both by himself and his relations. I have seen his Diploma from Leyden, and if you can without difficulty or hardship upon the rules of the University admit him ad eundem, you will gratify a very worthy person, and oblige

Sir
Your most assured
friend and brother

H. LONDON.

For the Reverend Doctor
Eachard,
Vice-Chancellor of Cambridge.

St Catharine's College, Cambridge.
MS. Tanner 35 (Bodleian Library, Oxford).

Decemb. 30th 1682
Cath. Hall

[May] it please your Grace

Although our poor and small College, since we began to rebuild it, have met with some encouragement from such who never had relation to us, nor reason to be concerned for us, but only as they were generously disposed to promote all undertakings of this nature; yet nothing ought so humbly and solemnly to be acknowledg'd as your Grace's singular bounty towards us, a blessing so great and advantageous we never durst have presumed to have entertained any thoughts of, knowing your Grace deeply engaged in the carrying on several more necessary and honourable designs, had not your Grace been pleased to shew some inclination that you would at least pardon such applications as might be made from the meanest endowed College in either of the Universities. It was not, My Lord any service or honour that your Grace could possibly expect from so despicable a place as we belong to, and such inconsiderable persons as we are: and that your Grace should be pleased to take any notice of that or us could not proceed from any thing else but a goodness as great as your See of Canterbury. We are

My Lord
your Grace's most devoted
and most dutiful Servants

JOHN EACHARD
NICHO. GOUGE
OFSP. BLACKALL
JOHN BRADOCK
J. WARREN.

Whitehall,
September 24th, 1691.

Sir,

It is some time since I wrote a letter to you by the Queen's command for an account of the names of such persons as in the several Colleges and Halls of the University had refused or neglected to take the Oaths, to which I received your answer with the returns made by the several Heads, which were expressed in such general and ambiguous terms for the most part as gave little satisfaction. I hope before this time all the Heads have fully and in due manner informed themselves what persons in their several Colleges and Halls have omitted to comply with the Act of Parliament by taking the Oaths, and therefore I am commanded to acquaint you that her Majesty expects they do every one of them forthwith proceed to fill up the vacant places in each College and Hall pursuant to the Act of Parliament without any connivance, in default whereof such directions will be given as shall be requisite for punishing the persons neglecting their duty herein. Her Majesty would therefore have you acquaint them with her pleasure in this matter, and send up to me a distinct and particular account of their proceedings in the execution of the Act of Parliament which you will please to do by the first opportunity.

I am,

Your most humble servant,

NOTTINGHAM.

Concordat cum originali

J. Holman Not. publ.

Letters of EACHARD *to* FRANKLAND, *in the possession of the Corporation of the City of Coventry.*

Now, Sir, as to your own business of your designed Fellowship; the Fellows with myself have lately considered of it, and are of opinion it will be every whit as convenient for the College (though heretofore we were of another mind) and as well for Coventry School to give as you first designed, two Scholarships of ten pounds a piece instead of a Fellowship. Which if you think fit to do your two Scholars in consideration of your sixty pounds shall be both free from Chamber Rent so that by that means each Scholarship will be worth about £12 per annum. You may be pleased likewise to take notice that you having paid your whole sixty pounds we are obliged to give to a second Scholar his chamber rent, and whoever you shall appoint shall enjoy that your kindness.

26 *July* 1683.

Whereas, Sir, you are pleased to value me so much as to ask my opinion about the best improvement of lads at school; having been used much to pupils, the greatest defect that I generally find is that they cannot turn common English readily into plain and tolerable Latin. And if more time were spent in translating out of English into Latin and less in composing of themes and speeches (though that need not be neglected wholly) I am confident it would be much to advantage. This is not, Sir, my opinion only but of many others; but particularly of Mr Milton; who though he was a man of very vile principles, yet he was a great wit and scholar, and most accurate in the Latin tongue.

15 *Jan* 1676

Letters

Letters referring to the Procter–Atkinson *quarrel.*

Atkinson *to* Procter.

Stapleford Decr 11th 1806.

Sir,

I was favoured with yours on Monday; and though, from my earnest desire to be permitted to be at Peace, I am sorry that the Proposal which out of Compliment to you I made in my last is not accepted, yet it is by no means my Wish, or for my Interest, that my Defence should be suppressed. If however you supposed that I mean to *publish* it, you misunderstood me: what I may do hereafter will depend upon Circumstances; but at present my Intention is only to apply the Antidote where I have reason to suppose the Poison may have been instilled. No one can possibly be more averse than I am to renew the Remembrance of past Differences and Animosities; and I agree with you that the Person who is the *Cause* of such an unpleasant Retrospect will appear in a very unfavourable Point of View not only to the University but to the whole World. But who it is that will *stand* in that unenviable Predicament—whether He who, after a general Amnesty had been recommended by the Visitor and acceded to by a Collegiate Act in which all Parties concurred, in a few Months after, without the least Provocation, accuses a Member of the Society of the base and disgraceful Crime of PERJURY, and founds the Charge upon Affidavits brought forward in the Cause in which all those Differences and Animosities were involved—or He who, reluctantly and tardily coming forward to *defend* himself against such a cruel Charge after all other means of procuring Redress have been tried in vain, is under the *Necessity* of commenting upon the Points contained in and alluded to in those Affidavits—which of these is the *Cause* of that unpleasant Retrospect and of all the Mischief that may follow, no Man sure of Common Sense and Common Honesty will hesitate a Moment to pronounce. You will allow me to observe farther on this Point that though you call what passed in the Combination-room when this injurious Charge was made "an unpleasant Altercation", there was no Altercation on my Side; for both you and the other Gentlemen present must remember, that I had not only not spoke a single Syllable to Mr Burrell, but had not even alluded to him or his Conduct in any way whatever when he broke out into the most gross Abuse of me, and accused me of the Crime of Wilful Perjury.—As to what passed betwixt him and me in the Hall,—I cannot allow—nor, I am persuaded will any candid Man whatever allow—that a hasty Expression called forth by a far more grievous Affront on his side, and used *previous to the Chancellors Decree* which he expressly declared was intended to restore and preserve the Peace of the College by an Oblivion of past Transactions,— I cannot, I say, allow Mr B. to confound or connect that paltry Squabble with an unprovoked Charge of Perjury brought forward *subsequent* to that Decree, and persisted in with the most rancorous Animosity.—To shew however that I do not require from others any Satisfaction for Injuries which I am not myself willing to give, and to deprive Mr B. even of *that* frivolous Plea for refusing to do me Justice, I now declare to you, that I am ready to retract the Words I made use of to Mr B. in the Hall, if he will in turn retract the Expressions by which they were provoked.

Forgiveness of Injuries is the most beautiful and striking Feature of that Religion which we profess, and he who does not practise it, whatever he may *call* himself, or whatever else he may be, is certainly no *Christian.*—For myself, I can with great Truth and Sincerity declare, that I bear no Ill-will or Hatred to any Human Creature;—but Christian Charity itself does not require us to forgive a ruinous Imputation upon our Character deliberately made and unrelentingly persisted in.

As to Mr Burrell's laying all the Affidavits before the Public in consequence of my presuming to defend myself against the infamous Crime of which he accuses me;— I think with you that he is capable of having recourse even to so absurd and intemperate a Step as that;—but what *End* it can be expected to answer, I am utterly at a Loss to conjecture. To those Affidavits on which *alone* he grounds his odious Charge and of which he sent me Copies, I have strictly confined myself in my Defence; and how those, which are in his own Opinion wholly *irrelevant* to that Charge will prove the *Justice* of it, I cannot conceive. I certainly shall not, on my *own* account, be sorry to have the Affidavits published, as they will, I have no doubt, of themselves diminish that Obloquy which has, by a partial Statement of them, been thrown upon my Character, and which, out of Respect to the Authority of the Visitor and a fixed Resolution to do nothing to disturb that Peace which his conciliatory Measures had restored to the College, I have hitherto taken no Steps whatever to remove. A candid and discerning Public will not fail to perceive, and to appreciate, the *Motives* by which *alone* Mr B. can be actuated in publishing a voluminous Mass of Affidavits which may excite Disquietude in the Minds of several unoffending Persons, whilst at the same time they have no Relation whatever to the Charge he brings against *Me*; and instead of their reflecting any Discredit upon me, as he may possibly expect,—the bringing them forward in that invidious manner will, I am confident, excite Disgust in every liberal and honourable Mind, and tend strongly to confirm the Justice of the Observations which I have made in my Defence upon Mr B.'s Temper and Conduct.—In *another* respect also the Publication of the Affidavits will, I am satisfied, be to my Advantage; for, as by such a Procedure, not only the Point at Issue betwixt Mr B. and myself but also all the Transactions to which those Affidavits relate will become Publici Juris, I shall then be at Liberty to defend myself at a Tribunal before which alone Questions of *this* nature can be impartially and justly decided. To the Judgement therefore, of an enlightened and unbiassed Public I shall probably, in that case, respectfully but fearlessly appeal; and I shall, at *any* rate, have the consoling Reflection that the *Verdict*, did it reach even to my Life, would not leave me in a worse Situation than that in which Mr B.'s *Accusation* has placed me;—for of what Value would be the Remnant of a wretched Existence which was to be dragged on under the blighting Imputation of a most disgraceful and degrading Crime!

I have already observed more than once, and I will again repeat it as it is a Circumstance of essential Consideration in forming a true Judgement of Mr B.'s Conduct in this Business,—that I consider, and *Lord Eldon* certainly considered, his Decree and the Return made to him in Consequence of it as forming, as it were, a new Æra in the College, and that all Differences and Disputes that had happened *prior* to that Period were by that Decree and Return entirely cancelled and done away.—On this Ground I take my Stand; and I doubt not but my Post will be perfectly tenable, as I have not, since the Time of the Decree and the Return made to it, done anything whatever to disturb the Peace or interrupt the Harmony of the Society; and I will study to act with such Candour and Moderation through the *Whole* of this unpleasant Business as may enable me, if I should find such a Step advisable, to appeal with a good Grace to the Visitor, and place myself and my Cause under his Protection.

You conclude with saying that "if my Pamphlet should be found to contain Expressions reflecting upon your Conduct, you shall feel it a Duty which you owe to yourself and Friends to reply to it, and to make the Reply as public as the Charge". The *former* part of your Letter gave me great Uneasiness, as the Object of it seemed to be to induce me, by Considerations which ought to have great Weight with *Mr B.* as an unprovoked *Accuser* but which apply not at all to *Me* as an unwilling *Defender*,—to acquiesce tamely and silently under the disgraceful Slur which Mr B. has thrown upon my Reputation;—but when you declare that you should consider it as an imperious Duty in *Yourself* to reply—not to *wilful Aspersions of your Character*, but to Expressions that merely may seem to reflect upon your Conduct, it is plain that I was mistaken, and that after such a Declaration you will never condemn *Me* for replying to an odious Charge by which, if unrefuted, my Reputation must be completely blasted and, of course, all the Credit and Happiness of my whole Future Life entirely destroyed.—In the present Case however your laudable Promptitude to vindicate your conduct will not be called forth;—for never, be assured, will I, without the most urgent Necessity, call you, or any Man, to the hard and mortifying Task which Mr B.'s unrelenting Hatred has imposed upon myself.

To *You*, I have not merely been anxiously desirous not to give offence, but to mention both your Name and Conduct with willing Deference and Respect; and if, contrary to my Intention and Conception, there should after all be any thing in my Defence which you conceive capable of being misconstrued to your Prejudice, I will immediately come forward to do you ample Justice either to Individuals or to the Public. *More* than this I *cannot* say; and after so frank and, I trust, you will allow so honourable a Procedure on *my* part, I will venture to hope that if in this disagreeable Business I may not be allowed to rank you among my Friends, I shall at least not have the Mortification of seeing you range yourself under the Banners of my Enemy.—I have only to add that though the Offer made in my last has not been productive of the Effects that might have been expected from it, yet I will take no farther Steps in the Business till I hear again from you. If your Letter *confirms* the Rejection of that Offer I will then produce my Defence—and may God defend and prosper the righteous Cause.

I am, Sir, your obed[t] Serv[t]

W. ATKINSON

[*Copy of rough draft of a letter from* PROCTER *to* ATKINSON.]

Sir,

Never before having had occasion to reply to a Letter replete with coarse Expressions, and not being addicted to the Use of them, I feel myself unable to answer your in the Style in which it is written, even if I were disposed to make the Attempt.

My principal object in addressing you, is, to correct a Mistake you have made, in putting a different Construction from what I intended on one part of my last Letter. Whether this was, or was not, done intentionally, that you might have some Plea for writing such a Letter as I never read before, you best know. When I said, you had no Claim to particular Indulgence, I did not allude to your Literary Merits. I had in view the great Length of Time, the many years you have kept the College in a State of perpetual Warfare, and the Large sum you had compelled us to expend in Law. I state this in my own Justification, and not for the purpose of averting your displeasure. I shall now make an extract from your Letter—(a Letter which does little credit either to your Head or to your Heart). [*This in brackets has been erased.*]

In your Judgment, then, it is nothing to the question, whether your Fellowship has been declared vacant, *justly*, or *unjustly* and this opinion forms Part of a Sentence in which you charge another with a Want of Common Sense, or Common Honesty. But this, considering what has past, does not surprise me, and I am disposed to make some allowance for a rash and greatly disappointed Man.

You pretend to have found some difficulty in reconciling my Practice with my Professions. I am at a loss how to reconcile one Part of your Letter with another. In the two first Pages, I see Strong, unfounded Charges made, with a Free use of very unbecoming Language; in the last I read something about a Heart o'erflowing with Gratitude to Heaven. I would ask, can a Heart o'erflow with Gratitude to God, and, at the same Time, with the very Gall of Bitterness to Man?

Here I close our correspondence.

[ATKINSON *to* PROCTER.]

Stapleford, Nov. 8th, 1808.

Sir,

I am sorry to find that my last Letter which I hoped would have produced some Apology for the unprovoked Abuse of which it complained, has occasioned a more copious and acrimonious Effusion of Bile than usual.

If you never before received such a Letter as mine, you must either have treated your *other* Correspondents in a very different manner from what you have done me, or *they* must have treated *you* very differently from what you deserved. As to your Inability to answer me in the same Style as mine, it is a modest Disclaiming of a Talent which in the same Breath you shew yourself possessed of in a *much* more eminent degree than *I* can pretend to be. I do not, indeed, think that you excel in that light and *ornamental* Branch of this Science which consists in *delicate Irony* and *elegant Repartee*; but in the plain, substantial, and—to use the Term with which you compliment *me*—in the *coarse* Work of the Business you stand unrivalled.

As to the *mistake* which you say it "was the Principal Object of your last to correct", there certainly was no mistake on *my* side; and I should pay a bad compliment to your penetration did I believe that you really *thought* I had made one. In speaking of the unprovoked Attack you made upon me in your former Letter I did not use the word Merit,—though *that* Word, if used absolutely and without an Adjunct always, I believe, means *moral* Merit,—but, I made use of the Term Deserts, which *never*, as every tolerably advanced *School-boy* knows, is applied to anything *but* Morals. Neither will I think so hardly of you as to believe that, if you really *had* fancied that I understood you as alluding to my *literary* Merit, you would deliberately hold that forth as furnishing a better Plea for my daring to resent that wanton Attack upon me than if I had understood it in the only Sense in which it *could* be understood by any but an Idiot.

What, Sir! shall it be allowable for a Man to be offended by a Depreciation of his *literary* Merit, and shall he need an Apology for expressing his Resentment when his *Moral* Character is traduced? Had my *literary* Merit only been arraigned, I should not have thought it worth while to stand forth in its Defence but should have left it to shift for itself as well as it could. No—it is of artful Misrepresentation, of unceasing Calumny, and of base Aspersions of my *moral* character that I complain; and which, whenever they dare to shew themselves *openly*, I will not fail to attack and to expose in such Language as a just Indignation dictates. When I first entered upon that part of your Letter in which you mention this supposed *Mistake* of mine, I was much puzzled to conceive for what *Purpose* this strange Supposition could be made: but when I came to the *end* of the Passage, the Secret was out. I saw *then* it was evidently introduced to give you an Opportunity of repeating the Attack, and of specifying the *Particulars* of the general and lumping Abuse contained in your former Letter. It appears *now*, that I forfeited my Claim to particular Indulgence by "the great Length of Time"—even "many Years"; in which I had kept the College in a State of perpetual *Warfare*—"and the large sums I had compelled you to spend in *Law*"!!!. I now see *plainly* how my *Sins* have been magnified by viewing them through this shocking long Telescope, but I was at a loss to conceive how the *Warfare* you mention could be imputed to me, till I recollected the old Adage that "It is the *Second* Blow that makes the Battle". A still *more* extraordinary Inversion of Fact is your accusing me of having put the College to great Expense in Law. That the College Money was wasted in such a way, I greatly lament, but the ruinous expence brought upon me by that cruel Prosecution was all defrayed out of my own Pocket or out of that of a friend, and not out of the *Funds* of the *Society*;—it was *your* Expences, not *mine*, that were thrown upon the *College Stock*. This Attempt however to shift the Blame in such Cases from ourselves to others is no more than what we see practised every Day. If two Fellows quarrel and fight in the Street, the *Aggressor* is generally most loud in charging the other as the Author of the Fray; and if a *Pick-pocket* is detected in the Fact and pursued, he is always the first and the most vociferous in crying "Stop Thief!"

You have quoted *that* Part of my last Letter in which I discuss the Point of your declaring my Fellowship vacant, and by an unaccountable Misconception of Words which are incapable of *Misconstruction*, you draw from it a similar charge of Inconsistency to that which I brought against *you*. I said—and I am perfectly *correct* in saying it—that, "Whether your depriving me of my Fellowship was done justly or unjustly was nothing to the question". Nothing to *what* Question? Why, to the Question I was *discussing*, to be sure,—to the Question of the *Inconsistency* of your *Professions* with your *Practice*. Had I said, that, whether the Action was just or unjust was the same in the *Nature* of the *Thing* or in a *moral* Sense, what you call a "strange Opinion" would have deserved a much harsher Appellation.

I must in Justice both to you and myself observe *farther* upon this point, that I can hardly think that you seriously understood what I said in discussing it, as "charging you with a Want of Common Sense or Common Honesty". In speaking of the Inconsistency of your Professions with your Conduct, the Difficulty of reconciling them with plain Sense and common Fairness was a Position which I had a right to use in the support of my Argument, but it was evidently confined to that particular Point and, even *then*, it was not stated as a *Fact* but urged as a *Contradiction* which I knew not how to reconcile. To charge you with a Want of *Sense* or *Integrity* in the *Abstract*, was an idea that never entered my Mind, and would certainly have been a Piece of low as well as ridiculous Abuse of which I should scorn to be guilty.

The *Pity* you are so kind as to offer me as a "rash and greatly *disappointed* Man" I reject upon the same grounds as those on which the Jester in the Fable declined the Acceptance of the Bishop's *Blessing*.

The Idea affixed to the Term "*Rash*" in *your* Vocabulary is, I have no Doubt, the same as *Dictionaries* explain by the Words *frank, open, sincere*; and as to the *Disappointment* you speak of it exists nowhere but in your own Imagination. *Disappointment!* No, Sir, *I have attained the highest Object of my Ambition*, and I am not only contented and happy but in perfect Good-humour with all the World, yourself not excepted.

You proceed to say that "you see strong unfounded *Charges* made in the first two pages of my Letter with a liberal use of very unbecoming *Language*". If you see any Charges *at all* in the first two Pages of my Letter your Sight must be a great deal quicker than mine is. I *have* indeed complained of the Malevolence, the Insults and Injuries which I have experienced at Catharine Hall, and if your Conscience, by *applying* those Complaints, has converted them into *Charges*, the Fault is not in *me*.

To the Accusation of "using very unbecoming Language", I will reply that it is the common Cant of those who having long insulted and abused with Impunity those who were so unfortunate as to be in their Power, have at last met with their Deserts, and are writhing under the Pain of a just Retaliation. They *then* talk of "*coarse Expressions*" and "*unbecoming Language*", and affect to be *surprized* and *astonished* at the Retort which their own wanton Aggression provoked.

You insinuate a Doubt of the *Sincerity* of the Gratitude I expressed to Providence for the Asylum it has lately afforded me, and you sneeringly ask, "Whether a Heart can o'erflow with Gratitude to God and at the same time with the bitterest Gall to Man"? I answer that it would seem from *some* Appearances, as if it *may*. You *yourself*, for instance, would be justly offended if I should express a Doubt of your being grateful to God for having permitted you to be Master of Catharine Hall, and yet do not your last two Letters to me clearly prove, that the *Gratitude* of your Heart has not been able to dislodge all its *Gall*?

You conclude with saying that "here you close our correspondence". You certainly may close it on *your* side when you please; but I will never close it on *mine* whilst you *continue* those Attacks upon my Character by which it has already been so unpleasantly prolonged.

I am, Sir,

You very humble Servant,

W. J. Atkinson.

Letters from pupils to Dr Corrie.

Bridlington June 22 [1843]

My Dear Sir,

I will take the liberty of writing you a few lines to inform you how I am going on. I was ordained to the curacy of Bridlington on Trinity Sunday, and rather a laborious one I think it will be. Since I have been here I have had ten funerals and other occasional duty in proportion, and as the vicar is confined to his room you may conceive that I am fully occupied. There is service on a Wednesday so that I have three sermons a week at present. I fear my strength will not be too much for all this. I see sometimes a Mr Banks of St. Cath's, and hear from him a little Cambridge news. He mentions you as being very kind to him.

I am afraid my accounts at College are considerable. I should be very glad if you would let me have an account of them. With every kind wish towards you, and trusting that we shall meet in heaven. Believe me

My dear Sir

Your very sincere friend

H. Cantley Holmes

Mrs Barnby's
Quay Road
Bridlington.

Letters

Rectory Kettering Jany 24, 1843

Dear Sir,

I felt much disappointed on my arrival here yesterday evening to find that you had left for Cambridge. I here enclose you £5. 0. 0 towards the liquidation of my bill—the remainder I must pay from time to time as I am able—of course, I write this on the assumption of your kind permission.

My bill I will thank you to forward to me again.

If you have any spare garments in the shape of coats etc. perhaps you would be so good as to lay one aside for me.

. . . .

I remain, dear Sir,
Your obliged Friend,

J. C. Glarey.

Carlton Colville
July 6th 1843.

Rev[d] Sir,

My friend the Rev[d] F. Cunningham having informed me, that he had entered me as a pensioner at Catharine Hall, I have taken the liberty, as I consider it my duty, to write to you, that you may know what my studies are, and that I may obtain your good advice respecting them. It was in last March that I began the Latin and Greek, having fully determined upon entering the ministry of the ever blessed Gospel of our God. I have read Grotius de Vertute and am now reading Virgil....I fear I am very backward, but I know he that hath called me to this work will enable me to go through it if it pleases him. If we had sufficient faith I believe all would be easy to us....

I remain, Rev[d] Sir,
Your humble S[t]

C. W. Woodthorpe,

Rev[d] Professor Corrie
Catherine Hall.

Carlton Colville
N[r] Lowestoft,
Suffolk.

Flysheet issued after the ROBINSON *election.*

[*PRIVATE.*]

TO THE MEMBERS OF THE SENATE.

A recent printed correspondence concerning the election of the present Master of St Catharine's College has given occasion and opportunity for putting forth the following statement, embodying facts which have been for some time in our possession.

1. It is the recognized custom in the College that Candidates for the Mastership vote for themselves. Mr Robinson voted in accordance with this custom. Nothing but an explicit declaration from him could give real ground for expecting that he would vote otherwise.

2. Mr Jameson has always admitted that Mr Robinson made no promise directly or indirectly to vote for him.

3. Mr Robinson never asked Mr Jameson for his vote. Mr Jameson promised it to Mr Robinson unconditionally. He stated that he gave it under a sense of personal obligation, and made no secret of his unconditional offer. A common friend of both, still resident in the University, pointed out to him two months before the election the certain consequences of an unconditional vote for Mr Robinson, and urged him to recall his promise, which he refused to do.

4. Mr Robinson never gave any promise to Mr Jameson to abstain from voting for himself, and has never admitted nor will admit that he gave Mr Jameson any ground for expecting that he intended to abstain from voting for himself.[1]

[1] It has been argued from the published document, dated Dec. 14, 1861, that Mr Robinson in giving full credit to Mr Jameson's assertion that he entertained this expectation, admitted that Mr Jameson had grounds for his expectation. If this be so, Mr Jameson equally admitted that Mr Robinson had grounds for believing Mr Jameson's vote to be a *bona fide* unconditional vote in his favour. We understand the document to mean that

5. Mr Robinson had for some time intended to vote for himself, as he was urged by friends to do. The day before the election he told a friend that he had a few minutes before informed Mr Jameson of his intention to vote for himself, had recommended Mr Jameson to do the same, and had added that this was the only way of declaring their willingness to undertake the responsibilities of the office. Our proof of this is contained in a letter written in October, 1861, by the gentleman referred to. We are informed that Mr Jameson has no recollection of this communication being made to him.

6. On the morning of the election one of the Fellows who voted for Mr Jameson informed Mr Robinson that the four votes excluding Mr Robinson's were to be equally divided, and remarked that by voting for himself Mr Robinson might have the Mastership.

7. On the morning of the election Mr Robinson went to Mr Jameson's rooms and found there the senior Fellow (Mr Milner) breakfasting alone with Mr Jameson. Mr Jameson then announced to Mr Robinson that they had both decided to vote for him. Mr Robinson once more advised Mr Jameson not to do so, but Mr Jameson declared that he had made up his mind in the matter, and that Mr Robinson must not think of him in any way in the vote he gave. At the election, which took place immediately afterwards, Mr Milner gave the deciding vote in favour of Mr Robinson, after Mr Robinson had voted for himself. A fortnight afterwards Mr Milner stated in writing that he knew Mr Robinson's vote was given with perfect honour.

8. Immediately after the election Mr Robinson thanked Mr Jameson in the presence of the Fellows, and declared that he owed his election entirely to him. Mr Jameson treated Mr Robinson with the utmost kindness of manner, and expressed gratification at the result to him then, and to others afterwards. He accepted from Mr Robinson the office of President, which is in the gift of the Master. Mr Robinson presided at a College meeting, at which Mr Jameson was present, three days after the election; but neither then nor at any time during Mr Robinson's stay in Cambridge did Mr Jameson express to Mr Robinson by word or by manner any dissatisfaction with Mr Robinson's vote. Five days after the election Mr Robinson left Cambridge, and it was nearly a fortnight before he heard that any misapprehension existed.

neither Mr Jameson nor Mr Robinson could doubt the direct assertion of the other. That Mr Robinson cannot have meant more than this is clear from a statement which we possess in his handwriting, dated Dec. 8th, 1861.

We may add, that some weeks subsequently, when Mr Robinson returned to Cambridge, he called upon Mr Jameson and asked him whether he wished him to resign. Mr Jameson disclaimed any such wish.

We are convinced that nothing can destroy the force of these facts as completely exonerating Dr Robinson from the charges which have been put in circulation against him; and we wish to declare our perfect confidence in his honour.

E. T. S. CARR, *President and Tutor.*
A. W. SPRATT, *Fellow and Prælector.*
A. PHILLIPS, *Fellow.*
W. F. KIMM, *Fellow.*
G. F. BROWNE, *Conduct Fellow.*

ST CATHARINE'S COLLEGE,
June 10, 1868.

Copy of letter from MAJOR H. B. LUARD, '*Woodlands,*' *Little Baddow, Chelmsford.*

Dear Sir, 23 *August* 1935

I went up to St. Catharine's from Malvern College in 1881 with a small Classical scholarship, but changed over to science and took a first class in the Natural Sciences Tripos in 1884, with a view to entering the medical profession.

I well remember the inferiority complex of that time, which must have been the lowest ebb of the life of the College, overshadowed by the Master's long ostracism. There were only about 40 men in residence, half of them scholars, the rest non-descripts and leavings from other Colleges. The Tutor was quite a character in his way, who received and dismissed us at the beginning and end of term with exeats and redeats scrawled on the backs of envelopes: the Dean was Dr. Lumby, succeeded later by G. F. Browne, who was indeed a man: both he and the Tutor preached well in Chapel: We had to keep five chapels a week, but I kept few except the surplice chapels on Saturday evening and the two Sunday ones as a rule. I never attended a morning chapel (at 7 or 8 a.m.!) but the afternoon chapel was at 5 p.m. and we and Mr. Browne the chaplain used to get these over in a quarter of an hour, as we put on a great pace, indeed halved the time of the psalms and canticles by the Chaplain cutting our verse short in the middle by a harsh grating voice beginning the next verse, which we reciprocated by cutting him short in his verse! Hall—

there was only one—was at 5 p.m.—very plain fare in two courses. A feature of dinner was the big pewter 3-handled sconce belonging to each term, which had to be filled with beer and passed round the table by anyone inadvertently talking "shop", and in default of a delinquent each of us would order a sconce in turn for good fellowship. There were rarely more than two at the High Table. Out of 40 residents there were not more than about 18 who went in for sport, so whatever our own game we played all the others to keep the clubs going. We could just manage to put two trial eights on the river (I stroked one though I had never pulled an oar before) and in football we kept up a team in both Rugger and Soccer by playing both games and playing them in alternate matches!

There was no intercourse between Dons and undergraduates except in the lecture room. I must say the Master was a very gentle harmless old man, who used to invite us once a term to luncheon, when his son was an undergraduate, and we used to go through the Master's lodge to a swimming pool at the back of his house, which was much appreciated. I had rooms on the right ground floor of Walnut Tree Court, and we made much use of an Eton fives court there, which I believe was later on pulled down by some vandal to make a choristers' room! The fine old trees in front of the College were quite a feature then. Of the six scholars of my year, one became a schoolmaster and took orders, another became an eloquent preacher in Bradford and ended his days in a country living in Essex: another had a varied career of adventure in many lands (he was our cox and a very bright little fellow) but went downhill eventually: another one, choral scholar, never took his degree, but had an honourable life which ended—I do not know if he is still alive—as a pensioner in the old Charterhouse.

As an undergraduate I had a very happy time, and was a member of the Union and had several friends in other Colleges, and I think we kept our end up in spite of the cloud overhanging the College. It is very pleasant to know that the College has recovered its prestige, its eminence in sport, and has 250 undergraduates, drawn from all the public schools: and a vigorous executive led so long by Rushmore, a St. Catharine's man whose acquaintance I was glad to make a few years ago, when I dined with him at the High Table for the first and only time in my life.

Yours faithfully,

H. B. Luard

Letters

An answer to the Appeal for the Rushmore Memorial
(*written in pencil*)

Dear Sir,

Though I have never heard of the person you mention, for the sake of gentleman Browne of Cats, the very best Proctor ever known in 1870, as all undergrads admitted, because he always caught his man fair and square and treated him properly afterwards, I am sending you £1. He became a Bishop later, but even that could not spoil him.

I am nearly quite blind so pardon me for writing thus.

Plate XXII

Dr G. F. Browne, Fellow, and Bishop of Bristol

III. STATUTES

There is printed here an abstract of the statutes drawn up (1) by the Founder, (2) by the Commission of Edward VI, (3) & (4) by the two Commissions of Queen Victoria. The first three are in Latin, that of Woodlark being barbarous in the extreme. The composers of the Edwardian statutes take the Founder's name in vain by writing their preamble in the first person singular! The last of the four sets is printed practically in its entirety. The history of the College is epitomised in these codes.

FOUNDER'S STATUTES

Preamble

This recites that "I Robert Wodelarke have founded a College or Hall in Mylstrete for the increase of the sciences and faculties of philosophy and of sacred theology, and after taking the advice of learned men have drawn up these statutes".

1. *On the office of Master*

There is to be a Master, superior to the Fellows and to the others living in the College, to rule and govern it according to the statutes, but in graver matters to consult the Fellows. He must be at least thirty years of age and Master or Bachelor of sacred theology.

The Master's stipend is to be a hundred shillings a year, paid in equal parts at the end of the four "terms" of the year. The Master may hold ecclesiastical preferment.

STATUTES OF EDWARD VI 1549

Preamble

This recites that "I Robert Wodelarke have founded a College or Hall in the University of Cambridge to increase the knowledge of sacred theology, philosophy and the other arts.[1] In which College there are to be a Master and six Fellows, more or fewer according to the revenues, and for their right government after taking the advice of learned and prudent men I have drawn up these statutes".

1. *On the office of Master*

Few changes. The Master is to be over all the Fellows and other students and to receive six pounds a year with eight pence a week for a servant.

[1] This seems to exclude both Law and Medicine.

STATUTES CONFIRMED BY ORDER OF QUEEN VICTORIA IN COUNCIL 10 MAY 1860

[These were the first statutes after the Edwardian of 1549]

The preamble recites that the College was founded by Robert Wodelarke, and goes on to mention its chief benefactors.

STATUTES OF 3 MAY 1882

Preface or preamble

Chapter I

On the office of Master

This chapter is very like the Edwardian. The Master is to be at least thirty years old, a priest of the Church of England, a Master of Arts or Law or a Doctor of Theology, Law or Medicine. He is to have twice the dividend of a Fellow and a fair allowance for a servant. He is not to be absent from Cambridge for more than six months in the year.

1. *The Master*

There shall be in the College a Master or Keeper, of good life and conversation, well qualified by learning and experience of business, of at least thirty years of age, a Priest in Holy Orders of the Church of England, and a Master of Arts or of some equal or superior degree in the University of Cambridge or Oxford.

He shall preside over and govern the Fellows, Scholars, and all other Members of the College, according to the Statutes. He shall manage the property of the College, and see that its revenues are duly applied to their proper objects, and that the surplus remaining in any year is properly invested or applied for the benefit of the College as a place of education, religion, learning, and research.

The Master shall receive in every year out of the revenues of the College

2. *On the election of a Master*

Within three days from a vacancy the senior Fellow in residence is to warn the Fellows to assemble after three days in the Chapel before 7 A.M. to elect a Master. After Mass all except the Fellows are to retire. If the Fellows cannot agree, another "scrutiny" is to be held within two days from the beginning of the first scrutiny, and so on until a majority agree on one person. Before acting as Master the person elected is to take an oath.

2. *On the election of a Master*

The only important change is the substitution of "prayers" for "Mass".

as herein-after provided a sum equal to two dividends of a Fellow, together with a sufficient allowance for the maintenance of a servant.

He shall not be absent from the College more than one hundred and eighty days in any year except on account of illness or other grave cause; nor shall he be absent from the College more than one-third of any term except on account of illness or other grave cause or necessary residence on his canonry at Norwich.

Chapter II

On the election of a Master

Within three days of hearing of a vacancy, the senior Fellow is to inform the others of the day of election, which is to be not less than the fourteenth, nor more than the thirtieth, day from the receipt of the news. But if the news arrive between the Friday following the Great Congregation and the 16 September, the election may be postponed to any day before the 3 October. The rest of the chapter shows little or no change from the Edwardian statute.

2. *The election of Master*

When the office of Master becomes vacant, the Senior Fellow resident in College shall, within three days after the vacancy is made known to him, give notice of the vacancy to all the other Fellows, whether present in College or absent, and summon them to meet for the election of a new Master on some day not less than fourteen days nor more than thirty days after the date of such notice.

If, however, the vacancy of the office of Master is first made known to the said Senior Fellow in the vacation after the Easter Term and before the sixteenth day of September in any year, the meeting for the election of a new Master shall be held on some day in the first week of the ensuing Michaelmas Term.

On the day appointed for the election the Fellows shall meet together at noon in the College Chapel. The prayers "Veni Sancte Spiritus", and "Deus qui corda", shall be said; and the Fellows shall proceed severally to nominate and elect a person duly qualified according to the preceding Statute for the office of Master.

If upon a first scrutiny there be no person nominated and elected by a majority of the whole body of existing Fellows, they shall proceed to nominate and elect a second time; and the process of nominating and electing shall be repeated as often as the Fellows think proper within forty-eight hours after the commencement of the first scrutiny. If at the end of the said forty-eight hours there be no person nominated and elected by a majority of the whole body of existing Fellows, the appointment of a Master for that turn shall be vested in the Visitor.

The person nominated and elected or appointed shall make the following declaration before he acts as Master, "Ego N. do fidem quod collegium sive aulam divæ catharinæ virginis, terras et tenementa, possessiones, redditus temporales et ecclesiasticos, jura et bona quæcunque collegii sive aulæ prædictæ regam, defendam, custodiam et gubernabo, et per alios regi, custodiri et gubernari faciam quantum potero. Item statuta ejusdem collegii edita, et in posterum edenda, firmiter observabo. Item collegium sive aulam prædictam cum omnibus bonis ejusdem contra omnes adversarios ejus quantum potero

Statutes of 1882

tuebor et defendam. Et quantum in me fuerit, correctiones, punitiones et reformationes justas et debitas faciam et exercebo, ac per alios fieri et exerceri, quantum in me est, curabo."

4. *Deprivation of the Master*

If the Master shall have been convicted by a court of competent jurisdiction of any crime, the Visitor may, if he think fit, proceed to inquire into the fact of such conviction, and if it be established may deprive the Master of his office.

If any three or more of the Fellows shall prefer to the Visitor a charge against the Master of disgraceful conduct, or of malversation in his office, or of gross neglect of duty, whereby he has in their judgment become unfit to preside over the College, the Visitor shall with all convenient speed proceed to inquire into the facts of the case, and if the charge be established, may deprive the Master of his office.

5. *Appointment of Vice-Master in case of the Incapacity of the Master*

If the Master shall at any time become incapable of performing the duties of his office, the Visitor on being satisfied thereof shall, upon the application of a majority of the Fellows present at a meeting convened for the purpose of taking the matter into consideration, such majority consisting of at least a moiety of the whole number of Fellows, or upon the application of the Master himself, have power to appoint one of

Statutes of 1882

the Fellows to act in the Master's place during his incapacity, and to assign to the person so appointed such portion as the Visitor shall think fit, not exceeding one-third, of the income assigned to the Master by these Statutes.

It shall be incumbent upon the Senior Fellow in residence to convene the meeting of the Fellows for the purpose mentioned in the foregoing paragraph, upon the request of any three or more of the Fellows, and to cause notice of such meeting to be sent to each of the Fellows.

The Fellow who shall be appointed by the Visitor to act in the Master's place shall be called Vice-Master. He shall retain his office, and receive the portion of the Master's income which shall have been assigned to him, until the Master shall be reinstated in his functions and powers, or shall cease to be Master. He shall exercise and perform all the functions and duties, and shall have all the powers and authorities of the Master, except the power of consenting to any change of the Master's emoluments, and shall be bound to residence in the same manner, and be liable to deprivation for the same causes and in like manner, as the Master.

If the Vice-Master shall die or resign his office, or vacate his Fellowship, or become incapable of discharging his duties, the Visitor shall have the like power upon the like application of appointing another of the Fellows to be Vice-Master in his room, and of assigning an income, limited as aforesaid, to such Vice-Master.

If the Master shall at any time after the appointment of a Vice-Master again become capable of performing his duties, the Visitor on being satisfied thereof shall have power to reinstate him in his functions and powers and in receipt of all his emoluments.

Founder's Statutes

3. *On the number of Fellows and the form of election*

There are to be three or more Fellows, English, in orders, Masters of Arts or at least "better" Bachelors. A majority consisting of the Master and at least half the Fellows is necessary for an election. If this cannot be secured, the choice is to devolve on the Master and two Fellows. Not more than two Fellows can be chosen from one county. Fellows are to take the degrees of their faculties, and are to "dispute" once a week for two hours at least, unless the Master (or President) think fit to alter the time. From this exercise the Master is excused.

Statutes of Edward VI 1549

3. *On the number of Fellows and the form of election*

There are to be six Fellows, fewer or more according to the revenues.[1] They are to be English, Masters of Arts or at least Bachelors "of the more learned kind". Priests or deacons are to be preferred, and of the six, two at least shall be priests and one a deacon. On a vacancy occurring among those in orders, the senior of those not in orders shall take them within a year, unless a junior shall be ready to take orders in his stead. The rest follows closely the Founder's statutes, except that the "disputes" are for two whole hours, no variation being mentioned, but Doctors in Theology (as well as the Master) are excused.

[1] Who is to decide whether the number of Fellows is to be more or less than six? To leave this point vague (unless there is a Visitor) is to allow the Society to choose its own numbers.

Statutes of 1860

Chapter III

On the number of Fellows and form of election

The number of Fellows is to be nine[1] or more. They must have a degree, be British subjects and of the Church of England. Three at least of the Fellows are to be in orders, two at least in priest's. The Master is to have a casting vote, a clear majority being necessary for a valid election. If this cannot be obtained, then the election devolves on the Master and two Fellows chosen by a majority of the Fellows. Fellows who are Bachelors of Arts or Law must proceed in due course to the degree of Master; Bachelors of Medicine to the degree of Doctor. Marriage involves vacation of Fellowship, but Professors with a stipend not exceeding £500 a year may marry, though they cannot have rooms in College.

Each Fellow is to have a "dividend", which is not to exceed £300 in any year. A vacancy must be filled up within a year or, in exceptional circumstances, two years.

Statutes of 1882

6. *The Fellows and their election*

Besides the Master, there shall be in the College six Fellows, or more if the revenues of the College are sufficient to provide for the maintenance of more than six.

Every vacant Fellowship shall be filled within one year from the date of vacancy, unless the majority of the Master and Fellows, for reasons to be set forth in a College Order, defer the election for a further period not exceeding one year.

The election of a Fellow shall always be made in Term time, and the Master shall give not less than fourteen days' notice to all the Fellows, whether present in College or absent, of the day and hour appointed for election.

The persons elected shall have taken some degree in the University of Cambridge or Oxford, and shall be such as in the judgment of the Master and Fellows are well qualified to be Fellows of the College as a place of education, religion, learning, and research.

If in the election of a Fellow the votes of the Master and Fellows present are divided into two equal parts, the Master shall have a second or casting vote.

If upon a first scrutiny there be no person for whom a majority, or at least one half, of the Master and Fellows pre-

[1] The number of Fellows was never more than six while these statutes were in force. It does not appear how the statute was evaded.

Statutes of 1882

sent have voted, the scrutiny shall be repeated as often as the Master and Fellows think fit within forty-eight hours from the time of the commencement of the first scrutiny. If at the end of the said forty-eight hours there be no person for whom a majority, or at least one half, of the Master and Fellows present have voted, the Fellows present shall elect two of their own number, to whom, in conjunction with the Master, the election of a Fellow for that turn shall be committed, so that the election may be made by the Master and one of the said two elected Fellows.

The Fellow elect shall make the following declaration before admission: "Ego N. do fidem quod omnia statuta et ordinationes collegii sive aulæ divæ catharinæ virginis, quatenus me concernunt, pro viribus observabo, et quantum in me est ab aliis sociis faciam observari; magistro seu præfecto dicti collegii sive aulæ, qui pro tempore fuerit, in iis quæ ad officium ipsius et statuta collegii prædicti pertinent obtemperabo; bonorum, terrarum, possessionum ac reddituum ejusdem collegii conservationem, defensionem et amplificationem, quantum in me est, procurabo."

The seniority of the Fellows in College shall be determined by the dates of their admission as Fellows, and not by the times of graduation.

Fellows who are Bachelors in Arts, or Law, or Surgery, shall proceed in due course to the degree of Master in Arts, or Law, or Surgery, and Fellows who are Bachelors in Medicine shall proceed in due course to the degree of Doctor in Medicine, unless prevented by illness or other cause approved by the Master and Fellows as sufficient.

In any special case in which the interests of the College so require, the Master and Fellows may make it a condition of the tenure of a Fellowship at the time of election that the Fellow shall, if called upon to do so within one year from the time of election, accept any specified College office, and hold it for such time as they require. On any breach of such condition the Fellowship shall become vacant.

7. *Election of Eminent Men as Fellows*

The Master and Fellows may elect to a Fellowship any eminent person whether or not he be a Graduate of Cambridge or Oxford, provided that the election be made by the votes of not less than two-thirds of the whole body of Master and Fellows, and provided also that not more than one Fellowship be held under the provisions of this Statute at the same time.

8. *Professorial Fellowship*

One of the Fellowships shall be deemed to be and shall be a Professorial Fellowship, and shall be held according to the terms and conditions prescribed by the Statutes of the University for Professorial Fellowships made under the powers of the Universities of Oxford and Cambridge Act, 1877. Provided that if at the time when these Statutes come into operation there be in the College six Fellows or more, the Master and Fellows may elect a Professor to a Fellowship and may suppress the Fellowships which thereafter fall vacant until the number is reduced to six.

9. *Supernumerary Fellows*

Any Fellow other than the Fellow holding the Professorial Fellowship may declare in writing to the Master his wish to become a Supernumerary Fellow.

If the Master and Fellows consent, he shall become a Supernumerary Fellow and shall be a Fellow to all intents and purposes, and hold his Fellowship for the time and in the manner provided by the Statutes, and enjoy all the benefits of the same, except that he shall not be entitled to any dividend. He shall not, however, count towards making up the number of Fellows required by the Statutes, but a new Fellow shall be elected after the declaration made, as aforesaid, by which he became a Supernumerary Fellow.

10. *Honorary Fellows*

The Master and Fellows may elect any person, whom they consider it desirable so to distinguish, to be an Honorary Fellow.

Such Honorary Fellow shall not have any voice or authority in the affairs of the College, nor be entitled to any dividend or presentation to a Benefice,

but he shall enjoy such other privileges and advantages as the Master and Fellows may from time to time determine.

The Master and Fellows may at any time terminate the tenure of an Honorary Fellowship.

Founder's Statutes

4. Form and manner of the oath at the election of Fellows

The oath to be taken before admission is: to observe the statutes, to obey the Master, to reveal no secrets to the harm of the College, to help to improve its revenues, to consent to no Fellow proceeding to any degree except in philosophy and sacred theology, to defend the College, to obtain or make use of no dispensation from this oath. The stipend of a Fellow is to be four pounds a year, payable quarterly. No ecclesiastical benefice, with or without cure of souls, can be held with a Fellowship for more than a year. But a Fellow can keep a "free Chapel", when residence is not required.

Statutes of Edward VI 1549

4. Form and manner of the oath at the election of Fellows

The oath is much simplified—to observe the statutes, to obey the Master, to reveal no harmful secrets, to defend and increase the possessions of the College.

The stipend is to be five pounds a year.

Chapter IV

On the Scholars (de discipulis) of the College

Besides the Frankland and Ramsden Scholars there are to be eleven others, two with stipends not less than £50 and nine with stipends not less than £25. Scholars, as far as possible, are to be called after the names of the donors of the Scholarships. The election lies with the Master and Fellows, but no account is to be taken of place of birth or school. Scholars may be elected after admission or matriculation. Scholarships are normally to cease with the B.A. degree, but in exceptional cases may be prolonged.

Scholars may be elected before admission, but may receive no emolu-

13. *The Scholars*

The Scholars shall be elected by the Master and Fellows without regard to their place of birth or school of education from among the Students of the College or of the University, or according to the results of examinations instituted for the purpose from among persons who have not been admitted to the College or to the University: provided that in the case of the latter persons they are not more than nineteen years of age at the time of examination, and that the Scholarships awarded to them be not tenable for a longer period than for two years certain, and that the

The following extract from the Order Book throws light on the attitude of the College just before 1860 to Royal Commissions and to constitutional changes imposed from without.

November 22, 1851.

Communications having been received from the Commissioners appointed by Her Majesty to enquire into the State, discipline, studies, and revenues of the University and Colleges of Cambridge, requesting information and answers to questions proposed by them, it was agreed by the Master and major part of the Fellows (the minority desiring that no answers whatever should be sent) that such answers should be returned as shall be agreed upon by the Master and Fellows, and that the answers should be sent accompanied by the following declaration by way of protest:

1. That the College of St Catharine the Virgin was founded by the private munificence of Robert Wodelarke, D.D. (who obtained a Royal Charter for the purpose) to the praise, glory, and honour of our Lord Jesus Christ, for the service of his Church, the administration of the Word of God, and the advancement of knowledge in Theology, Philosophy and other learning, and that the said College is governed by Statutes by him provided for that purpose.
2. That no power, other than the Visitor of the College acting in the manner appointed by law, has authority to require answers to questions respecting the affairs of the College.
3. That the College itself is competent to decide upon the desirableness or necessity of introducing changes or modifications into its system of administration, and has long possessed the power, subject to the authority afore mentioned, of carrying such changes or modifications into effect, and we therefore feel bound respectfully to protest against any violation of its established customs and privileges.
4. That we are induced to return the said answers solely because we desire, so far as our duty will permit, to protect the College (whose interest we are bound to serve & defend to the utmost of our power) from the injurious effect of partial statements, & ignorant misrepresentations.

H. Philpott, Master,
L. S. Purton.
G. W. Coopland.
C K Robinson.

Statutes of 1860	*Statutes of 1882*
ments before coming into residence. A Scholar may be promoted from an inferior to a superior Scholarship and (apparently) may for distinguished merit hold two Scholarships. A term's absence without permission, or failure to take the B.A. degree, is to involve loss of Scholarship. The Master and Fellows may take away, wholly or in part, a Scholarship in cases of bad conduct. The Master and Fellows may increase or lessen the number of Scholars or the emoluments of the Scholarships according to the state of the Scholarship Fund.	annual value of each of such Scholarships do not exceed eighty pounds inclusive of rent of rooms and all allowances. Every Scholarship, including the Scholarship on Bishop Sherlock's Foundation in connection with the Library, shall become vacant when the holder of it is of sufficient standing for the degree of Bachelor of Arts, unless the Master and Fellows shall think fit in cases of special merit to prolong the tenure for a further period not exceeding the time when the holder is of sufficient standing for the degree of Master of Arts. The Master and Fellows may promote a deserving Student from one Scholarship to another, and in cases of special merit may give two Scholarships to the same person, and may at their discretion award gratuities out of the Scholarship fund to poor and deserving students. If a Scholar shall have been absent from the College for the whole of any term without the permission of the Master and Fellows, his Scholarship shall thereby become vacant. The Master and Fellows may deprive a Student of his Scholarship or suspend his receipt of the emoluments for a definite time in case of neglect of study, or in case of failure in any University or College Examination, or in case of unbecoming or disgraceful conduct.

5. On increasing the number of Fellows

If revenues permit, the number of Fellows may be increased. These extra Fellows must be elected "juxta formam, modum et conditiones" as are laid down in the statute governing the election of Fellows, "et non aliter quoquo modo".[1]

Master and Fellows are to have their meals together "in communi aula sive parlura",[2] and the Master is to assign chambers to the Fellows so that two share a set. The Master may reserve for his own use "the principal room, the better room over the Hall, and the room between the aforesaid room and the Library". Other persons admitted *commensales* are to pay for their lodging into the College stock, and to "dispute" with the other Fellows. During meals "sive in aula sive in parlura"[3] the Bible or Fathers to be read "more ecclesiasticae lectionis" by a young person to be called *biblista* or *biblicus*, during which reading there is to be no noise, chatter or laughter. Latin is to be normally used at meals. The President is to be nominated by the Master.

5. Observances at table, the assigning of rooms and the officers of the same house

There is little change except in details. Only the Bible is mentioned as the book to be read at meals; the reader is "puer sive discipulus" instead of "puer sive clericus"; to the Master are assigned "the principal bedroom over the Hall and another between that bedroom and the Library"; a *commensalis* is now called *pensionarius*; an annual stipend of 6*s.* 8*d.* is assigned to the President; and a *senescallus seu receptor* is appointed at an annual stipend of 40*s.* to receive revenues and carry out repairs.

[1] This is rather obscure, but seems to be designed to prevent the election of inferior or bye-Fellows.

[2] It is unfortunate that the language of our records sometimes identifies *aula* and *parlura*, sometimes separates them.

[3] Here *parlura* certainly seems to mean "Combination Room".

Statutes of 1860

Chapter V

Dinner, assignment of rooms and officers of the College

Little change. Reading the Bible during meals is dropped. Fellows have a room assigned to them by the Master. The President is to receive a fair stipend, and so is the Bursar. The Master may hold the latter office.

Statutes of 1882

18. *Commons and Assignment of Rooms*

The Fellows shall receive out of the revenues of the College during residence a moderate sum for commons, to be determined by the Master and Fellows, and the Master shall receive during residence twice the amount allowed to each Fellow. The Master and Fellows shall have power to determine from time to time what shall be held to constitute residence for the purposes of this Statute.

The Master shall assign rooms in College to the Fellows severally, having regard to their seniority.

The use of rooms may be allowed to other members of the College by the Master and Fellows at their discretion, and the rents of such rooms shall be fixed by the Master and Fellows, and shall be paid as income to the College.

No Fellow shall be allowed to bring his wife or family to reside in College, unless special provision be made for that purpose and permission given by the Master and Fellows at a meeting called for the purpose of considering the question.

3. *The President*

The Master shall appoint in writing from time to time one of the Fellows of the degree of Master of Arts, or of some equal or superior degree, to represent him in his absence.

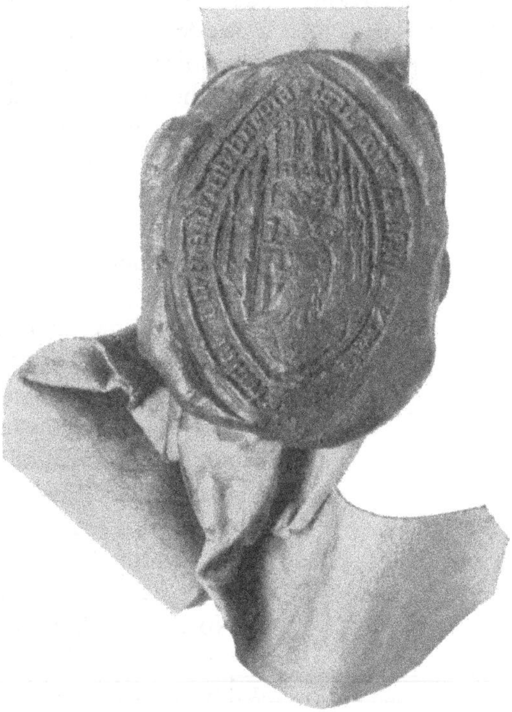

The Seal of St Catharine's College.

The seal, of which the above figure is an impression, is probably the one used by the Founder. It represents St Catharine kneeling, with the wheel on her back. The legend probably is:

SIGILLUM COLLEGII SIVE AULE SCTE
KATERINE VIRGINIS DE CĀTEBRIGIA

Statutes of 1882

Such Fellow shall be called the President, and shall have the authority of the Master when absent in all College business except in the use of the College seal which shall not be affixed to any document in the absence of the Master or at least without his consent in writing.

The President shall receive out of the revenues of the College a yearly stipend determined by the Master and Fellows, and shall hold the office until such time as the Master shall appoint in writing some other of the Fellows in his stead.

16. *College Officers*

A meeting of the Master and Fellows shall be held in every year on the fourth Monday in October at noon for the election of a Bursar, a Dean, a Steward, a Prælector, and a Chaplain.

The election shall be made in every case by the votes of a majority of the Master and Fellows present.

The Dean shall be elected, so far as conveniently may be done, from among the Fellows who are in Holy Orders.

The above-named officers shall receive out of the revenues of the College such stipends as the Master and Fellows may determine.

15. *Educational Staff, Tuition Fees, and Caution Fund*

The Tutor or Tutors shall be appointed by the Master for a probationary period of three years; and on the expiration of that period the Master and Fellows may confirm the appointment.

The Lecturers shall be appointed by the Master and Fellows for such periods as they may from time to time determine.

A Tutor may be deprived of his office at any time for grave cause by the votes of not less than two-thirds of the whole body of Master and Fellows at a College meeting.

The Master and Fellows shall determine the fees to be paid by the students of the College for tuition, and shall determine in what proportions the aggregate sum shall be distributed among the Tutors and Lecturers.

All Caution money, and also all moneys due to the College from any of its members, shall be received and collected as the Master and Fellows may determine. All the Caution money shall be placed to the credit of a fund called the Caution Fund. The Caution Fund shall be managed and the income thereof applied as the Master and Fellows may from time to time determine. The accounts of receipt and expenditure shall be kept by such officer as the Master and Fellows may appoint for the purpose, and shall be audited in every year together with the other accounts of the College.

6. *On the custody of the common seal and of the muniments*

The common seal is to be kept in the Tower, in a purse under three seals, those of the Master and two Fellows, in a box with three locks of different pattern. Every document before sealing is to be copied into a register.[1] Sealing is to take place only in the Tower, which is also to be called the Treasury. The muniments are to be kept in a chest with a register,[1] which is to contain copies. In the same chest are to be kept the statutes and catalogues of books, plate etc. with the names of benefactors and their benefactions, so that these can be commemorated at the feast of St. Catharine. Muniments are not to be taken from the Tower except to protect the possessions of the College.

The same rules are expressed in clearer and better Latin, with the addition of an audit ("ratio seu computus") to be held at the feast of St. Catharine.

[1] It is not clear whether the Founder meant two registers or one. The early Society in practice kept one only.

Statutes of 1860

Chapter VI

On the custody of the common seal, muniments and books

Practically identical with the corresponding Edwardian statute.

Statutes of 1882

25. *College Seal and Muniments*

The College seal shall be kept in a box secured by three locks of different patterns, the keys of which shall be kept by the Master and the two senior Fellows in residence respectively.

Before the seal is affixed to any document it shall be copied into the College Register and read openly at a meeting of the Master and Fellows called for the purpose.

All deeds of importance affecting the property or interests of the College shall be copied into the College Register, and be kept in the Treasury, nor shall they be taken therefrom except for the defence of the rights of the College or other grave cause approved as sufficient by the Master and Fellows.

20. *College Finances and Revenues*

The moneys received by the Bursar on account of the College shall be deposited by him in some bank or banks approved by the Master and Fellows, or shall be invested according to their orders.

Before declaring the dividend in any year, all things shall be done and paid which are required to be done and paid by the Statutes of the College, or by the Statutes of the University, or by the ancient and approved customs of the College, or by the unrepealed ordinances contained in wills, indentures, or writings of what kind soever, or by any

Statutes of 1882

other lawful ordinance; and a sufficient sum of money shall be applied or reserved for repairing, rebuilding, enlarging, or ornamenting the building of the College, for defraying the expenses of managing the College property, and for any other purpose which the Master and Fellows may deem to be necessary or advantageous to the College as a place of education, religion, learning, and research.

Subject as aforesaid, the yearly income of the College shall be divided and distributed among the Master and Fellows as follows, viz., to every Fellow such sum as the Master and Fellows shall fix for the dividend of the year, being not greater than two hundred and fifty pounds exclusive of rooms and commons, but including all other allowances, and to the Master a sum equal to twice such dividend. Both the dividend and also the stipends and other fixed pecuniary emoluments of the Master, Fellows, and Officers, shall be considered as accruing from day to day, and shall be apportionable accordingly.

21. *Payments for University Purposes*

The College shall pay in every year to the University the sum authorised by the Statutes of the University made under the powers of the Universities of Oxford and Cambridge Act, 1877, to be levied from the College.

22. *Surplus Revenue*

If at any time it shall appear to the Master and Fellows that the revenues of the College are greater than the amount required to afford to every Fellow a dividend of two hundred and fifty pounds a year, exclusive of rooms and commons, but inclusive of all other allowances, they may submit to the Visitor a scheme, approved by a majority of the whole body of Master and Fellows, for increasing the number of Fellowships or Scholarships or for providing a fund for granting gratuities to poor and deserving members of the College *in statu pupillari*, or for applying the surplus in some other way for the benefit of the College or of the University, and the said scheme, if approved by the Visitor, shall thenceforth have the same force and effect as if it formed part of these Statutes.

The Visitor shall not approve any scheme for diminishing the number of Fellowships below the minimum number prescribed by these Statutes.

23. *College Accounts and Audit*

The College financial year shall end always on the twenty-ninth day of September.

As soon as may be after the twenty-fifth day of November, St. Catharine's day, accounts of all receipts and disbursements for the preceding financial year shall be submitted by the Bursar to the Master and Fellows at a College

Statutes of 1882

meeting. Not less than fourteen days' notice of such meeting shall be given by the Master to the Fellows, whether present in the College or absent. The Master and Fellows shall examine the accounts, verify the vouchers, ascertain the balances due, comparing the same with the balances in the College banks, and sign the accounts if found correct.

An abstract of the several accounts of the College relating to funds administered for general purposes, or in trust, or otherwise, shall be sent on or before the thirty-first day of December in each year to the Vice-Chancellor of the University for publication. The abstract shall be made as nearly as practicable in the form contained in the Schedule attached to these Statutes. An account of the receipts and disbursements of money, if any, raised under the borrowing powers of the College shall be sent yearly at the same time to the Vice-Chancellor for publication.

Founder's Statutes	*Statutes of Edward VI 1549*
7. *On the prayers, Masses and suffrages for the Founder in life and after death*	
This section is very full and detailed. See p. 56.	This is replaced by a section (the last) containing orders for prayers and Holy Communion instead of Masses and exsequies, concluding with an exhortation to all "Fellows and students of this College" to remember their benefits and the kindness of God.
8. *For what crimes and misdemeanours Fellows are to be deprived of their Fellowships*	
If any Fellow be convicted of any serious crime, or be guilty of any grave offence, after confirmation thereof before the Master or, in his absence, the President, such Fellow is to be excluded from the College, neither the Master nor anyone else having any right of remission or dispensation.	8. The title of this section is the same, but no mention is made of confirmation before the Master or President. The offending Fellow is *ipso facto* excluded and ejected without any right of appeal or remedy at law.

Chapter VII

For what crimes and misdemeanours Fellows should be deprived of their Fellowships

1. If a Fellow leave the Church of England, the Master and the rest of the Fellows, after careful inquiry, must deprive him of his Fellowship.

2. A Fellow convicted of a crime may, if the Master and Fellows think fit, be deprived.

3. If two Fellows bring a charge of a serious nature against a Fellow, the Master and Fellows (except the three concerned) may deprive him.

4. If the Master consider a Fellow guilty of a serious offence, the Master and Fellows after due inquiry may deprive the offender.

11. *Suspension and deprivation of Fellows*

If any Fellow shall pertinaciously disturb the concord or discipline of the College, or shall wilfully violate or neglect to comply with any of the Statutes, it shall be the duty of the Master and Fellows at a College meeting, on proof of such misconduct, to admonish such Fellow; and if, notwithstanding such admonition, he shall contumaciously persist in such misconduct, the Master may, with the concurrence of the majority of such Fellows, other than the Fellow whose conduct is impugned, as are present at a College meeting to which all the Fellows shall have been summoned, suspend such Fellow from the enjoyment of his Fellowship for such time as they shall think fit, or deprive him altogether of his Fellowship.

If any Fellow shall be convicted by a court of competent jurisdiction of any crime, the Master shall, with all con-

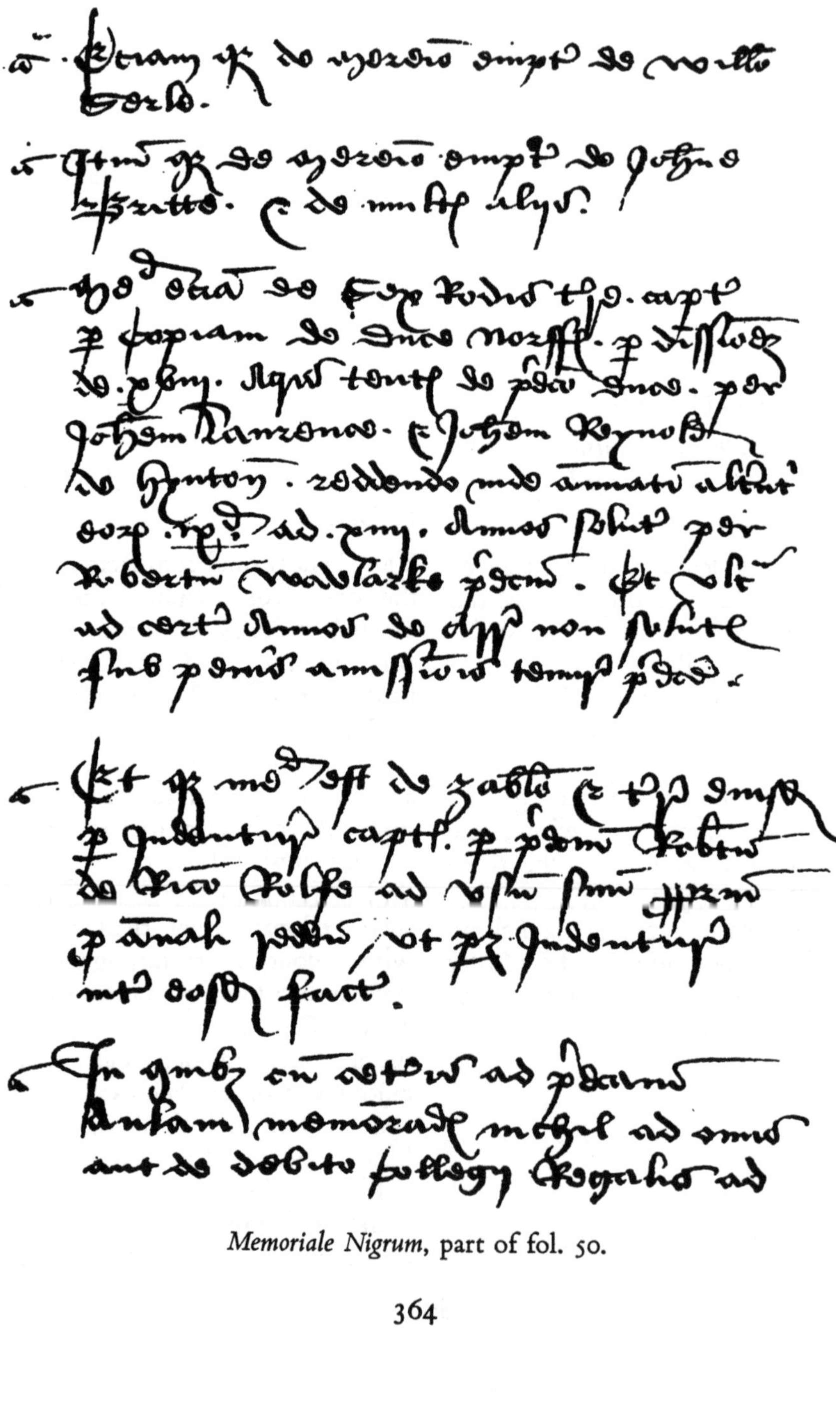

Memoriale Nigrum, part of fol. 50.

Statutes of 1882

venient speed, summon a meeting of all the Fellows, exclusive of such Fellow. The Master and Fellows assembled at such meeting may, if they think fit, proceed to investigate the case and if the fact of such conviction be established, the Master shall, if the majority of those present so determine, deprive such Fellow of his Fellowship and expel him from the College.

If the Master shall in any case think it proper to cause an inquiry to be instituted as to whether or not the conduct of any Fellow has been disgraceful and such as to render him unfit to be a Fellow of the College, or if any two Fellows shall prefer before the Master against any Fellow a charge of disgraceful conduct rendering him unfit in their judgment to be a Fellow of the College, the Master shall summon a meeting of all the Fellows other than the accused and the Fellows, if any, preferring such charge. The Master and Fellows assembled at such meeting shall proceed to investigate the case, giving the accused person an opportunity of being heard in his defence, and if such disgraceful conduct be proved, the Master shall, if the majority of those present so determine, deprive the offending Fellow of his Fellowship and expel him from the College.

In any case of a sentence of suspension or deprivation and expulsion of a Fellow there shall be a right of appeal to the Visitor, who shall have power to annul the sentence or vary it at his discretion.

Founder's Statutes	*Statutes of Edward VI 1549*
9. *On the keeping of the books, which must not be alienated*	
This section has been described, pp. 56–7.	Omitted, the audit being considered sufficient precaution.
10. *When the Master should ask for the consent of the Fellows*	10. The title is the same.
A list of occasions is given, including change of tenants, presentation to benefices, lawsuits in which the College is concerned etc. The College meetings are to be "in the Chapel or other convenient place". The statutes are to be read to the Fellows once a year. Richard Roche, the then Master, is allowed to hold any ecclesiastical benefice or dignity.	No change, the clause about Roche being of course omitted.

Chapter VIII

When the Master should seek the consent of the Fellows

There is no essential difference between this chapter and previous statutes. College meetings are to be held "in a convenient place within the College", and the Master is given a casting vote.

14. *College Meetings*

There shall be one College meeting in the Michaelmas term in every year, on a day to be fixed by the Master, of which fourteen days' notice shall be given to each of the Fellows. If any of the Fellows be absent from the meeting in any year, he shall be fined a sum of five pounds, and such fine shall be applied to such purposes as the Master and Fellows think fit.

The Master shall call meetings of the Master and Fellows whenever he may think it necessary, and when a majority of the Fellows shall require him to do so, such requisition to be made in writing.

No Fellow shall be absent without sufficient reason from a College meeting duly called.

No business shall be done at a College meeting unless at least one half of the whole body of Master and Fellows be present; but the Master and Fellows may delegate to the Master and resident Fellows the transaction of such business as may seem to them fit.

The Master shall have only one vote, but where the votes are equally divided he shall have a second or casting vote.

11. *Fellows are not permitted "devillare" outside the University without permission*

If a Fellow wishes *devillare* beyond a distance of four miles, he is to ask permission from the Master or President, who however is not to be harsh in granting it. No Fellow is to pass the night outside the College in Cambridge or within four miles of it except through illness, his parents' illness, or other cause deemed sufficient by the Master (President). More than sixty days' absence without permission involves loss of Fellowship without right of appeal. The head of the College is to see to it that Fellows are never all absent together.

11. *Fellows are not permitted to depart from the University without permission*

This section shows few changes. The limit of four miles is kept in the case of absence from the University, but is omitted in the clause forbidding pernoctation outside the College within Cambridge or its suburbs. At the end a clause is added permitting all the Fellows to be absent together in case of a serious epidemic of plague, when care is to be taken for the safety and custody of the College.

No Fellow *in statu pupillari* shall be allowed to vote at any meeting until the expiration of one year from the date of his admission as Fellow.

Chapter IX

Absence of Fellows from the University

Reasonable absence is permitted, but refusal to return when summoned is to bring loss of Fellowship. The Edwardian clause about leaving the College guarded when epidemics force the Society to retire from Cambridge is repeated.

17. *Residence of Fellows and Officers*

During full term at least one College officer other than the Master shall reside in College; during that part of the vacation between Easter and Michaelmas terms in which members of the College *in statu pupillari* are allowed to reside, at least one College officer or Fellow shall reside in College; and the Master and Fellows shall make such provision as may seem to them expedient for the residence of Fellows and College officers during the other vacations.

The Master and Fellows shall have power to require any College officer to reside in College during full term time, and during such part of the vacation between Easter and Michaelmas terms as they may think necessary for the due maintenance of discipline.

Every College officer or Fellow who is fulfilling the duty of residence in College under this Statute shall sleep in College at least five nights in every week, and if he is absent on either of the remaining nights, he shall have a deputy approved by the Master, and such deputy shall sleep in College: provided always, that a house communicating

12. *For what reasonable and honourable causes Fellows should retire from their Fellowships*

These are: (1) entering a religious order; (2) absence for more than sixty days in one year; (3) receipt of property, bringing in ten marks yearly. In the third case six months' grace is allowed.

12. *For what other causes Fellows should retire from their Fellowships*

(1) is omitted, as being unnecessary after the Reformation; (2) is omitted, as occurring elsewhere; (3) is retained. The period of grace is extended to one year, and ecclesiastical preferment, except such as does not exceed the annual value of ten marks and does not involve residence and cure of souls, is also a bar to holding a Fellowship.

Conclusion. After an exhortation to interpret and obey the statutes without subterfuge, the Founder reserves the right to emend or add to the present statutes. He also orders that there should always be a Fellow in priest's orders to pray for the soul of Iohanna de Barnston, in return for a gift of one hundred marks.

with the College and approved by the Master and Fellows shall be deemed to be within the College.

Chapter X

Other causes requiring Fellows to give up their Fellowships

The acquisition of patrimony, legacy etc. bringing in a revenue one third larger than the average dividend for the last seven years, or ecclesiastical preferment, is to bring loss of Fellowship after one year. A Fellow however may hold with his Fellowship ecclesiastical positions in Cambridge, provided that the above value is not exceeded.

12. *Vacation of Fellowships*

Every Fellow shall vacate his Fellowship at the end of six years from his election, except in the cases herein-after specified. No one who has thus vacated his Fellowship shall be eligible for re-election except to the Professorial Fellowship.

If a Fellow become the Head or a Fellow of any University or of any other College in any University, and if any stipend be attached to such Headship or Fellowship, his Fellowship shall thereupon become *ipso facto* vacant.

If a Fellow be admitted Master of the College, his Fellowship shall thereupon become *ipso facto* vacant.

If a Fellow be instituted to a benefice in the gift of the College, the clear annual value of which, after deducting all legal charges other than the pension, if any, of a previous incumbent, is not less than four hundred pounds, his Fellowship shall become vacant at the end of one year from the date of presentation.

If a Fellow accept a Professorship to which a Fellowship at another College is attached, his Fellowship shall thereupon become *ipso facto* vacant.

If a Fellow at the end of six years' tenure of his Fellowship hold a Professorship to which no Fellowship at another College is attached, he may hold his Fellowship as long as he holds such office.

If at the end of six years' tenure of his Fellowship a Fellow hold in the College the office of Tutor, Senior Mathematical Lecturer, or Senior Classical Lecturer, he shall continue to hold his Fellowship so long as he holds any one of such offices; and if his tenure of any one or more of the said offices shall have exceeded twenty years, he shall be entitled to continue to hold his Fellowship for life unless disqualified by any other reason than the lapse of time. For the purposes of this Statute election to any of these offices within three months after ceasing to hold any of them shall be considered as continuous tenure.

Chapter XI

Prayers and pious exercises, and faithful observance of the Statutes

19. *Divine Service and Religious Instruction*

Whereas by the fifth and sixth sections of the Universities Tests Act, 1871, it is enacted as follows:

"The Governing Body of every College subsisting at the time of the passing of this Act in any of the said Universities shall provide sufficient religious instruction for all members thereof *in statu pupillari* belonging to the Established Church.

"The morning and evening prayer according to the Order of the Book of Common Prayer shall continue to be used daily as heretofore in the chapel of every College subsisting at the time of the passing of this Act in any of the said Universities; but notwithstanding anything contained in the statute thirteenth and fourteenth Charles the Second, chapter four, or in this Act, it shall be lawful for the Visitor of any such College, on the request of the Governing Body thereof, to authorise from time to time in writing the use on week days only of any abridgment or adaptation of the said morning and evening prayer in the chapel of such College instead of the order set forth in the Book of Common Prayer:"—

The Master and Fellows shall, if necessary, provide stipends from the revenues of the College for persons whom they may appoint to carry out these provisions, and shall also make such regulations as they may deem expedient for the due celebration of Divine Service and for the due maintenance of religious worship and discipline.

24. *Change in the Value of Money*

An Appendix allows the Master and Fellows, with the approval of the Visitor, to vary the sums of money mentioned in the statutes if such variation is required by changes in the value of money.

No alteration in the specific sums mentioned in these Statutes shall be made in consequence of any change in the value of money, or for any other reason, except by Statute made in accordance with the provisions of the fifty-fourth and fifty-fifth sections of the Universities of Oxford and Cambridge Act, 1877.

28. *The Visitor*

The Visitor of the College shall be, as heretofore, the Crown acting through the Lord Chancellor of Great Britain for the time being.

29. *Mrs Ramsden's Foundation*

The net produce in any year of the estates devised to the College by Mrs. Ramsden being divided into four equal parts, one of such equal parts shall be applied exclusively to the payment of Scholars of the College, and the remaining three parts shall be deemed to be part of the yearly income of the College, and shall be applied in the manner defined in Statute 20.

Plate XXIII

Library

IV. THE LIBRARY

The Founder was very anxious about keeping safe the books he gave to the Library, and Corrie has written a good account of his work in this direction, which is printed below, with the kind permission of the Cambridge Antiquarian Society (Vol. 1).

There are no accounts of receipt and expenditure down to 1683, and from that date to 1740 the only regular emolument of the Library was £2 from each Fellow Commoner.

After 1740 a rent of £5 is brought to account from lands at Over, but we do not know how these lands came into the possession of the College. Various gifts came to the Library from Francis Tilney in 1703, Francis Neale in 1705, John Addenbrooke in 1718, Dr Crosse in 1728, Mr Halfhyde in 1730 and Thomas Bence in 1737. But the great benefactor was Dr Sherlock, once Master, who in 1756 gave £600 for the renovation of the Library and £21. 9*s.* 1*d.* in 1760. He left the College by will his books and lands in order to pay £20 a year to a Librarian Scholar and £4 a year for his rooms. Sherlock also put up the rails in Queens' Lane, leaving money to keep them in repair.

Soon after 1871 the Junior Library of modern text-books was separated from the Fellows' Library, and the volumes were housed in the Sherlock Building, pulled down in 1935. In 1919 the books were removed to Old Lodge and in 1933 to the basement of 68 Trumpington Street.

Two modern catalogues deserve to be mentioned:

(1) Early Printed Books in the Library of St Catharine's College, Cambridge, by J. B. Bilderbeck (1911).

(2) A Descriptive Catalogue of the Manuscripts in the Library of St Catharine's College, Cambridge, by Montague Rhodes James (1925).

Both were published by the Cambridge University Press.

THE FOLLOWING

CATALOGUE OF BOOKS

HAS BEEN TRANSCRIBED FROM THE

REGISTER OF ST CATHARINE'S HALL

LIBRI EX DONO ROBERTI WODLARKE PRIMARII FUNDATORIS HUJUS COLLEGII CATHENATI IN LIBRARIA

PRIMA STALLA

—— Liber vocatus Unus ex quatuor cujus 2^m fo. '*tis ab ea.*'
—— Petrus in aurora cujus 2^m fo. '*illi quos.*'
—— Lincolniensis de oculo morali cujus 2^m to. '*infudit.*'
—— Interpretaciones bibli*e* cujus 2^m fo. '*abiatt pater meus.*'
—— Egisippus istoriographus cujus 2^m fo. '*in societatem.*'
—— Radulphus super levitici (*sic*) cujus 2^m fo. '*si dicam.*'
—— Ffranciscus Petrarcha de remediis utriusque fortun*e* cujus 2^m fo. '*ex me percipi.*'
—— Baryngwys super apocalipsim cujus 2^m fo. '*deus erat verbum.*'
—— Postilla super pentateucum cujus 2^m fo. '*iussit.*'
—— Stephanus Cantuariensis super ecclesiastem cujus 2^m fo. '*et similiter.*'
—— Beger cujus 2^m fo. '*apparuit gloria tua.*'
—— Lira super novum testamentum cujus 2^m fo. '*tocius scientie et partis.*'
—— Nycolaus hanhaps de exemplis sacr*e* scriptur*e* cujus 2^m fo. '*que ex pacto.*'
—— Magister historiarum cujus 2^m fo. '*binarius in sanus.*'
—— Concordanti*e* cujus 2^m fo. '*peccasset edom.*'
—— Pariensis de viciis et virtute cujus 2^m fo. '*quod mundus.*'
—— Biblia magna cujus 2^m fo. '*uxorem suam.*'
—— Liber sermonum de tempore cujus 2^m fo. '*prima in tentacionum.*'

SECUNDA STALLA

—— Lira super vetus testamentum cujus 2^m fo. '*idemque locus.*'
—— Lira super prophetas cujus 2^m fo. '*a fidelibus doctrinarum.*'
—— Hugo super hisaiam (*sic*) cujus 2^m fo. '*mangni* (sic) *consilii angelis.*'
—— Hugo de Vianna super libros sapiensiales cujus 2^m fo. '*na in se.*'
—— Hugo super salterium (*sic*) cujus 2^m fo. '*possunt hæc.*'
—— Hugo super vetus testamentum cujus 2^m fo. '*mendavit.*'

TERTIA STALLA

—— Hugo super quatuor evangelia cujus 2^m^ fo. '*tribulaciones.*'
—— Hugo super duodecim prophetas cujus 2^m^ fo. '*tertio capitilo* (sic).'
—— Hugo super esichielem (*sic*) cujus 2^m^ fo. '*ordinationes oracionesque.*'
—— Hugo super Jeremium et lathbury super threnos cujus 2^m^ fo. '*non tocius.*'
—— Jannansis de sermonibus dominicalibus et sanctorum cujus 2^m^ fo. '*tres divinas.*'
—— Summa de rovlande cujus 2^m^ folia (*sic*) '*ne disjuncti.*'
—— Communis glosa (*sic*) super actibus (*sic*) apostolorum cujus 2^m^ fo. '*sancti quo xtus.*'
—— Hugo super apocalipsim cujus 2^m^ fo. '*drm Job quis.*'
—— Hugo super epistolas paulli (*sic*) et Canonicas cujus 2^m^ fo. '*plus valerent.*'

QUARTA STALLA

—— Thomas in prima parte Summ*e* cujus 2^m^ fo. '*oribus ancillis.*'
—— Thomas in opere.
—— Thomas in prima secund*e* cujus 2^m^ fo. '*omnino aliquis.*'
—— Thomas in secunda secund*e* cujus 2^m^ fo. '*manifestum est.*'
—— Thomas super quartum cujus 2^m^ fo. '*sacra sacramenta.*'
—— Magister sententiarum cujus 2^m^ fo. '*An posse.*'
Thomas de potentia Dei.
Thomas de spiritualibus creaturis.
Thomas in questionibus de Anima.
Thomas in questionibus de virtutibus.
Thomas in questionibus de resurrectione.
Thomas in correctorio secunda secund*e*.
Thomas in correctorio de veritate.
Thomas in correctorio questionum de Anima.
Thomas in correctorio questionum de caritate.
Thomas in correctorio questionum de potencia Dei.
Thomas in correctorio questionum de quodlibetis.
Thomas in correctorio super primam sententiarum.
Thomas in quodlibetis et incipit tractatus in Xto et sic finis.
In uno volumine cujus 2^m^ fo. '*litate et magnitudine.*'
—— Thomas de veritatibus cujus 2^m^ fo. '*ergo Deum.*'
—— Brevarium super Salterium cum tabula Sancti Thom*e* cujus 2^m^ fo. '*magnam.*'

—— Scotus super primum cujus 2^{m} fo. '*eue supremam.*'
—— Scotus super quartum cujus 2^{m} fo. '*effectus.*'
—— Thomas super Lucam cujus 2^{m} fo. '*ubus namque.*'
—— Thomas de virtutibus cujus 2^{m} fo. '*ti aliquis sicut.*'

QUINTA STALLA

—— Gregorius in omeliis et multis aliis cujus 2^{m} fo. '*Ita.*'
—— Prima pars moralium beati Gregorii cujus 2^{m} fo. '*dicta nisi.*'
—— Secunda pars moralium beati Gregorii cujus 2^{m} fo. '*vita sapiens.*'
—— Augustinus in soliloquiis super Genesim et de trinitate cujus 2^{m} fo. '*a et hominis.*'
—— Augustinus de agone Xtiano cujus 2^{m} fo. '*quidem appetens.*'
—— Augustinus in encheridion cujus 2^{m} fo. '*sensu experti.*'
—— B*a*rnardus de amore Dei cum multis operibus cujus 2^{m} fo. '*imprimum eo cui.*'
—— Compendium Chrisostomi super Matheum cujus 2^{m} fo. '*tegantur attenti.*'
—— Liber Sermonum vocatus Provincialis summa cujus 2^{m} fo. '*ctuasque ipso.*'
—— B*a*rnardus de dispensatione et precepto cum aliis cujus 2^{m} fo. '*et reliqua.*'
—— Distinciones Jennensis cujus 2^{m} fo. '*ut Deum videat.*'
—— Distinciones Holcote super Sapientiam cujus 2^{m} fo. '*natur.*'
—— Liber cum oracionibus et tractatu Lotarii de miseria hominis cujus 2^{m} fo. '*peccatis meis.*'
—— Historia Scholastica super Novum Testamentum cum aliis cujus 2^{m} fo. '*voluit eam.*'
—— Fflorarium bartholomei cujus 2^{m} fo. '*lus palmam.*'
—— Bartholomeus de proprietatibus cujus 2^{m} fo. '*in Domino.*'
—— Sermones repyngton cujus 2^{m} fo. '*urem super eum.*'
—— Eusebius in ecclesiastica historia cujus 2^{m} fo. '*que.*'

SEXTA STALLA

—— Pupilla ocul*e* cujus 2^{m} fo. '*legis justificatur.*'
—— Regimen animarum cujus 2^{m} fo. '*ponderitis.*'
—— Polici*e* Platonis cujus 2^{m} fo.
—— Ans*c*elmus de eterna beatitudine cujus 2^{m} fo. '*sum itaque.*'
—— Commentarium super Libros Ethicorum cujus fo. '*habet bene.*'
—— Liber vocatus Confessionale cujus 2^{m} fo. '*et hoc verum eum.*'

—— Policronica cum aliis cujus 2^{m} fo. '*Cambriensis.*'
—— Liber de vita et passione Sancti Thome marteris (*sic*) cujus 2^{m} fo. '*in illo compendio.*'
—— Prosper de vita contemplativa cujus 2^{m} fo. '*gratia et agat.*'
—— Guido de bello Trojano cum aliis cujus 2^{m} fo. '*militis.*'
—— Johannes Salisburiensis de pollicrotico cujus 2^{m} fo. '*quid.*'
—— Bocasius in Anglicis de viris illustribus cujus 2^{m} fo. '*thys sayde.*'

SEPTIMA STALLA

—— Liber eticorum Aristotilis cujus 2^{m} fo. '*et quum ita se.*'
—— Liber ratoricorum (*sic*) Aristotilis et iconomicorum de secretis secretorum cujus 2^{m} fo. '*de illo.*'
—— Policie Aristotilis cujus 2^{m} fo. '*quo actu.*'
—— Liber de remediis utriusque fortune cujus 2^{m} fo. '*in nobilia.*'
—— Tullius de Officiis cujus 2^{m} fo. '*si cum altero.*'
—— Questiones practice de phisica cujus 2^{m} fo. '*membra.*'
—— Liber perspective et geomatrie cujus 2^{m} fo. '*que continent.*'
—— Liber Augustini de fuga mulierum cujus 2^{m} fo. '*faciat.*'
—— Historie cronicales Anglie Francie et aliarum regionum cujus 2^{m} fo. '*inde sub.*'
—— Isidorus et ethimologiis (*sic*) cujus 2^{m} fo. '*de spectaculis.*'
—— Egidius de anima de generacione et aliis cujus 2^{m} fo. '*excepte.*'

LIBRI IN CAPELLA EX DONO FUNDATORIS ET ALIORUM

Imprimis tria Missalia scripta.
Unum Magnum Brevarium sine notis cujus 2^{m} fo. '*sedendo.*'
Alium Brevarium anticum cum notis cujus 2^{m} fo. '*sque libera.*'
Alium Brevarium anticum sine coopertorio cum notis cujus 2^{m} fo. '*Deus.*'
Legenda sanctorum cathenata cujus 2^{m} fo. '*et umbra.*'
Unum Brevarium cum placebo et derige cathenatum cujus 2^{m} fo. '*major.*'
Unum Primarium cum placebo et derige cujus 2^{m} fo. '*major.*'
Unum pervum Gradale cum Missis de sancta Katrina de sancta Maria et de requiem ligatum in bordis cujus 2^{m} fo. '*sum nata.*'
Alium parvum Gradale ligatum in parchmento cum eisdem Missis cujus 2^{m} fo. '*tat Domine Maria.*'
Una sequencia cum notis cujus 2^{m} fo. '*quem fuit.*'
Unum Manuale cujus 2^{m} fo. '*cujus est.*'
Istoria Ste Katrine cum notis in tribus libellis.

Legenda St*e* Katrin*e* cum istoria sine notis.
Unum Gradale ex dono Magistri Johannis Leche cujus 2^m^ fo. '*forenses.*'
Unum Brevarium cum notis ex dono ejusdem cujus 2^m^ fo. '*respondeantur.*'
Unum Brevarium impressum cathenatum ex dono Magistri Hale cujus 2^m^ fo. '*in nomine.*'
Unum parvus liber de s*i*nodalibus cathenatus ex dono Magistri Garnet cujus 2^m^ fo. '*munita.*'
Unum Missale impressum ex dono Magistri Balsston cujus 2^m^ fo. '*manus.*'

LIBRI EX DONO MAGISTRI NELSON SUB EA INTENCIONE DATI QUOD SEMPER REMANERENT CUM TRIBUS SOCIIS

Imprimis Thomas in prima parte.
Item Thomas in secunda secund*e* cujus 2^m^ fo.
Item Thomas super quartam sententiarum cujus 2^m^ fo. '*sacramentum.*'
Item Epistol*e* Jeronim*e* cujus 2^m^ fo. '*commentarios,*' ex dono Johannis Fyscher Episcopi Roffensis.

LIBRI EX DONO DOCTORIS BRIAN

Imprimis Dominicus super secundam partem sexti libri Decretalium.
Item Franciscus Zabarella.
Item Liber Institucionum.
Item Liber de casibus juris in scriptis.
Item tertius Liber Abbatis.
Item Dominicus super primam partem sexti libri Decretalium.
Item liber de casibus juris cum copia bull*e* natus beat*e* Mari*e* observand*e*.
Item prima pars Abbatis super secundam Decretalium.
Item Repertorium Doctoris Caldrine.
Item rubrica de accusacionibus in scriptis cum repeticione Domini Petri de Ancharano.
Item Iohannis Mon*i*cus Cardinalis Ordinaria Glossa.
Item Liber Decretalium in scriptis.
Item Lamphranck.
Item tertia pars Abbatis.
Decisiones non*e* Dominorum Auditorum de rota.

Catalogue of Books

In the following Notes upon the Catalogue of the Books given by the Founder to St Catharine's Hall, it is not intended to do much more than to give brief sketches of those English Authors whose writings occur in the Catalogue. By a comparison of the Catalogue itself with those possessed by similar and contemporary Foundations, many interesting particulars might doubtless be collected illustrative of the line of Study then pursued at our University; as by an examination of the several works enumerated in the Catalogue much information might be elicited respecting the Theology then popular among our Divines. For the present, however, I must content myself with the hope that I may find time to make occasional contributions to the Cambridge Antiquarian Society with reference to those objects; or that some one, having leisure, and better qualified for the task than I profess to be, may, in the meanwhile, be induced to turn his attention to so interesting an undertaking.

G. E. C.

NOTES

UPON THE CATALOGUE OF THE BOOKS FORMING THE FOUNDER'S LIBRARY OF ST CATHARINE'S HALL

PRIMA STALLA

1. *Liber vocatus*, &c.]—This mode of designating a book (the author of which, I suppose, was unknown) is very common in old catalogues. Thus in an old catalogue of the books in Durham Cathedral we find such entries as the following: "Liber qui dicitur 'Quid est tibi mare quod fugisti':" "De Libro qui vocatus 'Pauperum' XII quaterniones." See the "Catalogi Veteres Librorum, &c." published by the Surtees Society, p. 9.

It may here be observed, also, once for all, that the constantly recurring phrase "cujus 2^m fo." followed by certain words, such as "tis ab ea" in No. 1, "illi quos" in No. 2, &c., is equivalent to—"the second folio of which begins with (*tis ab ea*), &c.:" and is the method used by the literati of those times to distinguish different copies of the same work. Transcribers, then as now, would rarely if ever so exactly write in the same sized hand, as that, in copying out the same author, the second folio-leaf of one scribe's performance would begin with the very same word which commenced the second leaf of the copy written by another scribe: hence the method of distinguishing copies of the same work by giving the first words of the "second leaf."

2. *Petrus in Aurora.*]—This is a metrical version of the whole, or portions, of the Bible by PETER DE RIGA, Canon of Reims, who flourished about 1170. He gave the name of "AURORA" to this singular performance. From the great number of MS. copies of the work that are found existing, it may be concluded that the "Aurora" was popular in its day. Specimens of this work may be seen in Possevin's "Apparatus Sacer," Tom. II, and in Oudin's Commentarii de Scriptor. et Script. Eccles. Tom. II, under the word "*Petrus de Riga.*"

3. *Lincolniensis de oculo morali,* &c.]—This author was WILLIAM OF LINCOLN, a learned Carmelite of that city. He lived in the reign of Edward III, about the year 1360. In one of the ancient catalogues of books belonging to the Cathedral of Durham, he is mentioned as the Chancellor of the Diocese of Lincoln.

See *Pits,* p. 492; *Tanner,* Biblioth. Britan. p. 385; Catalogi Vet. Librar. Eccles. Cath. Dunelm. pp. 21, 53, 97, published by the Surtees Society, 1838.

4. *Ffranciscus Petrarcha de remediis utriusque fortune,* &c.]—This is one of those works of PETRARCH which appear in the Index Librorum Prohibitorum, p. 426, Madrit. 1667; *Oudin,* Comment. de Scriptor. Tom. III, col. 950.

5. *Baryngwys super apocalipsim.*]—The name of this author is variously written: BARENGUIDDUS, BARENGALDUS, BERENGARIUS, and BARENGUEDUS. There is no doubt, however, respecting his identity. He was an Englishman; and his name seems to survive in those of BARWIS and BARWICK, which are not now uncommon. He lived, according to some, about 1446; but Nasmith asserts that a MS. copy of this work of BARYNGWYS on the Apocalypse, which is in the Parker Library of Corpus Christi College, was evidently written before the 12th century. The work itself is printed at the end of the second volume of the Benedictine edition of the Works of St Ambrose.

See *Tanner,* Bibl. Brit. p. 97; *Nasmith,* Catalog. Libr. MSS. in Coll. Corp. Christi, p. 209.

6. *Stephanus Cantuariensis super ecclesiastem.*]—The author of this treatise was STEPHEN LANGTON, Archbishop of Canterbury for twenty-two years, and who died in 1228. He was a voluminous writer; his works being chiefly commentaries on detached books of Scripture. To him, also, has been attributed the division of the Bible into chapters as we now have it. Of the work here mentioned, a copy is preserved among the MSS. in the Parker Library of Corpus Christi College, under the title: *Tractatus venerabilis Stephani* [*de Langetune*] *Archiepiscopi Cantuariensis super Ecclesiastem.*

See *Tanner,* Bibl. Brit. pp. 446 et seq.; *Parker,* Antiq. Brit. p. 154; *Godwin,* De Præsul. (edit. Richardson), p. 88; *Nasmith,* Catalog. p. 35.

7. *Beger.*]—It is possible that the author here intended may be JOHN BEVER, a Benedictine Monk (A.D. 1290), who wrote a Chronicle of England commencing with the arrival of Brutus in Britain, and continued down to the reign of Henry III.

Or it may be WALTER BAKER, a Monk of St Mary Osney, near Oxford, who died about 1420, and who wrote the Lives of King Edward I and Edward II as well as a chronicle of remarkable events, chiefly relating to England.

Yet I think it more probable that PETER BERCHOR or BERCHEUR is meant, whose three works, the REPERTORIUM, REDUCTORIUM, and DICTIONARIUM *morale utriusque Testamenti*, formed a kind of treasure-house of Theology for biblical students in those days. BERCHOR has the reputation, moreover, of being the author of the *Gesta Romanorum*.

See *Clarke*, Succession of Sacr. Liter. Vol. II, p. 761; *Warton*, Hist. of Engl. Poetry, Vol. I, p. 114, *note*; p. 258, edit. 1824; *Tanner*, Bibl. Brit. p. 65; *Cave*, Hist. Liter. Sæc. XIV, p. 65.

8. *Concordantiæ.*]—I take this to be the work of JOHN OF DARLINGTON, an English Monk about 1284, who was afterwards Archbishop of Dublin. He was a person of commanding influence from his studious habits and general probity of life. Walsingham (in Edward I, p. 47) observes respecting him, "*Hujus studio et industria editæ sunt* CONCORDANTIÆ *magnæ, quæ Anglicanæ vocantur.*"

See *Tanner*, Bibl. Brit. p. 225.

TERTIA STALLA

1. *Lathbury super Threnos.*]—JOHN LATHBURY, the author here mentioned, was a Franciscan Monk of Reading; and distinguished as a Philosopher as well as a Divine. In the latter character he is known by his *Distinctiones Theologicæ*; but chiefly by this Commentary on the Lamentations of Jeremiah, which was in such repute as to be used in Oxford, at the time, as a theological text-book. This commentary was completed in the year 1406.

See *Tanner*, Bibl. Brit. p. 469; *Oudin*, Comment. de Scriptor. Tom. III, col. 2212.

2. *Summa de Rovlande.*]—I suppose, ROLLAND or ROWLAND, Sub-dean of Glasgow, a contemporary of Dr Woodlark. But I find no treatise entitled "Summa" ascribed to that Ecclesiastic. Condensed theological treatises were, however, frequently called *Summæ*, and that term was even applied to commentaries. Thus in the old catalogues of books belonging to the Cathedral of Durham we find "Summa Magistri Stephani de Langton super Ecclesiasticum."

See *Tanner*, Bibl. Brit. p. 641.

QUINTA STALLA

1. *Distinctiones Holcote super Sapientiam.*]—ROBERT HOLCOTE of Holcot in Northamptonshire and a Dominican Friar at Northampton, was a voluminous writer, and regarded as one of the most eminent schoolmen and eloquent preachers of his time. He died of the plague at Northampton in the year 1349.

See *Tanner*, Bibl. Brit. p. 407; *Cave*, Hist. Lit. Sæc. xiv, p. 40; *Bridges*, Hist. of Northamptonshire, Vol. ii, p. 147.

2. *Fflorarium Bartholomei.*]—BARTHOLOMEW, usually known by the surname of FLORARIUS, was a learned Englishman, who seems to have been almost always embroiled in controversy and disputations with the monastic Orders of the time. He lived in the beginning of the 15th century (1420). So obnoxious did he render himself to his opponents, that they procured the suppression of his writings, as being contrary to "good morals and Christian modesty." Bartholomew obtained his surname from the titles of his works: these were, (1) *Florarium*; (2) *Flores Sanctorum*; (3) *Flores Virtutum*: though these, probably, are all the same work under varied titles. It is certain, however, that among the *Libri prohibiti* enumerated in the Index of Pope Alexander VII are "*Flores Sanctorum* and *Flores Virtutum—ubicumque et quacumque lingua impressi*; *donec corrigantur*."

See *Oudin*, Commentar. de Scriptor. Eccles. Tom. iii, col. 2328 et seq.; Index Libror. prohibit. p. 50, *Romæ*, 1667.

3. *Bartolomæus de proprietatibus rerum.*]—Of this work the author was BARTHOLOMEW GRANVILLE or GLANVILLE, commonly known as BARTOLOMÆUS ANGLUS. He flourished about the middle of the 14th century (1360), and was descended from the Earls of Suffolk. If we may judge from the number of MS. copies of this work now extant, it must have been very popular in its day. An English translation of it by John de Trevisa appeared in 1398.

See *Tanner*, Bibl. Brit. pp. 326, 720; *Cave*, Hist. Liter. Sæc. xiv, p. 66; *Oudin*, Tom. iii, col. 969; *Hallam*, Literature of Europe, Vol. i, p. 161.

4. *Sermones Repyngton.*]—PHILIP REPYNGTON, REPPINGTON, or REPINDON, sometimes RAMPINGTON, was a Canon of Leicester, afterwards Bishop of Lincoln, and a Cardinal. He lived in the reigns of Richard II and Henry IV. In earlier life he was one of those, in the University of Oxford, who adopted and defended the religious opinions of Wyclif; but he afterwards recanted, and in the end became a bitter persecutor of the followers of Wyclif. He seems to have been an eminent Philosopher as well as Divine.

See *Tanner*, Bibl. Brit. p. 622; *Wood*, Hist. et Antiq. Univ. Oxon. Lib. I, pp. 189 et seq.; *Godwin*, De Præsul. (edit. Richardson), p. 296; *Foxe*, Acts and Monuments, Vol. III, pp. 24 et seq.; 257, edit. 1837.

SEXTA STALLA

1. *Pupilla ocule.*]—The complete title of this treatise is "PUPILLA OCULI, *omnibus Sacerdotibus tam Curatis quam non Curatis, summe necessarie, in qua tractatur de septem Sacramentorum administratione, de decem Præceptis Decalogi, et de reliquis Ecclesiasticorum officiis, quae oportet Sacerdotem rite institutam non ignorare.*" Many MS. copies exist of this once popular work, not to mention that it has several times been printed. The author of it was JOHN DE BURGH, an English Divine who was Chancellor of the University of Cambridge in 1385.

See *Cave*, Hist. Liter. Sæc. XIV, p. 81; *Fuller*, Hist. University of Camb. p. 119, *note*, edit. 1840.

2. *Anscelmus de eterna beatitudine.*]—The author here intended is ANSELM, Archbishop of Canterbury; but I believe the treatise itself is that entitled "*De beatitudine cœlestis patriæ,*" which, though ascribed to ANSELM, was the work of Eadmer, his pupil and intimate friend.

See *Tanner*, Bibl. Brit. p. 43; *Cave*, Hist. Liter. Sæc. XII, p. 209.

3. *Johannes Salisburiensis de Policratico.*]—JOHN OF SALISBURY flourished in the reign of Henry II; and, next to THEODORE, Archbishop of Canterbury, and the Abbot ADRIAN, was one of the greatest restorers of classical literature in this country. He was the intimate friend of Thomas à Becket, and seems to have witnessed the murder of that Prelate. He was afterwards (A.D. 1172) by the good offices of Henry II chosen Bishop of Chartres. The Book here mentioned is POLICRATICUS, *sive De nugis Curialium et vestigiis Philosophorum,* Lib. VIII *&c.*

See *Tanner*, Bibl. Brit. p. 438; *Cave*, Sæc. XII, p. 243; *Hallam*, Literature of Europe, Vol. I, pp. 98, 99.

SEPTIMA STALLA

Historiæ cronicales, &c.]—Most probably some of those *Regnorum Chronicæ*, or Metrical Histories of nations, which were at that time recited in college halls after dinner or supper on festival days, for the entertainment of the society.

See *Warton*, Hist. of Engl. Poetry, Vol. I, p. 96, edit. 1824.

V. ESTATES AND INCOME

GRANT OF PLATE TO SIR CHARLES CAESAR IN DISCHARGE OF A DEBT OF £200

Whereas We, the said Master or Keeper and Fellows of the said College or Hall have borrowed and received of Sir Charles Caesar of Bennington in the County of Hertford, Knight, the sum of £200 of lawful English money for the use of the said College, and have expended the same in and towards the new Buildings thereof, and which said sum is now justly due and owing by us to the said Sir Charles Caesar, BE IT NOW KNOWN,

That We, for and in satisfaction and discharge of £100 of the said debt of £200 by us owing—have given, granted, bargained and sold unto the said Sir Charles Caesar,

All and sundry Silver Tankards and pieces of plate herein after mentioned; i.e. One Silver Tankard called Mr Soothby's Tankard, weighing twenty-five ounces and ten pennyweight; One large two-eared Silver plate weighing thirty ounces; One Silver Tankard called Sir John Rouse's Tankard weighing fifty ounces; One Silver Tankard called Mr Peter Pleasant's Tankard weighing twenty-nine ounces and ten pennyweight; One Silver Tankard called Mr Robert Brookes' Tankard weighing twenty-four ounces and ten pennyweight; One Silver two-eared plate called Mr Potts' plate weighing twenty ounces; One other Silver two-eared plate with the College arms on it weighing twenty-one ounces; One other Silver Tankard called Mr Boothby's Tankard weighing nineteen ounces and 10 pennyweight; One Silver Tankard called Mr Rolt's Tankard weighing twenty ounces and ten pennyweight; One Silver Tankard called Mr Pierce's Tankard weighing forty-three ounces, One Silver Tankard called Mr Peter Hussey's Tankard weighing forty-five ounces; One Silver Tankard called Mr John Whiting's Tankard weighing nineteen ounces and ten pennyweight; One Silver Tankard called Mr Robert Fagg's Tankard weighing twenty-two ounces and ten pennyweight; One other Silver two-eared plate with the College arms on it weighing twenty-two ounces, and one Silver drum Salt with the College Arms on it weighing nine ounces and ten pennyweight.

22 November, 1688.

Plate XXIV

Specimens of the College Plate

Most, perhaps all, of the plate now in the possession of the College was acquired after the sale to Sir Charles Caesar. The smaller pieces were mostly given by Fellow Commoners in the Mastership of Procter.

COLLEGE ESTATES ABOUT THE YEAR 1800

TRUST ESTATES

District	Trust	a.	r.	p.
Adlingfleet and Whitgift	Skerne Scholarships	97	1	29
Braintree	Hobbes Scholarships	31	0	9
Bruisyard	Chapel	94	1	2
Cubbington and Histon	Frankland foundation	37	0	0
		24	0	15
Guilden Morden	Chaplain (leasehold)	263	0	34
	Master's stipend	7	3	2
Harlow	Stafford Scholarships	[£20 annually from estates never legally conveyed]		
Barrington	Barnardiston Scholarships [Sold 23 April 1801 for £1400 to redeem Land Taxes]	70	0	0
Over	Library	5	3	24
Therfield	Master's Sizar	36	3	15
Nether Whitacre	Library	80	2	32

MRS RAMSDEN'S FOUNDATION

	a.	r.	p.
Fockerby and Adlingfleet	865	1	10
	43	1	29
Garthorpe and Luddington	181	0	23
Linton	182	0	37
Norton	289	0	4
Barton	132	1	30

FELLOWSHIP FARMS

	a.	r.	p.
Barton tenement	6	0	19
Barton farm	68	2	38
Brinkley	17	1	31
Cambridge, St Giles	4	2	16
Chesterton	88	3	28
Coton	275	3	36
Fulbourn	15	0	32
Grantchester	15	0	26
Harlton	9	2	0
Layer Breton	32	1	3
Over	54	1	13
Paxton	27	3	0
Ridgewell Parsonage	[£420]		
Ridgewell Rectorial Glebe	38	2	24
Ridgewell Norton	3	3	2
Whitwell	93	1	11
Wilbraham	3	0	0
Rent charge on Mrs Ramsden's Barton Farm	[£10. 1. 7]		

INCOMES OF FOUNDATION FELLOWS AND SKERNE FELLOWS

Year	Foundation Fellow		Skerne Fellow	
1773	£5. 13. 4 (stipend) + £28. 16. 10 + £37. 4. 5 + £4. 1. 8	= £75. 16. 3	£52. 0. 0	
1778	£5. 13. 4 + £26. 6. 9 + £4. 13. 1 + £15 (Ramsden surplus)	= £51. 13. 2	£52. 0. 0	
1791	£5. 13. 4 + £56. 9. 10 + £4. 5. 5 + 10. 6 weekly	= £66. 8. 7 +	£52. 0. 0 + 10. 6 weekly	
1808	£5. 13. 4 + £125. 6. 0 + 10. 6 weekly	= £130. 19. 4 +	£52 + £68 from Ramsden surplus + 10. 6 weekly.	= £120 +
1855	£5. 13. 4 + dividend		£52 + £48 + 10. 6 weekly	= £100 +

FELLOWS' DIVIDENDS

Year	Corn money	Degrees	Beer	Bread	Scholars' absence	Rents	Dividend	Dividend from fines	Dividend from coal (first in 1731)
1684	71. 2. 9	52. 16. 0	11. 2. 0	17. 2. 6	19. 18. 0	3. 0. 0	24. 18. 0	—	
1690	52. 7. 8	5. 8. 0	7. 0. 0	4. 3. 0	16. 0. 0	3. 0. 0	12. 11. 3	7. 5. 0	
1700	85. 4. 9	24. 2. 4	7. 1. 0	13. 6. 2	13. 18. 0	4. 0. 0	21. 1. 9	7. 10. 0	
1707	43. 0. 9	10. 16. 0	6. 16. 0	13. 16. 1	19. 4. 0	4. 0. 0	13. 18. 11	10. 5. 8	
1715	75. 9. 3	39. 7. 8	5. 6. 6	22. 12. 2	29. 14. 0	4. 0. 0	25. 15. 5	8. 10. 6	
1726	89. 19. 10	22. 0. 0	26. 19. 6	12. 6. 8	31. 0. 0	4. 0. 0	26. 12. 3	46. 1. 5	
1744	52. 4. 5	14. 16. 0	26. 1. 8		25. 15. 0	4. 0. 0	17. 11. 0	12. 5	3. 1. 10
1765	104. 5. 8	27. 10. 8	24. 11. 3		31. 3. 0	11. 12. 0	28. 8. 9	1. 2. 5	1. 16. 6
1773	120. 9. 11	23. 6. 8	36. 19. 10		11. 0. 0	10. 1. 7	28. 16. 10	37. 4. 5	4. 1. 8
1782	94. 14. 5	10. 16. 0	24. 11. 5		17. 15. 0	10. 1. 7	22. 11. 2	4. 12. 0	—
1787	281. 2. 4	23. 8. 0	23. 15. 5		22. 1. 0	10. 1. 7	51. 9. 9	9. 7. 0	5. 2. 0
1799	512. 4. 9	20. 6. 8	21. 5. 6		22. 9. 0	10. 1. 7	107. 10. 0	37. 6. 9	11. 17. 7

AFTER 1806 THE MASTER'S DIVIDEND WAS INCREASED BY ORDER OF THE COURT OF CHANCERY SO AS TO BEAR TO A FELLOW'S DIVIDEND THE PROPORTION OF 6 TO 5

Year	Corn money and rents	Degrees	Beer	Coals	Scholars' absence	Porter's House etc.	Fellow's Dividend	Dividend from fines & wood
1807	681. 1. 3	8. 12. 0	10. 11. 8	—	6. 9. 0	10. 1. 7	99. 11. 0	2. 6. 10
1809	1075. 6. 1	15. 4. 0	10. 12. 0	21. 10. 3	13. 3. 0	10. 1. 7	159. 2. 10	—
1813	1107. 9. 5	21. 8. 0	9. 7. 0	29. 3. 11	17. 14. 0	10. 1. 7	165. 19. 11	—
1816	1356. 9. 7	33. 2. 8	8. 6. 0	109. 17. 4	16. 13. 0	10. 1. 7	213. 2. 6	—
1828	1432. 16. 4	85. 5. 4	10. 16. 0	99. 5. 9	30. 2. 0	10. 1. 7	231. 14. 3	—
1842	1452. 0. 8	115. 2. 8	9. 0. 0	58. 2. 10	13. 4. 0	10. 1. 7	230. 4. 5	—
1843	1446. 7. 10	84. 10. 8	—	88. 13. 2	18. 15. 0	10. 1. 7	228. 18. 11	—
1852	1287. 18. 5	87. 13. 4	—	70. 3. 8	—	10. 1. 7	202. 4. 0	—
1853	1195. 19. 5	109. 9. 4	—	42. 4. 8	—	10. 1. 7	188. 11. 6	—

THE REVENUES OF THE RAMSDEN ESTATE

Year	New Building	Fellows	Scholars	Surplus
1773	£209. 18. 2	£312. 0. 0	£41. 5. 0	£222. 1. 9
1774	206. 13. 10	229. 10. 0	104. 0. 0	404. 18. 11
1775	136. 12. 5	229. 9. 2	94. 5. 0	433. 17. 0
1776	875. 12. 5	209. 10. 0	72. 5. 0	243. 3. 11
1777	142. 18. 8	146. 3. 4	50. 0. 0	491. 4. 4
1778	745. 0. 1	186. 10. 0	38. 0. 0	36. 9. 4
1779	94. 19. 10	187. 0. 0	81. 5. 0	878. 12. 11
1780	115. 5. 4	157. 0. 0	54. 15. 0	617. 19. 8
1781	586. 8. 3	147. 0. 4	103. 0. 0	215. 13. 5
1782	576. 11. 3	182. 0. 0	62. 15. 0	53. 13. 7
1783	45. 12. 1	182. 0. 0	84. 10. 0	717. 3. 6
1784	44. 7. 5	182. 0. 0	87. 10. 0	654. 6. 10
1785	45. 6. 4	116. 10. 0	98. 0. 0	734. 2. 2
1786	58. 4. 3	95. 6. 8	99. 5. 0	738. 11. 4
1787	40. 7. 0	97. 3. 0	81. 5. 0	755. 13. 8
1788	44. 1. 0	138. 13. 4	51. 0. 0	556. 17. 7
1789	54. 8. 7	218. 16. 0	54. 11. 0	689. 0. 4
1790	54. 18. 8	225. 6. 8	114. 10. 0	605. 16. 11
1791	53. 15. 6	268. 13. 4	135. 10. 0	441. 11. 7
1792	53. 2. 1	227. 10. 0	102. 13. 0	622. 12. 5
1793	—	225. 6. 8	107. 11. 0	762. 4. 6
1794	55. 3. 10	193. 3. 4	81. 0. 0	935. 16. 1
1795	51. 14. 4	191. 3. 4	73. 15. 0	659. 2. 7
1796	56. 8. 3	184. 10. 0	64. 5. 0	757. 6. 4
1797	60. 7. 7	225. 6. 8	55. 15. 0	373. 15. 6
1798	53. 6. 5	225. 6. 8	45. 0. 0	529. 9. 8
1799	48. 19. 10	168. 13. 4	55. 10. 0	626. 18. 2
1800	50. 6. 5	186. 3. 4	56. 4. 0	822. 4. 8
1801	56. 16. 11	222. 6. 8	47. 13. 0	810. 8. 11
1802	46. 5. 3	186. 3. 4	28. 15. 0	596. 13. 7
1803	59. 16. 2	225. 6. 8	17. 5. 0	883. 14. 1
1804	97. 2. 10	228. 13. 4	13. 5. 0	523. 8. 6
1805	83. 15. 7	182. 0. 0	19. 15. 0	609. 16. 2
1806	64. 19. 3	183. 13. 4	38. 0. 0	755. 2. 7
1807	68. 18. 7	176. 6. 8	23. 5. 0	1293. 19. 4
1808	71. 7. 6	223. 18. 4	15. 0. 0	1139. 3. 2
1809	63. 15. 8	218. 0. 0	36. 5. 0	854. 7. 7
1810	62. 14. 11	186. 0. 0	86. 5. 0	1022. 7. 0

Year	New Building	Fellows	Scholars	Surplus
1811	£61. 10. 7	£146. 13. 4	£78. 0. 0	£1871. 12. 1
1812	63. 17. 0	190. 6. 8	93. 0. 0	1451. 7. 6
1813	66. 10. 10	186. 3. 4	73. 10. 0	1302. 12. 6
1814	66. 11. 8	184. 10. 0	89. 5. 0	1234. 2. 2
1815	66. 0. 2	182. 0. 0	109. 0. 0	881. 3. 10
1816	72. 1. 3	151. 3. 4	127. 0. 0	971. 0. 6
1817	70. 10. 9	147. 0. 0	129. 15. 0	1343. 14. 7
1818	73. 10. 4	105. 6. 8	110. 0. 0	1456. 10. 2
1819	73. 9. 1	141. 6. 8	94. 15. 0	1517. 18. 4
1820	71. 13. 6	142. 0. 0	89. 15. 0	1346. 2. 7
1821	77. 9. 2	120. 10. 0	95. 0. 0	1053. 14. 1
1822	74. 0. 11	142. 3. 4	97. 5. 0	1376. 11. 5
1823	74. 16. 7	203. 10. 0	93. 10. 0	941. 8. 10
1824	79. 15. 3	142. 0. 0	84. 15. 0	1341. 16. 9
1825	70. 3. 3	141. 3. 4	82. 0. 0	1713. 6. 3
1826	66. 13. 7	187. 16. 8	87. 5. 0	984. 9. 11
1827	83. 9. 11	141. 3. 4	80. 2. 0	1022. 3. 3
1828	90. 10. 8	142. 0. 0	67. 5. 0	1117. 6. 6
1829	95. 13. 4	142. 0. 0	87. 5. 0	197. 11. 8
1830	83. 18. 3	97. 16. 8	103. 15. 0	1773. 7. 5

The following is a good example of an early Audit. It is taken from the first ledger, which contains the accounts from 1623 to 1684.

Computus Johannis Savage a Festo S^{ti}
Michaelis 1645 ad Festum praedictum
1646

[Page 1] Recepta Casualia

Chamber Rents

1 Q^{r}	£14	6	4
2 Q^{r}	13	10	0
3 Q^{r}	15	6	8
4 Q^{r}	16	6	8
	59	9	8

Admissions

1 Quarter

Mr Whiteway, Ellis sen: sizar	0	6	0

2 Quarter

Chaplyn, Savage, Lyndsey sizars	£0	3	0

3 Quarter

Mr Ellerker, both Mr Wisemans, Mr Bracey, Denny, Golty, West, Viner, Triplet, White, Ellis jun: Rookby, Marriot, Warren, pension: Cox, Biker, Moore, sizars	2	8	0

4 Quarter

Mr Culpeper, Deans, Millington pens:	0	11	0
	3	8	0

College detriments

1 Quarter	1	16	8
2 Quarter	1	17	6
3 Quarter	1	16	0
4 Quarter	1	15	10
	7	6	0
The Surplussage of Cookes wages	9	17	0
Admission money to the Cooke	3	8	0
Eleven Mrs of Arts and 15 Batchelors Comencers	17	6	8
[*sic*]	30	17	8
Sum: hujus paginae	100	15	4

[Page 2]

Recepta Ordinaria

Of Margaret Ivett, Widdow of Coton	0	0	0
Of Elizabeth Fensham, Widdow of Coton ...	0	0	0
	0	0	0

Recepta per Chartam

A Liberis Tenentibus

Of Kings Colledge	0	13	6
Of Sir John Cook for the Lordship	8	0	0
Of Mrs Elvys for the 4 Mark Lands	3	6	8

		£	s.	d.
Coton	Of Mr Howard for the Dove close	£0	16	4
	Of Moulton for his lease of the 4^ll lands, and the 2^ll and a quit rent	6	1	5
Granchester	Of Mr Clench for Copthall	0	6	0
Barton	Of Sir Thomas Martyn	4	6	8
	Of Thomas Scargill for Dorringtons lease ...	0	9	0
Whitwell	Of Sir Thomas Martyn	3	6	8
Harleton	Of Mr Pentlow	1	0	0
Chesterton	Of Mr Rose	9	13	0
	Of Mr Bumsted	2	0	0
Willbraham	Of Thomas Moore	0	13	0
Fullborne	Of William Troughton	2	0	0
Over	Of Thomas Killburne	4	0	0
	Of William Miles	0	7	0
Paxton parva	Of Peter Wakelyn	1	13	4
Riddeswell	Of John Pearson	8	0	0
Burrow-green	Of Mr Westly	0	13	4
Layer Bretton	Of Mr Stansby	3	6	8
Cambridge	Of Mrs Williams for the black Bull	36	0	0
	Of Mr Cholmely	0	0	0
	Of Mr Thexton	10	13	4
	Sūm: hujus pag:	107	6	3
				[*sic*]

[Page 3]

Exitus liberi

To Trinity Colledge	0	9	0
To the Mannour of Vauches	0	2	8
	0	11	8

Solutiones in Collegio

Magistro Collegij	7	0	0
Magistro Ellis	5	13	4
Magistro Lynford	5	13	4
Magistro Brookes	5	13	4
Magistro Blake	5	13	4
Magistro Savage	5	13	4
Magistro Wait	5	13	4

Praesidi	£0	6	8
Collectori reddituum	2	0	0
Praelectori	0	6	8
Bibliotistae	1	14	8
Duobus Scholaribus D^ni^ Johannis Claypole	5	6	8
Duobus Scholaribus D^nae^ Payne	6	13	4
Scholari Magistri Cholmly	2	10	0
Scholari D^nae^ Cocket	4	0	0
Sex Scholaribus Doctoris Gostlin	24	0	0
Scholari D^ris^ Sibs	4	0	0
Bibliothecario	0	6	8
Summa	92	4	8

Stipendia Servorum

Magistri famulo	1	14	8
Promo	0	6	8
Lotrici	1	16	0
Mancipi	0	0	4
Ostiario	2	0	0
	5	17	8

Elocata Ordinaria

for rent of the back Court by Archers house	3	0	0
To the Bedles	0	2	8
To the Keeper of the Hall	2	4	0
To the Vniversity Waits	0	2	6
To the town of Cambridge for ground rented	0	1	0
To the Marshall for his yeares wages	0	4	0
To the Plummer for keeping the gutters	0	4	0
To the Sweeper of the Courts	2	0	0
To the Towne Cryer	0	2	0
	8	0	2
Sūm tot. pag	106	14	2

[Page 4]

Solutiones Ordinariae
expended by M[r] Blake before I took
the Stewardship

	£	s	d
paid Bell for Gardening ...	£0	7	7
paid for 1000 of tiles, and 500 bricks ...	1	7	0
for laths, tile pins, nailes etc. ...	0	10	6
To the pump mender for his quartridge ...	0	2	0
To the chymney sweeper for the kitchin ...	0	2	0
For a dozen of sawcers and a stamp with the Colledge Armes ...	0	5	6
To Westly, Cook, and Sadler for 9 daies worke ...	1	6	6
For 1000 of tiles—0 14[s] 8[d] for a load of lime—0 13[s] 4[d] ...	1	8	0
To the Vniversity Bedle for October to the poor ...	0	2	0
Wine on a Thanksgiving day ...	0	2	0
Two bushels of haire and half a bushell of tile pins ...	0	2	4
Mending the kitchin bellowes ...	0	1	8
for 4 Morning courses at S[t] Maries ...	0	2	8
Westly, Sadler and Cook 12 daies work ...	2	1	6
For carrying away the dunghill ...	0	1	10
For 6 load of Sand ...	0	6	0
For a fire 5 of November ...	0	2	0
Wine 5 of November ...	0	6	0
paid Westly for repayring the chimney, and mending the gable end next M[r] Hues house ...	3	8	0
the Glasier for mending the chappell, buttery, and Hall windowes	0	7	0
Given to the poore ...	0	3	0
	12	15	1

Laid out afterwards by my selfe

	£	s	d
delivered Sadler Novemb. 17 for a load of lime ...	0	13	4
For laths haire and nailes ...	0	4	2
Paid Batty Novemb. 24 for Colledge worke ...	1	14	0
To Westly and Sadler Novemb. 22 for Colledge worke ...	1	0	2
paid for mowing the bowling green 1[s] 6[d], for carying away the dunghill 1[s] 10[d] ...	0	3	4

	£	s.	d.
For carrying of six chaldren of Coales, and to Cook and Sadler for measuring them	£0	9	0
To Sadler Febr. 14 for 500 bricks and cariage	0	12	0
For 500 tiles—0–8s–0 for 4 bush. hair 8d the bush:—0–2–8—nailes 0–0–4d	0	11	0
To Westly for wood, a peny a foot, Febr: 18	0	15	0
To Sadler for 4 daies work Febr. 28—0–4–0 and to Westly for 4: d. w. 0–6–9	0	10	9
To Westly June 20 for 10 daies work about the new building ...	0	15	0
Paid him for his man—0–8–4. pd him for another man—0–4–2 ...	0	12	6
For another man to help him 5 daies	0	7	6
To another man	0	6	0
paid Sadler for serving Westly 10 daies, and Cook for serving him 5 daies	0	12	6
For nailes for the tiles—0–0–9. For 5 load of sand for the same works —0–5–0	0	5	9
paid for a load of lime	0	13	0
paid Westly for his worke about the new building	2	2	2
	12	7	2

For a load of lime—0–12–0. For 6 load of sand—0–6–0	0	18	0
For carying away 3 load of rubbish	0	1	6
paid Westly July 25—3–0–0—paid him Aug. 1—1–6–0	4	6	0
paid Batty for mending the ladders	0	10	4
For tiles for Mr Lynfords building	1	2	3
To the plummer for mending the leads	0	6	6
paid the pump mender for 4 quarters	0	8	0
To the Marshall for the whole yeare	0	4	0
To the Oyster cryer for 4 quarters	0	2	0
To the bible Clark for snuffers and mending the Lanthorne ...	0	1	2
To the Brewers men for their Christmasse box	0	7	0
To Mr Buck for 3 Colledge courses	0	3	4
paid Mr Thomas Buck for Painters inlargement	0	4	0
To John Ayers for 2 messe for the Commencers	0	6	8
To the Cryer of Lanth: and candles for a yeare	0	2	6
To Akred for the poor for a whole yeare	0	13	0
To Holden for the visited one moneths rate for the poore ...	0	1	0

To Goldsborough for wrong done to his house	£0	5	0
To the chimney sweeper	0	2	0
For mending the windowes in the chamber over Mr Ellis	0	8	0
	10	12	3
Sum: Hujus paginae	35	14	6

[Page 5] [Solutiones Ordinariae]

To the Smith for work—0–8s–0 given him to his box—0–0–6 ...	0	8	6
To Sadler for work	0	9	0
The Chimney Sweeper to his box—0–1s–0. The Baker to his box —0–1–6	0	2	6
To the Cook for a pewterers bill	0	17	4
To the town treasurer for an acquittance	0	0	4
To Stanton for cleansing the Communion plate	0	0	4
To the Joiner for mending the fourmes	0	1	0
To the Smith for a lock to the bull gate	0	5	6
paid him for the Kitchin hangers	0	1	6
paid him at another time—0–2–6 at another time—0–2–8— ...	0	5	2
paid him for a lock for the Colledge gate	0	5	0
pd him for a key of the gate and mending the lock of the green ...	0	1	0
paid him for a gnomon for the diall	0	13	0
paid him for other work about the kitchin	0	2	2
To Stanton for kindling the Hall fiers	0	3	6
for mowing the Green and twice carying away the dunghill ...	0	5	2
To the Cook for a pewterers bill	0	13	0
For mending 5 pieces of plate Apr. 6, and 2 pieces May 18 ...	0	14	0
For 4 salts 1s 4d a piece	0	5	4
To Cook and Sadler for emptying the sellar well	0	1	0
paid Mr Collins Feb. 6 for Colledge linnen	1	3	2
paid him at another time for more	1	13	7½
For a load of lime—0–12–0, for carrying of rubbish 0–2–0 for 2 load sād 0–2–0	0	16	0
	9	7	1½

Laid out for Doctor Gostlins Com̄emoration dinner	£3	5	9
Laid out for wine at the dinner, and wine and tobacco after din̄er ...	0	18	0
To the M^r^, Fellowes, preacher, and Schollars	2	8	4
For the Supper on Com̄encement night	4	5	4
For wine at Supper	1	3	6
For wine in the Hall on Kath: night	0	5	4
Wine for the Hall at the Thanksgiving for the Associatiō	0	3	2
Wine for the Hall ō another thanksgiving day	0	3	6
Wine for the Hall on Christmasse day, dinner and supper	0	5	1
Wine for the Hall on Shrove Tuesday	0	2	0
To the Sophisters for a bonfire at two severall thanksgiving daies ...	0	10	0
For wine in the Hall on two severall fish dayes	0	3	1
	13	13	1

For mowing the bowling green	0	1	8
For mending and new laying the bowling green March 12	2	12	8
To Batty for mending the bog house	0	3	7
To the plum̄er March 28 for worke	0	4	0
For 2 load of sand March 28	0	2	0
To the painter for painting part of the railes and a gutter	0	2	6
To Bell for gardning and seeds, and other things	0	6	2
For mowing the greene at 2 severall times	0	3	0
To Westly for 2 daies work	0	2	8
For carying 7 chaldron and halfe of coales	0	11	3
For carying 6 chaldron and half of coales	0	9	9
For changing the basin and ewer	0	5	0
For a book for the butteries	0	3	4
To the Gleasure for Work in the Hall and the kitchin	0	15	0
For sweeping the Kitchin chimneys Apr: 10	0	2	0
For sweeping the Hall chimney	0	1	0
To the painter for whiting the cloysters	0	5	0
For papers for divers library bookes	0	5	6
To Bell Aug. 3 for work: 7^s^–6^d^ and Octob. 9, 4^s^	0	11	6
To Cook for keeping the gates in the sicknesse time	0	11	0
To the Cook for meat which was allowed Cook when he kept the gates	0	4	4
For sweeping the kitchin chimneyes Aug. 2	0	2	0

Given to the Poor in the whole yeare	£5	7	10
Colledge detriments for the whole yeare	4	11	7
Colledge sisings for the whole yeare	6	11	4½
The Colledge gift to the Steward	1	2	0
	25	17	8½
Sum: hujus pag:	48	17	11

Summa receptorum huius anni	207	13	11
Summa expensarum huius anni	191	6	7
Debetur Collegio	16	15	0
Rd of ye monie that was due from Mr Duckfeild to ye College which was in Mr Lynford's hands	25	0	0
Memorandum yt ye rest of ye sayd debt of Mr Duckfeild, which is to be charged vpō Mr Waite for his chamber income	16	0	0
Arreragia still due from Mr Thextō from Gimmingham and Trunch	19	6	4
Due from Mr Chomlie for 5 yeares	12	10	0
Due from Mr Ellis as formerlie	12	0	7½
From Mr Blake vpon his account	7	3	2

Plate not giuen in
Ld Clynton
Mr Leigh
Mr Armin Bookes and plate
Mr Whitehead
Both Mr Deanes
Mr Bracey

Guliel: Spurstowe
Joh: Ellis
Samuel Brooke
Guilel Blake
Jos. Waite

[End of this account]

[*Discovered in Record Office S.P.D.* 12/75/78 *by* MR E. E. RICH]

THE SUMMES THAT THE COLLEDGES IN CAMBRIDGE DID SPEND, OF WHEAT FOR BREADE AND MAULTE FOR DRINKE IN THE SPACE OF ONE WHOLE YEARE. 1570.

	The summe of bread	The summe of the quarters of wheat, everie quarter at xiii^{s} iiii^{d}.	The summe of the barrels of Drinke every barrell of single beere at ii^{s} iiii^{d} and of double iii^{s} viii^{d} and of everie quarter of mault to be made v barrels of single bere and ii and di. of double bere.		The number of the quarters of mault every quarter at vii^{s} iiii^{d}
Collegium Trinitatis	cccciiii^{xxli}	vii^{c} quarters sixe score to ye Hundred	Ther is onely one kind of bere in that Colledge whereof is made iiii barrels and a kilderkin of everie quarter mmii^{c}l barrels		v^{c} quarters
			Single beere	Double beere	
Coll. Regale	clx^{li}	ii^{c} quarters	ii^{c}iiii^{xx}v barrels	xlii barrels	iiii^{xx}ii quarters
Coll. S. Johis	cccciiii^{xx}li	vi^{c} quarters	vi^{c}iiii^{xx}viii barrels	x barrels	clxv quarters
Coll. Christi	cclxxxii^{li}vi^{s}	iii^{c}lxiii quarters	ccciiii^{xx}viii barrels	x barrels	iiii^{xx}xvi quarters
Coll. Regine	ccliii^{li}vi^{s}viii^{d}	iii^{c}xx quarters	iii^{c}xlii barrels	xvii br. 1 kilde kin	iiii^{xx}vii quarters
Coll. Jesu	clix li iiiis.	cc quarters	iii^{c} barrels	lxvi barrels	iiii^{xx}xviii quarters
Aula Pembr.	lxxx^{li}	vi^{xx} quarters	ix^{xx}xiii barrels	xii barrels	xliiii quarters
Domus Petr.	iiii^{xx}xiii li vi^{s}.viii^{d}	vii^{xx} quarters	ix^{xx}ix barrels	x barrels	xliii quarters
Coll. cor. Christi	ccc li.	vii^{xx}x quarters	ix^{xx} barrels	x barrels	xliiii quarters
Aula Clare	lxix li xi^{s} vi^{d}	v^{xx}iiii quarters	ccc li barrels	iii^{xx}viii barrels	v^{xx}x quarters
Gunville and Caius	xlviii li x^{s}.	lxxiii quarters	xliiii barrels	lxx barrels	xxxvii quarters
Aula Trinitatis	l li	lxxv quarters	iiii^{xx}xiiii barrels	ciiii barrels	lxix quarters
Coll. Magdalene	lii li	lxxviii quarters	1 barrels	1 barrels	xxx quarters
Aula Catherine	xxxvi li	liiii quarters	lxiiii barrels	lxiii barrels	xxxviii quarters
Smā totlis	MMDXLiiijli.iiijs.xd.	MMIX^{c}xxxvij quarters	MMIX^{c} xxvj barr.	MMvij^{c}iiij^{xx}xv barrels and j kilde kins	Mij^{c}j^{xx}vj quarters

VI. THE AGRICULTURAL PROPERTY OF ST CATHARINE'S COLLEGE

DOCUMENT DRAWN UP BY THE BURSAR IN 1922

Before the days of national and municipal borrowing practically no form of investment was open to the College except land and houses. Most benefactions consisted of land or tenements, and in the few cases where a gift of money was made, it was usually invested at once in estate. The disadvantages of the system, especially in the case of distant property, are obvious; the advantages are less easily recognised. But the necessity of managing estates doubtless prevented the Society being wholly unacquainted with business; the memory of donors was kept alive; above all, the value of land was far more stable than the value of money.

In the nineteenth century, while considerable portions of income, and new benefactions, were put into stocks, few of the old estates were sold, chiefly because of the conservatism of collegiate corporations. But the enhanced value of agricultural land during the war of 1914–1918, the increased burdens laid upon landlords, and the high rates of interest to be obtained from investments, induced St Catharine's to sell nearly all its purely agricultural property, and to retain only land valuable as potential building sites or for the minerals beneath the surface.

The chief properties of the College were acquired in the following way:

Bull Inn Estate. Devised by Dr Gostlin 1626.

Barton tenement. Manner of acquisition unknown, first lease 1529.

Barton Farm. Acquired by purchases and donations of Dr Woodlark and others.

Chesterton. By purchase in 1556 and 1557.

Coton. By purchase at different times and by the donations of Dr Woodlark and others.

Fulbourn. Bought 1507.

Harlton. Bought 1507.

Layer Breton. Bought 1506.

Over. Bought by Dr Woodlark 1474. The part belonging to the Library has been assigned to that Trust since 1740, for unknown reasons.

Ridgewell. Bought by Mr Burrell, Fellow of the College, in 1838, and given by him to the Society.

Wilbraham. Bought 1507.

Ramsden Estate. Given by Mrs Ramsden in 1743. A part of the estate (20 acres) was bought by the College in 1807.

Braintree. Bequeathed by Thomas Hobbes 1631.

Bruisyard. Bequeathed by Matthew Scrivener 1687.

Cubbington and Histon. Bequeathed by Mr Samuel Frankland 1691.

Guilden Morden. Purchased by the Society and Mr Moses Holway 1695.

Master's Freehold at Guilden Morden. Conveyed to the College by Mr F. Procter 1847.

Therfield. Bequeathed by Bishop Sherlock 1758.

Nether Whitacre. Received in 1822 in exchange for estate at Congeston bequeathed by Bishop Sherlock.

The first large sale took place on 26 July 1919, when the following properties were sold:

(1) At Over in Cambridgeshire about 64 acres, bringing in £100 net rents annually. The net proceeds were thus apportioned:

	£	*s.*	*d.*
Burrell Patronage Fund ...	390	10	0
Library Fund	244	0	0
Corporate Income	3377	0	0
Total	£4011	10	0

(2) Barton and Grantchester, about 184 acres. Net rental £120. The net proceeds of the sale were apportioned thus:

	£	*s.*	*d.*
Ramsden Trust	3616	0	0
Corporate Income	2299	7	6
Total	£5915	7	6

(3) Fulbourn, about 3½ acres. Net rental £7. The net proceeds of the sale were £263. 10*s*. The estate belonged to Corporate Income.

(4) Little Wilbraham, about 5¼ acres. Net rental £6. Net proceeds £169 (Corporate Income).

(5) Ridgewell, about 34 acres. Net rental £20. Net proceeds £809. 10*s*. (Corporate Income).

There were also sold about this time:

(1) Bruisyard Estate (Chapel); 94½ acres. Net rental £15. Net proceeds £1384. 17*s*. 6*d*.

(2) Layer Breton Estate (Corporate Income); 35 acres. Net rental £18. Net proceeds £382.

(3) Cubbington Estate (Scholarship); House, Shop and Garden. Net rental £15. Net proceeds £388.

The total sum realised by these sales, £13,323. 15*s*., was thus used:

(1) The proceeds from the Bruisyard Estate were invested in Funding Loan.

(2) £2792. 14*s*. 1*d*. was invested in Consols.

(3) The rest was lent to the Ramsden Trust to pay the costs of the actions in defence of the coal rights at Norton.

On 21 July 1920 was sold the Linton (Yorks) Estate, 183 acres, net rental about £160, for about £10,000 (net). The property belonged to the Ramsden Trust.

On 14 September 1920 was sold the Braintree Estate, 31 acres, net rental £40, for £1680 (gross). The Estate belonged to St Catharine's, Pembroke, and Emmanuel conjointly (Scholarship).

On 20 September 1920 were sold the estates at Coton and Harlton, 340 acres, net rental about £185, for £9865 (gross). Of this about £8800 belongs to Corporate Income, the rest to the Burrell Patronage Trust.

On 24 November 1920 was sold a great part of the Ramsden Estate in Fockerby, Garthorpe, Adlingfleet, Luddington, Haldenby, and Eastoft. About 658 acres fetched about £35,000 (gross). Of this all but about 17¾ acres belonging to Corporate Income belonged to the Ramsden Trust. The rental of the parts sold was about £900 net.

Agricultural Property

The College now holds, besides the unsold lots at Fockerby [1], comprising about 562 acres, rental £1100 (gross), the following:

Ramsden. At Norton 290 acres, rental £366 (gross). At Barton 40 acres, rental £50 (gross).

Master's Sizar. At Therfield 34 acres, rental £30 (gross).

Master's Freehold. At Guilden Morden $7\frac{3}{4}$ acres, rental £12. 10*s*. (gross).

Library. At Nether Whitacre $78\frac{3}{4}$ acres, rental £138 (gross).

Scholarship. At Cubbington 37 acres, rental £55 (gross). At Histon and Impington 24 acres, rental £70 (gross).

Yorke. At Grantchester, the playing-field.

Corporate Income. At Chesterton $88\frac{3}{4}$ acres, rental £145 (gross).

The Bull Farm (Barton Road) 58 acres, rental £164. 8*s*. 6*d*.

Thus the College has sold 1631 acres, net rental £1586, for about £65,000 nett, retaining 1220 acres bringing in £2130 (gross).

The reasons for retaining these agricultural properties are either because they are potential building or mining sites, or because they are let on lease.

The proceeds of the sales are being invested in Funding Loan, 5 per cent. War Loan, War Bonds, Nigeria 6 per cent. Stock and Treasury Bills. The last, while producing a high rate of interest, are redeemable every quarter, thus permitting the Society to invest in the best securities as they become available.

The result of the sales is, roughly, that the income is doubled. Outgoings and expenses of management are avoided. Ultimately, when the sales are completed and the proceeds apportioned, it is hoped that the Scholarship Income will be raised from £900 to £1300, Corporate Income from £2600 (net) to £3600.

Besides the financial side of this change there is also a sentimental side. It is to be hoped that, when concrete estate becomes prosaic stocks and shares, the names and intentions of the donors will not be forgotten, even though it is no longer possible to fulfil to the letter the conditions on which the benefactions were given.

[1] Since sold.

INDEX OF CHIEF SUBJECTS

Index of Chief Subjects

Index of Chief Subjects

INDEX OF NAMES IN PART I

[This index does not include the lists on pp. 198–204, pp. 248–59, and pp. 282–9.]

Index of Names in Part I

Index of Names in Part I

Index of Names in Part I

Index of Names in Part I

Index of Names in Part I

CAMBRIDGE: PRINTED BY W. LEWIS, M.A., AT THE UNIVERSITY PRESS

Milton Keynes UK
Ingram Content Group UK Ltd.
UKHW022249051024
449250UK00006B/34

9 781108 008969